WITHDRAWN

THE POLITICAL THOUGHT
OF THOMAS AQUINAS

THE POLITICAL THOUGHT
OF THOMAS AQUINAS

By

Thomas Gilby

THE UNIVERSITY OF CHICAGO PRESS

Library of Congress Catalog Number 58-5539

THE UNIVERSITY OF CHICAGO PRESS, CHICAGO 37
Longmans, Green & Co., Ltd., London W.1, England.
The University of Toronto Press, Toronto 5, Canada

Copyright in the International Copyright Union. Published 1958
Printed in Great Britain

TO
HARRY WALSTON

Attendendum est quod aliter sumunt politicum vel civile apud Philosophum et aliter apud Juristas.

Commentary, *V Ethics*, *lect.* 12

CONTENTS

SYNOPSIS

INTRODUCTION

Rise of the European State from feudalism—Frederick II and the *Regnum*—St Thomas's background—His four new principles: 1, Political authority based on nature, not convention; 2, Not derived from ecclesiastical authority; 3, Limited to the maintenance of external justice; 4, Exercised as art, not expansion of ethics—Political science subsumed in a wider philosophical and theological doctrine.

PART ONE

THE INFLUENCES AT WORK

Augustinian theology—Roman Law—Medieval culture—Aristotelean philosophy.

ACKNOWLEDGMENTS

In the first place I thank Professor Dom David Knowles, of Peterhouse, but for whose encouragement this study would never have been started, and then Fr Kenelm Foster, O.P., of Blackfriars, Cambridge, Fr John-Baptist Reeves, O.P., of the Dominican House, Edinburgh, Professor Michael Oakeshott, of the London School of Economics, and Professor Yves R. Simon, of Notre Dame, but for whose critical comments it would have appeared with more defects.

THOMAS GILBY

Blackfriars, Cambridge
29 June 1957

ABBREVIATIONS

AFP.   *Archivum Fratrum Ordinis Praedicatorum*. Rome.

AHDL.   *Archives d'histoire doctrinale et littéraire du moyen âge*. Paris.

Beiträge. *Beiträge zur Geschichte der Philosophie des Mittelalters*. Münster.

DTC.   *Dictionnaire de théologie catholique*. Paris.

LMA.   *The Legacy of the Middle Ages*, ed. C. G. Crump and E. F. Jacob. Oxford, 1926.

MS.   *Mediaeval Studies*. Toronto.

PL.   Migne, *Patrologiae cursus completus. Series latina*.

RPL.   *Revue philosophique de Louvain*.

RSPT.   *Revue des sciences philosophique et théologiques*. Paris.

RTAM.   *Recherches de théologie ancienne et médiévale*. Louvain.

References without ascribed authorship are to St Thomas Aquinas and without title are to his *Summa Theologiae*, commonly known as the *Summa Theologica*. Thus, 2a–2ae. lviii, 8 signifies the second half of the Second Part, Question 58, article 8.

INTRODUCTION

WESTERN EUROPE received the social teaching of classical Greece when, about the middle of the thirteenth century, Aristotle's *Ethics* and *Politics* were translated into Latin by the Oxford scholar, Robert Grosseteste, Bishop of Lincoln, and the Flemish Dominican, William of Moerbeke, later Archbishop of Corinth. The texts were soon followed by commentaries on them by St Albert of Cologne—Albertus Magnus—and St Thomas Aquinas. The *Timaeus* was known and admired, but Plato's political teaching remained undiscovered until the Renaissance except from fragmentary quotations at second-hand. The image of the Aristotelean *Polis*, pictured sometimes as but a stage on the journey to the *Civitas Dei* and sometimes as a settlement which provided for every social need, dominated debate on human government.

The reconstruction, which made little claim to archaeological accuracy, met the historical occasion, for feudalism, an agrarian and warrior economy, was being transformed into mercantile and civilian arrangements; the process was slow and lasted from the twelfth century to the fifteenth. The West lagged behind the East where social organization was based on the cities and the great estates were not economically isolated.[1] But already the manor, self-supporting at least for bare necessities, was looking towards the borough and the rural commune was being taken into the city. The centre of gravity was moving from country to town, and to a condition where the instrument of power was money, not land. At the bottom of the social scale some sort of rural democracy was appearing among the serfs; at the top suzerainty was acquiring the style of sovereignty. A system of land-tenure in which men were held together by personal engagements and services between men at adjacent levels, appropriate to a pioneering period when the tribes were settling down and drawing the national divisions of Europe,

---

[1] L. M. Hartmann. *The Early Medieval State: Byzantium, Italy and the West.* Tr. H. Liebeschütz. London, 1949.

was evolving into a more political type of community, economically more complex, administratively more unified, socially
more official, and legally more impersonal.

The State, as the modern world knows it, was being born.
Soon the reflection followed that politics or statecraft constituted a special discipline with rules of its own. Previous
social and political convictions were a mixture, in proportions
different according to region, of maxims from Patristic Theology
and Stoic Philosophy, together with remnants of Roman Law,
worked into the folk-customs of invaders from across the North
Sea, the Elbe and the Danube. They were quickened by an
evangelical spirit, swept by a fugitive enthusiasm and touched
by a not unsophisticated romanticism. Now they were infused
by the ideals of enlightened self-interest and civic reasonableness.

Improvements in what may be called social plumbing,
chiefly matters of amenity or luxury, had been copied from
the Moslems to the south. Their courtly culture was spread
through the Angevin lands and beyond: the range of Eleanor
of Aquitaine's influence rivalled that of Queen Victoria
centuries later, though she set a different tone. It penetrated
the brilliant society of Provence and Languedoc, the scene of
St Dominic's first preaching mission and of the ruin wrought by
his friend, Simon de Montfort—that thirteenth-century Iron-
side. Salimbene, the Franciscan chronicler, gives us a glimpse
of the orientalized mode of life enjoyed by the great merchant
houses of Pisa. Algazel, the medieval Islamic philosopher, and
Averroes after him had interpreted Plato's *Republic* in the light
of Aristotle's *Ethics* and dealt with contemporary conditions.[1]
Yet the contribution of the Arabs to the social thought of the
West was slender and not to be compared with their influence
in the natural and metaphysical sciences. The Koran marked
no advance on the Mosaic Law, and the revival of political
theory was nourished from other sources, from the Roman Law
and the new translations of Aristotle out of Greek.

---

[1] E. I. J. Rosenthal. 'The Place of Politics in the Philosophy of Ibn Rushd.'
  Bulletin of the London School of Oriental and African Studies, xv, 2, 1953.
  For Salimbene's Chronicle see G. G. Coulton, *From St Francis to Dante*, London,
  1908.

Nor was the political influence of the Byzantines much stronger. Their administrative genius was scarcely appreciated, and Europe showed little to match their regular civil service, trained military cadres, or the whole disciplined order which the Eastern Empire maintained against Slavs and Saracens for a thousand years. Even in the art of war the Franks looked to them chiefly for siege-apparatus, and learnt the need of close formation less from the precepts of Commenus than from bitter experience of the Turkish light-horse.[1] Greek juristic studies may have underlain the teaching at Bologna, the nursery of the revived Roman Law in Europe, which lay near the borders of what had been the Exarchate of Ravenna, and only two days' march from the lagoons where the sway of the Basileus had last been acknowledged in Italy. Nevertheless no direct connection has been traced between the Greek universities and the early medieval law-schools of Italy and France. The intricate legal and commercial system of the Eastern Empire stood a world apart from the rudimentary structures of the West.[2] How different was its undebased gold *solidus*, so suitable for large-scale commerce, from the silver coins, often clipped, which served the economy of feudalism.

A gold florin was struck at Florence in 1252 and Henry III's beautiful gold penny followed in 1257. The new gold coinages which made their appearance in Europe during the thirteenth century were signs that the West was becoming an important export area. Genoa and Venice controlled the pilgrim traffic and monopolized exchanges with the Levant; both were as western in their social thoughts and habits as the East India Company was British. Men looked to the East for glamour, not for a lesson in civics. When the Latins seized and sacked Constantinople during the Fourth Crusade the Empire was partitioned into seignories and its centralized organization and institutions broken down. 'A new France,' so at first Innocent III acclaimed the effect. Yet not from his heart, for, perhaps prescient of its fatal consequences of schism and animosity

---

[1] R. C. Smail. *Crusading Warfare* (1097–1193). Cambridge, 1956.

[2] N. H. Baynes and H. St L. Moss. *Byzantium: An Introduction to East Roman Civilization*. Oxford, 1948.

   G. Ostrogorsky. *History of the Byzantine State*. Tr. J. M. Hussey. Oxford, 1956.

between Western and Eastern Christendom, he mistrusted the adventure. In fact it was to endure only for an anarchic half-century.

In the West the Emperor Frederick II was never undisputed master of the Reich; on his death (1250) the Great Interregnum began, and with it the collapse of his grandfather Barbarossa's plan for the hegemony of Europe. The defeat of Hohenstaufen imperialism was bloodily sealed when his grandson Conradin was beheaded after the battle of Tagliacozzo (1268), and the victorious Charles of Anjou wrote to Pope Clement IV 'to arise and eat of his son's venison'. Papal plans were less concerned with theory than with practice during the closing years of the struggle, for territorial dispositions in Italy bulked larger than any sweeping claim to jurisdiction on the part of secular rulers. The policy was to avoid the more immediate danger of being squeezed between two combined powers, the *Regnum Italicum* of the Holy Roman Empire in the northern part of the peninsula, and the *Regno*, the Kingdom of Sicily taken by Norman conquest from the Byzantines and inherited by Frederick II from his mother, the Empress Constance, daughter of Roger II; this covered the island itself and the peninsula northward to the Gulf of Gaeta. Frederick was a man of the south, 'the boy from Apulia,' and it was in his own realm already prepared by the administrative genius of Eugenio of Palermo that he created a State as a work of art, as Burckhardt called it, when the *Liber Augustialis*, which became law in 1231 and was immediately translated into Greek, stamped an official style on the racial medley of its inhabitants, and altered feudal devolution into a disposition of direct control from the centre.[1]

A similar process was at work elsewhere in other realms. The energy of Henry II of England and of Philip entitled Augustus extended the close sway of the monarch beyond the Home Counties and the Ile de France. But frequently local interests counted for more than the action of the whole nation brought to bear from the centre; fief-holders might compose governments within the government and over-mighty subjects might

---

[1] E. Jamison. *Admiral Eugenius of Sicily*. Oxford University Press for the British Academy. 1957.

eclipse the crown. A Clare might rouse the West Country, a
Lusignan the County of Anjou; Londoners could act for
themselves. The nearest approach to the constitutional State
was found in Spain where popular liberties were secured and
citizens, protected by charter or *fueros*, participated in the
Cortes. A freeman able to keep a horse might be advanced to
knighthood in Castille and Leon. Elsewhere in Europe it was
becoming a privilege reserved to men of gentle birth. The fleet
of Aragon, united with mercantile Catalonia in 1135, commanded the Western Mediterranean. The main Spanish effort,
however, was concentrated on the Reconquest; in 1248 Seville
was taken by Ferdinand II who, when urged to go campaigning
in the Holy Land, replied, 'We are always on Crusade.'

In Germany trade and the free cities grew together; Cologne,
a bourgeois community ruled by a Prince-Archbishop, long
held out against the Reich which rallied to the magic
of the Hohenstaufen name. Even there, as in most of the cities
of Northern Italy, independence lay under the shadow of
imperial claims which might suddenly and ruthlessly exact
acknowledgment. Venice, a conspicuous exception and never
feudal-minded, was expanding her rich commercial empire
and, wedded to the sea with the ring earned by Doge Ziani for
prevailing upon Barbarossa to kiss Alexander III's foot and
hold the stirrup of the papal mule, could defy Popes and
Emperors, and presented the nearest likeness to the classical
autonomous State of the pre-atomic age.

Most advanced politically was the realm of Sicily, ruled
from the court of Frederick II, *Stupor Mundi*. The cultures of
Phoenicians, Greeks, Carthaginians, Berbers, Romans, Goths,
Arabs, Byzantines, Lombards, Normans and Suabians mingled
together, and there even now you are told that houses are
colour-washed to show the origin of the families that occupy
them—blue for the Greek, red for the Saracen, white for the
Norman, and yellow for the converted Jew. On its northern
mainland frontier above the Liri valley Thomas Aquinas was
born, about 1225, less than two centuries after it had been part
of the Eastern Empire, from a family high in the royal and
imperial service. He was educated at Naples, the only medieval
university outside Spain founded by the secular power. During

his lifetime the French marched in with the blessing of the Pope, and Frederick's officials faded away. The Aquino family was caught in a tangle of shifting loyalties between the Houses of Hohenstaufen and Anjou, the policies of the Pope and their own ambitions. He died in 1274, eight years before the Sicilian Vespers massacred the oppressors and avenged the memory of Manfred and Conradin. Henceforth the island, more and more sundered from the mainland, fell under the rule of foreigners, Spanish and Austrian, and, though the independence of the *Regno* was restored under Charles III in the eighteenth century, it never rose again to its old greatness.[1]

Other foundations for the modern State, in France, England, and the Iberian Peninsula, were to prove more lasting, but it was by a man of Sicily that its theory was re-established. Henceforth politics began to be cultivated as a special discipline and *Staatsräson* or 'statism' emerged in its own right. Parts of the Greek City of Reason were dug up from the layers of centuries, imperial, barbarian, and ecclesiastical. What was discovered was the polity of Aristotle and later the republic of Plato, not the Athens of Pericles. An ideal was restored, not a historical plan, and the ideal was coloured to the medieval background.

Elsewhere will be found a sketch of St Thomas's social dialectic together with some account of his conclusions on the conciliation of authority and freedom, of group-discipline and individual expression, of company and privacy, of legalism and lyricism.[2] Our present purpose is to observe the influences at

---

[1] A. Walz. *San Tommaso d'Aquino. Studi Biografici sul Dottore Angelico.* Rome, 1945. Hastings Rashdall. *The Universities of Europe in the Middle Ages.* (ed. F. M. Powicke and A. B. Emden), ii, pp. 21–6. Oxford, 1936.

H. Acton. *The Bourbons of Naples.* London, 1956.

[2] T. Gilby. *Between Community and Society. A Philosophy and Theology of the State.* London, 1952.

O. Schilling. *Die Staats- und Soziallehre des hl. Thomas von Aquin.* 2nd ed. Munich, 1930.

C. Riedl. *The Social Theory of St Thomas Aquinas.* Philadelphia, 1934.

L. Lachance. *L'humanisme politique de saint Thomas.* Ottawa, 1939.

For general background, see F. C. Copleston, *Aquinas.* London, 1956. E. Gilson, *Le Thomisme.* Paris, 1948. *The Christian Philosophy of St Thomas Aquinas.* tr. L. K. Shook. London. 1957.

M. D. Chenu. *Introduction à l'étude de saint Thomas d'Aquin.* Paris, 1950.

work which formed his thought, and if we look for the rising naturalism as the Aristotelean stream flowed stronger we may plead that our study is not purely historical. Let us be warned, however, not to demand of him a complete and self-contained system, the formation of which can be studied in isolation from the exceptions and incongruities of the epoch. Although his politics were subsidiary to his philosophy and theology, they represented his response to his situation; they cannot be properly exhibited by moving a sort of permanent Thomist platform backwards into history.

No more than Matthew Paris, the chief journalist of the age, did he assess the constitutional changes which were going on before his eyes, yet he brought out some significant ruling principles, four of which may be enumerated. First, that the right of political authority to command derived from social needs inherent to human nature as such, and was not postulated merely because of corrupt proclivities due to original sin. Law was not restricted to the criminal code; power had the positive function of encouraging virtue as well as the negative function of checking vice; civic obedience would have been required even had the Fall not introduced the threat of compulsion. All this was a departure from the patristic doctrine and the consensus of scholastic opinion that political dominion, and private property and slavery as well, were *propter peccatum* and grounded on convention not on the nature of things: the old view was like that of Freud on neurosis, and found the origins of human inequality in our early environment, not our genetical constitution.

Secondly, this authority, at least in the abstract, was distinct from and not of itself beholden to the authority of the Church. Western tradition in the main held to the Gelasian conception of twin authorities for spiritual and temporal power each without visible superior in its own domain.[1] The prince did not claim the divinity of Augustus, nor even the ecclesiastical wardenship of Charlemagne. There was but faint reflection in the West to the caesaro-papism of Byzantium which had taken over the trappings and ceremonial of Persian monarchy —rather the reverse, for the effort of the extreme Papalists to

[1] Pope St Gelasius I. d. 497. *Epistolae*, viii. PL. lix, 42.

absorb all power in the pontifical power tended towards a
papo-caesarism. A powerful minority among churchmen, they
were fighting a losing battle, though their defeat was not
evident until the humiliation at Anagni and the death of Pope
Boniface VIII (1303).

Few claimed that all was Church, somewhat as the Mono-
physites had said that all was divine in Christ; fewer wanted to
separate the Church from secular social life, somewhat as the
Nestorians had divided Christ into two persons. The terms
Church and *State* in this context do not bear their later meaning,
namely of two quite separate corporations more or less tolerant
of one another when they have no quarrel. What men held to
was still a condominium of the two *dignitates*, the *sacerdotium* and
the *imperium* or *regnum*, within the single body of the Christian
commonwealth. Their problem was still the practical one of
distinguishing between two social obligations without merging
them under the direct control either of the ecclesiastical power
or, as the secularists vying with the clericalists were later to
advocate, of the civil power.

Two teachings were simultaneously accepted, that secular
power was flawed with sin and that submission to it was a
Christian duty: they were not felt to be inconsistent. The
religious climate had changed since the persecutions of the
early Church. Christianity was no longer a minority religion,
nervous, separatist and severe. Instead it was at ease with the
contemporary culture and social order, both of which were
largely of its own making. The contrast between the heavenly
and the earthly was less harsh. Everybody recognized the
supremacy of the spiritual over the temporal but were not
thereby defenders of what nowadays is labelled clericalism.
St Thomas, for instance, was a prominent figure at the Papal
Court, the forerunner of the present Master of the Sacred
Palace. All the same he held aloof from the party cause, promoted by canonists rather than by theologians, which derived
all dominion from the Pope. The Papacy had acquired particular overlordship through deeds of grant in certain areas,
and throughout Europe was acknowledged as the highest
arbiter, but that it possessed the plenitude of earthly power was
by no means general teaching. Thus it was held that the

temporal prince's power to rule was part of the order of natural justice, from which grace and ecclesiastical power could not derogate.[1]

There was then no cleavage between the sacred and profane organization of social life, and only a pale foreshadowing of Cavour's formula, 'a free Church in a free State,' adopted by nineteenth-century Liberalism when it would disestablish organized religion but leave it in peace. All the same the theoretic distinction between spiritualities and temporalities was sufficiently clear, and the Dominican, John of Paris (d. 1306), one of the ablest early Thomists, represented common central opinion when he allowed clerical power no direct control over the secular power and required each to respect the other.[2]

From this followed the third principle, that temporal power was immediately concerned only with temporal affairs although its purpose was to promote social virtue and its just commands obliged in conscience. St Thomas was free from the later cynicism of religious men to whom civil laws were like Customs' regulations, to be observed, they held, only because otherwise you will be fined. He was free also from their disillusionment which leaves them to take political decisions in accord with the principle of the lesser evil. The foremost task of government was to establish and maintain those objective conditions, principally matters of justice, which allowed citizens to lead the good life. Its protective rôle concerned crime rather than sin; it was out to prevent disturbances of the public order rather than moral wickedness it was unable to judge. Here Civil Law was like Canon Law, and operated in an *external forum* without prejudging the sentence of God who alone searches the heart and

---

[1] 2a–2ae.civ, 6.

[2] Jean Quidort, Joannes Dormiens. *Tractatus de Potestate Regia et Papali.* Ed. J. Leclercq, Paris, 1942.

C. H. McIlwain. *The Growth of Political Thought in the West*, pp. 263–7. New York, 1932.

J. Rivière. *Le problème de l'église et de l'état du temps de Philippe Le Bel.* Louvain, 1926.

A. J. Carlyle. *A History of Medieval Political Theory in the West*, v, pp. 422–37. London, 1928.

J. Lecler. *L'Eglise et la souveraineté de l'Etat.* Paris, 1946. Tr. *The Two Sovereignties.* London, 1952.

A. L. Smith. *Church and State in the Middle Ages.* Oxford, 1913.

the reins. The ordinances of human law should be reduced to
a minimum consonant with the needs of the community; too
fussy an improving spirit in legislators was deprecated. Let laws
be sufficiently stable for subjects to know where they stand,
but what was just varied according to changing conditions, and
therefore they were not to be flatly applied, but modulated by
equity as circumstances required.[1]

For, and this was his fourth principle, government and
legislation were more directly functions of art than of ethics.
Sound political judgment, which answers to what is practicable,
must in some cases decide between alternatives both of which
may have good moral reasons in their favour, and reach a
resolve by a kind of poetic freedom, not by the determinism
proper to the deductive sciences, where conclusions are brought
out from principles by logical implication. Not that St Thomas
entertained the idea of 'pure politics', in the sense that statecraft could be divorced from morality; he merely proposed that
political prudence or statesmanship should have the courage of
its own convictions and not strain for abstract reassurance that
its judgment was orthodox. The material could not provide it.
The issue was one of practice, not theory. The object was
particular, not general. The decision was contingent on events,
not necessary given the premisses, and therefore could never be
entirely evaluated by theological and philosophical reasons.[2]

He finished no formal political treatise, and the four principles we have picked out were advanced in various parts of
his philosophical and theological writings composed during the
twenty years of his teaching career (1254–74). As his Aristoteleanism grew so the need for State action was more firmly
emphasized. Its field, however, was not extended. No steady
development is noticeable. When he is called an Aristotelean
it is well to remember that his speculation was more pregnant
than his scholarship; his effort was to form a living wisdom,
not a reconstruction of the past. Then also his reputation as a
thinker who advanced in a progression of theorems is modern
and undeserved. He himself praised a certain obliqueness in

---

[1] 1a–2ae, xci, 4. xcvi, 2, 3, 4, 6. xcvii, 1. 2a–2ae, lxxvii, 1, *ad* 1. cxx, 1. *V Ethic.*
lect. 16.

[2] 1a–2ae. xcv, 2.

discourse, and his ideas move more like knights than rooks and are no less difficult to corner.[1]

Moreover they are never purely political. Hence his argument can be appreciated only by ranging widely and touching on topics, such as the psycho-physical unity of man or the primacy of intelligence in mystical union with God, apparently remote from social issues. Primarily a theologian, he preached no party line in the institutional conflicts of his time. The balance he struck between political Augustinism and Aristoteleanism was tilted after his death, on the right by the clericals, on the left by the secularists. Both sides could cite him in support: he had clearly defended the universal primacy of the Pope, he had also acknowledged the existence of political rights which needed no prior ecclesiastical ratification.

The difference was discovered in the divergence of the continuators of his two unfinished political works. The first, the treatise *de Regimine Principum*, was completed by Ptolemy of Lucca (d. 1326), his Dominican disciple, a clericalist and a republican, who would have tightened the organization of Christendom under the supreme jurisdiction of the Pope; his work, says W. E. V. Reade, is 'remarkable as a combination of traditional points of view with anticipations of a later type of political theory, and is as modern in spirit as it is medieval in outward form and style'. The second, the *Commentary on the Politics*, was completed by Peter of Auvergne (d. 1304), who seems to have been more at home in the Faculty of Arts than of Theology; the commonwealth he pictured was a regional state smaller than Christendom and unaffected by the Church.[2] As the rifts opened in Western social psychology between religious and civic forms, and between private and public life,

---

[1] 2a–2ae. clxxx, 6.
  Mortimer Adler. *St Thomas and the Gentiles*, p. 46. Milwaukee, 1938.

[2] See *de Regimine Principum*, iii, 10, 12, 13, iv, 4, 9, 12.
  W. E. V. Reade. *Political Theory to c.* 1300. Cambridge Mediaeval History, vi, pp. 629–32. 1929.
  E. Hocedez. 'La vie et les oeuvres de Pierre d'Auvergne.' *Gregorianum*, xix, pp. 3–36. Rome 1933.
  E. Amann. 'Pierre d'Auvergne.' *DTC.* xii, 2, 1882. Paris, 1935.
  G. de Lagarde. *La naissance de l'esprit laique au déclin du moyen âge.* iii, 'Secteur sociale de la scolastique.' Paris, 1942.

the contrary causes St Thomas had stated as abstract values hardened into exclusive concrete situations. Before them his thought may seem well to hesitate, like the Chinese sage who was asked to adjudicate between rival queens of beauty and replied, 'Both are worse.'

The following study is divided into two parts. The first is introductory, a selection of events, institutions, sentiments and ideas which he had to reckon with, arranged under four chapter-headings, on theology, law, social history, and philosophy. What he made of these sometimes conflicting elements is discussed in the four corresponding chapters of the second part, and recapitulated in the concluding summary.

1 Simplification is dangerous, and not least about the ways ideas work out in history, or when personalities are narrowed to a cause. When the label *Political Augustinism* is attached to the religious suspicion of secular power and coupled with the attempt to draw its teeth by subjecting it to the Church, we may reflect that St Augustine was about as much a political Augustinist as St Thomas was a fanatical Thomist. Jerusalem is the heavenly city, Babylon the earthly city, but this does not always stand for the *civitas iniqua* leagued against God, for in the temporal order lay validity and justice. Similarly *saeculum* was not only this wicked world but also a providential if provisional system. A moralism stemming from St Gregory and St Isidore may have been content with a political discipline consisting of exhortations to princely virtue and piety, but another movement among theologians, jurists and statesmen also discerned with St Augustine a proper *scientia regendi populos* and defended the rightfulness within the civil order. It was to be reinforced by St Thomas drawing from the resources of the Aristotelean philosophy and elsewhere, but already at the time of the Lateran Council in 1179 it was expressed by Rufinus. There were really three cities, he said: Jerusalem, the *christianae societatis fraternitas*, Egypt, the *malorum conspiratio*, and, as it were in between, Babylon the *tuta conversatio* of both the good and the bad, that is, of average men, in external justice and humanity. (Y.M.-J. Congar. *Maître Rufin et son* de Bono Pacis. RSPT. xli, pp. 428-44. 1957.)

Part One

THE INFLUENCES AT WORK

THE INFLUENCES AT WORK

FOUR main streams, theological, legal, literary and philosophical, rose from different sources and converged in the thirteenth century. They are here artificially canalized for convenience of treatment and made to flow, as it were, along separate channels. The first was that of Patristic Theology which bore along a neo-Platonic idealism coloured by the speculations of Arab and Jewish philosophers, notably Avicenna (d. 1037). Christianity was essentially a social religion for, as St John the Divine had taught, right standing to God was defined by right standing to the fellowship; hence it is not surprising that political lessons in the Fathers also reflected the ethical teaching of the Roman Stoics on the prominence of public duty. This movement came to a head with the Augustinian Scholastics, among them the pre-Scotist Franciscans, pre-Thomist Dominicans and the objectors to St Thomas's 'naturalism' who effected its temporary condemnation in Paris and Oxford.[1]

Next came the revival of the Roman Law, destined to have a profound effect on contitutional history. Starting at Bologna towards the end of the eleventh century, it produced the codification of Church Law in the twelfth century whence issued the political action of the Canonists in the thirteenth. Their work was later matched by the Civilians in the secular realm. Both made the moulds in which legal and political forms were cast in the countries of Europe outside England where the

---

[1] E. Gilson, *History of Christian Philosophy in the Middle Ages*. ix. 'The Condemnation of 1277,' pp. 387-427. London, 1955. For general background see:

M. M. Gorce. *L'Essor de la pensée au moyen âge*. Paris, 1933.

D. J. B. Hawkins. *A Sketch of Mediaeval Philosophy*. London, 1946.

R. W. Southern. *The Making of the Middle Ages*. London, 1953.

A. Forest, F. van Steenbergen, M. de Gandillac. *Le mouvement doctrinale du XIe. auXIVe siècle*. Paris, 1950.

H. Daniel-Rops. *Cathedral and Crusade*. Tr. John Warrington. London, 1957.

From Alexander to Constantine: Passages and Documents Illustrating the History of Social and Political Ideas. 336 B.Ç.–A.D. 337. Translated with Introductions, Notes and Essays by Ernest Barker. Oxford, 1956.

C. N. Cochrane. *Christianity and Classical Culture*. Oxford, 1940.

Common Law, though affected by the Canon Law, was true to its own genius and strong enough to hold its own. From the political philosopher's point of view the lawyer's first task was to define the proper relationship between the powers of the supreme governor and the rights of the people.

Thirdly are to be set factors which make up the character of a group yet cannot be reduced to a set of systematic conclusions or tabulated regulations. The processes of community-life cannot be portrayed as successions of rigid forms, although never more than in the Middle Ages was social theory expressed in clear-cut concepts. Men educated in definite principles were not thin upon the ground, and they were confident they could control social processes. Their logical and legal terminology, however, should not lead us into simplifications which do violence to the movement of history.

The current was flowing from literary and scientific humanism to speculative theology. For all that St Thomas excogitated, whatever his followers have done since, no cloistered scholasticism removed from the jostling interests of the world, but a dialectic racy enough for the *artistae*, the students of the liberal arts and the sciences who mourned his death more than did the divines of Paris University. We must read between the lines of his argument and respond to poetic images descending from the mountains of myth, to the beat of folk-rhythms half-heard, to heroes of romance, to customs rooted in the tribal mass and to causes which inspired troubadours, evangelicals and spiritual tramps when they questioned the conventions of a property-minded community.

Finally, the onset of the new Aristoteleanism. Its desiccated later effects are more easily described than its exciting humanity at the time. It was then neither obscurantist nor did it hug an exclusively *a priori* method, which later invited the contempt of post-Renaissance scientists. The rational investigation into Nature was conducted in a temper that was empirical and not at all servile to accepted authorities. Its political science discovered a City of Reason which could be studied apart from the teaching of the Church, and from which, some contended, priestly interests should be banished.

A scientific social doctrine slowly emerged from the academic and homiletic literature of the medieval clerks. A political rationalism began to shrug off the theology set forth by Church authority. Seized on by propagandists and ministers of the Nation-States, a secular jurisprudence eventually dissolved Christendom into an uneasy concert of Christian nations and then, after the divisions of the Reformation, into an agreement of ethical moods between Christian individuals. That consequence was long delayed, but already before the Renaissance the idol of the Prince, clad according to the Roman Law and divested of ecclesiastical trappings, was being erected in majesty. And to each State its Caesar. The vision was translated into a method of government, and lay authority was furnished with an instrument for the complete control of public life: the stricter legalism which tightened internal civil discipline was paralleled in the life of the Church. Citizens became subjects. Equity was reduced from a general virtue to a special function of the legal executive. The State might or might not tolerate an authority, whether of personal conscience or of a free association, the judgments of which ran counter to its own.[1]

The premisses were present in the high Middle Ages. Divines, decretalists, post-Glossators, wandering poets, gospellers, minstrels, masters of arts, prelates, politicians, crusaders, land-hungry adventurers—all had different ideas about how men should live together. Like other schoolmen, St Thomas was a plagiarist and a nimble one, for often he improved on the original and on occasion, taking an argument from its context and placing it in his own, changed it almost out of recognition. In his writings can be discerned, sometimes developed and sometimes in germ, many of the leading themes of Western political philosophy.

---

[1] R. M. McIver. *The Modern State.* Oxford, 1926.

I

THEOLOGIANS

ST ISIDORE's encyclopedia, the twenty books of *Etymologiae*, was the main quarry for medieval writers who tried to build in continuity with the past. Or rather, it was like a stonemason's junk-yard in which fragments of social doctrine from classical antiquity were heaped rather than arranged, ill-fitting pieces of different stones and styles, waiting to be worked into a coherent edifice of jurisprudence.[1] Hence it came about that details from Plato and Aristotle were used before their political theories were known, and odd bits of the Roman Law before its general shape appeared.

Acquaintance with the Greek Fathers was scrappy, at first through anthologies, *Flores* and *Excerpta*, later through chains of quotations in scriptural commentaries, *Catenae*. Latin translations of St John Chrysostom's *Homilies* on St Matthew's Gospel were in circulation and parts of St John Damascene's *de Fide Orthodoxa* had been brought home like relics from the Crusades by a lawyer of Pisa and were enshrined in Peter Lombard's *Sentences*. St Cyril of Alexandria was quoted, also the Cappadocian Fathers, St Basil, St Gregory of Nyssa and, more frequently, St Gregory Nazianzen, a congenial spirit to the gentler days which were dawning. An interesting line of contact with the Greek Fathers and the religious thought of Byzantium stretched through the Cistercians of Austria and Hungary.[2]

---

[1] St Isidore, Bishop of Seville (d. 636). *Opera* PL, lxxxi–lxxxiv.

W. M. Lindsay. *Isidori Hispalensis Etymologiarum seu Originum* libri xx. 2 vols. Oxford, 1911. Quoted about 100 times in the *Summa Theologica*, 90 times in the Second Part which deals with moral and social science. For the difficulty of squaring different texts see 1a–2ae. xcv, 4 and 2a–2ae. lvii, 3.

[2] G. Hofman. 'Johannes Damaskenos, Rom und Byzanz.' *Orientalia Christiana*, xvi, pp. 177–90. Rome, 1950.

See E. M. Buytaert on the influence of Damascene and the versions of Burgundio and Cerbanus. *Franciscan Studies*, x, pp. 434–43; xi, pp. 30–9, 50–3. Franciscan Institute Publications. Text Series 8. St Bonaventure, New York, 1950, 1951, 1955.

Extracts were not always authentic or verified and accurately rendered: thus an early text about the vivifying influence of Christians in the Empire was ascribed to St Gregory Nazianzen and taken to declare that two social principles existed corresponding to man's dual nature, the Church being compared to the soul and the State to the body.[1] Medieval dialectics delighted in such Pythagorean pairing; spiritual power was compared with material power, male to female, light to darkness, the new Adam to the old, the sun to the moon, and usually to the advantage of Church authority. St Thomas's knowledge of Greek was slight; even so he drew more fully than his scholastic predecessors and contemporaries on Greek Christian literature, and was reported to have remarked that he would exchange the whole city of Paris for Chrysostom on Matthew.[2]

Robert Grosseteste, the leading Hellenist of the thirteenth century, possessed Origen's *Homilies*, Basil's *Hexameron* and works by or ascribed to John Chrysostom, John Damascene and the Pseudo-Dionysius, but his main reference was to the four great Latin Fathers, Ambrose, Jerome, Augustine, Gregory, and to Isidore and Bede.[3] It was from them that the medieval writers gleaned what they knew about the institutions of Roman antiquity, though the histories of Julius Caesar and Livy and the social satire of Juvenal were also referred to. The glories of Rome which were their inheritance were gains from the fall of Troy. As Hildebert, Archbishop of Tours (d. 1134) wrote:

sic ex Aenea crescunt Romana trophaea,
sic gens Romulea surgit ab Hectorea.

---

[1] 2a–2ae, lx, 6, *ad* 3.

[2] H. F. Dondaine. 'Les scholastiques citent-ils les Pères de première main?' *RSPT*, xxxvi, pp. 231–43. Paris, 1952.

C. Baur. 'L'entrée littéraire de saint Chrysostome dans le monde latin.' *Revue d'histoire ecclésiastique.* viii, pp. 249–65. Louvain, 1907.

A. Wilmart. 'La collection des 38 homilies latines de saint Jean Chrysostome.' *Journal of Theological Studies.* xix. pp. 305 sqq. Oxford, 1918.

G. Greenen. 'Thomas d'Aquin: documentation patristique.' *DTC.* xv. 1. 741. Paris, 1946.

[3] R. W. Hunt. 'The Library of Robert Grosseteste.' *Robert Grosseteste, Bishop and Scholar.* p. 125. Ed. D. A. Callus. Oxford, 1955.

Ciceronian sentiments—Cicero was a favourite author with St Augustine—were echoed which cannot always be found in so many words by consulting the original author: thus St Albert appealed to Cicero for his definition of law—right written down to further what is virtuous and block what is contrary, *dicit Tullius quod lex est jus scriptum, assistens honestum, prohibens contrarium.*[1] St Ambrose's *de Officiis Ministrorum* was modelled on Cicero's *de Officiis*; he taught that the Emperor was within not above the Church, and was less deferential to the temporal power than another revered authority, St Gregory the Great, who said that if the ruler did what was uncanonical then we had to put up with it as well as we might without sin. Paradoxically St Gregory did more than any pope before Hildebrand to give political weight to the spiritual power. St Irenaeus and Tertullian, known during the Carolingian period, were little cited in the thirteenth century, and the ante-Nicene writers, with the exception of Origen, constituted no significant portion of its patriotic documentation.

Far and away the leading authority was St Augustine, the master of the theological movement of which the *Sentences* of Peter Lombard (d. 1160) remain the most famous monument. They provided the favourite text for commentary, but were improved on by the work of the later Augustinian schoolmen, William of Auxerre (d. 1231), William of Auvergne (d. 1249), John of Rochelle (d. 1245), Alexander of Hales his debtor and St Bonaventure (d. 1274).[2] Early writings of St Thomas were in this tradition, yet already they forecast a new response to natural ethics and the dignity of secular law.

Augustinian Scholasticism proposed no distinction between the theology of the Christian Revelation and rational philosophy. Devout reflections from the Scriptures about the vanity of earthly things were combined with vigorous and sustained speculations about them, a tribute to the interest they held. The literature of Neo-Platonism was tapped, as to a lesser extent was that of Arabic Aristoteleanism: Proclus and Avicenna were consulted, and the Pseudo-Dionysius was an esteemed

[1] Commentary *I Politics. cap.* 1

[2] J. de Ghellinck. *Le mouvement théologique du XIIe. siècle.* 2nd ed. Brussels, 1948.
   P. M. Perantoni. *Prologemena to the Summa of Alexander of Hales.* Quaracchi, 1948.

and frequently quoted authority. Social philosophy was absent
from the searching and synthetic *Summa Philosophiae*, once
attributed to Robert Grosseteste, the organizer of philosophical
studies at Oxford, but now with more likelihood to Robert
Kilwardby (d. 1274), Provincial of the English Dominicans
and Archbishop of Canterbury.[1] It showed no advance beyond
the political position of St Augustine.

This was best discovered in his writings against the Donatists,
for the *de Civitate Dei* was less a treatise on political theory than
on Christian apologetics.[2] The old Stoic and Patristic contrast
between innocence and convention was sustained. The social
application of force was defended because otherwise the community would not hang together. Nevertheless the memory of a
Golden Age, when men were fresh from the hand of the Creator
and were free and equal, still lurked. Innocence was enmeshed
in the bonds if not of sin then of practical needs wrapped round
us by the facts of life after human nature's lapse from original
righteousness. As Newman said, material force was the *ultima
ratio* of political society everywhere. Slavery, private property
and coercive authority were all institutions set up with divine
approval to make the best of a bad job—sex and marriage were
similarly extenuated.

The unanimous conviction that all power came from God
was shot through with the suspicion that there was something
of the bully in secular authority; it was an imposition, tolerable
only because the alternative was worse. Abel lived the simple
life, Cain built the first city. Was not the title to ownership
merely prescriptive, and dominion not much better than
robbery grown respectable? The Apostle had spoken of the
rulers of the world of this darkness; Satan was free to roam, and

---

[1] C. K. McKeon. *A Study of the Summa Philosophiae of the Pseudo-Grosseteste.* New
York, 1949.
E. Gilson. *The Unity of Philosophical Experience.* London, 1938.
Reason and Revelation in the Middle Ages. New York, 1939.

[2] J. N. Figgis. *The Political Aspects of St Augustine's City of God.* London, 1924.
G. Combes, *La doctrine politique de saint Augustine.* Paris, 1927.
N. H. Baynes. *The Political Idea of St Augustine's de Civitate Dei.* London, 1936.
R. H. Barrow, *Introduction to St Augustine, The City of God.* London, 1950.
H. Eibl. *Augustinus vom Göttereich zum Gottesstaat.* Freiburg, 1951.
A. Lauras and H. Rondet. 'Le thème des deux cités dans l'oeuvre de saint
Augustine.' *Etudes augustiniennes*, pp. 99–160. Paris, 1953.

the spiritual principalities and the powers of nature they
governed were not entirely subservient to God's sovereignty.[1]
Indeed such political doctrines as can be pieced together from
stray references in sermons and scriptural commentaries may
be made to look like essays in social pathology. At most they
accorded the State only an interim respect.

St Peter and St Paul had impressed the duty of obedience,
nevertheless to some early Christians civil authority represented
Anti-Christ. They found reasons for refusing to co-operate in
the life of the secular community and for anticipating the
millenium. Had not the Apocalypse pronounced a doom on
Rome for spilling the blood of the prophets and saints? Even
the less shaggily devout joined in the dirge, *Alas, alas, that great
city!* However otherworldly their aspirations, they lamented that
the craftsmen were gone, the trumpeters and pipers heard no
more. They too joined in rebuilding the Empire. Europe
became Christian, the leaders of the Carolingian Renaissance
were clerics, and Charlemagne was the Frankish Justinian and
the *Rector Ecclesiae*. All the same, Radbert styled him Pharaoh,
the oppressor of his people, and Walafrid Strabo depicted him
as a tyrant.[2] The persuasion that political subjection was a
curse lingered in theological tradition; indeed it has never
died, like the sympathy with primitive anarchism which is
evoked by the myths of the West. Traces of it appear even in St
Thomas, who was the first to take up a stand against the
propter peccatum hypothesis of secular power associated with the
name of political Augustinism.[3]

The Church on earth had never regarded itself as the society
of the godly and elect, and had never so separated itself from
sin as to become a clique. Under the guidance of pontiffs like
Gregory VII and Innocent III, austere and saintly but prepared to deal with the world as they found it, Church policy
and discipline accepted property and sought to possess secular
power. The idea, discoverable in St Augustine, that the State
might be founded on crime and lack the true justice which

---

[1] C. B. Caird. *Principalities and Powers: A Study of Pauline Theology.* Oxford, 1956.
   O. Cullmann. *The State in the New Testament.* London, 1957.
[2] H. Fichtenau. *Das Karolingische Imperium*, pp. 255, 333. Zurich, 1949.
[3] H. X. Arquillière. *L'augustinisme politique.* Paris, 1934.

hinged on righteousness and the Christian religion, was already losing its force. Against it could be set the Church's practice of consecrating rulers after they had taken their Gospel-oath to rule as Christian men. All power, whether to bear arms as a knight or to teach as a doctor, must be blessed before it could be exercised. Nor would the inherent worldliness of secular authority be so evident in an age when Church and State were not separate and the social soil was fertile of such Christian growths as free associations protected by law, parliaments and universities.

For other reasons also religious writers might hesitate to condemn the earthly city as wicked Babylon. Prelates exercised great temporal power, and wanted more; the Canonists of the Curia claimed universal lordship for the Pope. Many clerks from a higher spiritual level made a concerted attempt to charge the workings of government with Christian virtue. Power must declare the majesty of God, justice must be done and be shown to be done. Many of the beneficiaries of the devout humanism which was a legacy left by the twelfth century, were men of affairs.[1] In brief a Christian culture was being transformed into a civilization which accepted with confidence the things of this world.

That the effects were manifest in widespread social reforms and a growth of public spirit is not maintained, still less that men were better then than now. It is merely noted that a lightening of political pessimism prepared for St Thomas's entrance. He would not have shared Pascal's censure that true justice was absent from what the State prescribed and guaranteed by its laws, or Newman's pathos that the sight of the world is nothing else than the prophet's scroll, full of lamentations and mournings and woe. Let us look first at the biblical theologians who ventured into civics prompted by Solomon's wisdom, and secondly at the speculative theologians who traced the prolongations of Eternal Law into social psychology.[2]

1. *The Bible as Mundane Guide*

The Sapiential Books—Proverbs, Ecclesiastes, the Song of

---

[1] G. Paré, A. Brunet, P. Tremblais. *La Renaissance du XIIe siècle. Les écoles et l'enseignement.* Ottawa, 1933.

[2] O. Lottin. *Psychologie et Morale aux XIIe et XIIIe siècles.* i, 'Problèmes de Psychologie.' Louvain, 1942.

Songs, Wisdom, and Ecclesiasticus—make for more profane reading than the other canonical books of the Bible; there is about them something sophisticated and almost epicurean. It was this, not their spiritual sense, which increasingly attracted the interest of the thirteenth century. In St Thomas's unfinished *Commentary on the Politics* five out of the eight scriptural quotations were from the Sapiential Books, in his *de Regimine Principum* twenty-one out of forty-eight, and in the discussion on political authority in his commentary on Romans xiii twenty-three out of seventy. St Albert's *Commentary on the Politics* showed the same leaning, a sign that attention was shifting from the emblematic to the intrinsic interest of worldly things.

Fashions were changing from the days when texts were used as pegs on which to hang moralities and when Solomon was consulted less for his secular advice than for the mystical teaching of his Canticle. Not for centuries, however, did history aim at verisimilitude, not edification. Writers such as Peter the Chanter (d. 1197) and Stephen Langton (d. 1228) were faithful to the method of Alexandrine tropology and the symbolism of St Gregory's *Moralia*; allegories in the Bible explained universal history, and this was the same as Church History. *Veni sponsa mea de Libano*, cried the Song of Songs; it was Christ speaking, commented St Optatus, the spouse was the Church and Lebanon the Roman Empire because of its sacredness and decency.[1] *Assumptus est Moyses de aqua*, they read in Exodus, and back came the echo from the Institutes of Justinian, *eligitur rite magistratus de populo*.[2]

William of St Thierry (d. 1148), the intimate of St Bernard, treated *urbanitas* as charity in the City of God, not as the lubricant for good citizenship.[3] His humanist opponent, William of Conches (d. 1154) wrote a gloss on the *de Consolatione Philosophiae* of Boethius, the statesman who looked to eternity to compensate for the ruin of his career in this world, and also a *Summa Moralium Philosophorum* consisting of precepts mostly from Seneca and Cicero. Boethius was a major philosophical

---

[1] *de Schismate Donatistarum*, 3. PL xi, 1000.
[2] H. Kantorowicz and B. Smalley. 'An English Theologian's view of Roman Law: Pepo, Irnerius, Ralph Niger.' *Medieval and Renaissance Studies*, i, pp. 237–52. London, 1941.
[3] See 2a–2ae, cxiv.

influence on the School of Chartres which combined an elementary Platonism with a classical culture. It was the Victorines, Hugh of St Victor (d. 1141) and Richard of St Victor (d. 1173) who began to open out the literal sense of the Scriptures. They noticed the threefold division, ethics, economics, politics; thereafter the indications increased that a new science was about to be entertained, the proper study of which was the earthly city.[1]

The earliest political treatise was the *Policraticus* of John of Salisbury (d. 1180), a systematic account of the duties of a Christian prince unmentioned by St Thomas.[2] As a description of the conditions of an organic Christian commonwealth it surpassed the later *de Instructione Principum* of Giraldus Cambrensis (d. 1220).[3] The *Respublica* was the Western world, the *orbis latinus*. The soul of the body politic was the Christian faith and priests guided by the Pope discharged its functions.[4] All the laws were religious and holy since their purpose was right living. John stood without rival among his contemporaries for his knowledge of the ideas and institutions of the ancient world; he followed the footprints of philosophers, yet reached no scientific theory about the nature of the political community. A third of his scriptural quotations were from the Sapiential Books.

The scientific humanism of the period looked to the same sources; thus Alexander Neckham (d. 1217), the foster-brother of Richard Coeur-de-Lion, whose five books *de Natura Rerum* were the earliest to consider such subjects as the use of the magnet in nautical science and *synderesis*, the basis of natural ethics. Biblical exegesis began to blend theological devotion after the manner of the Victorines with the drier philosophical

---

[1] *Didascalion*, ii, 30. *Practica* divided into (1) *solitaria, ethica, moralis*; (2) *privata, oeconomica, dispensativa*; (3) *publica, politica, civilis*. PL clxxxvi, col. 759.

[2] C. C. J. Webb. *Ioannis Sarisburiensis Episcopi Carnotensis Policratici sive de Nugis Curialium et Vestigiis Philosophorum Libri viii.* Oxford, 1909.

J. Dickinson. *The Statesman's Book of John of Salisbury.* New York, 1927.

H. Liebeschütz. *Medieval Humanism in the life and writings of John of Salisbury.* Warburg Institute, xvii. London, 1950.

P. Delhaye, 'Le bien suprême d'après le Policraticus de Jean de Salisbury,' *RTAM*, xx, pp. 203–21. Louvain, 1953.

[3] See *Policraticus* iv, 3; v, 2; viii, 17.

[4] See *Policraticus* iv, 3; v, 2; viii, 17.

interests of the Parisian Summists. William of Auvergne, a pioneer into Aristotle's natural philosophy, wrote commentaries on Proverbs, Ecclesiastes, and the Song of Songs before 1225. Afterwards Bishop of Paris, he encouraged the friars and was the friend of Roland of Cremona (d. 1253), the first Dominican Master and Regent of Studies at Paris, who wrote a commentary on Job not insensitive to profane values.[1] To his regency succeeded Guerric of St Quentin (1233–42) whose commentaries on the Sapiential Books were perhaps more imbued with the new Aristoleanism than were the parallel works of Hugh of St Cher (d. 1263) who occupied the other Dominican chair at Paris and epitomized the biblical scholarship of the age. Both connected the Natural Law with the inner drives of things towards their full stature, towards *esse sive bonum*; they began to look towards purposes working within physical processes, not only at mental patterns constituted outside them, and to venture a scientific, as opposed to a dramatic reading of the world. Hugh spoke of Ecclesiastes as an instruction in ethics, physics and theology. High in the administration of his Order during St Thomas's early academic career, he was the first Dominican to be created cardinal. A patriotic Frenchman, he alluded proudly to Philip Augustus— Bouvines had been won in 1214—and would not allow the Emperor to be sole successor to Roman power and referee in the game of international politics.[2]

St Bonaventure's commentary on Proverbs, which became a standard work, was written for piety (1257). The focus remained fixed on heaven, not on earth, even in the later Dominican commentaries of William of Tournay (d. 1272), William of Alton—the Regent who succeeded St Thomas at Paris (1259)—and John of Varzy (d. 1278). Their purpose was

---

[1] E. Filthaut. *Roland von Cremona, O.P. und die Anfänge der Scholastik im Predigerorden.* Vechta, 1936.

[2] A. Dondaine. 'Un commentaire scripturaire de Roland de Cremone: Le livre de Job.' *AFP* xi, pp. 109–37. Rome, 1941.

F. M. Henriquet. 'Les écrits de frere Guèrric de Saint-Quentin.' *RTAM*, vi, pp. 191–2. Louvain, 1934.

O. Lottin. *Psychologie et Morale aux XIIe et XIIIe siècles.* ii, p. 83. Louvain, 1948.

P. Glorieux. *Répertoire des maîtres de theologie de Paris au XIIIe siecle.* Paris, 1933.

B. Smalley. 'Some Thirteenth Century Commentators on the Sapiential Books.' *Dominican Studies*, ii, pp. 318–55. iii, pp. 41–77, 236–74. Oxford, 1949, 1950.

homiletic rather than civic. Proverbs taught us how to live virtuously, Ecclesiastes how to despise worldly vanity, the Canticle how to love God. A *scientia legum* was mentioned but its nature was not explored. The prospect of the City of Reason had not been delineated and for many years men looked to the Bible rather than to the classical authors for their philosophy. St Albert died in 1280; *phoenix doctorum, philosophorum princeps*, declared the epitaph inscribed on his tomb in Cologne, *major Platone, vix inferior Salamone*—greater than Plato, scarcely less than Solomon. It was the epitome of praise, and the epilogue to the age.

The Dominican Vincent of Beauvais (d. 1264) was a typical witness to the state of social theory before the entry of Aristotle's *Ethics* and *Politics*. A familiar of the royal court, he composed his *Speculum Majus*, an omnium gatherum of information, for the education of Louis IX's family. He was no theological, philosophical or legal specialist, but five books of the *Speculum Morale* provide a fair picture of contemporary social science.[1] The first, on *scientia oeconomica*, consists mainly of good advice on household management, including poultry-keeping; the next broaches, but no more, the subject of *scientia politica*, for, after fifteen short chapters about nations and States and eighteen about rulers, 109 chapters deal with laws; the remaining three books treat of legal processes and crimes. The proportion suggests the difference between the 1240s when he wrote and the 1250s when Aristotle was coming into his own, and the 1260s when St Thomas began his expositions of moral and natural philosophy. Vincent meditates on his wide collection of heterogeneous facts, but he is not a synthetic thinker and, despite the theological bearing of his interests, one looks in vain for an ordered body of thought. He died only ten years before St Thomas, yet he belonged to quite a different academic generation.

---

[1] *Speculum Doctrinale*, vi–x. The whole work, the *Speculum Majus*, also known as the *Bibliotheca Mundai* (Benedictine edition, Douai, 1624) was divided into three parts, the *Speculum Naturale*, the *Speculum Doctrinale*, and the *Speculum Historiale*. The *Speculum Morale* was a fourteenth-century compilation from the writings of St Thomas, Peter of Tarentaise, Stephen of Bourbon and others.

A. Steiner. *Vincent de Beauvais: de eruditione filiorum nobilium*. Medieval Society of America. Cambridge (Mass.), 1938.

His preface apologises that only a few small blooms from Aristotle are arranged, *nonnullos Aristotelis flosculos*, and those chiefly on physical and mathematical subjects. He refers to the *Ethica Nova*, the early thirteenth century translation of the first book of the *Nicomachean Ethics*, and repeats Aristotle's division of moral science into the monastic, the economic and the political. He shows none of the familiarity with Aristotle's social and political doctrine evident in St Thomas's early systematic work, the *Commentary on the Sentences* (1253–5). He makes no mention of the *Politics*, but paraphrases—possibly from Michael Scot—a conspectus of *scientia civilis* by Alfarabi, whose commentary on the *Posterior Analytics* and treatise *de Ortu Scientiarum* were accepted authorities on scientific method. He faithfully reproduces the features, historical, moral, and legal, which his contemporaries considered essential in public life. He emphasizes the importance of custom, continuity, and stability; next, he inquires into the virtues which should invest the ruler; third, he measures social conduct by laws enacted, having regard, however, to the legislator's intention.[1]

His approach to politics is not pedantic, for practice is engaged as well as theory; the *tact des choses possibles* should go with agreement on the meaning of words, *rationes nominum*. Words call for definition, otherwise reasoned discussion is out of the question; a city, for instance, is constituted by its inhabitants not its buildings, a people by its citizens not the populace. Government should be accommodated to the ways in which human groups do work in fact, though opportunism is no substitute for a doctrine.[2] Politics and jurisprudence are treated as identical studies. He accepts Azo's datum, that law is sometimes strictly taken to mean the authentic constitutions made by the Roman people, sometimes more widely to include every reasonable statute, and insists the legality should be clear and manifest; nothing so becomes the legislator as plain speaking. On divisions of law his terminology is no more exact than St Isidore's; Civil and Canon Law are both included under human law, and their principles are common. He reminds himself that definition is dangerous in civil law, but

---

[1] *Speculum Naturale*, i, 10. *Speculum Doctrinale*, iv, 4. vii, 4, 5.
[2] *Speculum Doctrinale*. vii, 6.

that God's Law of Nature is constant under all surface variations.[1]

Vincent of Beauvais almost warms to a properly political
dialectic, but he has not shed a moral rhetoric. He narrates and
moralises about the practice of *regia virtus*, but does not reach
to the origins and nature of political power. Plutarch has finely
described the model ruler—*qualis debet esse princeps eleganter
descripsit in libello pulcherrimo, qui inscribitur Institutio Trajani*—and
this sets his own tone. His inspiration comes from biblical
theology, not from philosophy, and his vast florilegium is not a
scientific study. About it lingers the glow of the humanism of
Chartres already fading from the schools, and his mirror
reflects the decoration of the high-medieval French Gothic
rather than its structure.[2]

2. *The Theology of Natural Law*

Another advance towards political theory was conducted by
the theologians, mainly from their own resources without
drawing on the jurists. Until the end of the thirteenth century
their inquiries into the origins of political authority remained
more searching than those of the philosophers. They went back
to the very beginning of law. *Doth not wisdom cry 'I was set up
from everlasting, from the beginning, before ever the earth was.'?*[3] They
had meditated on St Augustine's exaltation of the Eternal
Law which is the *Ratio Divina* behind all law: *by me kings reign,
and princes decree justice.*[4] The far peaks seemed to close in as they
surveyed the slopes sweeping down to the valleys. *When he
appointed the foundations of the earth, then I was sent by him rejoicing
in the habitable parts of the earth; and my delights were with the sons
of men.*[5] Human beings were invited to receive the divine

---

[1] Ibid. vii, 34, 35, 36, 43, 54.
With reference to St Isidore's distinction between *fas* and *jus*, vii, 57 may be
compared with 2a–2ae, lvii, 1, *ad* 3.

[2] E. Mâle. *Art religieux du XIIIe siècle en France*. Paris, 1931.

[3] *Proverbs*, viii, 23.

[4] Ibid. viii, 16. *Contra Faustum*, xxii, 27, PL xlii, 418. *de Libero arbitrio*, i, 6. PL
xxxii, 1229.
A. Schubert. 'Augustinus Lex-aeterna Lehr nach Inhalt und Quellen.' *Beitrage*,
xxiv, 2. Münster, 1924.

[5] *Proverbs*, viii, 29–31.

exemplars by embracing them *per modum cognitionis*, not by being subjected to them without choice *per modum actionis et passionis*.[1] The Eternal Law thus brought into human psychology was called the Natural Law. This was no abstraction of Stoic philosophy, but a historical command, heralded by the Jewish Revelation and effectively maintained by the Christian Church. The theologians set themselves to investigate its workings through moral and legal acts.

An immemorial conviction persisted that a right existed more primitive than any instituted by custom or legislative acts, a law in nature which set bounds to human will. In the *Antigone* it held sway over the gods themselves: Aristotle had taken the allusion and contrasted a universal *logos* at work within natural processes with the particular regulations imposed by man. The Roman Law itself, historically a majestic piece of pragmatism composed from governmental edicts, half-consciously seemed to imply an ethical feeling for an underlying decency in things. Its foundations were not altogether arbitrary, and if particular details were determined by empirical observation and methodic positivism, not by religious, mystical or philosophical insight, it represented on the whole a norm of social behaviour which corresponded with common convictions. Its teachers and practitioners, though concerned less with philosophical speculations than with the fulfilment of obligations arising out of existing social conditions, discerned a difference between the 'natural' and the 'artificial', at least to the extent that a juridical 'logic of facts' could be discerned underneath particular rules grounded on political expediency.

Classical jurisprudence, however, was not backed by a dogmatic theology nor was public life watched by a Church which was no department of the State but an independent witness to eternal moral values. The litigiousness of the Greeks bred commercial attornies, but their philosophical bent was not towards legal analysis. Between the traders busied with exchanges and the moralists and statesmen engaged with high questions of the commonweal no dignified class of jurists appeared, as with the Romans, who reflected on the theory and shaped the legal instrument of government. Even the Romans,

---

[1] See 1a–2ae, xci, 1, 2. xciii, 1, 3, 4, 5, 6. xciv, 1, 2.

despite their use of such terms as *jus naturae* and *lex naturae*, were lawyers first and philosophers afterwards; probably they arrived at the *jus naturale* through their dealings with the *jus gentium*. Concerned with practical solutions, they were tolerant of what did not in fact conflict with the interests of the State, but their habit of mind anticipated no collision between a higher law and administrative needs. Unlike the medievals they never asserted that Natural Law could override concrete and positive ordinances; their appeals to ethical ideals were scarcely more important than rhetorical decorations.[1] The Christianization of the Empire tended to change that, yet the *Institutes* accepted the legal fact of slavery while agreeing it was against natural rights.

The term *Nature* would not ring with the same tone to third-century authors and to the compilers of the *Corpus Juris* under Justinian and, still less, to the thirteenth-century philosophers and theologians of law. From natural instincts, however suspiciously regarded in ascetical literature, followed certain corollaries, among them the notion of primeval justice. Inborn rights were given us by our Creator, and these, with the growth of Christianity as an organized social force, were made politically more telling. They could be, and were, invoked against civil tyranny and backed by the Church. The early Scholastics learnt from St Augustine the lesson that the Natural Law reflected the exemplars of the heavenly city set above this world, and that the codes men devise for themselves are but artificial shifts to deal with shadows, sometimes no more than accommodations to sin. Its nobility was in no sense diminished when writers of a later generation discovered from Aristotle a new respect for physical reality. They left the positivism of the working order to the lawyers, and while scarcely noticing the literary adumbrations of a social *ratio* which had appealed to the Stoics, they were intent on rights apparently not created by

---

[1] E. Barker. *Introduction to O. Gierke, Natural Law and the Theory of Society*, i, p. xxxvii. Cambridge, 1934.

J. W. Jones. *Historical Introduction to the Theory of Law*, p. 103. Oxford, 1940. *The Law and Legal Theory of the Greeks*. Oxford, 1957.

P. Vinogradoff. *Outlines of Historical Jurisprudence:* Vol. ii.

The Jurisprudence of the Greek City, pp. 11, 12, 82, 173, 250. Odxford, 1922.

G. M. Calhoun. *A Working Bibliography of Greek Law.*Cambrige (Mass.), 1927.

the will of any human legislator, and by digging into them they cleared the ground for political science.

The non-Aristoteleans were worried by the problem, how man was born free and yet everywhere was in chains. If their idea of liberty was richer than Rousseau's their idea of bondage was correspondingly more tragic. The liberty and equality of our original state were etched against the restrictions and exclusions of our present lot. The memory of Eden still lingered underneath accepted conventions. Slavery, private ownership and civil subjection, they thought, had been ordained *propter peccatum* in order to establish some discipline where otherwise anarchy would reign. Was not the strength of such institutions that of positive and coercive law rather than of the gracious plan proper to the state of human innocence? Certainly they commanded respect and obedience, for they had divine warrant and the apostolic injunction was forthright about subjection to the powers that be. All the same the first Christian millenium was not propitious for political idealism. Submission to secular authority could be recommended almost in the mood of making the best of a bad job, and judgment on the best type of political regime be determined by which was likely to do the least harm.

The issue, moreover, was clouded by ambiguity: *natural* might be taken either in contradistinction to *artificial* and signify what was innocent and straight from the hand of God or to *supernatural* and signify what was primitive and unregenerate. The attraction the Augustinists felt for the unspoilt was offset by their hesitations about the uninhibited. Then, also, *natural* could mean animal as opposed to *rational*, and, as in the classification of 'unnatural' sins, this could deepen the division between instinctive adaptations to social environment and reasoned contrivances to civilize it.

Nor was the confusion lessened by St Isidore who transmitted inconsistent texts describing the Natural Law. On one side Gaius (d. 160) represented it as the ordinances pronounced by natural reason and uniformly observed by all peoples; so it could be identified with the *jus gentium*, and set off against the positive law or *jus civile* which was peculiar to the State. On the other side Ulpian (d. 228) described it as what nature teaches all animals; it was natural in that it was not deliberately enacted, and so could cover unperplexed adjustments to group-living. Obviously it needed to be complemented by set agreements if men were to come to terms with actual social divisions and conflicts. For instance belligerents commonly agreed to respect the persons of ambassadors. Such widespread rational additions to the Natural Law were found in the *jus gentium*; they became part of the *jus civile* when officially adopted by the State. On this view human law could be represented as an accommodation to disorders arising from sin: one had to look for a fault somewhere when captives were allowed to be sold into slavery. That ordinances were burdensome and bound up with penalties was in keeping with Augustinist sentiment, and may partly have accounted for Ulpian's popularity. On the other hand it was embarrassing to agree with him and leave Natural Law on the animal level, not least because of the Stoic teaching that reason in Nature was answered by reason in our mind and that Law was a pronouncement of Reason.

The difficulty, if largely a matter of terminology, was enough to exercise the schoolmen, profoundly respectful of the words of received authorities. It was complicated by the fact that animal, rational and spiritual were treated as so many separate layers not fused together, and it was not eased until the developed Aristoteleanism of St Thomas brought out the family-likeness of things and the analogies running through all creation. Then it was marked how natural appetites aspired from lowest to highest, and some continuity between biology and law was confirmed.

Huguccio (d. 1210), whose *Summa* on the *Decretum* has been called the greatest achievement of twelfth century Decretist scholarship, was content to repeat both formulas without harmonizing them. Slowly the distinction came to be drawn between what is instinctive, *natura ut natura*, and what is deliberate, *natura ut ratio*. Put forward by Philip the Chancellor (d. 1236), it was elaborated by the early Dominican and Franciscan doctors, Roland of Cremona, Guerric of St Quentin, Hugh of St Cher, John of Rochelle, Alexander of Hales, and St Albert.[1] They were exploring the psychological and moral

---

[1] O. Lottin. *Le droit naturel chez saint Thomas d'Aquin et ses prédécesseurs*, p. 74. Bruges, 1931.

medium in which the Eternal Law was received, and in the process discovered an outline design for social living and principles of law more profound than a pattern imposed as a corrective to sin. An order was inherent in the human community which was antecedent to any method of governing its potentially recalcitrant elements. In that liverty-loving age men sought to make their theory and institutions of a piece. No wonder, then, that St Bonaventure recognized the *jus naturale* properly so called in the Gospels, though he recurred to the time-worn descriptions—in its more proper sense it was common to all nations, and in its most proper sense was impressed on all animals.[1]

Still more questions confused the issue. Was the Natural Law the Divine Law? Was the Mosaic Law the Natural Law? And under what heading should its ceremonial precepts be placed? And where the 'other law in my members' of which St Paul spoke? Was Canon Law the continuation of Gospel Law? Not until St Thomas's *Summa Theologica* defined and divided the field was a common grammar for discussion available. It was then, when the specific element in Original Sin was isolated, that animal appetites were distinguished from sinful *concupiscentia*, and associative impulses were accepted as essential to human nature and able to be infused with grace.[2] Then also Aristotle's *Ethics* and *Politics* made themselves felt.

Social theology had prepared the ground. A blend of meditations on charity and the reign of law, inspired by the *Timaeus* and St Augustine, of homilies on the duties of rulers and of discussions about ecclesiastical and feudal rights, it had also caught a glimpse of the divine reason working through world events. Its history was sacred history, its book the Bible, its theme the acts in time of the eternal Father, the Logos, and the Spirit. Its drama began with the Creation and Fall and would end only with the final restoration of mankind. Its classic was the *de Civitate Dei*.[3]

---

[1] C. Baur. 'Die Lehre vom Naturrecht bei Bonaventura.' *Festgabe f. C. Bäumker*, pp. 217–39. Münster, 1913.

[2] 1a–2ae, lxxxii, 3.

[3] E. C. Rust. *The Christian Understanding of History*. London, 1947.

J. Daniélou. *Essai sur le mystère de l'histoire*. Paris, 1953.

R. L. P. Milburn. *Early Christian Interpretations of History*. London, 1954.

K. Young. *The Drama of the Medieval Church*. Oxford, 1933.

P. Geyl. *Use and Abuse of History*. Oxford, 1956.

Moreover the divines were in the seats of power. They knew the world, and they knew how to rule it. They had been engaged victoriously in the great contest between spiritual and temporal dignities within the single community; they had formulated the notion of sacramental jurisdiction, and tightened the early medieval penitential discipline of the Church; they were familiar with legal processes, and keenly interested in maintaining prescriptive rights and exemptions.[1] Yet their practice was clearer than their theory, their grip on administration was firmer than their reflections about the corruption within power, and their position was the reverse of that of the British Socialists in the 1920s, who had a doctrine but had yet to learn the arts of government.

They were to discover that blunter claims to earthly rule were to be pushed, and that in order to face the new secular temper more was required than the exposition of the moral law or expertise with the law of the land, more than advice on how to save your soul or maintain your existing rights. The State was being born, a natural group which enacted laws in response to its present needs and without seeking ecclesiastical approval. At Mantes in 1203 Philip Augustus had declared that matters of feudal law which involved no moral issues were not for the Pope to decide; by the end of the century the temporal power of the Church encountered a resistance more consolidated than any that had been shown by the Emperors, and soon to be supplied with a political doctrine. A philosophy of the State was only gradually formed, and as late as 1266 Roger Bacon noted the gap, which detailed investigation into points of law did not fill. 'A part of moral philosophy sets forth the public laws, first about divine worship, and then about the commonwealth, cities, and kingdom: under it is contained the civil law of emperors and kings throughout the world, and many have written much on this. It is to be lamented, however, that this section is not dwelt on by the Latins, except in a legal and positive manner (*nisi laicaliter*) occupied with what in fact has been enacted, not in a philosophical manner, as by Aristotle and Theophrastus.'[2]

---

[1] A. Luchaire. *Le Concile du Latran et la réforme de l'Eglise.* Paris, 1908.
[2] *Opus Tertium*, xiv. Ed. J. S. Brewer. London, 1859.

II

JURISTS

Roman justice was a heritage from classical times and men schooled by Virgil, Cicero and St Augustine admired its ideals. Lawfulness however, stood for more than a temper in the thirteenth century since the Roman Law had come on the scene, a definite code and an expanding instrument of government. Its practitioners were among the gainers. Their prestige was heightened with the improvement of their studies and techniques. Jokes, of course, were made at their expense, then as now. Could you be a lawyer and an honest man? Could archdeacons be saved? The civil lawyers were jealously watched by the ecclesiastical authorities, the canon lawyers were criticized as careerists by religious reformers. Their practices grew and juridical concepts spilled over into theology, for example the distinction between the *clavis ordinis* possessed by all priests and the *clavis jurisdictionis* which had to be conveyed to them by higher authority. Legalism set the style for social life both sacred and profane.[1]

It was the era of the great lawyer-Popes and of travelling Justices upholding the Common Law. No question then arose of government being allowed to override the law or to improvise a code at will; rulers were required to maintain old traditions and to find warrant for their acts in custom or in the *Corpus Juris* as adapted to the needs of a community in transition from feudalism to capitalism. Social decisions turned on points of order, indeed political action and warranted action went together in that legal-minded age.[2]

Nevertheless social psychology exhibited an easy-going

---

[1] *IV Sentences* XIX, i, 2, *iii*.

[2] F. M. Powicke. 'Reflections on the Medieval State.' *Transactions of the Royal Historical Society*, 4th Series. xix, p. 6.

P. Vinogradoff. *Roman and Canon Law in Medieval Europe*. Oxford, 1929.

T. F. T. Plucknett. *Legislation of Edward I*. Oxford, 1949.

attitude towards the sanctity of law, a certain swagger more easily recognized than defined—it was less a matter of unsubmissive conduct, for that is present and even prominent in the most legalistic communities, than of a mood not awestruck by its own inventions. Our Lord had said that the sabbath was made for man not man for the sabbath, and those who cherished the spiritual law of the Gospel, about which St Augustine had written so eloquently, were not inclined to hold lesser texts in excessive reverence. The forms of human law should be punctiliously observed—so much was granted, and to that extent the proprieties were strict—but moral teaching was not cluttered with legal injunctions. The rhythms of social and religious life were not mechanized according to the complex measures of a code. The liturgy re-enacted the mysteries of Christ's life, and was not regarded as a sort of court-ceremonial before the eucharistic throne.[1] Conscience was not yet caught in systems of canonico-moral casuistry—although these must be allowed the credit of having brought home the distinction between the external and the internal forums, between crime before the community and sin before God.

True, the wages of sin was death to the soul; on the other hand, a crime or delict could be taken in your stride, at least with regard to its temporal consequences, if you were prepared to appeal and make use of all the resources of the law, and, if these failed, to take your medicine. Sanctions were severe, for the extreme penalties of death or excommunication were commonly imposed. The human texture was perhaps tougher then than now; the penances accepted, if physically more painful, were psychologically less taxing. Schism was condemned because it broke the fellowship of charity and heresy against faith was a sin held in peculiar horror. Nevertheless men were not obsequious and could criticize a dominant party-line in religion without doubting their own orthodoxy or undermining well-accepted institutions.

The distinction between public office and private person was robustly maintained; the dignity was one thing, the individual worth of its holder was another. The English Dominican, Thomas Wallis, for reasons since confirmed, objected to a pet

---

[1] L. Bouyer. *Life and Liturgy*. London, 1957.

theological theory of Pope John XXII, an ugly character to offend, and went off to beard him in his own court at Avignon.[1] This was not the procedure of later ages. There was a sturdiness in the life of devotion not easily abashed or haunted by the fear of not playing safe with a code. Obsessionals existed of course, but scrupulosity was not prominent in spiritual literature, and sufferers were not treated with a quasi-legal reflex apparatus to allay them with assurance of security. Not that controversies were conducted delicately, for it was an age of fierce and often coarse invective; a condemnation could be charged with curses which were sometimes the fruits of fertile imaginations working on the allegorical senses of the Old Testament. Perhaps familiarity bred contempt, perhaps some of the spiritual menaces—and inducements—were like a currency which loses its weight with inflation, perhaps, best of all, it was just a sense of proportion. Anyhow a meticulous regard for human authority was no more generally evident then than now if you eavesdrop on canon lawyers talking among themselves.

To the theologians belongs the credit of holding off the threat of a legal system being imposed like the Prussian State as its own purpose and not as an instrument of a higher condition of society. The jurists came in for some rough handling from the conservative divines in the first half of the thirteenth century: at one moment Honorius III checked the teaching of Roman Law in the schools of Paris, though not precisely because of the dangers of the excessive claims pushed for it nor because of the edge it put on morals.[2] In the flush of their success the lawyers were not to be restrained: some of the early Civilians imagined themselves to be philosophers on alleged hints from Boethius about Aristotle's topology and methodology; some canonists equated Canon Law with theology, though in theory the distinction and subordination of the two disciplines seems to have been pretty well preserved outside legal circles. Ridiculous and disagreeable, remarked St Thomas, uncharacteristically tart, about the intrusion of decretalism into

---

[1] T. Käppeli. *Le procès contre Thomas Waleys. O.P. Etudes et documents.* Paris, 1936.

[2] M. M. Davy. *Les sermons universitaires parisiens de* 1230–31, *pp.* 88–90. Paris, 1931.

theology.[1] He had reason to be sensitive on the subject; the study of law was the main path to advancement, consequently the teaching of the Church might not always be presented in proper perspective by holders of high office. The qualities of a successful administrator were not necessarily those of a divine.

Against the dangers and the abuses of medieval legalism should be set its greater influence for good. It transformed a barbarism—whether that was savage or kindly depended on the extent of the social penetration of Christianity—into a civilization where human exchanges could be settled by rights made manifest by due show of evidence, not by combat or ordeal. Brute force was tamed and verdicts arrived at without appeal to preternatural intervention. The times compare favourably with our own, when barbarism has returned, sometimes crude and sometimes using subtle methods invented by modern science for breaking up the free personality and making it conform to the pattern imposed on the mass.[2] Then torture was used for eliciting evidence; this was not so bad, though bad enough. Roman practice was more ruthless than English practice, and Edward I's men resented the papal recommendation that torture should be used against the Templars; it was contrary to the decency of Common Law. Men should fight for their laws as for their wall, Heraclitus had declared, and in the thirteenth century the law was the acknowledged protector of their freedom. Bracton spoke of lawyers as dedicated to the art of the good and equitable; they were like priests, for they worship justice and minister sacred rights.[3]

Papal policy supported the north Italian communes in their struggle against the Emperor; Alessandria was named in gratitude after Alexander III.[4] Historical circumstances determined the alignment, yet not entirely, for it was decided not only on reasons of security for the States of the Church or to seize an advantage for future aggrandisement; it corresponded

---

[1] *Contra Retrahentes*, 13. XI *Quodlibets*, 9, *ad* 1. 2a–2ae, lxxxviii, 11.

[2] J. Rollin. *Police Drugs*. London, 1955.

[3] *de Legibus et Consuetudinibus Angliae*. iv, 3. Ed. T. Twiss. London, 1878.

[4] M. Pacaut. *Alexandre III: Etude sur la con~eption du pouvoir pontifical dans sa pensée et dans son oeuvre*. Paris, 1956.

to the sympathy of the Canonists for representative government. It is no exaggeration to say that on the whole their effect on secular history was on the side of the civil liberty and what now would be called constitutional democracy. They shared in the undying effort to have government carried on according to reason not appetite, and by mandarins not war-lords or palace-eunuchs.

Let us go back to the beginning of 'the ghost story', as it has been described, 'of the second life of the Roman Law after the demise of the body in which it first saw the light.'[1] Under Justinian the jumble of legislation which fell under the *jus vetus* (statutes passed under the Republic and early Empire, the decrees of the senate, and the writings of authoritative jurists) and the *jus novum* (ordinances of the middle and later Empires) was organized into a coherent *Corpus Juris*. This consisted of the *Code* (529) and of the *Digest* or *Pandects* (533) which organized the old and new regulations respectively, of the *Institutes* (533), an elementary outline, and of the *Novels* (565) or fresh constitutions.[2]

Byzantine State-philosophy may have derived from Eusebius who upheld the Emperor's right to rule 'by the grace and in the image of God'. Certainly Justinian's legislation was Christian in feeling. Dante recognized the fact when paying tribute to the vocation of Rome to pacify the world under *justitia* and *pietas*. Concerned with reformation as much as with punishment, its tone was hortatory; unlike the old Roman Law which proffered no sanctions for well-doing, it presumed that good should be done as well as evil avoided. Its judgments manifested a feeling for freedom, *favor libertatis*, and a tenderness which preferred *clementia* to *asperitas*, *benignitas* to *acerbitas*, *aequitas* to *duritia juris*. It was in this form, without the later modifications of the religious *Ecloga* of the Isaurian dynasty, and uninfluenced, so far as is known, by the great law schools of Beyrut and the East, that Justinian's masterpiece was received in the West: this was fitting, for he governed in Latin

[1] P. Vinogradoff. *Roman Law in Medieval Europe*, p. 13.

[2] *Corpus Juris Civilis*. i. *Institutiones*, edited by P. Kruger; *Digesta*, edited by T. Mommsen. Berlin, 1920.

i. *Codex Justinianus*, edited by P. Kruger. Berlin, 1915.

iii. *Novellae*, edited by R. Scholl and W. Kroll. Berlin 1912.

and was a westerner in his thought as he was in his military strategy.[1]

Whereas other Latin forms in Byzantium suffered a noiseless dissolution, the Roman Law prevailed for well nigh a thousand years until the fall of Constantinople to the Turk (1453). Swamped in the West by the tide of tribal invasions, it did not entirely disappear during the Dark Ages. Bits of it were copied and used. Cassiodorus, 'the last Roman Statesman', and a conserver of classical texts, was a faithful Home Secretary to Ostrogoth kings. Private apprenticeship to its forensic practice may have continued when academic instruction in its plan and details ceased. Some maxims were preserved by St Isidore and garbled texts appeared in the laws of the Visigoths and Burgundians who had been Roman allies of the Empire for two centuries before the collapse of imperial authority: service comradeship communicated a common style and, as in the case of the British with Ghurka regiments, left traces of procedure. Countryfolk have long memories, and the invaders were not always heathen or without respect for the institutions of the ancient provinces in which they settled. Hence *leges romanae* survived alongside the *leges barbarorum*, and legal *romanitas* impregnated the Carolingian Renaissance of the eighth century. Lanfranc, a lay-lawyer before he became a monk, is a pointer to the continuity of the juridical tradition in the north of Italy.

Nevertheless when the integral Roman Law was salvaged late in the eleventh century at Bologna only fifty miles from Ravenna, the last outpost of Byzantium in Italy, how technically superior it appeared when compared with the tribal and regional customs of the West. It was as if a pilgrim, marvelling at the marbles and mosaics, the splendour and symmetry of Santa Sophia, looked back to the rugged edifice and rude ornament of his cathedral at home. Ralph Niger, the contemporary of John of Salisbury, moralized the story of Absolom who slew his brother, Ammon, for seducing his sister:

[1] *Paradiso.* vi. *Monarchia.* ii, 5.

N. Lenkeith. *Dante and the Legend of Rome.* Warburg Institute. London, 1952.

R . G. Renard. 'Droit romain et pensée chrétienne.' *RSPT*, xxvii, pp. 57–62. Paris, 1938.

H. St L. Moss. *The Birth of the Middle Ages.* Oxford, 1935.

T. C. Sandars. *The Institutes of Justinian.* Introduction, p. xxx. London, 1898

in like manner, he concluded, the Roman Law killed the evil custom of trial by ordeal.[1] The violence of combat was superseded by the formal display of evidence for both parties in a dispute, the rough and ready justice of tribal courts by exact procedure according to cool reason.

The refining process was matched in theology. The Ransom Theory of the Atonement lingered in Peter Lombard, and Abelard (d. 1142) was in advance of his times—that was one of his troubles—when he rejected the idea that the devil was our jailer, yet slowly the story of a savage price and a double-deal, more appropriate to a saga than to doctrinal exposition, gave way to explanations more credible and devout.[2] The central argument on vicarious satisfaction of St Anselm's (d. 1109) dialogue, *Cur Deus Homo*, combined the *accipitatio* of the Roman Law and Germanic notions of making good.

The Church played the leading role in this legal revival. Ralph Niger went on to describe how the Roman Law dawned again and, under the patronage of the Papal Court, spread to the kingdoms of the West. To some extent the Church had never lost it, for its discipline embodied elements from the classical jurists handed on by such writers as St Isidore. At a time when folk-customs were becoming the laws of the realms founded on the ruins of the Roman provinces it was recognized that clerics and monks formed groups obedient to an older code: *Ecclesia vivit lege romana*.[3] The Papacy, moreover, inherited the Byzantine administration in Central Italy. Not surprisingly, therefore, the Canonists got off to a flying start in adapting the *Corpus* to the Church's own discipline. The Civilians were later in doing the same for the State. There were exceptions, Lanfranc for instance, yet in the main the West lacked an educated class of laymen corresponding to the Byzantine civil lawyers who were able to discuss questions of Church and State on equal terms with the clergy.

---

[1] II *Kings*, xiii.
  H. Kantorowicz and B. Smalley. 'An English Theologian's View of Roman Law: Pepo, Irnerius, Ralph Niger.' *Medieval and Renaissance Studies*, i, pp. 237–52. London, 1941.
  C. Leitmaier, *Die Kirche und die Gottesurteile*. Vienna, 1952.

[2] See 3a, xlviii, 4, 5. xlix, 2. 1a. xxi, 4.

[3] P. Fournier. *L'Eglise et le droit romain au XIIIe siècle*. Paris, 1921.

A century before Accursius (d. 1260) wrote his great Gloss,
which was the earliest major systematization of the Civil Law,
Gratian composed his *Decretum* between 1149 and 1151. Published privately, it soon came to enjoy in Canon Law a prestige
equal to that of Peter Lombard's *Sentences* in theology. Laying
under contribution the work of the Bologna doctors, he reduced
to some sort of order the Church's existing legislation, already a
rough imitation of Roman models.[1] Soon the Canonists were as
far ahead of the Civilians in exploiting the *Corpus* as the papal
officials were of the king's servants in the business of administration. At first their credit was greater, for a theological aura surrounded their proceedings and they could urge a higher
origin and more divine titles for their *Princeps*. When in 1200
Innocent III invoked the *Translatio Imperii* in assuming the
authority to provide an emperor during the disputes between
Hohenstaufen and Welf he was following common form. That
Caesar was Caesar only by will of the Pope was not felt to be
a far-fetched claim, nor that civil law should defer to the
canons of the Church.

The arts of government which flourished in the papal court
were expressed in its chancery style; the *modus dictaminis*, the
rhythm, the *forma scripturae*, all were brought to a consummate
pitch. Exact to the smallest detail in the seal of a document,
the rules of authentication were as fine as those of the Bank of
England for detecting forgeries. Its official impersonality anticipated the reforms of Frederick II and Piero della Vigna in
Sicily and worked more smoothly to more lasting effect. 'Criticise
it as we may', writes Dr. E. F. Jacob, 'and as most contemporaries did, for its delays and venality, in the Roman Curia men
moved in a different world to that of a State; a world where
subtle distinctions were heard, and delicately shaded opinions
expressed, the spiritual home of educated and intelligent
humanity.'[2] How sophisticated they must have felt and how
they must have dissembled their amusement when they adjudicated between Giraldus Cambrensis, with his Celtic imagina-

---

[1] J. Kantorowicz. *Studies in the Glossators of the Roman Law.* p. 80. Cambridge, 1938.
Studia Gratiana. Ed. J. Forchielli and A. M. Stickler, 2 vols. Bologna, 1953-4.

[2] 'Innocent III.' *Cambridge Medieval History*, vi, p. 36. 1929.
A. C. Clark. *The Cursus in Medieval and Vulgar Latin.* Oxford, 1910.

tion and sense of grievance, and his rough Norman opponents, with their accusations that the bishop-elect was a horse-thief.

Not until towards the end of the thirteenth century, when Church and State began to separate and solidify into distinct bodies, did Canonists and Civilians come into serious conflict, and even then the issues were ambiguous; there was no uniform taking of sides in the struggle between Papacy and Empire. Of course the ideal of the supreme *Princeps* emancipated from Church control was bound to attract the lay-minded, and Peter Crassus, the Ravenna jurist, in his *Defence of Henry IV*, a treatise which announced 'the entry of Roman Law into medieval political thought', denied the deposing power of the Pope, or 'the monk Hildebrand', as he called Gregory VII.[1] On the other hand, some of the eminent lawyers of Bologna, Orleans and Naples had no cause to support the Emperor, and not all Canonists were by any means Papalists either by temperament or conviction; in fact many, particularly among the cardinals, developed the theory, which was to lead to the Conciliar Movement, that the Pope was the constitutional representative of the *congregatio fidelium* and stood to the College of Cardinals as a bishop to a cathedral chapter.[2] Bishops, too, zealous for their rights as 'ordinaries', and for diocesan and provincial rights and franchises, were prepared to support Regalism in order to maintain themselves against the *Curia*, and this episcopal temper persisted during the Gallican controversies and until the Vatican Council.

1. *Canonists*

Eventually made shapely and consistent, the Canon Law in the early Middle Ages was still unformed and muddled. A patchwork of precepts drawn from Jewish, New Testament, Conciliar, and Pontifical sources was mixed with Roman maxims and rubrics, and diversified according to regional compilations. The change was wrought by the masterpiece of the Camaldolese monk, Master Gratian (d. before 1173), the *Concordia Discord-*

---

[1] C. N. S. Woolf. *Bartolus of Sassoferrato*, p. 70. Cambridge, 1913.

[2] W. Ullmann. *Origins of the Great Schism*. London, 1948.

B. Tierney. *Foundations of the Conciliar Theory: The Contribution of the Medieval Canonists from Gratian to the Great Schism*. Cambridge, 1955.

antium Canonum. This was no mere miscellany of tests in chronological order of publication but their systematic distribution
according to topics in a running argument according to the *sic
et non* method of the schools. Known as the *Decretum Gratiani,* a
standard text-book not an authoritative code possessing the
weight of law, it was complemented by various compilations,
more or less methodical, of synodical canons, notably of the
two Lateran Councils of 1179 and 1215, and of the decrees of
the lawyer-popes, Alexander III (Roland Bandinelli, d. 1181),
Innocent III (d. 1216) and Honorius III (d. 1227). These
collections were later replaced by the famous *Decretals* of
Gregory IX (d. 1241), into which were later inserted the
decrees of Innocent IV (Sinibald Fieschi, d. 1254).[1]

The *Decretals* formed the *novum jus,* which went beyond the
academic moderation of Gratian's *vetus jus* and declared the
centralizing policy which consolidated and expanded the
achievements of Innocent III. Officially promulgated by the
Bull *Rex Pacificus* (1234), they were compiled by St Raymund
of Pennafort (d. 1275), who was praised by Vincent of Beauvais
for pruning—somewhat roughly, some have complained—five
volumes to the size of one and twenty-five distinctions to five.[2]
A Catalan and already an expert jurist when he joined the
Dominicans, afterwards legal adviser to the Pope and for a
short period Master-General of his Order, whose primitive
constitutions he edited in the form that survived for nearly
seven centuries, he was the *doctor decretorum,* a specialist in the
jurisprudentia divina of Church discipline—the very phrase
indicates the mixture of theology and law effected when the

---

[1] A. L. Richter and E. Friedberg. *Corpus Juris Canonici:* 1. *Decretum Magistri
   Gratiani.* Leipzig, 1879. ii. *Decretalium Collectiones.* Leipzig, 1881.

   P. Fournier and G. le Bras. *Histoire des Collections canoniques en occident depuis les
   Fausses Décrétales jusqu'au Décret de Gratien.* 2 vols. Paris, 1931–2.

   G. le Bras. *Histoire du Droit et des Institutions de l'Eglise en Occident.* Prologomènes.
   Paris, 1955.

   A. van Hove. *Commentarium Lovaniense ad Codicem Juris Canonici. Prologemena.* 2nd
   ed. Malines, 1945.

   F. Cimitier. *Les Sources du Droit canonique.* Paris, 1930.

   F. Thaner. *Die Summa Magistri Rolandi.* Innsbruck, 1874.

[2] *Speculum Doctrinale,* vii, 49.

   F. Balme and C. Paban. *Raymundiana.* Monumenta Ordinis Praedicatorum
   Historica. Rome, 1898, 1901.

doctrine of sacramental repentance passed into the external forum of penance. Gratian had spoken of the *potestas ligandi et solvendi* in one context to mean the apostolic power of remitting sins, in another to mean the power of jurisdiction over the public order. Raymund's *Summa Juris* and *Summa Casuum* systematized the penitential doctrines and disciplines promoted by the Lateran Decrees, and developed the distinction drawn by Alexander III between two results of sin; the offence to God was amended *per cordis contritionem* and the scandal to the Church *per oris confessionem et operis satisfactionem* according to officially determined scales of satisfactions or indulgences.[1]

A religiously-charged dialectic was at once a political strength and a juridical weakness in the cause of the political Canonists. An academic impurity was a characteristic of its partisans, particularly when they engaged in polemics.[2] For they were promiscuous. Strict argumentation from legal premises was mingled with biblical allegories and moralities, *a priori* philosophism with political opportunism, divine ordinances with appeals to historical titles, sometimes authentic and sometimes spurious: a case in point was the Donation of Constantine, the exposure of which by Lorenzo Valla inaugurated the critical treatment of sources.[3] They were makers rather than students of history. Theological excurses compose much of Gratian's collection, and two works by St Thomas, which from their titles might be expected to be devoted to legal topics, turn out to be discussions of heresies concerning the Trinity and the

[1] P. Anciaux. *La Théologie du sacrement de pénitence au XIIe siècle*. Louvain, 1949.

J. MacNeill and H. Gamer. *Medieval Handbooks of Penance*. New York, 1938.

G. le Bras. 'Pénitentiels.' *DTC*, xii, 1, col. 1160–79. Paris, 1933.

E. J. Arnould. *Le Manuel des Péchés*. Paris, 1940.

M. van de Kerckhove. *La notion de juridiction dans le doctrine des Décrétistes et des premiers Décrétalistes*. Assisi, 1937.

R. Mortimer. *The Origin of Private Penance in the Western Church*. Oxford, 1939.

[2] J. de Ghellinck. *Le mouvement théologique du XIIe siècle*, ii, 3. 'Melange des matières théologiques et juridiques.'

'Gratien, La théologie dans ses sources et chez les glossateurs de son "Décret".' *DTC*. vi, 2. 1731–51. Paris, 1947.

A. van Hove. *Commentarium Lovaniense*. i, 3. De methodo scientiae canonicae ejusque connexionis cum scientia theologica et cum jure romano.

[3] G. P. Gooch. 'Modern Historiography,' in *Maria Teresa and Other Studies'*, p. 219· London, 1951.

Incarnation, with an eye to Abbot Joachim's followers.[1] Roger
Bacon would have liked Canon Law purged of the waste of
civil law and kept for theology.[2]

Canon Law eventually formed a coherent system of genuine
laws ·many of which were not entirely new. All emanated from
an authority whose credentials could not be challenged. The
entrance of theological externals into such a system was fair
enough. More troublesome was the intrusion of Canon Law
into theology. As legalism spread so devotion sometimes tended
to be clogged and some distinctions were blurred; thus there
was some confusion in theory between sacramental validity and
liceity.[3] In practice clerical students who were careerists forsook
theology for the *scientia lucrativa*. Gregory in cobwebs, wrote
Dante to the Italian cardinals, Ambrose in forgotten corners,
Augustine given up, together with Dionysius, Damascene, and
Bede, and they hold forth about I know not what manner of
laws, Innocent, and Hostiensis—and why not?—the first sought
God our noblest ends, from the others come prebends and
benefices.[4]

The strict lawyers among the Canonists were well able on
occasion to examine and expand a case in the purity of their
own technical medium. Crime could be considered in abstraction from sin; it was a public offence which earthly authority
could judge so long as it kept to outward deeds and did not
refine on motives it could only guess at. Accordingly a verdict
was to be arrived at in the light of the evidence brought forward
according to the due procedure, and sentence pronounced
secundum allegata even when privately its justice might be
doubted.[5]

Nevertheless the policy of the Papalists was to extend rather
than to limit the bounds of Canon Law. Not rash, but relentless

---

[1] *Expositio* 1ae *decretalis ad archidiaconum Tridentinum. Expositio super* 2a *mdecretalem ad
eumdem. Opusc.* xxiii, xxiv.

[2] *Obus Tertium,* xxiv.

[3] L.   Saltet. *Les réordinations. Etude sur le sacrement de l'ordre.* pp. 289–96. Paris, 1907.

[4] *Epistolae* xi, 7. Innocent was Sinibald Fieschi, Innocent IV; Hostiensis was Henry
of Susa, Cardinal Bishop of Ostia (d. 1277), author of the famous *Summa
Hostiensis.* See *Paradiso* xii, 82–5, in praise of St Dominic.   ix, 133–6.*a*,
Monarchia ii, 3.

[5] See 2a–2ae, lxiv, 6 *ad* 3. lxvii, 2.

and persevering, they were banded together to advance their cause. This was the ideal of the spiritual control of the government of Europe, advanced by Hildebrand and enlarged by Innocent III, who at his consecration preached on the text, *I will suddenly speak against a nation and kingdom, to root out and to pull down, and I will suddenly speak of a nation and of a kingdom, to build up and plant it*: his views were not generally regarded as immoderate.[1] Theirs was not merely a system of academic law nor of domestic discipline for the Church; it was an engine to bring the entire social organization under control. They knew that the permanence of institutions lies in religion, not in legal forms, and these they based on Natural Law of which the Church was the guardian.[2] They interpreted history to suit their ends and shaped events in the process. Their uncompromising doctrine of Papal monarchy was the logical outcome of a Christendom still united but which had burst the seams of the Empire. The Pope had rightfully taken the Emperor's place. Past facts were enrolled and broken in to suit present and future needs. The political Canonists possessed the quality which has been admired in the Whigs—but with this difference, they did not succeed.

It was as theocratic statesmen not as jurists, then, that some of them identified their law with the divine law, and that more would have enlarged its sway for the sake of the welfare of a united Europe. As such they should be judged. They cannot be dismissed on the pretence that their position was based only on doubtful texts, mystical historicism and symbolical theology, and maintained with a mixture of naivety and chicanery. Their attempt at a spiritual despotism, not ignoble in its ambitions, was impressive in its results. The Old Empire was long dead, the New Empire was already declining; it had never been so strong as it claimed and passed unmentioned by St Thomas. The Church, on the other hand, was very much alive, and unafraid of power.

---

[1] *Jer.* xviii, 7–9.

M. Maccarrone. *Chiesa e Stato nella dottrina di Papa Innocenzio III*. Rome, 1955.

[2] O. Lottin. *Le droit naturel chez saint Thomas d'Aquin et ses prédecesseurs*, ii, 3.

S. Kuttner. *Repertorium der Kanonistik* (1140–1234). *Prodromus Corporis Glossarum*, i. Vatican City, 1937.

The effect was perhaps happier for civilization than for simple devotion. To some extent a sacerdotal hierarchy was transformed into a hierarchy of lawyers, 'and in all ages the lawyers, invaluable as a conservative force, have been as a body greater enemies of reform than the priests'.[1] The change was more perhaps a matter of social psychology than of institutional structure. The confident assumption of responsibility by the clerics and their administrative technique combined to produce a system in which the secular power was humanized and the arts and sciences fostered. In that high culture and law-building civilization organized religion was not a dead weight but a quickening force and grace.[2]

The achievement answered the unanimous conviction that the Church could magisterially judge all causes where sin was involved. Innocent III had formulated the prerogative when, after urging peace with King John of England, he had been snubbed by Philip Augustus for meddling in a matter between lord and vassal. Moreover, Rome was the repository of justice, the *sedes justitiae* to which recourse could be had when justice was denied in civil courts. A far-reaching moral surveillance protected the orphan and defenceless against the avarice and greed of magnates. Canon lawyers possessed the monopoly of matrimonial legislation. They developed Roman principles of law and created new ones which have since been recognized by International Law—for instance, rules concerning safe-conduct of envoys, diplomatic confidence, condemnation of treaty violations, the humane treatment of prisoners, the protection of minorities, sanctions against aggression, the conditions of treaties and peace settlements. They insisted on promulgation as a necessary condition of law, for otherwise law would not be addressed to the reason of its subjects. Their rules for discovering evidence have served as models for judicial procedure. Many key positions in the State were held by clerics, so were lectureships in Civil Law.

---

[1] H. Rashdall. *The Universities of Europe in the Middle Ages*, i, p. 139.
   W. Ullmann. *The Growth of Papal Government in the Middle Ages. A Study in the Ideological Relation of Clerical to Lay Power.* London, 1955.

[2] G. Schnürer. *Kirche und Kultur im Mittelalter*, ii. Paderborn, 1926.
   R. Hull. *Medieval Theories of the Papacy.* London, 1934.

Altogether, when control over the disposal of benefices and the temporalities annexed to ecclesiastical dignities are also taken into account, the Papacy was a formidable social force, indeed the greatest, and its servants the political Canonists were at the peak of their power.[1] They could legislate against such practices as the docking of horses; the zealots among them could compare the gold of the mitre to the lead of the crown, and compute that the sacerdotal power surpassed the regal power 7,644 times, that being the sun's excess of size over the moon.[2] None would have agreed that canons could be enacted only with the consent of the temporal ruler or in agreement with the law of the land. It was natural they should be champions of the power which had created their class.

Humanly speaking the Canonists almost, but not quite, succeeded in committing the Church to a temporal theocracy. The strained interpretation of the text, *here are two swords*, according to which both spiritual and temporal power had been entrusted to the Church, was not generally accepted by the theologians. If both were entrusted to one authority neither would be fittingly used, wrote the Papal Chancellor, Robert Pullen (d. 1146), and a century later theologians of the centre were equally moderate.[3] Official claims were more circumspect

---

[1] G. B. Pallieri and G. Vismara. *Acta pontificia juris gentium.* Milan, 1946.

S. Z. Ehler and J. B. Morrall, *Church and State through the Centuries.* Illustrative documents, ii, iii, iv. London, 1954.

A. Potthast. *Regesta Pontificium Romanorum ab anno 1198 ad annum 1304.* Berlin, 1874-5

A. Fliche. *Le réforme Gregorienne et la reconquête chrétienne.* Paris, 1947.

Z. N. Brooke. *The English Church and the Papacy.* Cambridge, 1931.

M. Maccarrone. *Vicarius Christi: Storia del titolo papale.* Rome, 1952.

G. Barraclough. *Papal Provisions: Aspects of Church History, Constitutional, Legal and Administrative, in the Later Middle Ages.* Oxford, 1935.

M. Pacaut. *Alexandre III.* Ch. ix., pp. 335-69. 'Les doctrines politiques des canonistes.'

For a summary of the Church's teaching on International Law see

J. Folliet. *Morale internationale.* Paris, 1935.

D. A. O'Connor. *Catholic Social Doctrine.* Westminster, Md., 1956.

[2] W. Ullmann. *Medieval Papalism. The Political Theories of the Medieval Canonists.* London, 1949.

[3] *Luke,* xx, 38.

F. Courtney. *Cardinal Robert Pullen. An English Theologian of the Twelfth Century,* pp. 259-62. Rome, 1954.

J. Lecler. 'L'argument des deux glaives.' *Recherches de science religieuse,* xxi, pp. 299-339. Paris, 1932.

than those of the publicists of the Canonical vogue. Boniface
VIII may personally have agreed with these young Turks,
nevertheless his Bulls *Ausculta Fili* and *Unam Sanctam* advanced
no novel and explicit claim to direct dominion over the world,
and when in 1298 he settled the dispute between England and
France he arbitrated in his private capacity as Benedetto
Gaetani.[1] Not rarely the Pope was the only potentate who
acted as a good European, and strove to reconcile jealousies in
face of the common danger from the East. Despite the venality
and arrogance of the Curia, it spoke for the commonwealth of
undivided Christendom.

Civilian lawyers and politicians who supported the increase
of regal power in the Nation-States sought to restrict pretensions
to universal jurisdiction. They were anticipated by many
churchmen who were chary about pushing ecclesiastical
claims if that meant more centralization and tighter control
from the Papal Curia. Bishops had no wish to diminish their
local rights and shared their countrymen's resentment about
being taxed for the benefit of foreigners.[2] Even the friars,
influential in the highest circles, for they enjoyed pontifical
approbation and popular esteem—there was then a flourish
about them like that of the Light Division in Wellington's
army—were not committed to the politics of the Canonist
Movement. The Franciscans, the leaders of an evangelical
movement, were neither hag-ridden by legal forms nor likely
to be awed by titles to power, however respectable, which
turned on ownership. Roger Bacon disliked the juridical
clatter, *strepitus juris*, of Church government, and Jacopone da
Todi, the author of the *Stabat Mater*, was an outspoken critic of
Boniface VIII.[3]

The Dominicans compared themselves to Jacob and the
Franciscans to Esau. They were more clerical in constitution
and perhaps more classical in temper—less emotional, Hastings
Rashdall judged—yet as a body they tried to resist Popes and

---

[1] F. M. Powicke. *The Thirteenth Century*, 1216–1307, pp. 650–3. Oxford, 1953.
Christian Life in the Middle Ages, pp. 48–73. Oxford, 1935.
T. S. R. Boase. *Boniface VIII*. London, 1933.

[2] *Opus Tertium*, xxiv.

[3] W. E. Lunt. *Papal Revenues in the Middle Ages*. New York, 1934.

rulers who appointed their men to administrative posts and to
back out of the work of the Inquisition which was thrust on
them: hints were dropped of their characteristic irony about
the man in possession.[1] St. Albert was created Bishop of
Ratisbon in 1260; he resigned after one year, and reflected that
a prelate was expected to behave more like Sardanapulus than
like Christ. They could always be trusted to take an independent line, as the Plantagenets discovered who planted
them in Wales and Ireland. The scientific exposition of natural
and revealed religion, which was their special calling, lifted
them out of the ruck of current prescriptions, and, though
doctrinally committed to the supremacy of the Pope, their
main bases were in places like Oxford and Paris where the
pretensions of the Curialists could be unperplexedly resisted by
Church figures as orthodox as Grosseteste and St Louis. Their
strength lay in England, France, North Italy, the Rhineland
and the Low Countries, regions where nationalist feeling was
detached about the claims to empire asserted either by Caesar
or by Pontifex. When Nicholas IV sought to depose their
Master-General, Munio of Zamora, their representatives at the
General Chapter of Palencia (1291) acted like Nelson at
Copenhagen.[2] Another Master-General, Hervé de Nédéllec (d.
1323), was a strong supporter of the rights of ordinaries.

It may be assumed that the distinction of the temporal and
spiritual spheres as maintained by the *de Potestate Regia et
Papali* of John of Paris (d. 1306) represented their common
opinion, at least in England and France.[3] Apart from St
Raymund of Pennafort who was in a class by himself—though
mention may be made of Monaldus (d. before 1285), the author
of the *Summa Monaldina*, and Martinus Polonus (d. 1279), a
chronicler who drew up an alphabetical guide to the *Decretum*—
no prominent Canonist authorities came from the ranks of the

---

[1] L. de Lacger. '*L'Albigeois* au siècle de saint Louis.' *Revue d'histoire ecclésiastique*.
lii, 1, pp. 26–50. Louvain, 1957.

[2] A. Mortier. *Histoire des maîtres généraux de l'ordre des frères Precheurs*, ii, pp. 260–315.
Paris, 1905.

[3] J. Leclercq. *Jean de Paris et l'ecclésiologie du XIIIe siècle*. Paris, 1942.
  M. Grabmann. *Studien zu Joannes Quidort von Paris*, *O.P.* Munich, 1922.
  G. Digard. *Phillippe le Bel et le Saint Siège*. Paris, 1936.

5

friars. They compiled directories which worked law into
morals, but rarely took degrees in the schools of law. The legal
activity of the English Dominicans John of Bromyard (d. after
1310) and William of Hotham (d. 1299), the favourite minister
of Edward I, was exceptional. Nicholas Trivet (d. 1328) and
Robert Holcot (d. 1349) were more typical; both were volu-
minous writers and the sons of judges—the latter indeed was a
lawyer at Oxford and Cambridge before he became a preacher
—but they left Canon Law and civil law severely alone.[1] It is
noteworthy, too, that Positive Law was not overstressed by
John of Freiburg (d. 1314), *tuba evangelica*, whose *Summa
Confessorum* both carried on the work of St Raymund of Pennafort and ran into the devotional movement of the fourteenth
century. It was a capital work of pastoral theology which
systematized the multiplicity of decrees and practical rules in
canonical and casuistical writings without doing violence to the
principles of living morality set forth in the second part of St
Thomas's *Summa Theologica*.[2]

The Dominican Ptolemy of Lucca argued that the Pope was
the true and proper lord of the Emperor, and two Austin friars,
Giles of Rome (d. 1315) and James of Viterbo (d. 1308),
combining Aristotelean and Thomist political theory with the
Augustinist criticism of secular power as lacking true justice,
were the publicists of a theocracy which gathered in all earthly
dominium, so much so that princes were subordinate to the
Pope even in the secular administration of their own realms.[3]
Yet in the main the doctrine of the papal *plenitudo potestatis*
came from the political Canonists rather than from the treatises
of the theologians; the Dominican and Franciscan masters
were curiously uncommitted to the theory when it is remembered how active both Orders were in the business of the
Roman See.

---

[1] B. Jarrett. *The English Dominicans*. p. 61. London, 1921.

[2] M. D. Chenu. 'Jean de Fribourg,' *DTC*, viii, 1, col. 761–2. Paris, 1924.

[3] Ptolemy of Lucca. *Determinatio Compendiosa de Jurisdictione Imperii*. Ed. M. Kram-
    mer. Hanover, 1909.

    Aegidius Romanus, de Ecclestica Potestate. Ed. R. Scholz. Weimar, 1929.

    H. X. Arquillière. *Le plus ancien traité de l'église, Jacques de Viterbe*, de Regimine
    Christiano. *Etude des sources et édition critique*. Paris, 1926.

    D. Gutiérez. *De Jacobi Viterbiensis vita, operibus et doctrina theologica*. Rome, 1939.

Moreover, stiffish opposition was encountered from the dioceses and ecclesiastical provinces. Devotion to the See of Peter implied no tame acceptance of the fiscal charges and administrative interference which went with centralization. A new pharisaeism, engendered by the increase of positive laws and the multitude of regulations, was resented, and the condemnation came to men's lips, *Woe to you, lawyers, because you load men with burdens grievous to be borne.*[1] A great line of schoolmen-bishops, the products of the movement which brought in the universities and friars, succeeded the monk-bishops of the twelfth century and preceded the civil-servant bishops of the fourteenth and after. There were exceptions, such as Hubert Walter, a commanding figure in the period who reserved his best energies for secular affairs, but men like Langton, Edmund Rich, Grosseteste, Kilwardby, Peckham, Winchelsey, and the Dominican Innocent V looked beyond the mechanism of Church government to the urgency of preaching and instruction. To the high theologians, especially those inspired with the old humanism and the new hellenism, the Canonists were workers in a subordinate department, to be watched lest because of them the Church Militant acquired too large an administrative tail. Roger Bacon's flings at the ecclesiastical commissars and St Thomas's firm drawing of bounds to Positive Law witness how little they intimidated the life of devotion. Shrillness is no sign of strength, and when their claims became exorbitant they were no longer able to enforce them, for by then civil authority had grown in dignity and ability to protect its own.

It must be admitted, however, that the pride of the Canonists was not unfounded. Their organization has been compared to that of Standard Oil in our own day. The association of medieval clerks stretched across the Western World, from the Shannon to the headwaters of the Euphrates, from the Tagus to the Vistula; their establishments were linked together and supervised by the system of visitation; they achieved a legal unity

---

[1] W. A. Pantin. 'Grosseteste's Relations with Papacy and Crown,' in *Robert Grosseteste, Scholar and Bishop*. Oxford, 1955.

   C. R. Cheney. *From Becket to Langton. English Church Government*, 1170–1213. Manchester, 1956.

which transcended frontiers and proposed an equality which contrasted with the class-distinctions outside. Famous professional soldiers of the fourteenth century and great mercantile families of an earlier period might spring from obscurity, but ordinarily it was only through the Church that the way lay open for the character and talent of a boy of humble birth. By making it possible for a peasant's son to get learning and enter on a high career, churchmen helped to break up a system in which a man was tied to the land or to service founded on territorial occupation.

Their active ideas which helped to humanize political institutions and civil law may be considered under three headings. First, the spiritual ability to master or at least to modify the consequences of physical processes; secondly, the importance of contract in public agreements; third, the need of election according to proper procedure in the constitution of authority.

The conviction that justice, a Christian virtue, was spiritually free and could break out of merely material bonds might be expected of the organizers of an eternal salvation scheme. If the canon lawyers were not theologians themselves, at least they were the servants of theology. They were not backward in appealing to the secular arm or squeamish about the use of brute-force. All the same they were not hypocritical when, for instance, they avoided the death-sentence and handed its execution over to the secular arm; let no clerks at all be judges of blood, said a canon of the Council of Westminster in 1102. The fiction deferred to the idea that ministers of the New Law should not be *percussores aut occisores*.[1] They had no prejudice against blood-letting, yet surgery was more severely forbidden to clerics than the practice of medicine; here also symbolic reasons were at work —*Ecclesia abhorret a sanguine*. They were not so spiritual as to escape altogether the tendency common to all medieval systems of lumping the innocent with the guilty, and exacted reparation from the families or corporations of offenders who had injured the rights of the Church. Nevertheless Canon Law maintained the principle of personal responsibility for faults, and the feeling for it prompted the

---

[1] 2a–2ae. lxiv, 4.

abandonment of collective excommunication by Innocent IV.[1]

The determination that events should not be merely allowed to take their course entered into the arguments of Alexander III on the Lateran decrees and of Grosseteste's letters to William of Raleigh, that such was the force of matrimony that it could legitimize a child born out of wedlock.[2] In seeking to convey the effects of legitimacy the churchmen fell foul of an old custom founded on a tribal and social instinct against 'outsiders'. There were sound reasons for it, yet it is not fanciful to relate its laws to male vanity and conjugal jealousy, and to a closed community which excluded bastards, eunuchs, and foreigners. When they sought to bring the secular law into line with Canon Law at the Council of Merton (1234) the prelates were refused with the famous answer, *Nolumus leges Angliae mutare*. Divine grace, however, knows none of these exclusions, as the Canonists recognized for all their show of 'impediments'. The Church is not a peculiar connection of 'insiders'; even its juridical constitution does not shut it in. It is not a primitive group. A Christian society, faithful to the teaching of St Paul, aware of the mystery of spiritual procreation and of sonship by adoption, and uncommitted to a blood-and-soil fixation or to taboos on intercourse with strangers, will keep open house and resist *Apartheid. Neither let the son of a stranger, that hath joined himself to the Lord, speak saying, the Lord hath utterly separated me from his people. Neither let the eunuch say, Behold I am a dry tree.*[3]

A system constructed by human laws will inevitably be more rigid and artificial than one formed by theology. It has been said that an English court may shut its eyes to the facts of life, and, not entertaining illegitimacy, may rule that a child may be *filius nullius*, that is, not a child of lawful parents.[4] To the Church's Law, however, all children, whether illegitimate or

---

[1] I. T. Eschmann. 'St Thomas and the Decretal of Innocent IV, Romana Ecclesia: A New Argumentation in Innocent IV's Apparatus.' *MS*. viii, p. 1. Toronto, 1946.

G. le Bras. 'Canon Law.' *LMA*., p. 357. Oxford, 1926.

[2] *Roberti Grossetesti Epistolae*. xxiii, xxiv. Ed. by H. R. Luard, pp. 71–97. Rolls Series. London, 1861.

[3] *Is*. lvi, 3.
1a–2ae. cv, 3, *ad* 2.

[4] Chancery Division. *In Re* T. and T. *The Times*, 13 Oct., 1956.

not, belong by baptism to the household of the Faith and, by dispensation if necessary, may reach the highest office.

A written code will also lack the springiness of custom, for it is more arbitrary, less natural—a tower rather than a tree. The Roman Law was no exception. All the same it was charged with Christian values, both at its origins under Justinian and during its development by the medieval clerics; its effect on the community was not wholly one of mechanization. If to some extent its official modes stiffened suppler folk-rhythms, it also prepared for the exercise of a more civil conception of liberty than was allowed by the *leges barbarorum*. Popular lore might credit a love-child with exceptional gifts of mind and body whereas illegitimacy was an impediment to the sacrament of Holy Order according to the canons; on the other hand the clerics were readier than the lay-lawyers to master natural processes, or at least to modify their results or break down the barriers by legal action. Primitive groups, closed in on themselves, may live according to a kind of incest, which prevents free communication and the *multiplicatio amicorum*.[1] The influence of Canon Law tended to make the community wider and more welcoming. The stranger to the tribe, no longer an enemy, became the *advena* of the civil law or *peregrinus* of the canons, and was granted rights accordingly.

The idea of marriage as a purchase, a barter between two families represented by the bridegroom and the father who gave away the bride, was being changed into a more personal relationship. Canonists and theologians emphasized the sacramental union of hearts; that was more important than the property-bargain or actual procreation. Marriage was a partnership of the man and woman concerned, which could be valid by the contract of the two persons, *per verba de praesenti* without witness or presence of a priest. This was little to the liking of the Common Lawyers, who refused dower save in the case of marriage *ad ostium ecclesiae*, and saved the situation, as best they could, by insisting on banns, made obligatory by the Lateran Council of 1215—it was there that Innocent III revoked the existing legislation on the prohibited degrees of

---

[1] 2a–2ae, cliv, 9.

consanguinity, a humane decision but one that ran counter to ancient sentiment. The rights and wrongs of the dispute may be left aside; the point is the value ascribed to individual personality.

Canonists held that marriage was private contract and not, as the older lawyers had taught, merely a *consortium* the consequences of which were fixed by law; most moralists agreed that marriage was ratified by consent, not copulation.[1] The maxim, *consensus facit nuptias*, ran through the fourth book of Gregory IX's *Decretals*. The theory was that the contracting parties in marriage should be unforced; in fact an heiress was still a pawn in the game of feudal power. The divines affirmed that a wife was not owned by her husband and that the role of children was not entirely submissive. The praise of virginity, weaker perhaps than it had been in the days of St Jerome, recognized a woman's right to be just herself and was a persistent factor in the history of female emancipation.

The person, rather than the head of a family was the centre of responsibility in the political community if he were a male and a property-owner. Civil or political association was preferred to despotic or patriarchal aggregation. These ideas, not entirely foreign to classical Roman teaching, were strengthened by the medieval progression from Status to Contract. The theory and practice of making wills was warrant for the individual's ability to transfer domestic property rights. Legally binding agreements could be entered into with strangers to the family group. Jurisprudence entered into the spirit of the current philosophy and theology of freedom, and personal dignity and independence were seen in a fresh light. The credit for bringing this about belongs jointly to the disciples of Gratian and Peter Lombard.

In this temper, too, the machinery of representation by voting was devised. The weight of quality as well as of quantity had to be allowed for, and the *sanior pars* balanced with the *major pars*; the classical view was that worth should prevail

---

[1] See 3a. xxix, 2. 2a–2ae. lvii 4. clii, 2, *ad* 1. *V Ethics, lect.* 9.

J. Dauvillier. *Le mariage dans le droit classique de l'Eglise depuis le Décret de Gratien jusqu'à la mort de Clément V*. Paris, 1893.

even when in the numerical minority.[1] Other reasons, apart
from ecclesiastical practice in the promotion of cathedral,
collegial and monastic dignitaries, conspired to make the
canonists favour the transmission of authority through due
election, not through birth or the fact of possession. One was
their bent towards reasonable debate in the settlement of
difference. Another could be found in the circumstances of
their opposition to imperial or regal power, which made them
dwell on some act of popular consent as an essential condition
of legitimate sovereignty.

A working distinction between the office and the person,
originating in patristic literature, notably in the exegesis of
Romans xiii, had been developed by the theological and juristic
schoolmen. It was officially defined that sacramental power was
not dependent on the private worth of the minister.[2] Office in
the Church was constituted by spiritual or pastoral status, and
this was apart from personal merit or performance according to
gifts of the spirit. All might be ministers of grace in the sense
that they were commissioned to teach, give the sacraments and
rule in the juridical body instituted by God. The difference has
been upheld on appeal to the House of Lords, which decided
that a leading Jehovah's Witness had no right to exemption
from military service since his denomination did not allow for
the co-existence of two elements, a ministering or clerical
element and a lay element to which it could act as a regular
minister.[3]

The power of order, too, was distinct from ownership on a
personal title. The distinction in Church order had its counter-
part in social philosophy: official position was neither a matter
of individual excellence nor held by the magnetism of the hero.
'It is impermissible and foreign to the spirit of Marxism-
Leninism,' said Mr Khrushchev when detailing Stalin's
enormities, 'to elevate one person and to transform him into a
superman possessing supernatural characteristics akin to those

---

[1] F. M. Powicke. *Stephen Langton*, p. 81. Oxford, 1928.

[2] Denzinger, 424, 436, 584. See 3a, lxiv, 5.
   D. E. Heintschel. *The Mediaeval Concept of an Ecclesiastical Office*. Washington, 1956.

[3] *Walsh v. Lord Advocate. The Times*, 20 July 1956.

of a god.'[1] When the Summists appealed to the authority of a
saint or doctor it was not of his personal originality and excellence they were thinking, but of a quasi-juridical guarantee
offered by the text that the doctrine so supported was worthy
of credit.[2] So also the identification of an individual with his
social authority would have been a deviation from the social
doctrine of the Middle Ages. Will may set up power, but only
reason can make it right—and the reason in question was a
social reason articulated in the terms of a law well-understood,
commonly accepted, and binding on all.

Needless to say, political motives also entered into the
Curia's attempt to ensure the rule of men most likely to protect
natural rights and religion. It intervened decisively against
dynastic power on occasion, for instance when Innocent III
ruled out Philip of Suabia. Sensitive to the dangers of being
threatened by imperial power from its southern flank in Sicily,
it took the side of the democratic communes in North Italy.
The policy was opportunist; it was also faithful to canonical
notions of order, which lay closer to the Greek feeling for the
ruler's political virtue than to the German respect for the
leader's family and person. The canon lawyers were strong
constitutionalists to a man.

The point of right, at least in theory, was decided almost
impersonally, certainly without any warm mystique about the
blood royal. Moreover, the officials of the Curia themselves
belonged to a hierarchic system and were suspicious of a rival
rex et sacerdos. The ritual annointing of the Emperor's head was
replaced after the time of Innocent III by the anointing of the
right arm and between the shoulder blades.[3] Power was
invested with a quasi-sacramental character, but on condition that the ruler made a contract into which the Church
entered. Alexander III roundly told Barbarossa that he held
the Empire only as a benefice. Some canonists taught that the
transfer of power to the *Princeps* could be revoked by the

---

[1] *Speech to Congress of Communist Party of Soviet Union. The Times*, 5 June 1956.

[2] M. D. Chenu. 'Authentica' et 'Magistralia'. *Divus Thomas.*, pp. 257–85. Piacenza,
1925.

[3] F. Kern. *Kingship and Law in the Middle Ages*. Tr. S. B. Chrimes., p. 55. Oxford,
1939.

Populus: thus two Papalists, the cardinals Goffredus Tranensis
(d.1245) and Hostiensis (d. 1271) held that the Roman people
of their day could still make laws, for it had not wholly abdicated
its power, which is said to have been translated, that is conceded.[1]

Finally, and not least important when comparing spiritual
and temporal power, allowances should be made for the dignity
accorded the poor and weak by Christian teaching. The
expectation that churchmen would show sympathy with the
underdog was not always disappointed. As they waxed in
power and pomp, less as ministers of the Gospel than as servants
of the State, it may have become less apparent. Yet apart from
genuine pity, the cynicism of churchmen about the pretensions
of worldly power and their absence of servility towards potentates should be no matter of surprise. The Church had not lost
its popular touch with the Parisians at the time of the Catholic
League, and later still, perhaps with less respectability, with
the *lazzaroni* under the Risorgimento and the Irish immigrants
during the palmy days of Tammany.

2. *Civilians*

Canon Law prepared the way for the full reception of the
Roman Law in Europe, and helped clear the ground for the
building of the Modern State. This was largely the work of
civil lawyers. Their ideas also were shaped by canonical conceptions of dominion, rule and jurisdiction. Even in England
where the native Common Law, based on Anglo-Saxon customs
and feudal techniques and developed more by the practice of
the courts than by academic teaching, was vigorous enough to
resist the Code, lawyers could not but consult the regulations
of an organized religion which entered into so many interests.
Bracton referred to the *Decretum* of Gratian, the Lateran
Constitution of Alexander III, and the *Decretals* of Gregory IX.[2]

---

[1] W. Ullmann. *Medieval Papalism*, p. 166.
   Godfrey of Trano. *Summa in Titulos Decretalium*. Venice, 1601.
   Henry of Susa, Cardinal-Bishop of Ostia. *Summa Aurea super Titulis Decretalium*.
      Cologne, 1612.
[2] S. Mochi Onory. *Fonti canonistiche dell' idea moderna dello Stato*. Milan, 1951.
   F. W. Maitland. *Roman Canon Law in the Church of England*. London, 1898.
   Bracton and Azo. Publications of the Selden Society, viii, 1895.

Forms and procedure of civil law were framed after the ecclesiastical model.

The revival of Roman civil law, well under way before Gratian's time, started with Irnerius, the *jurisperitissimus*, who was teaching at Bologna in 1088, and continued through a famous line of masters, 'the four doctors', Bulgarus, Martinus, Jacobus and Hugo, summoned by Barbarossa as imperial counsel to sit in the Diet of Roncaglia (1158). They were followed by Joannes, Roger and Placentinus in the next generation, and by Azo and Hugolinus in the thirteenth century. All based themselves on the law books of Justinian, for when it is said that 'the Bolognese had the Romans for their masters and none but the Romans', what they learnt was not the classical law of the Antonines but its later development.[1] They fashioned a formal discipline according to exact and proper rules, so that the study of the law, no longer merely a training for the conduct of litigation, was emancipated from subservience to grammar and rhetoric.

During the early period of Glossators, the *Corpus Juris* was explained by phrases run into the text and meaningless apart from it. At first these were written between the lines—the interlinear gloss; afterwards they spread to the margin—the marginal gloss. This method culminated in Accursius (1182–1262), the author of the *Glossa Ordinaria* or *Accursiana*, whose authority was such that it became almost axiomatic that a court would not recognize what the Gloss did not, *quidquid non agnoscit glossa nec agnoscit curia*.

A cramped commentary on an old text was no more fitted to the political development of the thirteenth century than was a running commentary on the Bible or on a received authority, such as Dionysius or Peter Lombard, to its theological systematizing. A new scholastic jurisprudence emulated the assimilation and restatement of Aristotelean philosophy by the Summists who were substituting the more systematically developed *quaestio* for the meditative and traditional *lectio* on a text. The gloss writers, themselves practising lawyers as well as teachers,

---

[1] H. Kantorowicz. *Studies in the Glossators of the Roman Law*, p. 3.
H. F. Jolowicz. *Roman Foundations of Modern Law*. Oxford, 1957.

soon perceived that features in existing institutions could not be
fitted to Roman patterns. During the lifetime of Accursius the
schools of Post-Glossators were rising; the glosses were giving
way to paraphrases, and then to text-books or *summae*. Azo (d.
1230), the master of Accursius, had composed a *Summa* on the
Justinian *Institutes* and *Code*, and the saw, *chi non ha Azzo non vada
a Palazzo*, reflected his reputation. The aim was less to discover
the past meaning of a text than to fashion an instrument of
living law, since rules which united a pagan community might
not commend themselves to Christians. The effort was backed
by the study of the definitions, principles, and divisions of law.
Recital gave place to debate, and it was related of Bartolus (d.
1357) that his habit was to begin with the solution of a problem
under discussion and then to call upon his pupils to adduce
passages in support.

As in philosophy so in law, the French communicated their own
elasticity of mind. They were the *Ultramontani*—in the reverse
sense, both in geography and ideology, to that of the nineteenth
century. Paris and Orleans laboured less than Montpellier and
the Italian schools under the weight of the *Corpus*. Custom and
equity was held in greater regard, and men were nursed who,
mincing no words, referred to the Gloss as *diabolica, fatua* and
obscura. They were ridiculed in return by the Italians as
ruminatores. In fact, by seeking to discover the spirit as well as
the letter, the French came to a better appreciation of historical
meaning and present occasion. In Paris, so ran the saying,
scholars seek the arts, in Orleans the authors, in Bologna the
codices.[1] Premature specialization was avoided at Orleans,
which as a law university ranked above Paris; all the same
premature specialization was avoided there, for, until the decay
of literary schools in the thirteenth century, law-students were
not admitted until they had taken a degree in arts. The professors are said to have been in the habit of lecturing partly in
French and partly in Latin. St Thomas was the contemporary
of James of Revigny (d. 1296), the luminary of the Orleans

---

[1] H. Waddell. *The Wandering Scholars*. 6th ed., p. 134. London, 1932.
    See the non-authentic work of St Thomas, *de vitiis et virtutibus deque aliis numero
    quaternario procedentibus*, 6, Opusc. lxxi, Editio Piana.

school, and, as will appear, the climate for his political theory
was that of Northern Europe.[1]

The jurists used the Roman Law as the theologians and
philosophers of Paris and Oxford used the Fathers and Aristotle.
When the text of the Code was insufficient they looked to the
glosses and elsewhere to discover the *jus commune*.[2] They
appealed to Church canons, imperial and town laws, feudal
and natural precepts, customs and statutes of the realm. The
ratio juris was not formed from Roman texts alone. The teaching-
method included debates, or *quaestiones disputatae*, as well as
lectures. The analysis of principles was combined with a sense
of fact; the argument, as in contemporary moral theology, was
both speculative and practical. As in moral theology, too,
teachers and judges more and more appealed to accepted
authorities and to the *communis opinio*, sometimes to safeguard
themselves from liability; thus they set up a chain-reaction
which sometimes subjected equity to the ruling of the majority
and substituted a mechanical return for a pondered pronouncement on the truth of the matter.

Without overmuch regard for archeological correctness, the
Roman Law was flexibly adapted to current needs, like the
grammar of the Church. The medieval lawyers did to it what
Coke was later to do with their own precedents. To take an
example: a vassal holding of a lord could not be credited with
full ownership, 'but by describing his remedy as an *actio utilis* of
the sort granted to the Roman *superficiarius*, a step was taken
towards ascribing to him a *dominum utile* as opposed to the
dominum directum of a lord'.[3] The ruler of a Nation-State was
credited with the powers of Caesar in the maxim, *princeps est
imperator in regno suo*. It was felt that lawyers were not merely
technicians spelling out the meaning of words, too much for

[1] P. Fournier. *Histoire de la science de droit en France* iii, Les universités françaises et
l'enseignement du droit en France au moyen âge. Paris, 1892.
   H. Rashdall. *The Universities of Europe in the Middle Ages*. ii, pp. 139–51.
[2] W. Ullmann. 'The Legal and Political Ideas of the Post-Glossators' in *Lucas de
Penna and the Medieval Idea of Law*, p. 45. Introduction by H. D. Hazeltine.
London, 1946.
[3] J. W. Jones. *Historical Introduction to the Theory of Law*, p. 14.
   E. Maynial. 'Notes sur la formation de la théorie du domaine divisé.' *Mélanges
Fitting*, ii, p. 419. Montpellier, 1908.
   For application to the morality of ownership see 2a–2ae, lxvi, 1–2.

law and too little for justice; law remained just only by responding to the actual conditions of an ever-changing social life.[1]

Two related principles of contemporary juridico-political doctrine may here be mentioned for they will appear later. First, that the administration of written laws should be tempered by the spirit of equity; secondly, that some sort of popular consent entered into the nomination of the supreme legislator.

The influence of Martinus who led the 'Equity Wing' against the strict legalism of Bulgarus and most of the Bologna masters may be traced through Placentinus (d. 1196) to the French law schools, in the country where Celtic Gauls and Norman Vikings had prepared the soil of freedom. It was recognized that the texts of the Law, or for that matter of any code or gloss, could not be stretched to fit every situation which arose. The fact was enlarged on by the Aristotelean moral philosophers when they taught that social justice called for a certain flexibility, since the common good which was its purpose consisted of a multitude of human persons, not a *bloc*. Law itself was a matter of social justice; it was made for the benefit of a commonwealth of human beings each apart and all together. Hence a legalistic justice which merely attended to the strict working of regulations and applied them without sense of situation fell short of the full idea of law and justice. For justice, like truth or beauty and the Eternal Law itself, is an analogical value which cannot be reduced to the set details of unvarying precepts: in every sense of the term, it means fair play.

It would not have occurred even to those jurists who were sticklers for the letter of the law that Positive Laws, that is, laws whose force depended on their enactment by human authority, could form a closed system imposed and expanded without reference to religion and natural rights. Nevertheless, with the growth of the Roman Law at the expense of customary law and of deference to its superior elegance and efficiency, a world was created, of rulers, officials and subjects, in which the legal machine began to work on its own almost to the exclusion

---

[1] A. Denning. *The Road to Justice*. London, 1955.

of other interests. This may be expected to happen when any specialist technique is elaborated and exploited apart from a controlling wisdom: analogies can be found with mathematics in the seventeenth century, the critique of knowledge in the eighteenth, physics in the nineteenth, and linguistic logic for a period in the twentieth.

One political result of this legal development was to elevate the ruler about the checks of popular custom and constitutional law. For John of Salisbury in the twelfth century the test of difference between a prince and a tyrant was whether he kept the bounds of his office; to Bracton in the following century the king was under the law.[1] But as the Romanizers gained ground so also did the notion of the *princeps solutus a lege*, the absolute sovereign who is the master, not the servant, of law, together with the corollary that government might act by decree without consulting the community at large. The conclusion was arrived at less by an appeal to examples from antiquity than by the interior dynamism of the Roman Law, and it was favoured by the decline of religion as an organized social force.

It is true that the early Civilians spoke of law rising from the people, from the *universitas, id est populus*. Placentinus, who left Bologna in disapproval of its stringent spirit and founded the school of Montpellier, referred to the Emperor as the people's vicar.[2] But to expect political Liberalism in the Middle Ages would be premature; the theory of popular representation was qualified by the famous *lex regia*—what pleases the prince has the force of law, since by regal law issued concerning his sway, the people have conferred on him and lodged in him all their rule and power.[3] Henceforth he was the legislative sovereign. The maxim, frequently truncated to the first clause, that the prince's pleasure has the force of law—and, as such, rejected by St

---

[1] F. Schulz. 'Bracton on Kingship.' *English Historical Review*, lx, p. 237. London, 1945.

[2] A. J. Carlyle. 'The Theory of Political Sovereignty in the Medieval Civilians to the time of Accursius.'
Mélanges Fitting, i, pp. 183–93. Montpellier, 1907.

[3] *Institutes* 1, 2, 6. *Digest* II, 1, 4.

Thomas at the very beginning of his treatise—was at first
restricted to the Holy Roman Emperor, the inheritor of the
prerogatives of the classical *Princeps*, but was later extended to
the rulers of kingdoms and city-states.[1]

Furthermore, most Civilians, including Placentinus, held that
this act of alienation could not be taken back. On the other
hand Bulgarus and Azo were among the important minority
which stressed the inherent right to act by custom, and can be
cited to testify that the transfer was not irrevocable—the names
show that the equity and legalistic wings among the jurists did
not correspond respectively to the theories of representation as
delegation or of representation as personification, nor to constitutionalist and absolutist policies.[2] Many of the Canonists
taught that the people could withdraw their mandate from the
prince; some that the people's right to legislate still remained.[3]
These views may have been determined by Guelf policies, but
they were also suggested by moral ideals of moderation, agreement, and shared responsibility, ideals which were thrown into
relief by the excesses of tyrants like Ezzelino.

Notwithstanding the force of custom, the trend was towards
centering legislative power in a single princely organ of
sovereignty. It began to be less spread out over the body politic.
Its possession and exercise began to be set up as a fact which
sought no justification—apart from success—and which was not
derived from religious or moral considerations or even from
popular consent. The practice was linked with the theory that
politics was an autonomous discipline, yet it was from the
Roman Law, not from Aristotle, that the lineaments of the
absolute monarch were drawn. It was reproduced as Europe
split into independent states and the ruler of each claimed to
be sole and supreme within his own domain.[4]

---

[1] 1a–2ae, xc, 1, *ad* 3.

C. N. S. Woolf. *Bartolus of Sassoferrato*, p. 35.

[2] F. Kern. *Kingship and Law in the Middle Ages*, p. 117.
A. J. Carlyle. *A History of Medieval Political Theory in the West*, v, p. 48, vi, p. 13.

[3] W. Ullmann. *Lucas de Penna and the Medieval Idea of Law.*, p. 48.

[4] W. Ullmann. 'The Development of the Medieval Idea of Sovereignty.' *English
Historical Review*, lxiv, pp. 1–33. London, 1949.

III

LANDED MEN AND WANDERERS

MEDIEVAL thought has been scouted for being over-academic. There was not enough experimentation, it has been said, nor attempt to control the processes which exploit human environment; the effort on peering into hollow objects of speculation would have been more profitably spent on the applied sciences. Let that pass, together with murmurs about scholastic cobwebs and dancing angels on a needlepoint, and, granting that technological progress lagged behind logic, turn the inquiry and ask to what extent the theorists were subject to the pressures set up by their living conditions.

How you think is affected by how you feel, and how you feel by the culture and material standards of your time. The presuppositions of a social theologian are formed by his history as well as by the relatively timeless factors of his religious creed and philosophy: to understand him we must receive an impression of his surroundings as well as make an abstraction of his ideas. St Thomas was no exception. Detached he may appear—certainly the tang of his times is better caught from some of his colleagues, for instance from Humbert of Romans or Albertus Magnus or Ptolemy of Lucca. All the same he is imperfectly appreciated from dwelling only on the debates of the schools. Theory, like art, is the result of collaboration. At the risk of being perfunctory let us adopt the ascending dialectic from material to formal which he himself would have approved, and glance at some of the customs and moods of the world in which he moved.

1. *The Social Scene*

Feudalism, variously evolved according to region and period but basically an order of land-tenure, was taking on a more

political and urban complexion. The effect was of greater
versatility for the community and greater instability for the
individual. It made for easier means of escape from the bondage
of food-production, for a peasant's son could go to the town and
rise by craft or trade; he could turn soldier. Merchandise was
more powerful than the sword. Even in the eastern Latin
principalities, achievements of the piety and land-hunger of
the Franks and of their colonizing capacity and administrative
energy, policy was sometimes decided by the interests and
rivalries more of commercial agents than of the nobles and
knights of Outremer. The power of Pisa was in decay, but
Venice and Genoa were gathering the fruits of a medieval
capitalism rooted in the commercial revival of the twelfth
century; their factories were to outlast the crusaders' castles.[1]

Planned economies were still the rule, for Free Trade came
in after the French Revolution and disappeared during the
First World War. All the same, personal initiative was breaking
the forms of privilege and protection. Credit was turning
enterprise into gold and local dealing opening out into freer
exchanges. Traders and travellers went farther afield—Marco
Polo set off from Venice in 1268—and producers, breaking
away from a tied system and neighbourhood-markets, bargained
for greater independence. To take one geographical condition
of prosperity: it was less important to be a strong place under
the protection of a lord or a pilgrimage-centre in the shadow
of a church than to be a market at a harbour, river-crossing
or mountain pass on a route which might stretch from the
Atlantic coast to the Baltic, the Black Sea or the Levant.
Opportunities for trade rather than advantages for defence
were the factors in the urban development of such places as
Southampton where there was a double tide or Innsbruck on
the road to the Brenner.[2]

Correspondingly the sentiments of social psychology were

---

[1] H. Pirenne. *Medieval Cities; their Origins and the Revival of Trade*. Princeton, 1925.
Economic and Social History of Medieval Europe. Tr. J. E. Clegg. London, 1936.
W. Heyd. *Histoire du commerce du Levant au moyen âge*. Tr. F. Reynard. Paris, 1923.
S. Runciman. *The Crusades*. 3 vols. Cambridge, 1951–4.
Cambridge Economic History of Europe, ii, 1952.

[2] J. W. F. Hill. *Medieval Lincoln*. Cambridge, 1948. An excellent history of the
growth of a city.

changing. Family and tribal loyalties were being lifted into a
wider political obedience and service. Dominion belonged to
the ruler less as the head of the kindred, *caput progeniei*, than as
the sovereign of the State. Power, once inherited from father to
son, as under the Capets, was now being decided by the conditions of contract, and the change was encouraged by the
Church. Knight-service no longer governed the holding of
property. The Military Orders, which had introduced a formal
discipline into the institutions of chivalry, were developing
almost into chartered companies. When power and fashion
were focussed on the court so much the more store was set on
manners and breeding. Stylishness was cultivated, luxury displayed, and conduct turned on punctilio. The feelings of some
marcher lord for the courtier were not unlike those of Wellington's or Wavell's fighting-man for the Belem Rangers or the
Gaderene Swine.

The moralists for their part now laid more stress on justice
than on honour and loyalty. The average man of the *Summa
Theologica* was a citizen, not a lord or vassal or serf, and the
social virtues there recommended were those of partnership in
a polity, not of gentility and courtliness. Panache and fame, a
handsome manner and fastidious taste did not pass unadmired
so long as they were contained in the reasonable virtues of
fortitude and temperance.[1] There was a shift of scene, and
rights and duties were now set against a civilian background of
temporal tranquillity; in some respects their assignment foreshadowed the social ideals of Locke. Whereas in the early
chansons de geste noble behaviour belonged to men of gentle
birth, by 1250 it was extended to the middle-class; a *vilain* was
not necessarily base, a noble could be guilty of *vilenie*.[2] Yet if
St Thomas reflected the contractual liberalism of the age his
influence on its later evolution was fainter—and when we
speak of liberalism in his regard we mean, not the dominating
political force of the nineteenth century, but the virtue of
social liberality pointing to the *esprit large* and away from the
idée fixe.[3]

---

[1] 2a–2ae, cxxix, cxxxiv, cxliv, cxlv, clxi, clxii, clxix.
[2] J. Crosland. *Medieval French Literature*. Oxford, 1956.
[3] 2a–2ae, cxvii. A. R. Vidler. *Essays in Liberality*. London, 1957.

The Germans were pushing into the Eastern Marches and colonizing the Baltic lands. Less massively the English were occupying Wales and Ireland and extending continental institutions to the West. More land was being brought under the plough. Despite mechanical advances in the early Middle Ages, notably with regard to animal-harness and the use of water-power for mills, agricultural methods scarcely improved from the eleventh to the fourteenth centuries, and a smiling country-side was not the result of the progressive expulsion of the Moors by the Christians from Spain.[1] Until the Black Death the increase of population pressed on the means of subsistence. Under the strain of new conditions a patriarchal economy was proving unequal, and its gradual break-up was at once the cause and effect of changes in social thinking. The scene was more urban, less manorial; obligations were more standardised, less individual; dues were beginning to be collected more as taxation than as rent, and knightly service might be commuted for a money payment.[1] The landed estates, less self-sufficient, were being subordinated to the centre, a rural economy to the gold-standard.

Other symptoms marked the transition. Lay lawyers displaced clerics in the administration, and royal officials the feudal barons. The nobility of France were eventually tamed to the condition of courtiers. Artistic patronage moved from the monastery to the prince's palace, and there the great figures, the seneschal, the constable, the butler, the chamberlain, were being promoted from servants of the household into ministers of the Crown and State. The changes were paralleled in the art of war. Early in the century the great rectangular barracks of Frederick II, such as still may be seen at Legnano, replaced rambling residential castles, and by its close Edward I's adoption of the long-bow after the Welsh Wars proved that the infantry was the decisive arm, not the cavalry of knight and men-at-arms. It was cheaper too, what with the rising cost of armour and horses. Feudal levies proved no match for professional soldiers, and nobles were discomfited by burghers and

---

[1] See A. L. Poole. *Obligations of Society in the Twelfth and Thirteenth Centuries.* Oxford, 1946.
    R. Latouche. *Les origines de l'économie occidentale.* Paris, 1957.

seamen. Chivalry was becoming an upper-class mannerism.

Merchantmen assembled in a crisis served instead of a permanent navy; they were used to transport armies overseas, and attack on the enemy's trade and fleet was secondary to the effort on land. Sea-power, decisive in the Carthaginian Wars, was scarcely appreciated outside England, Aragon, Genoa, and Venice; it was of limited effect until the rise of the Ottoman Turks and the oceanic discoveries, except for the maintenance of the Crusades which since the death of Barbarossa (1190) avoided land routes.

Officialism increased in academic life. Salaried occupants of university chairs and holders of lectureships succeeded itinerant scholars, teachers in monastic and cathedral schools, and masters who had set up on their own. Their following was becoming less personal, for education was becoming a means to finding a job, and a diploma counted for more than having been a disciple of some renowned scholar. The University of Naples, founded in 1224, was not a free association of masters or students, as originally at Paris or Bologna, but a training-school for civil servants.

The use of ancestral tokens and distinguishing emblems in a mêlée was stylized by the exact science of heraldry with rules as official as those now governing patents and trademarks. Its formal occasion was the tournament, a fashionable spectacle, like Wimbledon or Ascot, not the rough-and-ready occasion of ruder times. Altogether the community was moving from the condition of a domestic group loosely centred on the king's household to that of a civil order controlled by the royal court. The transition was from paternal precepts and *scientia oeconomica* to formal law and *scientia politica*.

The Christian West possessed within itself the resources to produce a genial polity from its high culture, and the twelfth century promised what the thirteenth century brought to such brief maturity. But a certain legal formalism set in and spread to both Church and State. Officialism in social life was increased by the reproduction of Roman models and encouraged by the study of the Roman Law, while at the apex of new power stood the *persona publica*, the public figure of the sole ruler who personified the power of the community.

Soon there was a suggestion that his official actions might be exempt from the rules of private morality, for the idea of the Common Good began to be coloured by the idea of the Public Good and the interests of the State. The terms have different implications, since the good of all is the good of each whereas the public life of the State can appear as a thing apart. *Persona* recovered its original histrionic sense and came to mean the outward face, the 'personage', overlying the intimate substance of a human being. A legal tone dulled its philosophical echoes ringing from the debates of the early Councils on the mysteries of the Trinity and Incarnation.[1]

Simultaneously a new method of making law was being introduced. Hitherto it had been a declaration of the customs of the people. Now more and more if became an administrative act expressing a will which exercised irresistible force and was answerable to nobody. It was the decree of a sovereign who differed from a first magistrate as much as a full owner did from an usufructuary or a trustee.

Previously a masterful king might have treated his realm as his own property, perhaps exploiting it without much regard to abstract justice or the well-being of the whole and issuing his decrees according to his own advantage, perhaps seeking to diminish sectional interests and unify the country. The assertion of imperial and regal power against feudal rights went back many years and was the theme of King John's difficulties with the English barons. Nevertheless any approach to tyrannical practice or absolutist theory encountered the resistance of immemorial convictions formulated by the feudal jurists. They acted in no doctrinaire spirit but merely sought practical ways of maintaining existing rights. The magnates considered themselves to be the repositories of these rights—which shows they were not speaking as liberal democrats—and invoked custom in their fight against the King. Law was upheld as a standard to rally the forces of tradition.

The customs of the people, their common heritage, were declared under the proper circumstances after consulting ancient usage; law was a restatement, not an innovation or a creation of the prince's will. Such was the sentiment of the

---

[1] See 1a, xxvii, 1. 3a, ii. 2. Below pp. 236–49.

Canonists and, at first, of the Civilians. It was uttered in many places, in the *Roman de la Rose*, in the aristocratic reaction to the Angevin kings, in the *Liber Feudorum* or *Consuetudines Feudorum*. This, published by the Consuls of Milan and annexed to the *Corpus Juris Civilis* by Hugolinus, revived the Emperor Constantine's declaration that ancient usage and custom could not be disregarded unless they ran counter to *lex*.[1]

The Lombard Law, more resistant to the Code than other tribal laws, was still ranked equal with the Roman Law in Sicily, if not indeed as its superior, until the early thirteenth century. By the fourteenth century, however, Lucas de Penna put custom below statutory enactment, though the prevailing view even then was that written and unwritten law were of equal weight.[2] Legislation required some co-operation between the prince and the people; in declaring a law he spoke for the whole community after taking counsel with the elders. The popular consent implied was the acknowledgment that a provision corresponded with custom, not an act of subsequent ratification; it was rather like the procedure by inquest which survives in the English trial by jury.

When Baldwin was crowned first Latin Emperor in Santa Sophia in 1204 he found himself little more than the chairman of a house of peers.[3] A prince was not free to dictate policy without seeking the accord of the landed magnates. As for his immunity from law, thirteenth-century sentiment would not have allowed that he was beyond its reach or that there was no effective authority who could control him, though its judicial organ might not be designated. The acceptance of duties qualified the enjoyment of power, and mutual obligations, sealed by oath and carrying with them limitations of rights were held to exist between a ruler and his people. Rulers were

---

[1] J. E. A. Joliffe. *Angevin Kingship*. London, 1955.

G. H. Sabine. *A History of Political Theory*. xi. 'The Folk and its Law.' London, 1937.

A. J. Carlyle. *A History of Medieval Political Theory in the West*. ii, 1. iii, 1.

C. H. McIlwain. *The Growth of Political Thought in the West*, p. 171. New York, 1932.

[2] M. Schipa. *Italy and Sicily under Frederick II*. Cambridge Medieval History, vi, p. 148. 1929.

W. Ullmann. *Lucas de Penna and the Medieval Idea of Law*, iv.

[3] S. Runciman. *A History of the Crusades*, iii, p. 125. Cambridge, 1954.

answerable in conscience for their actions and could not shelter behind the anonymity and impersonality of office: this was perhaps the most salutary political principle bequeathed by Christian feudalism to later generations.

Caballus, the pack-horse, became the war-horse, the beast of burden the chevalier's mount. The fortune-hunters who followed William the Conqueror were not unlike the men who opened up the Rand. Early chivalry cast no charm, it was an affair of service based on land-tenure. Later taking colour from the Moors and Saracens, it flowered into the decoration of a culture and served no essential function in the social organization. Its ideals, reflected only in brief parentheses of the *Summa Theologica*, were not unlike those of the horsey Victorian soldier who, when asked what was the use of cavalry in modern warfare, replied, Well, I suppose to give tone to what otherwise would be a mere vulgar brawl. The knight-errant was an absentee landlord, neither at home administering his domain nor doing his service. The chevalier was the gallant, detached from the humdrum round, the devotee of a courtly habit; he might be an adventurer, perhaps a fop, grumbled at by the territorial barons and sometimes a fallen favourite, the victim of their rough resentment.

He was matched by the new type of cleric, unbeneficed and wandering at large, looked at askance by incumbents and attacked by the Masters of Paris. Where did *he* fit into the social scheme? The question was not easy to answer, for the question of *status* was of primary importance to critics whose minds had been formed by the Roman Law; it was not as if they were Aristotelean philosophers to whom *situs* was one of the minor categories. The friars seemed no part of the structure of the Church; they held no property keyed to the discharge of an official function, they made no vow of stability in a monastery. All the same their opponents had to admit ruefully that they were official tramps blessed with pontifical approval, quite unlike the *vagantes* condemned by the canons of the Church Councils. Theirs was more the repute of the fifth-century Sophists, those travelling professional educators. Their demeanour was not picaresque. Among them were men of weight in the schools and in the counsels of Church and nation. Some were papal legates and cardinals, or occupants of the most venerable sees in Christendom; before the century was out a Dominican, Innocent V, and a Franciscan, Nicholas IV, were elected to the Chair of Peter itself. Under St Bonaventure's government the Franciscans assumed responsibilities seemingly far removed from a carefree life of poverty; John Peckham is better remembered as a successful estate-manager for his archbishopric than as a poet or theologian.[1]

The social movement which produced the friars also revealed other symptoms. Detachment about personal possessions changed to anxieties about obligations rooted in this world and about fair-dealing which hinged ponderously on material things, anxieties which the increasing subtilization of law was ineffective to satisfy. There were doubts concerning vested interests in spiritualities and temporalities, concerning the whole business of providing for yourself and your family in the ordinary way, and even concerning the precepts of institutional religion itself. A respect for the poor because they were poor was an authentic part of the Christian tradition. Not until after the Reformation was poverty considered a vice and prosperity a badge of godliness.[2]

A special contempt for what may be called the virtues of the good business-man showed itself in the thirteenth century. Although the Church for its part had settled the principle of its right to own property, ecclesiastical preoccupation with the affairs of this world was being increasingly challenged, and on devotional grounds; the rebels, thrown up by a religious culture, seem to have taken an extravagantly spiritual view of religion.[3] Landed property inevitably came to bulk larger than sacramental dignity in the concept of *estate*, and in the discharge of its functions. As the Church's possessions grew, so tender consciences mused how difficult it was to serve God and Mammon. Of course laicizers were ready to propose the ideal of a purely spiritual Church, without property or temporal power; they were not disinterested parties, but from the days of Arnold of Brescia (d. 1155) could sometimes count on the support of

---

[1] D. L. Douie. *John Pecham*. Oxford, 1952.
[2] W. Shewring. *Rich and Poor in Christian Tradition*. London, 1947.
[3] Denzinger, 494–6, 596, 619.

religious fanaticism, and in the early fourteenth century were to strike an uneasy alliance with the zealots for poverty.

Eccentrics and enthusiasts repudiated other responsibilities besides wealth. Marriage itself, so closely related to property, was discredited when Courtly Love turned sentimental and temptation to sin was lauded as ennobling romance. The possessive emphasis in the secondary precepts of the Decalogue did not pass unnoticed: thou shalt not covet thy neighbour's wife—nor his ass. Theologians themselves recognized that the Old Law was limited, material, and negative, and, unlike the post-Reformation manualists, preferred to construct their moral theology on the higher plan of the Christian virtues.[1]

Many forces, economic and literary, worldly and religious, mad and sober, delicate and coarse, cool and feverish, from the courts, the religious houses and the underworld, were undermining the old foundations. The settlements of weavers were centres of unrest, and the roads were thronged with merchants from foreign parts, vagrant scholars, *clerici ribaldi de familia Goliae*, gospellers, Manichees, singers of romantic love, men going on crusade, children led by pied pipers, pedlars of relics, pilgrims doing penance and much else on the way, itinerant officers of Church and State. All after their fashion combined to shake the stability of social convictions which grew from the roots of feudalism.

Nor could the unrest be wholly set down to aberrations of conduct or a wild spirit of protest and fun, which far from spreading to the clerics seems to have started with them. The discipline of a dozen Church Councils, from Germany across France to Spain, was applied to those who diced, wined, sang, took part in theatricals, did comic turns, and flaunted themselves in green and yellow garments.[2] The cause lay deeper than a passion for sport and spiced meats and wine. Their culture was charged with too many memories of spells from outside the classical world for men to accommodate themselves dutifully to an order formed from Greek philosophy and Roman

---

[1] 1a–2ae. c, 10, 11. cvii, 1. 2a–2ae. Prologue.

[2] J. D. Mansi. *Sacrorum Conciliorum Amplissima Collectio*. xxiii, 33, 215, 237, 512, 882, 935, 992, 997, 1055–7, 1086. xxiv, 140–1.

law. The anonymous thirteenth-century pastoral from the *Carmina Burana* was a parable of their condition:

> *Exiit diluculo*
> *Rustica puella*
> *Cum grege, cum baculo,*
> *Cum lana novella.*
>
> *Conspexit in caespite*
> *Scolarem sedere:*
> *'Quid tu facis, domine?*
> *Veni mecum ludere.'*

They might receive the pattern, and be obedient to the code of the *Princeps* and to the ecclesiastical order, but there was much else on the fringe. Their Scriptures witnessed to the strange and prophetic strains of the Jewish dispensation, their worship echoed the tones of Syrian music, their speculation could not forget the adventures of John Scot Eriugena. The vagabonds trod the routes of Celtic monks. The sagas were not spent; the Northmen were carrying their mediterranean conquests as far as Antioch, and it was not until the Varangian Guard broke that Constantinople fell to the Latins. The eastern frontier was open to Germans, Slavs, Hungarians, Bulgarians, Tartars. From the south were imported dainties and refinements from the Arabs. At the University of Naples the young Thomas Aquinas was instructed in literature and logic by Martin of Denmark, in natural philosophy by Peter the Irishman; both belonged to Michael Scot's Greco-Arabian circle round Frederick II, at whose court the first sonnet was composed. In the monastic guest-house might be found a Copt or an Armenian, a Venetian who had lived in Muscovy or Persia, a Flemish cloth-merchant who had dabbled in the secrets of the Bulgars. St Louis presented Henry III of England with an elephant in 1254. Experience was too rich, and the myths too varied to be epitomized in the contemporary *summae* of the scholastic theologians and lawyers: their scent lingers in the potpourri of the *Decameron*.[1]

---

[1] F. Lot. *La Fin du monde antique et les début du moyen âge.* Paris, 1927.
R. Flower. *Ireland and Medieval Europe.* Proceedings of the British Academy. London, 1927.
W. O. Ker. *The Dark Ages.* Edinburgh, 1956.
J. J. Jusserand. *English Wayfaring Life.* London, 1921.

Baroque hagiographers, like the heralds of the period who dwelt uncritically on legends of antique magnificence and honours, sought to flatter noble patrons who had a saint in the family tree. The Aquino family was granted a pedigree and panoply equal to any in Europe, whereas in fact St Thomas's immediate relatives were of more standing as officers of state than as landed lords. His father was Justiciar in the marches between the Kingdom of Sicily and the Patrimony of Peter, and his uncle and namesake, Thomas of Aquino, Count of Acerra, was posted as imperial regent to the Kingdom of Jerusalem (1226).[1] The ambitions of his parents that he should end up as Abbot of Monte Cassino and Archbishop of Naples were disappointed. He left behind the feudalism of the Castle of Rocca Secca where he was born, the patriarchalism of the Abbey of Monte Cassino where he was first educated, and the ecclesiastical career for which the University of Naples prepared him, in order to throw in his lot with the Dominicans (1243-4): characters who would have become monks in the grand Benedictine centuries were now joining the friars. The Dominicans had to rescue him from the energetic displeasure of his family who kidnapped him and held him in durance for months. He was sent across the Alps, probably to Cologne to study under St Albert, finally to teach in Paris (1252) at the *Studium* of St. Jacques on the left-bank of the Seine: thence the Dominicans came to be known as the Jacobins.

2. *The Order of Preachers*

The Dominicans, or Preachers, had been founded forty-six years before by St Dominic, a far-seeing and self-effacing Castilian who had exchanged the quiet life of a regular canon at Osma for the hurly-burly of preaching the Christian evidences to the Albigenses in Languedoc.[2] The first episcopal patron of his community was the ex-troubadour and Cistercian,

---

[1] F. Scandone. 'La vita, la famiglia e la patria di S. Tommaso.' *S. Tommaso d'Aquino, O.P. Miscellanea storicoartistica*, i, 3. Rome, 1924.

[2] H.M. Vicaire. *Saint Dominique de Caleruega d'après les documents du XIIIe siècle.* Paris, 1955.

H. C. Scheeben. *Der hl. Dominikus*. Freiburg, 1927.

B. Jarrett. *Life of St Dominic*. London, 1924.

Fulk of Toulouse; his followers came to England (1221) in the train of Peter des Roches, Bishop of Winchester, no friend of the baronage, and were befriended by Stephen Langton. A legal corporation of clerics confirmed by Honorius III (1216), they were coming to the height of their influence in the Western world; devoted to study by their profession—*contemplata aliis tradere* later became their motto—they still relied on their own wits rather than on the dignities they were acquiring, and were not yet side-tracked into administration.

Caught up in the mendicant and penitential movement, they were spared the tragic dissensions which later afflicted the Franciscans, partly because from the beginning they were self-governing according to a democratic constitution—in his own life St Dominic equably suffered himself to be overruled by a majority-vote in favour of a businesslike control of temporalities—partly because they were never profoundly committed to the ideal of corporate poverty, partly because of their bias towards a rational and classical order. Committed by their origins to canonical and liturgical observances, theirs was always a *canonica religio*. Their founder's shrine was at Bologna—stately and scholastic, grave and courteous—and there and at Paris alternately their earliest General Chapters were held, not at Rome. All superiors were elected and, except at first in the case of their Master General, held office for a temporary period, after which they returned to the ranks. They believed in representative institutions, and their practice in conjunction with other influences promoted the rise of parliamentary government.[1]

Unlike the monks they made no profession of local stability. They were affiliated to national provinces—of which England, founded in 1221, is now the ninth in order of seniority—but their work took them across territorial frontiers, and much of their life was spent tramping from one centre of learning to another. Benedict loved the mountains, ran the saying, Bernard

---

[1] G. R. Galbraith. *The Constitution of the Dominican Order,* 1218–1360. Manchester, 1925.

E. Barker. *The Dominican Order and Convocation.* Oxford, 1913.

M. Gaynes Post. '*Plena Potestas* and Consent in Medieval Assemblies. A Study in Romano-Canonical Procedure and the Rise of Representation, 1150–1325.' *Tradition,* i, p. 369. New York, 1943.

the valleys, Francis the towns, Dominic the universities—and
these, more secular than the monastic and cathedral schools
they superseded, were not retreats for academic meditation and
research but battlegrounds for ideas which shaped events. The
Dominicans adopted monastic ordinances, but theirs was no
monkish world. Their houses were built in the towns not in the
countryside, and nearer to the market than to the castle or
cathedral; their churches were not massive and dim, but
open spaces of light supported on slender piers. On arriving in
England, they tarried briefly in Canterbury, then moved on
to Oxford. Every priory was also a school which was open
to all. By 1248 they had established five *Studia Generalia* for
higher studies, Paris, Bologna, Oxford, Cologne, and Montpellier. The songs they heard were not merely the Gregorian
chants of their own choirs, but also the strains of romantic
poetry and courtly epic which succeeded the *chansons de geste*.
All helped to form the culture they shared.[1]

> *Temps s'en va*
> *Et rien n'ai fait.*
> *Temps s'en vient*
> *Et ne fais rien.*

The words rose up from the street to Guerric of Auxerre as
he sat at his window, and so moved his heart that he entered
the Dominicans, to become their first prior of Metz.[2] And on
the road they caught pieces in lighter vein, love-songs, spring-
songs, begging-songs, from restless clerks, poor scholars, and
jongleurs. In brief, the contemplatives, the Hellenic leisured-
class, were no longer enclosed or at home but abroad and at
large.

In Spain the friars appointed special convents for oriental
studies where they discoursed with rabbis and mullahs; at one
Dominican house the chair of Hebrew was held by a Jew.
Raymon Martinez was reputed to have been the first Christian

---

[1] C. Dawson. *Religion and the Rise of Western Culture*, viii.

G. Paré. *Le Roman de la Rose et la Scholastique courtéoise*. Paris–Ottawa, 1941.

C. S. Lewis. *The Allegory of Love: A Study in Medieval Tradition*. London, 1936.

W. P. Ker. *Epic and Romance*. London, 1896.

[2] H. Waddell. *The Wandering Scholars*, p. 145.

with a greater command of Hebrew than St Jerome's. Another Dominican, Pablo Cristiani, himself a Jew, engaged in public and temperate disputation with the great rabbi Nachman before King Jaime I and Raymund of Pennafort at Barcelona.[1] In general the Franciscans seem to have been more cordial than the Dominicans in their relations with the Jews.

The friars debated with Greeks in the Levant and fraternized with Armenians. Hakluyt wrote of 'the sending of certaine Friers Praedicants and Minorites to the Tartars'. Speak of Prester John or the Great Cham of Tartary, and they were ready to explore his dominions and enter his court. Andrew of Longjumeau and William of Rubruck were St Louis' ambassadors to the Mongols; others had preceded Marco Polo to China. The posts of the Dominican *Fratres Peregrinantes pro Christo* later stretched from the Crimea to Persia.[2] Since the Second Crusade a new respect for the Moslems had been discovered; the Dominican explorer, Ricoldo de Monte Croce (d. 1320) spoke warmly of the virtue and piety of Arab cameldrivers and held them up as examples to Christians.[3]

Nearer home, in southern France and northern Italy they rubbed shoulders with scepticism, pessimism, cynicism, anarchism, romanticism, and, after St Albert and St Thomas, with naturalism too. They showed little enthusiasm for the canonization by Innocent IV of Peter of Verona a year after he had been martyred for his zeal by heretics on the road from Como to Milan (1252) They first settled at Oxford in the Jewry, where they defended their neighbours against persecution. One of them, Lawrence of Reading, a well-known preacher, joined the

---

[1] O. S. Rankin. *Jewish Religious Polemic*. Edinburgh, 1956.

[2] R. Loernertz. *La Société des Frères Peregrinants*. Etude sur l'orient Dominicain. Rome, 1937.

W. A. Hinnebusch. *The Early English Friars Preachers*. Rome, 1951.

B. Jarrett. *The English Dominicans*, p. 99. London, 1921.

Richard Hakluyt. *The Voyages, Traffiques and Discoveries of Foreign Voyagers*, i. London, 1928.

William of Rubruck. *Itinerarium* (tr. Rockhall). Hakluyt Society, ii, 4. London, 1900.

C. Dawson ed. *The Mongol Mission: Narratives and Letters of the Franciscan Missionaries in Mongolia and China in the thirteenth and fourteenth centuries*. London, 1955.

[3] G. Grupp. *Kulturgeschichte des Mittelalters*, iv, pp. 251-2. Paderborn, 1924.

Jewish religion under the name of Haggai. They sailed from Barcelona in 1250 to found an Arabic University at Tunis, then the liveliest intellectual centre in Africa: 'I would freely pass the rest of my life in prison chains,' said St Louis, 'if as a result the King of Tunis and his people were converted to the Christian religion.'[1] Jean de Meung was their neighbour in Paris; though he had sided with the secular masters against the religious orders he asked to be buried among the Dominicans. Even the satire of Chaucer—who translated the *Roman de la Rose* as well as the *Golden Legend* of the Dominican James of Voragine—hints at the sympathy between the friars and the men of science and letters, and their shared raciness of expression.

Raynier Sacconi, formerly a leading Cathar in Lombardy and later head of the Inquisition at Milan, was with St Thomas at the Papal Court at Viterbo (1262). 'Once a heresiarch,' he described himself in his exposition of the teachings of the Cathars and Poor Men of Lyons, the *Summa de Catharis et Pauperibus de Lugduno*, 'now by God's grace a priest in the Order of Preachers though unworthy.' One item of doctrine noted is that secular authority does grave wrong by using force against criminals and heretics. The Cathar *Liber de Duobus Principiis* descanted on the dualism between a good and an evil God, and in two sections, *ad instructionem rudium* and *de persecutionibus* explained how the power which afflicts Christ and his followers is wielded by the evil God.[2] Not a few friars were like Raynier, who had felt the attraction of the complete renunciation of early possessions and power, for thereby a load of evil would be shed and the devil's thrall escaped. They anticipated Acton's sentiment, that all power corrupts. The persuasions of the Poor Men of Lyons, the Vaudois, and other groups, so sharply at variance with the habits and religious culture of feudalism, flowed into the Manichee rejection of the forces of the physical world. That the combination did not produce a widespread antinomianism was the work of St Dominic and

[1] A. Berthier. 'Un Maître Orientaliste du XIIIe siècle, Raymond Martin.' *AFP* vi, pp. 267–311. Rome, 1936.

[2] A. Dondaine. *Un Traité néo-manichéen du XIIIe siècle. Le Liber de Duobus Principiis, suivi d'un fragment de Rituel Cathare.* Paris, 1939.

S. Runciman. *The Medieval Manichee*, vi. Cambridge, 1947.

St Francis. The Franciscan dedication to absolute poverty was imitated more hesitantly by the Dominicans than by their founder; their adoption of corporate poverty lasted only for some decades, and even with respect to individual poverty they made an exception for books.

Extremists among the religious revivalists broke the bounds of law, and doctrines reappeared which St Augustine had known from the Montanists. The Spirituals merged with the followers of the Abbot Joachim of Fiore (1145–1202), who had prophesied a reign of love which would dispense with the adoption of physical force or a juridical Church. The Dominicans, cooler and perhaps more quizzical, were constitutionally less shaken than the Franciscans by these movements. They formed a confident corps, well-trained in philosophy and theology, united in discipline, not typically represented by John of Vicenza, a political thaumaturge finally discredited, but not before he had been entrusted with dictatorial powers by his native city. When they stood up to the imperial authorities or fell foul of the beneficial clergy they could feel confident of papal backing.[1] They on their side were the Pope's men and often employed in his service, although their conviction about his spiritual primacy did not commit them to the political cause of the Canonists and their sympathies were not settled in the early stages of the debate about his supremacy with regard to a General Council. John Torquemada, however, was the foremost defender of the Papal position after the Council of Basle, and a generation later Cajetan, the greatest theologian of the age, moved the whole question from Canon Law into theology.[2]

A self-assured caste seems to produce good eccentrics, and the outcrop of Dominican originals can be compared to that of other stable social strata—to the mannerisms of the Grand Whiggery, the bohemianism of the early nineteenth-century upper middle-classes, the singularities of old-fashioned dons, country parsons and naval officers. Inevitably they were

---

[1] D. L. Douie. *The Conflict between the Seculars and the Mendicants at the University of Paris in the Thirteenth Century.* London, 1954.

C. Sutter. *Johann von Vicenza.* Freiburg, 1891.

[2] H. Jedin. *A History of the Council of Trent.* Tr. E. Graf, i, pp. 27–31, 114. London, 1957.

accused of arrogance and a humble Dominican was said to be as rare a bird as a monk out of pocket. St Albert, Master Eckhart, St Catherine of Siena, Cajetan, Melchior Cano Bucer, Giordano Bruno, Campanella, de las Casas, Thomas Gage, Labat, Lacordaire, Gonzales, McNabb, and many more, a few to the point of heterodoxy, most to the Church's benefit, have not quite echoed the note of the men in office. Yet they have kept to the severity of St Thomas's principles, and their classical theology has been on the side of reason and law; perhaps they were steadied by their rivalry with the Franciscans.

The later alliance of *fraticelli*, Ockamites, Regalists and Louis of Bavaria shows what different types could combine to attack the established order. The century which saw the rise of the friars was certainly no period of dull and dutiful security. As property bulked larger so its very grounds were undermined. As the official forms of power were made more solemn so its consecration was attacked. As legality extended so anarchy had greater appeal. As sacramental discipline was tightened so sentimentality became looser and more libertine. The promise of the thirteenth century was not sustained; what may be called the disciplined liberalism of St Thomas's political thought was succeeded by a style which simultaneously allowed for private competitiveness and insisted on more corporative rigidity. Nevertheless, while it lasted it was an eager and promising age for the Church and civilization, full of life and spirited reasons. The picture is less of a Norman church decorated by Fragonard and Blake and Dali than of a Gothic cathedral which may look asymmetrical and askew and be traceried irregularly and riot with detail, some of it ribald, but which rises from deep foundations according to an efficiently engineered disposition of pillars, arches and buttresses.

IV

PHILOSOPHERS

IF strict rationalism be separated from theological typology then most of the philosophical topics which engaged the schoolmen before they discovered the Aristotelean corpus can be represented as extensions of material logic or inquiries into the attribution of abstract meaning to particular experience. That, of course, is to make a distinction not entertained in the twelfth century and to read history backwards. The main debate of the period concerned the bearing of general ideas, or 'universals' as they were called. Were they merely names, as the nominalists contended, or were the Platonists right who held they were more real than the individual shadows they cast? Or was the intermediate position of Gilbert de la Porrée (d. 1154) well-founded? If we may speak of pure speculation and leave out of account the humanist warmth of Chartres, the interest in the natural sciences elsewhere and the devotion to ancient wisdom nourished by *lectio* and *meditatio*, it may be said that philosophy, austerely pursuing conceptual analysis and lacking the Ionian sympathy with material nature to be learnt from Aristotle, almost seemed to consist in putting things into categories. It was anatomical rather than biological.

Despite the monism which appeared at the beginning of the thirteenth century, with Amaury of Bène who said we should laugh, not mourn, because of the divinity at play within the world, and with David of Dinant (or Dinan) who identified the divinity with matter itself, the metaphysical feel for dynamic processes was slight, and so was the appreciation that physical things were real in themselves and manifested a teleology through their inner workings.[1] Philosophers did not apply

---

[1] 1a. iii, 8. *IV Sentences II*, xvii, 1.
Vincent of Beauvais. *Speculum Historiale*, xxx, 107.
G. Théry. 'Essai sur David de Dinant d'après Albert le Grand et saint Thomas.' *Melanges Thomistes*, p. 402. Paris, 1923.
F. Copleston. *A History of Philosophy*, ii, pp. 136–85. London, 1950.
M. D. Chenu. 'L'Homme et la Nature. Perspectives sur la Renaissance du XIIe siècle.' *AHDL*, xix, pp. 39–66. Paris, 1952.

Aristotle's principle, that natures could be known from their proper ends. Instead the world was a drama in which things were presented as allegories of something else, a shadow-play conducted by ritual and interpreted by myth. As for purely rational criticism, then the human environment was read in schematic terms and its items were marked with a fixed and almost legal status. A pattern of meanings was read into rather than drawn from the world. A hierarchy of values was disclosed, not a biological flow. Men had a strong sense of material reality, but not a strong philosophy in its favour. It was as though the mind were a spiritual pilgrim through this life, not an active sharer with material forces. Aristotle's psychological teaching had not yet affected the schools, and the consequences drawn from it by St Thomas, that the mind is the only living substantial principle within the body and therefore belongs to the physical world, were to come as a shock.

The metaphysical mood, however, was pluralist. The followers of Avicenna and Averroes may have accentuated the contrasts between the realm of necessity contemplated by an aloof and possibly unique intellect and the series of contingent events touched by manifold sensations, but they left intact the Western conviction that human individuals were real, responsible and important.

The philosophy of human conduct reflected the ethics of the Stoics, simultaneously full of public zeal and cool before the natural warmth of huddling together and living in community. Detachment from passion, preached by the admired moralists, was strengthened by a strain of neo-Platonism. Plotinus described the virtue of the purged soul which, escaping from the mesh of relationships in the visible world, achieved a lonely poise.[1] He had soldiered in the East under the Emperor Gordian, but only to learn Persian and Indian ways of thought, and he seemed to have been destitute of social feeling. Traces of the teachings of the Cynics appear in the religious homilists— indeed their attitude towards secular power was touched by a certain cynicism in the modern sense of the word, also by an ascetical fastidiousness not uninfluenced by the Epicureans.

[1] 1a–2ae. lxi, 5.

The jurists, of course, were not given to meditations on an otherworldly mystery nor did they seek to escape out of the conditions of this world. Yet in those days, when the stream of thought did not run shallow, theological and philosophical questions were matters of public and even legal and political interest. The classical Roman authors themselves, though distrustful of definition and deduction after the Greek fashion, had not been merely legal practitioners pursuing an exclusively empirical method. *Nature*, a foil to convention in social thought, in some contexts could be referred to animal instinct, as by Ulpian, in others it could be identified with reason, as by Gaius; in both cases it stood for what was not, in the legal sense, civilized. The contrast was repeated in theology where nature was taken either as primitive and unregenerate or as original and innocent; there again it stood for what was overlaid by the economy of grace.

Consequently civilization could appear as a formal dignity and conventional politeness, a creation of the juridical order, an artificial achievement which concealed or crowned, according to the view taken of Nature, the underworld of rude or at least uninhibited forces. No literary cult of the noble savage was practiced, yet medieval Augustinism anticipated the feeling of the Enlightenment that civilization levied a heavy price. That the secular power of coercion was resented does not appear: the fact was accepted. Divines might sombrely discuss its origins, yet they saw no practical alternative if potentially criminal appetites were to be tamed. Religion itself was coming to be expressed more and more in juridical and institutional terms and invoking heavier sanctions. Except from partisans of Abelard and from evangelical movements which claimed greater freedom and familiarity with God than seemed allowed by the formularies of worship, few grievances were aired against the principle and practice of Church authority. The mien of orthodoxy became more ceremonious, but the inner life of devotion coursed as impetuously as ever.

1. *The New Naturalism*

The symbolic interpretation of this world was changed when Aristotle was discovered. Already writers were beginning to show a curiosity about nature, and in England especially empiricism had struck root. Frederick II's scientific coterie studied physical processes for their own sake, and he himself was a field-naturalist who was not content with old wives' tales but sought by first-hand observation and experiment to discover whether vultures had a sense of smell and what went on during human digestion.[1] His falconer was Rinaldo d'Aquino, brother to St Thomas and his kidnapper in a vain attempt to keep him away from the Dominicans. Naturalism was in the air. Learned men began to contemplate the parts of reality as all of one piece, continuous from top to bottom, and in effect opened the way for the scientific study of institutions both sacred and profane.

They perceived that a political community was fastened together less by a mesh of positive laws than by natural kinship, sympathy and sense of friendliness.[2] The pity was that the later Aristoteleans, insensitive to literature and unresponsive to *ens sensibile et mobile* which is the object of natural science, lost the pioneering spirit and found themselves left in logomachies. Not until the Renaissance were the absurdities of an excessive and exclusive *a priori* method derided and inductive pursuits intensified in the schools of serious research. Aristoteleanism, however, was still young and experimental in the thirteenth century.[3] Then it was that political science reappeared as the study of the fundamental laws of human association, and men came to see that the civilized group rose from the biological mass and might contribute to the spiritual expansion of personality. The State was neither artificial nor imposed, and its inherent power to command possessed a dignity greater than that of keeping original sin well battened down.

If Plato's problem-raising temper was not apparent in the dogmatic spirituality of the Neo-Platonists, his general philos-

---

[1] *de Arte venandi cum avibus. The Art of Falconry.* Ed. C. A. Wood and F. M. Fyfe. London, 1956.

[2] M. Hamburger. *Morals and Law: The Growth of Aristotle's Legal Theory.* New Haven, 1951.

[3] J. H. Randall. 'The Development of Scientific Method in the School of Padua'. *Journal of the History of Ideas,* i, p. 177. 1940.
    A. C. Crombie. *Robert Grosseteste and the Origins of Experimental Science.* Oxford, 1953.
    C. H. Haskins. *Studies in the History of Medieval Science.* Cambridge (Mass.), 1927.

ophy, transmitted through Themistius, Philoponus, Simplicius, Proclus, Plotinus and Boethius, and known to St Augustine, profoundly affected medieval ideas. When the theologians discoursed about there being no lasting city here below they were in general accord with Plato's school without knowing the cut of his political thought. No medieval translations of the *Republic* and *Laws* were in circulation. The *Timaeus* was received as Plato's political testament, the *Republic* was supposed to be its second part and vaguely mentioned as representing what Socrates thought about the civil order and its laws.[1] Until the Renaissance most of the references to Plato were taken from Aristotle. The texts of the Pseudo-Dionysius translated by John Scotus Eriugena (c.860) and his own speculations displayed a hierarchic universe in which the visible things were theophanies, symbols of a spiritual world, not profoundly real in themselves. The early schoolmen disavowed the pantheism, but not the sentiment.

To this tradition Aristotle, with his strong sense of present reality and unapologetic worldliness, threw down a challenge. Addressing themselves scientifically to the inner natures and purposes of material things in a fresh and bracing climate of naturalism, men discovered rational and therefore divinely given values in the ethics and politics of pre-Christian antiquity.[2] Its social ideas were rather different from their own, for no organized religion stood over the self-sufficiency of Aegean communities to question policy in the name of a higher law.[3] Few conceived of a natural order untroubled by the supernatural, but a civic cirtue was admired which was not beholden to the life of grace, and later a self-reliant rationalism was released which professed to be able to manage without the control of faith.

Its ideal was not that of the *Societas Christiana*, but of a self-sufficing civil community having the resources within itself to satisfy all reasonable social needs; it was developed by men

[1] St Albert. Commentary *I Politics*, *cap*. i, *e*.

[2] E. Gilson. 'Le moyen âge et le naturalisme antique.' *AHDL* vii, Paris, 1932.
M. T. d'Alverny. 'Le cosmos symbolique du XIIe siècle.' *AHDL*, xx, pp. 31–81. Paris, 1953.

[3] A. H. M. Jones. *The Greek City*. Oxford, 1940.

themselves from their own needs and its constitution was not given to them from above. The habit of reasoning about it combined with the dialectical expansion of the Roman Law, notably with respect to the power of the *Princeps* apart from the Roman Pontiff, to produce the secularism of later centuries. Both the *Polis* of Greece and the *Imperium* of Rome were thought to be models when the Nation-States were taking shape. The early Aristoteleans, however, were moved by no such cause; their immediate concern was merely to disengage a social and political discipline from the previous mixture of morals and law. Before Aristotle's *Ethics* and *Politics* were discovered, attention had been mainly directed to what had been done, as revealed in charters, capitularies, synodal acts, chronicles, homilies and controversial tracts, in order to keep continuity with the past and inculcate Christian social conduct. It was not until after commentaries on Aristotle were followed by formal and systematic expositions which drew from the sources of Greek social thought and Roman jurisprudence that political science freed itself and devoted itself to the study of *raison d'état*.

2. *Aristotle from the Arabic and Greek*

The drama of an orientalized Aristotle bursting in is now shelved. His entrance into the West was more gradual. His influence, first felt in logic, passed progressively into physics, astronomy, and biology, and then into metaphysics, psychology, ethics and politics. He was the central figure of controversies which mounted during St Thomas's teaching career and for a few years after his death and then sank down. The Dominicans' vindication of their master was sufficiently successful. A hundred years later and the Scholastics were using Aristotle's name as a substitute for first-hand inquiry.

To begin with logic. Lost Latin translations by Boethius had been recovered and embroidered by other hands. At the beginning of the twelfth century the 'Old Logic' of the *Categories* and *Perihermeneias* together with Porphyry's *Isagoge* were known, and by its end the Organon was completed by the 'New Logic' of the *Prior Analytics* and *Posterior Analytics*, the *Topics*, and the *de Sophisticis Elenchis*. So far Aristotle was no cause of contention,

but the admired master for dialectics. On the west front of
Chartres he sits meditating together with Cicero and Donatus,
an orator and a grammarian; the early Scholastics did not look
to him for the substance of their philosophy.

A change set in when his other works were put into circulation. The indoctrination spread first from Toledo on the
Christian frontier with Islam. Mingled with the teachings of
the schools of Baghdad and Cordova, the Latin texts of Aristotle
were taken from the Arabic. Gerard of Cremona (d. 1187)
translated the *de Coelo et Mundo, de Generatione et Corruptione*, and
the first three books of the *Meteorologica*. The centre then shifted
to the court of Frederick II, some of whose savants were no less
alien to the European tradition than his bodyguard of Saracen
archers. By the time of Michael Scot (d. before 1236), who
personified this passage from Spain to Italy, most of the
cosmological, psychological, and metaphysical treatises were
being studied.[1] Yet so far scholars had reached only the edge
of Greek science and philosophy.

The texts were ill-translated. They were presented together
with interpolations from the great Arab philosophers, Avicenna
(d. 1037) and Averroes (d. 1198)—the first an earlier and more
persuasive influence though not in political thought, the second
more pointed and controversial[2]—and ventilated opinions un-
welcome to Christian belief and sentiment. The result was that
a provincial council at Sens (1210), which also condemned the
pantheism of David of Dinan and his contemporary Amaury of
Bène (d. 1207), forbade public and private lectures at Paris on
the natural philosophy of Aristotle and his commentators.
Five years later the legate, Robert Curzon, renewed the ban:
the *Organon* and the *Ethics* were expected. It was not withdrawn
after the panic had died down, but became a dead letter; the
'English Nation' at Paris University officially organized public

---

[1] F. Ueberweg and B. Geyer. *Die Patristische und Scholastiche Philosophie*, pp. 342–5,
359–62, 368–71. Berlin, 1928.
S. D. Wingate. *The Medieval Latin Versions of the Aristotelean Latin Corpus*. London,
1931.
E. Gilson. *Christian Philosophy in the Middle Ages*. v, pp. 181–234. 'Arabian and
Jewish Philosophy.'

[2] K. Foster. 'Avicenna and Western Thought in the Thirteenth Century.' *Avicenna,
Scientist and Philosopher*. Ed. G. M. Wickens. London, 1952.

lectures on the whole Aristotelean corpus (1225),[1] and Gregory IX admitted the provisory character of the prohibition and called for corrected editions of Aristotle (1231).

The sack of Constantinople (1204) during the fourth Crusade furnished more manuscripts and opportunities for learning. From about the middle of the century the two most notable translators from the Greek were Robert Grosseteste and William of Moerbeke—an Englishman and a Fleming. Manfred in Naples followed the example of his father, Frederick II, and commissioned Bartholomew of Messina to translate the *Magna Moralia*; the *Economics* followed shortly afterwards. By then Oxford and the Papal Court had become the chief centres of an Aristoteleanism less perturbed than in Naples by civil war and in Paris by controversies about whether the reason could go its own way without reference to the truths of religion. In England a habit of studying this world in a soberly scientific and humanist spirit went back more than a hundred years through Alfred of Sareschel—Alfredus Anglicus—and his friend, Alexander Neckham, to Adelard of Bath. Rome kept its equanimity, for St Thomas's address secured the patronage of Urban IV (1261–4) and Clement IV (1265–8), both of them French.

Semi-authoritative hostility remained, nevertheless, and the tolerance show to Aristoteleanism by the Franciscan John of Rochelle (d. 1245) was not countenanced by his Order. The situation was complicated by those who mistook Averroes for Aristotle. Their teaching on human responsibility, personal immortality and God's particular Providence could not be reconciled with the truths of religion, and they seemed to be laying the foundations of a purely secular culture in defiance of the Christian social tradition.[2]

The threat offered by these Latin Averroists, as they came to

---

[1] M. de Wulf. *Histoire de la philosophie médiévale*, i, p.p 235–6. Louvain, 1924.

[2] F. Copleston. *A History of Philosophy*, ii, pp. 435–41, 'Latin Averroism'. London, 1950.

E. Gilson. *History of Christian Philosophy in the Middle Ages*. pp. 387–402. London, 1955.

D. H. Salman. 'Saint Thomas et les traductions latines des Métaphysiques d'Aristote,' and 'Jean de Rochelle et l'averroisme latin.' *AHDL*, viii and xvi. Paris, 1932, 1947.

be called, was one of the reasons why St Thomas was posted in 1269 by his Master General from the Papal Court to Paris. The distinction he drew, together with St Albert, between the proper reading of Aristotle, which of course he thought was his own, and that of Siger of Brabant, usually regarded as the leading Parisian Averroist, eventually came to be accepted, but not before he had been condemned in council in 1277 by Stephen Tempier, Bishop of Paris, Kilwardby and Peckham, Archbishops of Canterbury, followed the same tenor in dealing with Thomist teaching at Oxford, though less solemnly. Peckham noted that even among the Dominicans Thomas's position was pungently debated, *etiam a fratribus propriis arguebatur argute*; the Franciscans at their General Chapter held at Strassburg in 1284 forbade the circulation of the *Summa Theologica* except among lecturers who were *notabiliter intelligentes*, and with the proviso they must be provided with William de la Mare's *Correctorium Fratris Thomae*, which amended him on 117 counts.

The dispute was less about Averroes himself, who was held in general respect and referred to by St Thomas as the Commentator, than about the Latin Averroists. The questions round which it revolved, the eternity of the world, the individuation of human minds, and the relationship of reason and faith, were not of immediate political interest. The complete *Ethics* and *Politics* of Aristotle slipped in under cover of the smoke, and it was not until towards the close of the thirteenth century that the special problems they raised were made manifest or were used by the Averroists to disconcert orthodoxy. Before then the *Ethics* had taken its place in the curriculum of Dominican schools and university faculties. The *Politics* was not often mentioned.

The *Ethica Vetus* (*Ethics*, *ii* and *iii*) was available before the end of the twelfth century, the *Ethica Nova* (*Ethics*, *i*) by 1210. Fragments from elsewhere (particularly from *Ethics*, *vi*) were incorporated by Robert Grosseteste in the first complete Latin version made probably between 1245 and 1247. St Albert's lectures on the *Nicomachean Ethics* delivered at Cologne in 1249 and taken down by his student St Thomas were based on this *translatio Lincolniensis*. Touched up by the Dominican William of Moerbeke, afterwards chaplain to Pope Clement IV and Archbishop of Corinth, it served as the text for the earliest commentaries.[1]

The first Latin translation of the complete *Politics* seems to have been that made by William of Moerbeke about 1260[2]: he may have been the author of two extant manuscripts of an earlier translation of the first two books.[3] Unlike his other translations, it was not a revision of a text already in circulation, but was freshly done from Aristotle. From the promise in the *Ethics* of a programme on the State its existence had already been surmised.[4] To him belongs the credit of introducing it to the West.

The stage had long been set for this special discipline. The statesman Boethius (e. 524) wrote the much-studied *de Consolatione philosophiae*, which was not a political guide, for it looked away from the mishaps of earth to the serene order of eternity notwithstanding passages of Aristoteleanism and Stoicism.[5] Cassiodorus (d. c. 570) spoke of *civilis philosophia* ministering to the benefit of the whole city, and the text is duly noted by St Isidore and repeated by Hugh of St Victor.[6] The following century remembered the Victorines, but forgot the old Senator —only his *Exposition in Psalterium* was cited by St Thomas, a

---

[1] S. H. Thomson. *The Writings of Robert Grosseteste, Bishop of Lincoln.* Cambridge, 1940.

F. M. Powicke. *Robert Grosseteste and the Nicomachean Ethics.* Proceedings of the British Academy, xvi. London, 1930.

D. A. Callus. 'The date of Grosseteste's translation and Commentaries on the Pseudo-Dionysius and the Nicomachean Ethics.' *RTAM*, xiv, pp. 186–204. Louvain, 1947.

A. Pelzer. 'Le cours inédit d'Albert le Grand sur la Morale à Nicomaque recueilli et rédige par saint Thomas d'Aquin. *Revue néo-scholastique de philosophie*, xxiv, pp. 333–61, 479–520. Louvain, 1922.

A. Mansion. 'Quelques travaux récents sur les versions latines des Ethiques et d'autres ouvrages d'Aristote.' *Revue néo-scholastique*, xxxix, p. 86. Louvain, 1936.

E. Franceschini. 'La revisione Moerbekiana della.' *Translatio Lincolniensis* della Ethica Nicomachea, *Rivista Neo-Scolastica*, xxx, p. 159. Milan 1938.

[2] So dated from the first clear reference to it, *III Contra Gentes* 22.

[3] G. Lacombe. *Aristoteles Latinus*, i, pp. 74–5. Rome, 1939.

[4] 1135 a 12. 1181 b 12–33.

[5] Ed. A. Fortescue and G. D. Smith. London, 1925.

[6] PL clxxvi, 759.

R. A. B. Mynors. *Cassiodori Senatoris Institutiones.* Oxford, 1937.

sign of the decline of letters. Abelard discussed the *communis utilitas*.[1] Dominic Gundissalinus picked up from Alfarabi the mention of a *scientia politica sive civilis racio* and also a reference that Aristotle had written a work on politics.[2]

Among the Arabic philosophers of the East, Alfarabi did not discuss its contents, and Avicenna, though he devoted two summary chapters to political science at the end of his *Metaphysics*, made no mention of it. Among the Arabic philosophers of the West, Averroes had an active career as judge and physician; the *Politics* was not available to him, but his paraphrase of Plato's *Republic* showed the influence of the *Nicomachean Ethics*. His work was not translated into Latin until 1539, but a medieval Hebrew translation, by Solomon ben Yehuda of Marseilles, is evidence that a political terminology had yet to be coined.[3] The famous *Secretum Secretorum* by a pseudo-Aristotle, also entitled *Liber Moralium de Regimine Dominorum* or *de Regimine Principum Aristotelis*, supposedly addressed to Alexander the Great, was translated by Philip of Tripoli, quoted by Michael Scot, and commented on by Roger Bacon.[4]

The texts reached Europe at several removes, having first gone into Asia and Africa. The early translations neither conveyed the political preoccupations of Athens, for that would have required an effort of historical perceptiveness beyond the power of the medievals, nor rendered at first-hand the original phrases, for the Latin was based on the Arabic, which was based on the Chaldaic, and thus on the Greek. Cicero was the only author on social philosophy included in a reading list for Paris University which dates from between 1230 and 1240. It referred to economic ethics as *ypotica*—*ab ypos, quod est sub, quod est scientia de subditis*.[5] One could not go very far on such scraps. A decade or so later, St Albert's first lecture-course on the *Ethics* made no mention of the *Politics* although by then he was

---

[1] *Dialogus inter philosophum judaeum et christianum.* PL clxxviii, col. 1653.
  J. G. Sikes. *Peter Abailard.* Cambridge, 1932.

[2] *de Divisione Philosophiae.* Ed. L. Baur. *Beiträge*, iv. Munster, 1903.

[3] E. I. J. Rosenthal. *Averroes's Commentary on Plato's Republic.* Cambridge, 1956.

[4] G. Lacombe. *Aristoteles Latinus*, i, p. 93.
  R. Steele. *Opera hactenus inedita Rogeri Bacon.* Oxford, 1920.

[5] F. van Steenbergen. *Aristotle in the West.* Pp. 95–7. Louvain, 1955.

basing himself on a translation straight from the Greek. Robert Kilwardby, his contemporary, was equally silent; the *de Ortu Scientiarum* enumerated three interests of practical science, namely, *philosophia ethica, philosophia mechanica,* and *sermocinales*—the art of speech.[1]

From about 1260 onwards the situation changed. Aristotle opened a field of natural and theological philosophy which could be worked without recourse to Christian theology. The distinction, not accepted by the Franciscan and early Dominican doctors though employed as a valid abstraction by the later Dominicans, was pressed to extremes by the upholders of the 'Double-Truth' theory—that the truths of faith and of reason could contradict one another and both could still be sincerely professed. The abstraction was made concrete, and a distinction of complementary discipline became a separation of frames of mind. The fracture extended into social thought. A 'Double City' theory was proposed, and the lurking problem of divided allegiance was brought into the open, this time by the philosophers, not the theologians.

Before the reign of Constantine the Christian Church had stood apart from the State. After the breakdown of the Roman Empire it did not enter at first into the organic life of the new nations, and for various reasons. The pagan religion of the tribes was closely linked with kingship; they were migratory until the sixth century, and when they settled down their territorial boundaries did not always correspond to the ecclesiastical provinces which went back to the days of the undivided Empire; above all their government was frequently Arian. The situation changed with the ascendancy of the Catholic Franks and the conversion of the Goths. Matters civil and ecclesiastical then intermingled, and national churches were ruled by the king: Charlemagne conceived it his duty to rule the Church no less than the State.[2] There was a second dissolution during the 'Second Dark Age' when the Vikings from the north, the Magyars from the east, and Moslems from the south threatened the remains of the Carolingian Empire.[2] Again the barbarians were converted, and the reform of religious discipline was

---

[1] E. M. F. Sommer-Seckendorff. *Studies in the Life of Robert Kilwardby.* Rome, 1937.
[2] C. Dawson. *Religion and the Rise of Western Culture,* pp. 97–115.

consolidated when the great Hildebrand (d. 1085) freed
episcopal appointments from feudal control and maintained
against the German Emperor the supremacy of the spiritual
over the temporal power. The *sacerdotium* contained the *regnum*
within the single *Respublica Christiana*.

The ambiguous victory, however, was hard won, and when
Aristotle appeared on the scene his prestige was joined to the
growing majesty of the Roman Civil Law in order to set up
secular power in its own right. Aristotle's impact was all the
greater because it was disinterested; unlike many legists he had,
as it were, no axe to grind in the protracted disputes between
spiritual and temporal power. Men had thought of the *societas
christiana* descending from above, unified by the sacramental
act of baptism, but now they were shown a social instinct
working through an ascending process from the natural conjunction of male and female and the household and the
neighbourhood-group to a self-sufficing *communitas humana*.

The political community in ancient Greece had not depended
on supernatural religion—why then should the revival of its
purely reasonable system look to Church authority? The justice
described in the seventh book of the *Ethics* was a dynamic
virtue going beyond obedience to the Tables of the Law or
conformity to a code. The *humana civilitas* was no artificially
contrived institution but sprang from man's social nature; it
was no mere instrument but the end and purpose of virtue, no
mere remedy for sin but a noble object. The vision of a united
Christendom remained for centuries, but already it was
accepted that the authority of the State derived neither from
nor through the ceremonial, juridical, and official ordinances
of the Church.

How far St Thomas went in this direction the following pages
may show. He reverenced Aristotle as his leader in ethical and
political philosophy. Many of his contemporaries saw little
difference between him and Siger of Brabant, and the con-
demnations of 1277 lumped both together. Nevertheless the
creation of a purely secular enclave in a wider scene, a City of
Reason in which human nature as it actually existed could be
at home, was no part of his thought. He considered that the
rational animal was a true type and a proper study, that

natural justice was a necessary foundation of all morals, and that reason had its rights. Nevertheless good sense and good will were only part of the story. Men needed Divine Revelation and supernatural help, and their social organization should be open to and integrated in the kingdom of grace. The complete order should be considered in one sweep, and men taken as *wholes*, not as two things, one the body and the other the soul, one the material man and the other the spiritual man, one the subject of the State and the other a member of the Church. A theology which failed to see that could be but a sectarian discipline.

Church and State were not separate institutions before the fourteenth century; the conflicts between Popes and Emperors were between different dignitaries within a single united Christendom. If the early Parisian Averroists were an anxiety to the ecclesiastical authorities for doctrinal reasons, there is nothing to show that they were lacking in public respect for religion, or that they were disposed to set up a rival magisterium in the later manner of Marsiglio of Padua and his friend, John of Jandun. They claimed little more than the academic liberty of reasoning how they liked. The logic of the Double-Truth theory allowed a man to profess wholeheartedly, though scarcely single-mindedly, the truths of faith. After all a saint had said, *Credo quia impossibile*, and snubbing the reason was a fashion for holy men. Yet if the contradiction may serve very well as an interim attitude, its long-term effects on the psychological health of individuals and society are less happy.

A formal rejection of the Church's right to be in politics and the assertion that religion was a private affair would have sounded equally strange during the thirteenth century. All the same a secular political spirit was coming to grudge the claims of clerical power. Papal decrees tried to withdraw the clergy from secular employment and a new class of lay-lawyers was taking their place not only in the courts but also in the councils of State. They were the chief instruments of the change. It is difficult to assess the part played by the early Neo-Aristoleans. The Arab transmitters of Aristotle to the West were not politically minded. The evidence is scanty for the social views of the

early Latin Averroists, yet it is a safe conjecture that they
influenced the juridical and political thought of the period
since they were prominent in the Faculties of Arts.

There is no record of any practical consequences of their idea
of a world ruled by a determinism which might have been
expected to disallow our free responses to a freely-working
Providence. There are indications they extolled a model of the
good life in which Christian humility was not prominent. The
wilder spirits scoffed at poverty and chastity—'a folly to the
Greek'—but then so did the orthodox in unbuttoned moments.
Siger of Brabant and Boethius of Dacia—Boethius of Sweden,
said to have been a Dominican—left ethical pieces which
favoured practical self-sufficiency and a contented rationalism.
Siger adjudicated on problems arising from the *Politics*: for
instance, was the city better ruled by good laws than by good
men?[1] But that the doctrine of a single Cosmic Mind led him
and his followers to favour a State Monism or be indifferent to
individual rights is not borne out by what is known about them.
It would have been to their advantage to preach liberty.
Tolerance, however, was not a value actively respected by the
medievals, despite the teaching of some theologians that conscience should be respected and infidels not be forced to the
wedding-feast, and even they substituted the *compelle remanere*
for the *compelle intrare* and did not reprobate the death-penalty
for heresy.[2] Humanitarians were few in those days.

---

[1] A. P. D'Entrèves. *Dante as a Political Thinker*. Oxford, 1952.

E. Gilson. *Christian Philosophy in the Middle Ages*, pp. 399, 725. 'Boèce de Dacie et
la double verité, *AHDL*, xxii, 1955.

For the *Summa de Bono*, see M. Grabmann, *AHDL*, vi, p. 187. Paris, 1932.

F. van Steenbergen. *Siger de Brabant d'après les oeuvres inédits*, pp. 115, 299, 321,
534. 2 vols. Louvain, 1931, 1942.

G. de Lagarde. *Naissance de l'esprit laique au déclin du moyen âge*, iii, 2, 'Les facultes
des arts et l'averroisme.'

R. M. Giguère. *Jean de Sècheville, de principiis naturae*. Montreal, 1956.

[2] 2a–2ae. x, 8, 9, 11. *IV Sentences*, XIII, ii, 3.

J. Lecler. *Histoire de la tolérance au siècle de la Réforme*, pp. 65–123. Paris, 1955.

8

Part Two

THE DEVELOPMENT IN ST THOMAS

THE DEVELOPMENT IN ST THOMAS

THE *Politics* was already out of date as a practical plan during Aristotle's lifetime, for, when he wrote, the Greek City-States which provided his models had been subjugated by Philip of Macedon and by his own pupil, Alexander the Great, the mightiest empire-builder in history. Caesar succeeded to Alexander, Pope and Holy Roman Emperor to Caesar. The generalization is fair enough that from the days of Aristotle to those of St Thomas there was a movement from *Polis* to *Imperium*, though historically many types of social organization co-existed and a similar expansion was not found in all of them.[1]

After the barbarian invasions and the break-up of the Western Empire the fact of dominion was more important than any theory about it. The time was not ripe for any claim to universal sovereignty. Nevertheless the imperial attributes were never quite forgotten, and they were revived from the time of Charlemagne, the founder of what came to be known as the Holy Roman Empire. There was an Emperor but scarcely an Empire, for the *Imperium* was a symbolic function rather than an organized territorial power. The designation *Roman* first appeared in 1034, not to re-assert the world-wide pretensions of ancient Rome but for opportunist reasons of diplomacy, and *Holy* was adopted by Barbarossa in 1157 in order to compete on an equal footing with the Pope and *Sancta Ecclesia Romana*.[2] Both titles were thin, though real enough for Dante.

It was but a shadow of Rome, and lacked the communications, administrators, army, language and for many years the Law which were the strength of the old Empire whose preroga-

---

[1] M. Hammond. *City-State and World-State in Greek and Roman Political Theory until Augustus.* Cambridge, Mass., 1951.

[2] G. Barraclough. *The Medieval Empire: Idea and Reality.* London, 1950.
   R. Folz. *L'idée de l'Empire en occident du Ve. au XIVe. siècle.* Paris, 1953.
   A. Dempf. *Sacrum Imperium. Geschichts und Staatsphilosophie des Mittelalters und die politischen Renaissance.* Darmstadt, 1954.

tives it claimed. All the same there was no alternative in Europe to the Emperor as supreme ruler of temporalities until the nations achieved full political independence, except for premonitions, which grew stronger after Hildebrand, of the hieratic thesis that the Pope, *sacerdos regalis* and *caput* of the whole *corpus* of Christians, held the keys of the law, *claves juris*, as well as the keys of the kingdom of heaven, *claves regni caelorum*.

Local feeling was strong under feudalism, but national patriotism was not so focussed to the distance that a sharp image of the State still less of the Empire was held. A man would follow his lord and fight against the heathen even on the far frontiers of Christendom, yet small sense of official duty or service towards the *respublica* coloured his immediate allegiance and crusading devotion. In some respects he might be compared with an Irishman nowadays, proud of his country even if detached about its political constitution, who is ready to work in Great Britain, pay its taxes and enlist for its defence, who is loyal to his ship, regiment or squadron, without being committed to the national political cause.

All this began to change after the rise of the Italian Republics and of the proud and independent realms which occupied the territories of the old Roman provinces. A new type of political community emerged, claiming its own appropriate mode of service. The compact City-States and centralized Nation-States fulfilled the conditions of the perfect political community described in the *Politics*, and their completeness was capped when their rulers claimed the attributes of the *Princeps* of Roman Law: they were not of course like 'the godly prince' of the Reformation State who governed both temporalities and spiritualities. When it is said that Christendom was changed into a collection of self-contained national communities reflecting the ideas of Aristotle it is not suggested that Greek political institutions were restored. Greek influences were weaker than those of the Roman Law and of the economic forces that were changing the social order; even the Renaissance State was a modification of the medieval not a restoration of the antique.

Nevertheless Aristotle provided the theory to match the occasion when a thousand-year-old process was reversed and moved back from *Imperium* to *Polis*. There were many causes for the change. The lapse of imperial practice, national pride and mistrust for Italian Rome, lay dissatisfaction with the clerical theocracy, fiscal grievances and the increasing influence of civil lawyers and the mercantile classes were among the contributory factors. Feudalism was disintegrating, and with it the prestige of the warrior-class. Social virtue became more bourgeois, for the new *civility* used soldiers only for its own defence; *militaris* was but an adjunct to *regnativa* and *politica*.[1] The knightly classes protested that although they defended the city they could take no part in the public life of Dante's Florence, which was run by business-men, unless they demeaned themselves through being 'ennobled' in a guild. The cities of the Empire also underwent rapid constitutional and economic changes during the first half of the thirteenth century, and Cologne, St Thomas's first Dominican *studium*, was a formidable centre of opposition to the Hohenstaufen cause.

The reception and development of political ideas in his writings will be taken according to the order of the four chapter headings of the first part of this study. His indebtedness to his predecessors will be considered first in theology, next in jurisprudence, thirdly with respect to a friar's distinctive conception of group-life, finally in Aristotelean philosophy.

The method is convenient, yet not without the danger of pulling out the strands from a close-knit texture of analogies from every human interest. One of the most abstract of thinkers, paradoxically his body of thought is peculiarly liable to be misrepresented when subjected to specialist treatment. The separation of a purely rational philosophy from the *sacra doctrina* of the Christian Revelation can be forced enough without the further separation of a system of formal political categories from the product.[2] Inseparables may be made into distinct ideas, but never into things apart. As he remarks, realities which cannot be divided in actual fact may be separately considered by the reason.[3] It is allowable, indeed necessary, for scientific method to treat one class of values without attend-

---

[1] 2a–2ae. l, 1, 2, 4.

[2] T. Gilby. *St Thomas Aquinas: Philosophical Texts*, pp. xviii–xxi. *Theological Texts*, pp. xi–xiii.

[3] 1a. lxxxv, 1, *ad* 1. *de Hebdomadibus*, 4.

ing to another, and within that class systematically to go
through one part after another without losing sense of the
background. And so it should be possible to abstract the
theological, juristic, cultural and philosophical elements in his
social thought without tearing the whole.

The treatise on Law in the *Summa Theologica* contained his
only set piece on political theory: it should be supplemented
by sections from the treatises on Prudence and Justice.[1] The
commentary on the *Politics* was merely the start of a paraphrase
of Aristotle's text, the *de Regimine Principum* was a homiletic
instruction to the King of Cyprus left unfinished, and the *de
Regimine Judaeorum* was an answer to inquiries from the Duchess
of Brabant about discriminatory taxation at the expense of a
minority.[2] The absence of formal reflections on feudalism was
less surprising from him than from John of Salisbury a century
earlier. Oddly, since he lived in the midst of them at the Papal
Court for the middle period of his teaching life (1259–68), his
writings give no inkling of the political ambitions of the
Canonists. He did not contend that all dominion descends from
God through the Pope, nor did he dwell on juristic ecclesiology.

Of the three types of theology enumerated by Varro, poetical
theology *ad theatrum*, civil theology *ad urbem* and natural
theology *ad orbem*, the last prevailed in his thought.[3] His social
morality was systematically built into a philosophical and
theological structure, with few open references to the established order of his day and fewer to its myths; he carried on the
work of rational analysis and systematization begun by Abelard.
The *Summa Theologica* was unattached to the massive growth of
political Papalism, deep-rooted in history and bearing the
regalia and effective symbols of authority both sacred and

---

[1] Law, 1a–2ae. xc–cviii. Prudence, 2a–2ae. xlvii–lvi. Justice, 2a–2ae. lvii–cxii.

[2] 1a–2ae. xc–cviii. (c. 1270) *In viii libros politicorum Expositio* (c. 1269). Authentic to
iii, 6 inclusively (1280–7); the rest was by Peter of Auvergne. *de Regimine
Principum ad regem Cypri*, also entitled *de Regno* (c. 1266). Probably authentic
to ii, 4 inclusively: the rest by Ptolemy of Lucca. (cf. J. A. Endres. *De Regimine
Principum des hl. Thomas von Aquin.* Munster, 1913). *de Regimine Judaeorum ad
ducissam Brabantiae*, also addressed *ad comitissam Flandriae* (1261–72). The
authentic section of the *de Regimine Principum* is translated by A. P. D'Entrèves
and J. G. Dawson, *Aquinas, Selected Political Writings*. Oxford, 1948.

[3] See *de Civitate Dei*, iv, 27.

profane, which overspread the thirteenth century. Rome appeared to be set on the summit of the Western World and to possess the substance of monocratic power; in fact the political centre of gravity was moving north-west. St Thomas was in no doubt about the religious primacy of the successor of St Peter,[1] but the Dominicans generally were not ranged with such writers as Augustinus Triumphus of Ancona, the uncompromising spokesman for direct papal jurisdiction in secular matters.[2] His formative years and the final period of his mature thought were spent in the different political atmosphere of Paris and the *domaine royale*. There the soaring architecture reflected the new social scholasticism, and men translated their national pride into resistance to the idea of a single overlord in Christendom whether he were called Pope or Emperor.[3]

The political theory which can be composed from his writings is like his discourse on other topics—the dialectic doubles back, the advance is not straight and steady. Yet an advance can be detected: as his knowledge of Aristotle deepened so his account of political prudence and the reasonable ideal of citizenship became more technically assured. While he did not rule out what may be called the romantic and perhaps the wilder strains in human behaviour, his respect for political authority grew, and the face he turned to rebellion was bleaker at the end than at the beginning of his career. At the same time—heir to Abelard who had felt the hostility of legalism to the Gospel spirit—he brought out the pre-eminence of equity playing above the letter of the codes and the dignity of man's vocation to live beyond the measures of legal justice and political virtue. His pace and emphasis vary as he sought to resolve the tensions set up when persons live together; apparent inconsistencies can be corrected by fuller explication, not by rejection of one side or the other.

He taught for about twenty years, from 1252 when he received the degree of Bachelor of Theology at Paris, until his death in 1274 on his way from Naples to attend the Oecumenical Council of Lyons. His writing career falls into three

---

[1] 2a–2ae. 1, 10. xi, 2, *ad* 3. Disputations, X *de Potentia*, 4, *ad* 13.
[2] *Summa de Potestate Ecclesiastica ad Ioannem XXII.*
[3] L. Réau. *L'art gothique en France*, p. 11. Paris, 1945.

periods. First, seven years at Paris (1252–9) when, of the works which interest us, he composed his *Commentary on the Sentences* of Peter Lombard, the tract *Contra Impugnantes Dei Cultum*, against the opponents of the new religious Orders, and the Commentary on St Matthew's Gospel; he also began the *Contra Gentes*. Second, nine years in Italy at the Papal Court which travelled between Viterbo, Orvieto, and Anagni (1259–68); there he met William of Moerbeke and started his series of commentaries on Aristotle with the treatise on natural and metaphysical philosophy. The unfinished treatise de *Regimine Principum* was started and the first part of the *Summa Theologica* completed; he declined the Archbishopric of Naples. Third, the final six years of his life, when, to counter the threat of Latin Averroism, he was recalled to teach in Paris (1268–72), and then afterwards was charged with the organization of Dominican studies at Naples (1272–3). Here in the same community was a familiar friend, Ptolemy of Lucca, ten years younger than himself, who was to finish the *de Regime Principum*, and die at the age of 90 having witnessed the new lay concepts of political power being put into practice. The second part of the *Summa Theologica* on moral science (1269–72), the commentaries on the *Ethics*, the beginning of the *Politics* (1269–73), and the Epistle to the Romans (1272–3) belong to this final period.[1]

From his student days he was acquainted with the *Ethics* and drew on it for his first systematic work, the commentary on the *Sentences*. He came to know the *Politics* from about 1260. He began commentaries on both towards the end of his life when he was writing the second part of the *Summa Theologica*. Although their social teaching, notably their insistence on the naturalness of political authority and the virtues of political association, differed from Augustinism no dramatic caesura fell in the run of his argument, and he continued to quote St Augustine for support.[2] The impression is left that he was an Aristotelean

---

[1] Chronology according to A. Walz. 'Thomas d'Aquin : Ecrits.' *DTC*, xv, 1, 635–41. Paris, 1946.

B. Schmeidler. *Die Annalen des Tholomeus v. Lucca.* Monumenta Germaniae Historica: Scriptores Rerum Germanicarum. Nova Series, viii. Berlin, 1930.

[2] E. Gilson. 'Pourquoi saint Thomas a critiqué saint Augustin.' *AHDL*. i, pp. 5–127. Paris, 1926–7.

before he came to study the texts, and then found himself so much at ease with what he read that he could fill out the meaning; on occasion his intellectual sympathy could supply for the deficiencies of his scholarship or of the faulty translation in front of him.

He opened easily enough in his *Commentary on the Sentences* (1254–6) by mingling Apostolic counsels and Stoic sentiments in the style of his theological predecessors: the kingdoms of the earth pass away, yet rulers and magistrates were owed a duty of respect and obedience. All the same a difference was already betraying itself: this world was not so shadowy and shifty that our minds and wills cannot find a firm purchase there. It contained truths and fundamental rights. It was a proper scene for scientific certitude and for virtuous conduct. Hence he recognized a moral power within secular authority, which can bind *non tantum temporaliter sed etiam spiritualiter ut Apostolus dicit ad Romanos xiii*;[1] he produced a rudimentary sketch of political prudence—the trained ability of governing the community— which was to be redrawn in the *Summa Theologica*; he quoted freely from the *Ethics*.[2] Despite this the work as a whole belonged to the old theological tradition. Aims and objects were presented as descending from above the visible world, and the true community was the Church in which human persons commune with God, the angels and the saints.

Presently the difference grew more pronounced as his sense of the earthly community increased. The echoes of Neo-Platonism fell fainter, the notes of Aristoteleanism rang clearer. The far exemplars seemed to close in and become present ends. Men acted not only for a distant duty but for well-being here and now. The result was to accentuate the opposition between this world and the next. Thus, the *Contra Gentes* praised human nobility surpassing community-service, and then in the next chapter acquiesced without protest to slavery as an inevitable consequence of group-life.[3]

Similarly, the *Summa Theologica* extolled the virtues that spurn all earthly and political considerations, and then went on

---

[1] *II Sentences*, XLIV, ii, 2.
[2] *III Sentences*, XXXIII, iii, 1, 4a. XXXVI, i, 1. 2a–2ae. 1, 1. 2.
[3] III *Contra Gentes*, 80, 81. See 2a–2ae. civ, 6, *ad* 1.

to put the good life under the sway of civic and legal justice.[1] In one place he wrote of the heroism of the solitary life, in another of its monstrousness.[2] These points give some indication of the stresses to which his social and political dialectic was subject. This much may be ventured by way of simplification, that he began by bringing out the traditional dignity of persons against the threat of tyranny and ended by presenting an Aristoteleanism so mature and charged with Christianity that the power of the political community could be concentrated without danger of regimenting people like units in a mass.

He was fighting on two fronts: on one he took the offensive against a new rationalism, on the other he held a defensive position against an old obscurantism—the term is not altogether fair. He attacked the Latin Averroists and was attacked by the Augustinian theologians who granted no free field to reason and, occupied with noble essences, were spiritually fastidious about plunging the mind in matter. No doubt some of these were heresy-hunters, but others were no prescribers of scholarship; men like Robert Kilwardby and John Peckham were no less speculative than he was, and rather better versed in the natural sciences.

How common cause could have been joined from these opposite camps may be suggested by the reflection that a believer who allows that strictly rational conclusions can be elaborated contrary to faith may well find himself in partial agreement with the believer who has no use for pure philosophy and occupies himself solely with a religious philosophy based on faith and experience of the Christian fact: in their different ways both suppose that split between faith and rational science which St Thomas deprecated. Somewhat after the same fashion, a statesman who followed Machiavelli might easily adopt Traditionalism as a practical stand: thus some of the nineteenth-century publicists for Throne and Altar dismissed Rationalism together with the French Revolution and sought the foundations of social stability in a religion to which they did not subscribe.

---

[1] 1a–2ae. lxi, 5. 2a–2ae. lviii, 5. (1a–2ae. xxi, 4, *ad* 3 may also be contrasted with 2a–2ae. lxv, 1).

[2] 2a–2ae. clxxxviii, 8. *I Politics, lect.* 1.

The opposition of the conservative theologians to St Thomas did not come to a head until after his death. They esteemed his character but objected to his views as earthbound. Did he not reject the idealism of divine illumination for an empiricism derived from the senses, the soul as spirit for the soul as substantial form of body, the dominance of faith for the autonomy of reason? These are psychologico-theological questions, and their social and political implications were not yet drawn out and debated. Other signs of his innovating spirit also appeared. For instance, was he not sacrificing the sturdy temper of freedom by tightening the discipline of the political community?

The *Summa Theologica* was less prepared to resist trespass by the ruler than the *Commentary on the Sentences* was, and much less than John of Salisbury who put a tyrant under the ban of the law. There was a paradox here, for St Thomas had learnt from Aristotle the distinction between the *jus politicum* observed by equals among themselves and the *jus dominativum* and *paternum* exercised over dependents and that the first was more excellent, being justice pure and simple.[1] One might have expected a ruler to have been more subject to restraint in the polity of the thirteenth century than in the paternalism of the twelfth. This, however, is to leave out of account the diminishing force of custom due to the growing acceptance of the principle that the monarch is more than the people's vicar but a personified power who *motu proprio* can make laws. He did not favour these tendencies, rather the reverse, nevertheless they were in the logic of part of his thought, and as his Aristoteleanism developed so he favoured a closer political integration and the ruler's elevation above popular whim. The *bonum commune* was godlike and far transcended the *communitas domestica*. Men while still on earth were citizens of no mean city. The State was an institution more august than any mere combination against crime. The enhancement of its authority inevitably followed from such convictions.

We were not made to live as solitaries, he remarked, and only a strange grace made us such; by nature, that is by God, we are social and political animals. *Quod quidem naturalis necessitas declarat.*[2] St Albert, characteristically blunter, declared that the

---

[1] *Politics*, v, 10. 1134 b 8. St Thomas, *lect.* 11.   [2] *de Regimine Principum*, i, i.

good life was for a man who lived by himself, the better for a man who lived in his family, the best for a man who lived in his city or political community. A lonely man, Moerbeke remarked, was the *affectator belli* denounced by Homer—'clanless and lawless and heartless is he'.[1] St Thomas, however, remained sensitive to those supernatural virtues which did not directly and manifestly advance social welfare; they enhanced man in the individual, not man in the mass. Whereas St Albert took Diogenes the Cynic as his example of the recluse, he preferred St John the Baptist and St Anthony the Hermit. Despite his insistence on the claims of the community and the texts alleged by supporters of the Corporative State between the World Wars to prove him no liberal, he was concerned to emancipate persons from subjection to any human group or scheme, and his general social argument mounted to the teaching of the last two tracts in defence of the friars, *de Perfectione vitae spiritualis* (1269) and *contra Retrahentes a religione* (1270), that the contemplative life was superior to any career of administrative or productive usefulness.

He recognized, more so than his predecessors, the value and soundness of created things, God-given and inherent. The world might go on for ever—our reason could not tell us to the contrary. Human nature was not completely corrupted by sin— *id quod est naturale totaliter perdi non potest*. Moral activity revolved round certain enduring types and could be classified apart from the circumstances and personal motives which provided their special but passing individual interest.[2] His metaphysical theology extended and deepened the dependence of creatures on God; the first and creative cause was not just one factor which originated a process but was the sustaining ground and mover of the whole reality produced. Everything shivers on the brink of extinction but for divine power and mercy, yet God cherishes all the things he has made and by him they are real in themselves.[1] St Thomas wrote like a man quite at home in

---

[1] *Politics*, i, 2. *Ethics*, x, 10. 1180a 28. *Odyssey* ix, 114 was also quoted by Plato, *Laws*, iii, 680 B. St Thomas *I Politics*, *Lect*. 1, 2. See *X Ethics*, *Lect*. 10, 15 St Albert, *I Politics*, cap. i.

[2] 1a. xlvi, 1, 2. *Opusc.* xxv. *de Aeternitate Mundi contra murmurantes* (1270). 1a–2ae. lxxxv, 1, 2. 2a–2ae. lxxvi, 1. 1a–2ae. xviii, 1, 2.

T. Deman. *Aux origines de la théologie morale.* Montreal, 1951.

his surroundings as he found them; in accepting them we could not be too natural or in explaining them too rational. He was no ethical formalist who divorced right from good, or ought from can, or even, one may say, duty from pleasure. *Deus impossibilia non jubet*, said St Augustine.[2] And St Thomas would have spoken more strictly of potentiality rather than possibility, for, at a level more profound than that of miraculous intervention in a local scheme of reference, he never thought of omnipotence doing violence to the things it creates.

Of two typical Christian approaches to social problems, one takes the order of natural justice perceived in this world and trusts to good sense, since sin has not radically corrupted the human faculty of legislating; the other is more apocalyptic and certain of the vanity of everything apart from the revelation and grace of God. The difference between the Latin Catholic and the German Protestant outlooks which appears at oecumenical congresses is deep-rooted in theology; its historical consequences, which allow of no simple contrast, have been unexpected, for if, in fact, Protestant regions have offered more for the economist to admire, Catholic regions have offered less for the medical psychologist to deplore—success may be variously judged, and the test of making a living is not that of leading a happy life. It is clear that St Thomas must be ranged among those who start from this world and never arrive at the need for vilifying it.

His effect on the mentality of his own Order was perhaps deeper than that of its founder. Aristotle was not reckoned a Christian author, and the early Dominican authorities were guarded about welcoming him and legislated to keep profane knowledge within bounds; that was to be changed. Whereas St Albert grumbled at the obstructions to the study of natural philosophy put up by his brethren, St Thomas passed them by, and wrote in the manner of one taking it for granted that any topic of human interest should be studied, and that without detriment to theology. His was the confidence of a contemplative mind seeing truth everywhere, of an aristocratic temper not easily put out. It was not unjustified by his surroundings.

---

[1] 1a. xlv. 1, 2, 3. xlvi. 3, *ad* 2.
[2] *de Natura et Gratia*, 43. PL xliv, 271.

Individual life might be brief and bloody, his family from the border between Pope and Hohenstaufen was rent between divided loyalties and his own kin were killed when Charles of Anjou was establishing himself in Naples; all the same there were reasons to be sanguine. The joy of the world was sung by an Easter Sequence of the time—

> *merula, monedula, cuncta volucria,*
> *saecula futura canunt aurea.*

Manichaeism had been mastered, and the evangelical movement canalized in the friars; the Crusades were not yet a hopeless cause; Orthodox and Romans, despite the shock of the sack of Constantinople, were at least in communication; papal schisms and the Black Death had not brought decay. In England, soon to be ruled by Edward I, the Common Law was being formed; in France the king and fount of courtesy was St Louis who dispensed justice under an oak-tree and helped his subjects to heaven while striving to give them a good life now; in Germany the choir of Cologne and the west front of Strassburg testified to St Albert's versatile genius. Cathedrals, monasteries, parish churches were being rebuilt; universities were being founded; political institutions were being constructed. Stone was carved in more living shapes, glass glowed more brightly, painting found less hieratic forms and music sweeter modes.

The season was late spring and the shape of things, not yet covered by foliage, could still be seen. The light was gay not leaden, the climate clear despite the passing overcast of apocalyptic rumour—according to Joachimite prophecy the Eternal Gospel was expected to dawn in 1260. The Spirituals had not yet gone queer nor were they dubiously allied with secularists and positivists; the Children's Crusade was a memory and the mass-hysteria of wandering flagellants still in the future. More than a hundred years separated the religious revivalism of two Dominicans, Blessed Jordan of Saxony, second Master-General, and St Vincent Ferrer. How different they were—the first attracted young men *potius humanitate quam severitate*, conducted an inhibited correspondence with Blessed Diana d'Andalo and after his death in shipwreck off Acre appeared to his friends as a cheerful apparition; the second was the Angel of the Judgment who excited his hearers to God's love *terrore concussos atque a terrenis affectibus evulsos*.[1] By then the autumn had come and the religious devotion to sadness and death. We must be careful of simplification however; St Vincent, for instance, was a master of logical theory and his fame now grows in quarters unmoved by hell-fire sermons.

The times were unlike those of St Augustine when civilization was going down in ruins. Although the Turks were destroying the Latin principalities in the Levant and had occupied the hearthland of the Byzantine Army, the Cuman Tartars had been repelled and the frontiers of Western Christianity were being extended to the north-east and south-west. Cistercians and friars accompanied the soldiers. The land was reclaimed, great churches were built, schools were opened in the towns. Iconography shows St Thomas calm and sedate, a book on his lap, his fingers expository; he is not proclaiming, denouncing or wringing his hands. He was singularly free from the homilists' complaint of living in bad times. Perhaps he lacked the tragic sense. Both the glory that is to come and the present mystery of grace were grounded on physical things; the lowlier they were the better they shadowed divine light.[2] He really did hold that matter was real.

Pagan rulers possessed valid authority to govern Christians because the divine law, which is from revelation, did not abolish the human law, which is from natural reason; both mutually sustained one another according to the principle that grace perfected nature[3] He wrote nothing to support those chaplains who advised their lords on crusade that there was no duty of keeping faith with infidels. The divine exemplars were not only ideal types, high in the heavenly places, separate and remote from the world; they were present ends which entered into and shaped human activity. We were surrounded by real objects, to be respected and served for themselves and not merely as occasions for reaching out to something else; in

---

[1] M. Aron. *St Dominic's Successor*. London, 1955.

B. Altaner. *Jordans von Sachsen, Die Briefe*. Leipzig, 1925.

2nd Nocturn Lessons. *Dominican Breviary*, 15 February and 5 April.

[2] 1a. 1, 9, *ad* 3.

[3] 2a–2ae. x, 10.

1a. i, 8, *ad* 2. ii, 2, *ad* 1. lxii, 7. 1a–2ae. x, 4. *de Trinitate*, ii, 3.

particular the political community was endowed with true rights which depended on no supernatural intervention and deserved virtuous service apart from ecclesiastical command.

This acceptance of present reality countered a *contemptus mundi*, peevish or merely trite. His sympathy for living purposes coursing through physical processes and his insistence on the presence of sensibility in natural science and of individual appreciation in moral conclusions forbade a rigid grid being set on the social group. No Aristotelean philosopher could then be committed to an artificial scheme, an academic version of a medievalised Roman system, however august its genesis or successful its vogue. The Dominican Church at Bologna, where St Dominic lay buried, served as the headquarters of the jurists; there St Thomas attended a General Chapter of his Order, but his spirit was easier than theirs, and his jurisprudence closer to the humanism of Placentinus—'the only poet among the Glossators', remarks Kantorowicz[1]—who had emigrated to France weary of the unbending orthodoxy of the Italians.

He did not resent present earthiness, economic considerations or enlightened self-interest in morality, nor did he condemn the profit-motive. He made no apology for taking men as he found them. Private property meant the dignity of personal responsibility in administration, therefore to be advocated; exclusive enjoyment was an abuse, and therefore to be censured, for all should share in the fruits of the earth. Like Aristotle he was suspicious of short-cuts to Utopia, and agreed with the criticism that Communism was a specious benevolence, doctrinaire and indifferent to actual experience.[2] Repeatedly he insisted that a lively prudence should point and particularize the judgments of moral science, since these by their very generalization were too sweeping to fit unique individual cases. Social stability demanded that laws should be constant and not too easily repealed; on the other hand justice should not lay down a flat and unvarying *ought*.

A cleric gentle and generous about lay values, he was a man of Paris, not of Bologna.[3] The artists mourned his death, and

[1] *Glossators*, p. 203.
[2] *Politics*, ii, 5. 1263b, 1264a. St Thomas, *lect.* 4, 5.
[3] For a comparison of the two universities, see Rashdall, *Medieval Universities*, i, pp. 136-7, 262-4.

Siger of Brabant offered no mere conventional gesture of condolence to the Dominicans—possibly controversy had brought the two men closer together. Dante placed them together in the *Paradiso*. Both attempted to open up a field where reason could operate without interference from outside or servility to superior orders. What St Thomas strenuously opposed was the Double-Truth theory, that faith and reason could contradict one another without either being the worse; instead he pressed for a greater effort of penetration into the processes of each and of elaboration of their common analogies.

An ethical doctrine which issued from the study of Aristotle could be studied in abstraction from the supernatural. The difference lay in the nature of the abstraction. The system of the Latin Averroists could be represented as none of the Christian theologian's business: it could be alleged to respond to a concrete historical situation, namely the self-sufficient, self-governing civil community, and therefore might be developed apart from the rules of the Christian revelation. To the Thomists, however, the City was but one formal interest to be developed in harmony with many others. Their line of thought, the middle way between the extremes of political Averroism and political Augustinism, stretched through Godfrey of Fontaines, Giles of Rome, Ptolemy of Lucca, John of Paris, and Remigio di Girolami. It influenced writers such as Nicholas Trivet and Walter Burley, but not the men who shaped affairs.[1] Simplifications usually score the political success, and in the event the Averroists won, for the Augustinists were driven from one position after another until they played no more part in policy than Liberals in the age of Communism and Fascism. The Canonists had been their *corps d'élite* and when they were relegated to household duties within the Church secularism ceased to be disputed on the field of State.

The political theory of the early Latin Averroists, as already observed, can only be guessed at from the few texts which

---

[1] G. de Lagarde. 'La Philosophie sociale d'Henri de Gand et Godefroid de Fontaines.' *AHDL*. XIV, pp. 73–142. Paris, 1943–5.

Conor Martin. *The Commentaries on the Politics of Aristotle in the late thirteenth and early fourteenth centuries, with reference to the thought and political life of the time.* Bodleian MS. D.Phil. c. 211. Oxford, 1949.

remain to us.[1] It is possible to read back into them the idea of a City of Reason apart from Christendom, a *humana civilitas* not amenable to revealed religion, less preoccupied with rewards hereafter than with the proper conduct of affairs here and now. Yet no evidence is forthcoming that the supporters of the doctrine of the single *intellectus agens* in fact advocated an over-mastering State, or would lose the individual in the network of universal ideas. The play of ideas is less simple and consistent in history than in logical debate. In any case there seems to have been an ironical quality about the character of Siger and his friends, and about the *invidiosi veri* they argued, almost as though they were *frondeurs* with no stomach for a centralizing absolutism.[2]

The ecclesiastical prohibitions against philosophers dabbling in divinity probably widened the gap between reason and faith. The Faculties of Arts, now in possession of rich new material from Aristotle, could claim immunity so long as they made no theological pronouncements—perhaps the Double-Truth theory was more tactical than doctrinal, an attempt to seize an advantage, so that henceforward moral and political philosophy could be studied in isolation from the customary precepts of Christianity and the teachings of the theological moralists and canonists.[3]

The civil lawyers hastened the process. Indeed, lay control of the State was the work less of philosophers basing themselves on Aristotle's *Politics* than of legal scholastics developing the Roman Law. Both combined to establish the condition of a State which acknowledged no authority but its own, and where policies and laws could proceed without reference to ecclesiastical authority. Even in Venice, that *città apostolica e santa*, the Inquisition was admitted but reluctantly, and then on condition that it was supervised by three citizens of the Republic. In

---

[1] F. Stegmüller has edited a text which refers to the common good. 'Consequenter quaeritur utrum aliquis possit magis amare alium quam seipsum.' *RTAM*, iii, pp. 158–82. Louvain, 1931.

    R. A. Gaulthier. 'Trois commentaires avérroistes sur l'Ethique à Nicomaque. *AHDL*, xvi. Paris, 1947–8.

[2] Dante. *Paradiso*, x, 133–8.

[3] G. de Lagarde. *Naissance de l'esprit laïque au déclin du moyen âge.* iii, p. 46.

practice the silencing of the Church meant the silencing of religion. A purely secular social morality proved unable to stand on its own and Natural Law sentiments were to persist, and so were those of Christianity. All the same, when Machiavelli separated diplomacy and the mechanics of government from morals he split apart what had been cracked already two centuries before, and so prepared for the positivism of modern times. Before long the State was conceived as the organization of human wills for social ends about which revealed religion and personal morals could have no say. The vein of State policy was worked apart from other values, and *Staatsräson* came to exist for its own sake as a sufficient guide for action.[1] Similarly human law sought no outside justification, and was presented as what in fact had been enacted and what in fact will be enforced.

---

[1] F. Meinecke. *Machiavellism: The Doctrine of Raison d'Etat and its Place in Modern History.* Tr. D. Scott. London, 1957.

V

THE ADVANCE FROM THE THEOLOGIANS

To the extent that they determine the complexion and features of a community, political science is the study of the agreements and institutions of men living together, and of their laws, natural, customary and enacted.[1] This was especially true in the Middle Ages. In order to discover the social teaching of the theologians we must turn to their treatises on law. It will not surprise us if, by comparison with the jurists, we find them concerned less with the processes of legislation and more with the nature and underlying principles of law itself.

The Greeks cast forward to the purpose of political authority without dwelling on its legal titles; they required that it should serve the good life, and applied this test to the successive types of government under which they lived. The Romans, however, looked back to the origins of authority; they conceived the common good juridically as the public good. The questions arose, Where did power reside? and, By what right was it claimed? The philosophically-minded spoke of a pact entered into by the people on the grounds of ordered security, the legists translated that into a transference of power from the people to the prince. The academic cast of mind in the Middle Ages was more Roman than Greek, hence the theologians conducted their examination in terms rather of legal and religious rights than of biological design.

Influenced partly by the concepts of a juridical philosophy to which no *res publica* was possible without legal bonds, and which defined the people as the coming together of a considerable number of men who were united by a common agreement about rights and duties as well as the desire to participate in mutual advantages, and partly by the concepts of a religious philosophy which saw the whole universe ruled by the divine order revealed in the Scriptures, the medieval theologians were convinced that no just secular power existed which had not

---

[1] W. S. Holdsworth. *A History of English Law*, iv, p. 233. London, 1924.

been constituted by law, and that there is no law except from God.[1] Law is null, said John of Salisbury, when it does not bear the image of divine law.[2]

To their way of thinking law was much wider in scope than the civil law of the State, and by *law* they meant not just a claim on our emotions or our 'moral sense' but a rational command inducing a real obligation. This fact should be remembered; at the same time we must allow for an ambiguity of usage. Whereas legists sought for an historic pronouncement, moralists thought of a law present and operative before political institutions were devised and civil laws enacted. Both could claim obedience only in virtue of their emanation from or dependence on anterior divine precepts. The theologians described the moral conditions of just authority, and much farther than this they did not go. If some of them looked for a divine deed of grant and expected to discover the title to political power among Church documents either from the Scriptures or from Christian tradition, most of them did not inquire into the supposed historico-legal act which constituted sovereignty.

Here there was little advance in doctrine during St Thomas's lifetime. He underlined the moral requirements for the acquisition and exercise of power without which the ruler is an usurper who cannot command the obedience of Christian men; he set the State—and for that matter the Church as a juridical institution—under the Eternal and Natural Law; he encouraged no theory of a power able to maintain itself legally apart from the moral order. Yet, as will be seen in the next chapter, he would not thereby have all laws and political decisions drawn by logical inference from the precepts of social ethics.

The Natural Law in those days did not carry its eighteenth-century sense, namely the rational order consonant to man in a state of pure nature without the accretions of convention and superstition; nor was it a kind of super-system set above the

---

[1] *Populus est coetus multitudinis juris consensu et utilitatis communione sociatus.* Cicero, *de Re Publica*, i, 25. Trans. G. H. Sabine and S. B. Smith. *On the Commonwealth: Marcus Tullius Cicero.* Columbus, 1929.

Quoted 1a–2ae. lv, 2 from *de Civitate* Dei ii, 21. *De Re Publica* was not named as a source.

[2] *Policraticus*, iv, 6.

provincial bodies of civil law. By the thirteenth century men had learnt from Aristotle and contrasted the *naturale*, a thing's movement from within called the *voluntarium* in the case of activity aware of its goal, with the *violentum* or the *artificiale*, a movement imposed from without in which the subject did not co-operate. The contrast was developed when Natural Law, divinely implanted in us, was compared with Positive Law— whether civilian or canonical—which we ourselves constructed.

Now thoughtful theologians never had thought of the Gospel Law as an artificial code. Its rhythms were developed from the impulses of our deepest being. It was Natural Law taken to the heights. Yet not until the *Summa Theologica* was written were the harmonies found. For if we picture horizontal levels or strata when we adopt the term *supernatural*, then of course the laws of grace move in a region higher than those of nature. Whereas if we take a vertical system of reference for the ascending motion of men from their lowliest beginnings to their highest perfection and apply *supernatural* to the laws of grace, then we run the risk of making them preternatural, non-natural, and, by a fallacious slip, unnatural. Hagiography and the literature of conversion dramatically heighten the theme of the violence offered to nature by grace. They belong to individual psychology but may well be extended into social psychology by a system of external regulations, penitential and otherwise. Grace may then be made to appear against the grain; religion may be delivered bound up with protocol. The effect may be heroic or merely mannered, yet on a point of theology the effect of force, strain and violent invasion, the idea that God has to break before he can make, should be subordinated to the classical teaching that grace, although beyond our ability and merit to acquire, is connatural to us in its mode of activity.

Corresponding to these horizontal and vertical lines in our illustration, *nature* was also taken in two senses. One was Latin, and signified a thing's due position, stage, or status in an ordered scheme; the other was Greek, and signified rather the immanent purpose springing from within a thing and reaching out to its highest proper goal. When the two were confused then what was supernatural with respect to the first tended to be taken as unnatural with respect to the second. Similarly,

when the civilized was contrasted with our primitive condition
the suggestion followed that a certain artificiality was a condition of good society. This could cloak a subtle and complicated
sort of violence, as though true civilization did not make for
simplicity and ease of manner.

St Thomas was ahead of contemporary theologians when he
perceived that it was the business of rulers and lawyers, not
directly of moralists, to enact positive laws and to determine
their significance.[1] He voiced the change taking place in the
legislative functions of the State, for as the administration grew
more constructive so it was found that the new laws which had
to be made could no longer be described merely as restate-
ments of old customs. They were decided more by future
political advantage than by past habits—at least that was the
drift, and eventually, as we read in Burke, long established
natural rights discovered empirically in a continuous social
tradition were to be upset by a theory of doctrinaire politics,
and the French Revolution turned its back on dead French-
men.[2] Already an act of princely will was being substituted
for consultation with the people and their consent. Afterwards
as law grew more technical so the study of it concentrated
more on the details without reference to wider values.

Such is the logic of specialism. Aristotle had noted the saying
of Gorgias of Leontini that citizenship in Larissa depended on
the act of the magistrates or citizen-makers; this, commented
St Thomas, was merely a statement of fact which provided no
explanation.[3] A subaltern science can furnish no reason for
its premisses. These it can accept only from a higher science.
Legal science is no exception. Left to itself it cannot go much
farther than defining crime merely as what will in fact be
punished, and punishment merely as what will in fact be
imposed for crime.

There was no sudden break with the past in this trend
towards legal positivism in both Church and State. For that in
effect was going on. Once it was recognized that Positive Law

---

[1] O. Lottin. *La morale naturelle et la loi positive d'après saint Thomas.* Louvain, 1920.

[2] C. Parkin. *The Moral Basis of Burke's Political Thought.* Cambridge, 1957.

[3] *Politics*, iii, 1. 1275 b 27. St Thomas, *lect.* 1.

could not be wholly evaluated by moral premises it was bound to keep pace with an artificial technique for creating laws which slowly displaced the method of adapting old customs to meet new situations. Nevertheless all through the Middle Ages, and beyond, to the Spanish Scholasticism of the early Baroque and to the high Whig period, edicts which hampered men's moral and religious duties were not reputed to be laws at all. In other words, they were checked by standards outside the province of specialist lawyers.

1. *Law in Nature*

Lawfulness, then, represented an idea more far-reaching in medieval than in modern times; it stretched back to a primeval rightness in things and forward to justification through grace. Like the human mind itself as pictured by psychologists of the Unconscious, it could be compared to an iceberg most of which is underwater and out of sight. The political and legal shapes of conduct appearing above the surface of consciousness and deliberation were configured to a theological understructure; beneath lay a mystery apprehended only in the darkness of religious faith. The Roman Law itself, the classical monument of Empire and the rational instrument of public order, had its origins in the hearth and home; below the property pre-occupations were the rites, sacred and nocturnal, which were to the lucid forms of its later structure what falling in love was to the conventionalized concept of Roman *amicitia*.[1]

Ends as well as origins determined the organization, which contained its own purposes even less completely than it articulated all its material. Beyond this world rose another, and this, to which we were bidden by the moral precepts, was not contained within the visible structure of legality but overspread it from above. Cardinal Manning observed that all controversies were ultimately theological—even the denial that religion has anything to say was at bottom a theological statement. Our views on politics should be resolved by what we think men are and what they are for. And so political theories are largely our answers to questions about the nature and limits of

[1] See C. W. Westrup. *Introduction to Early Roman Law. Comparative Sociological Studies: The Patriarchal Joint Family.* 5 vols. Copenhagen–London, 1934–54.

the laws binding us together. Unless we grasp this our actual policies will be fumbling, for opportunism no more supplies for lack of principle than appeasement for not being provided with defensive and offensive plans together with the means of carrying them out.

Theoretic doctrine is implicit in most acts of State, and perhaps nowhere more forcibly than in Great Britain, where some principles of domestic and foreign policy and some social convictions are so firmly embedded in the instinctive layers of community-life and so taken for granted that they are scarcely talked about. It is difficult to overestimate the importance of extra-political factors: without them Alfred could not have restored Wessex, nor this country fought back after Dunkirk. They are necessary not only for national survival but also for the smooth running of the State. The acceptance of a law presupposes a sense of social obligation. A government's chief need is to be trusted. Even a contractual theory of the State fails if it forgets that contracts are binding only by virtue of the moral duty of keeping promises, which duty does not itself derive from contract. Public efficiency relies on motives of emotional, moral or religious colour. Cicero's saying, *fundamentum justitiae est fides*, faithfulness is the basis of justice, which anticipated Locke's notion of trust, was quoted with approval by Vincent of Beauvais.[1] In short, political and legal action alone cannot create the social impulses which are the conditions of its success.

St Thomas manifestly respected legality and on occasion showed himself well versed in a juridical medium. His interest, however, lay in the living social principles behind law, not in technical expertise; his thought was not built into the architecture of the Roman Law, but dwelt outside and looked to it merely for a convenient reference. He noted some points at which theology touched it, and occasionally developed a legal notion particularly on questions of Church order. For the rest, however, the *Summa Theologica* could have been composed had Accursius or Gratian never written, even perhaps had the Glossators and Canonists never made much stir. At a time when St Raymond of Pennafort's *Summa Casuum* and the

---

[1] *Speculum Doctrinale*, iv, 30.

alphabetical repertory of Monaldus were setting the fashion of
drawing theology into canon law, he preferred to settle an
issue by the inherent evidence and not by an appeal to an official
or semi-official ruling. He was a contemporary of Accursius
and Hostiensis, yet it is surprising how sparing was the use of
formal law in his argumentation. There was no hint at all that
the lawyers were going to dominate the following generations at
the expense of philosophers and theologians.

Legalism and rationalism are similar for liking their concepts
sharp, tidy and dispassionate. He shared the taste, yet kept
the continuity between the impulses rising from the racial
and cultural group which are at work in the making of law
and the intellectual content of its formulation. This closeness of
the *material* and the *formal* ran through his whole philosophy,
particularly in his psychology of man as one single substance
composed of body and spirit. His theory of knowledge saw no
deep gulf between the physical and the mental; material
existence was given the authentic kick of reality.[1] The same
conviction came out in his social doctrine which recognized
that physical power might be invested with moral right; in
other words, that virtue might use force, as in war and
capital punishment. *Naturalis ratio* was set in the flow of events
as well as in intellectual patterns. The antithesis of *Bios* and
Logos was not laboured. The Stoics had identified *natura* with
ratio, but for St Thomas this *ratio* or meaning was an actor not
a spectator, a shaping purpose not just a logical essence.[2]
Consequently he was more generous in extending the term
natural to all manifestations from within. It included unconscious and animal drives as well as deliberate choices. An
authentic Aristotelean, he held that the existence and nature of
a thing can be known only by an act of judgment charged with
sense-perception. All living things in this world, men not
excluded, reach to their final ends though physical movement
and passion. Accordingly he did not dichotomize what is
instinctive and what is construed, what is uninhibited and what
is conventional, what is found and what is enacted.

---

[1] T. Gilby. *Phoenix and Turtle: The Unity of Being and Knowing.* London, 1950.

[2] G. M. Manser. *Das Naturrecht in thomistischer Beleuchtung.* Freiburg, 1944.

It is as though his epistemology led him to reject the *propter peccatum* position of his predecessors, for the pressures proper to the earthly level of existence, the *contrapassum* or give-and-take of physical forces, the eat and be eaten, the inward organic changes, the burdens borne because we belonged to this world, were not in themselves punishments, though sin of course greatly aggravated the suffering.[1] Mechanics could be taken into morals—the terms were not profoundly opposed—might into right, this world into the Kingdom of God. He accepted the fact that power-politics has the last word but one. If the wicked are allowed they will do as they like; it is the job of the virtuous to stop them. Hence just laws must command superior force. About this he was not at all apologetic. Grace was not content with denunciation of abuses or with passive resistance to the powers of this world or with non-cooperation and pacificism. Physical force was not the ultimate form of persuasion, yet its exercise could be an inescapable duty. Material might by itself was admittedly brutal, but it could be ennobled by right, and then was not, as Augustinists held, merely excused.

The civilized community was not an arbitrary enclosure within a wilderness inhabited by forms and ideas, a select residential area, as it were, away from the slums of matter and the mob of facts. Surprisingly little pessimism came from St Thomas or talk about 'this wicked world', but instead a note of benign worldliness hitherto unsounded in theology. Of course the times were congenial to this liberal temperament. The tension had relaxed since St Augustine had defended Christianity when the 'evidences' of religion were still pagan: he yet had the vision to rise above his circumstances, and apprehended that the things above were better than the things below, but that both together were better than the things above by themselves.[2] Now, however, the general social assumptions were Christian, orthodox or not, and accepted to some extent by Moslems and Jews. The Church had assimilated the world, and theologians in consequence were not so edgy about it. St Thomas seems genuinely to have liked physical nature. It was the only basis on which he could think. He

---

[1] See 2a–2a. lxi, 4. *Ethics*, v, 5. 1132 b 21. St Thomas, *lect.* 8.
[2] *de Civitate Dei*, xxii, 24.

accepted its conditions, among them that men should mix together in order to live the good life and observe the conditions of their material environment.[1]

Furthermore he held that all departments of knowledge should respond to experience and to one another. If such contact be demanded of the theoretic sciences, such as dogmatic theology and metaphysics, then still more must those which deal with practical answers to problems of conduct keep close to the here and now. The moral, political and legal sciences are false to themselves if, like a die-hard dreaming of the good old days, they make imaginary constructions without reference to current history, psychology, and economics.[2] Statesmen and lawyers enjoy liberty within the limits of their business, nevertheless they should be sensitive to the infra-legal and supra-legal demands of social organisms. The State they serve should not be sealed off from a more universal human community and society. The Natural Law was neither the relic of a past Golden Age nor a bare external measure pronounced in a few simple statements, but a driving reason, supple and manifold, a *participatio legis aeternae* communicated to human beings which should run like the ground-bass through all political and legal activity. Hence political and legal science should consult theology, as theology should consult psychology, and psychology biology and physiology, and all should consult history and one another.

Imprinted on all natural beings, the Eternal Law charged all their activity with meaning and purpose, and this *impressio activi principii* was like the promulgation of a country's law to the subjects who are to obey it. The whole *universitas rerum* was a commonwealth in which non-rational creatures were gathered into God's reason, as our bodily members into ours, though there was no question of choice in the matter.[3] As hands can

---

[1] 2a–2ae. clxxxviii, 8. *III Politics, lect.* 5.

[2] E. Welty. *Vom Sinn und Wert der menschlichen Arbeit, aus der Gedankenwelt des hl. Thomas Aquina.* Heidelburg, 1946.

A. F. Utz. 'Aushöhlung oder Dynamik des Eigentumsbegriffes?' *Divus Thomas,* xxv, pp. 243–54. Fribourg, 1947. *Gemeinschaft und Einzelmensch, Eine sozial-metaphysische Untersuchung, bearbeitet nach den Grundsatzen des hl. Thomas von Aquin.* Salzburg, 1935.

[3] 1a–2ae. xciii, 5, *ad* 1, 2.

be thoughtful so physical things can be lawful. There in the
Eternal Law, said Bernard Sylvestris, is found whatever the
reason of angels and men can comprehend; there whatever
heaven holds under its wide arches.[1] Thus spoke the Nature-
welcoming humanism of Chartres when in the words of the
contemporary lyric,

> *hiemale tempus vale!*
> *aestas reddit cum laeticia.*

For St Thomas the worlds of mind and of matter were
never far apart. By securing the first link in the chain of
law to the material world he was spared the embarrassment of
those divines who could never theoretically reconcile the
application of force and the sway of love.

Their antithesis of Nature and Convention magnified the
results of the Fall. Man's original ease and freedom had gone
and henceforward the law which ruled him was profoundly
penal in effect. They were there to curb his sinful nature,
and though they were imposed by divine decree or by human
will with divine permission, they came to terms with evil
in order to limit its effects. They were concessions to the
reign of force and the rights so created were artificial, pragmatic and remedial rather than native, noble and valuable in
themselves. Slavery, governmental power of coercion and the
exclusions from ownership implicit in a system of private
property were institutions which prevented anarchy and
guaranteed some stability in social life. All three were grouped
together. Dig into their foundations and you would see that
they were built on past acts of forcible acquisition.

It is true that they had been afterwards validated by prescriptive rights, nevertheless the flaw of sin stretched underneath. The authority of the State was affected, since Christian
righteousness had not gone into its making. *Remota justitia quid
regna nisi magna latrocinia?* What was the realm but robbery
writ large?[2] Taken out of its context the phrase over-simplifies
St Augustine's thought and misses his Roman pride. To those,
however, who made a slogan of it, the core of political power
was in a sense unsound. True, Christians owed the duty of

---

[1] *de Mundi Universitate*, i, 2. Edited C. S. Barach. Innsbruck, 1876.
[2] *de Civitate Dei*, iv, 4.

obedience and, since the conversion of the West, temporal
power was vested and consecrated with a blessing; all the same
an Augustinian could never quite pay it the reverence possible
from a theologian of the Aristotelean School.

The relations of natural and positive rights were further
complicated by the prestige of Ulpian, called simply the
Jurist, *Jurisconsultus*, whose writings composed a third of
Justinian's *Digest*. One of his most-quoted texts treated Natural
Law as common to all animals. It ruled instinctive adaptation
to environment, thus the mating of male and female, whereas
human law was a business of deliberate and civilized adjustments.[1] This zoological reading was offset by the Stoic doctrine
that law was reason, *lex est summa ratio insita in natura*, and by
the authority of St Isidore who adapted Gaius and defined
natural law by the test of universal human acceptance, *commune
omni nationi*, not *commune omnibus animalibus*. All the same there
were grounds here for an exaggeration of the difference between primitive nature and cultivated reason, between the wild
and the domesticated, especially if the etymology of nature
from *nascitura* were emphasised.[2]

Then also a theological undercurrent of suspicion ran against
nature, whether accepted in a primitively animal or in a
sophisticatedly rational sense. The distinction between the
natural and supernatural worlds in which men live had not
been refined before religious writers discovered Aristotle. The
conflict between flesh and spirit was equated with the conflict
between nature and grace; the conflict between worldly and
heavenly wisdom was the conflict between reason and faith.
The corruption of the body could be vividly dramatized, that
of the soul was less sensible. The allurements of sin appeared in
secular guise. The dogma of bodily resurrection told the
theologians that flesh could be taken into spirit without being
etherealized; they were less convinced, however, that reason
could be taken into faith and remain reasonable. The Franciscan and early Dominican masters refused to entertain, even if
they considered, philosophy apart from theology. An exception
might be made for logic, and men like Grosseteste and

---

[1] 2a–2ae. lvii, 3.
[2] 1a–2ae. xciv, 4, *sed contra*. 3a. ii, 1. *Etymologies*, v, 4. PL lxxxii, 199.

Kilwardby, advancing beyond the findings of the Greeks and Arabs, ranged over the fields of pure mathematics, natural philosophy (with particular attention to the nature of light), scientific method and technology.[1]

Despite the influence of the schools of literary humanism and affective theology nourished by devout meditation on the Scriptures, religious thought was already tending to stiffen into a sabbatarianism which the growth of law inevitably aggravated. For a brief period the revival of Aristoteleanism halted the process and invigorated theology. A divine meaning and purpose running in and through natural processes was caught sight of, and law itself was then treated as part of the ascent of man to God. If Aristotelean Scholasticism presently hardened into its own sort of formalism, it bequeathed the lesson, never quite forgotten in theology, that nature should be confidently accepted and experimentally investigated.

It also averted the danger that the Christian precepts, because they inculcated conduct surpassing commonsense, should thereby flout the ordinary decencies—a sort of Léon Bloy heroism at its best, and, in decay, a system of magical thinking. They could have been made to appear like so many articles of positive law, august yet arbitrary, laid on from outside and above without respect for human nature. From *supra-national* to *extra-natural* is an easy transition, and thence to *artificial*. The descent into *sub-natural* is not unknown. The morals without religion of a secularist culture can be weighed against the religion without morals elsewhere. It is a matter of taste whether you find yourself more at home in Stockholm or in Dublin, and a matter of debate which is the less admirable.

St Thomas can scarcely be called a Pelagian—indeed during the controversies on efficacious grace which circled round the *Congregatio de Auxiliis* (1607) his followers were sometimes accused of being Jansenists—yet he brought nature in no attenuated sense into theology. He was certainly no Barthian either, for, pursuing the implications of Chalcedon, he taught that as in Christ two real and distinct natures were united in one person, so for our salvation a divine life was communicated

---

[1] A. C. Crombie. *Robert Grosseteste and the Origins of Experimental Science.*

through and to human nature.[1] Grace was not like a garment. It was not only imputed for righteousness. It did not obliterate its natural subject, and its activity, no naked escape from the conditions of life but a committal to the Christian fellowship, was a man's very own.

Indeed he was not given to forced contrasts, either between body and soul, or between nature and grace, or between the laws of animal life and those of reason. He did not regard the material world as if it were a volcano whose rumbling threatened the architecture of reason and religion erected on the crust of past eruptions. It was the good earth for God's grace. There was a *continuatio* of the spiritual into the material and a *communicatio* between them, an evolutionary surge from the first to the last day of creation.[2] Man's *ratio* shared in the *ratio* of the universe; both derived from the *ratio divina*. One single substance operated through all the manifestations of a human person; all motions from within the organism could be taken up mind and will, all meanings and volitions fused with sensibility and feeling. His teaching fits in very well with modern *Gestalt* Psychology, which stresses the unity of human responses to environment and is not misled by laboratory techniques of separating them into their components: the spiritual soul is entire throughout the body, and intelligence should be as much in the heart as affection should be in the head.[3] This applies also to the corporate personality of the political community.

Law is essentially a condition of communication, and the forms of expression and methods of signalling—the strokings of ants' antennae, the movement of a squirrel's tail, the jay's warning cry in the wood—which fall short of conceptual signification through speech should be observed with sympathy by the social moralist. The laws of animal life enter into and are transcended by the laws of rational life. The rudimentary and barbaric are developed into the civilized.[4] All in their turn are taken up into laws of grace. The organs of reproduction

---

[1] Y. M. J. Congar. *Christ, Our Lady and the Church*. Tr. H. St John. London, 1956.
[2] *III de Anima*, lect. 8. II *Contra Gentes*, 56, 57. *II Sentences, XII*, i, 2.
[3] 1a. lxxvi, 8. Disputations, *de Spiritualibus Creaturis*, 4: *de Anima*, 10.
[4] *II Politics, lect.* 12.

and excretion, so close to one another, call for privacy and
delicacy but not for shame, and medical psychologists know
what harm is done by over-fastidious censorship. Hence laws
should not seek to suppress natural instincts or to straitlace
their functions. Even arbitrary conventions, of secondary
importance to the essential adaptations of men and women, are
primarily means to the enlarging, not the cramping, of human
activity. In processes where there was a mingling of art and
nature, said St Thomas, art operated in the same manner and
through the same means as nature did.[1] The artificial became
the congenial, the 'artistic' or 'artful' treatment of a subject,
the 'natural stroke' praised by eighteenth-century writers:
modus artificialis dicitur cui competit materiae.[2]

To such a habit of mind civilization was less imposed from
without than developed from within; conversion to grace was
less a submission than an elevation. St Thomas brought out
how connatural was the inner springiness of grace. It is out
sharing in God's likeness by a rebirth, a new creation which
destroys only sin and in the end will restore all things in
Christ. For this reason he parted company with Peter Lombard,
who had taught that divine charity was the indwelling Holy
Ghost. On the contrary, its dignity as friendship demanded
that it should be a love which we ourselves elicited.[3]

His usage was not always consistent in pairing terms.
Spiritual was generally contrasted with *material*, and, in
questions of social authority, with *temporal* (which elsewhere
was contrasted with *eternal*). Other contrasts were *clerical* and
lay, *ecclesiastical* and *civil*, *sacerdotal* and *regal*, *sacred* and *profane*,
soul and *body*, *contemplative* and *active*, *theoretic* and *practical*,
internal and *external*, *private* and *public*, *religious* and *secular*. There
is some overlapping, but care should be taken in shifting from
one pair to another. *Religion* might mean the ordering of our
whole lives towards God, or the special virtue, a part of justice,
which governs divine worship, or the dedicated state of life.[4]
Switch the categories and his discourse is misreported. Thus, if

[1] Disputations, XI *de Veritate*, 1.
[2] *I Sentences*, Prologue, i, 5, *ad* 1.
[3] 1a–2ae. cx, 1, 4. 2a–2ae. xxiii, 2.
[4] 2a–2ae. lxxxi, 4, 8. clxxxvi, 1.

you identify *spiritual* with *religious*, and then with *private*. Or *material* with *civil*, and then with *natural*. Or *natural* with *temporal*, and then with *bodily*, *profane*, *public*. For the due response to State authority, he held, was from supernatural virtue, while on the other hand, the Church possessed natural and temporal claims which you met in the spirit of paying the rates: the Blessed Thomas of Canterbury demanded the restitution of Church property even to the scandal of the King.[1] He did not draw the comparison used by Papalists, that the spiritual power was to the civil power what the sun was to the moon, or the soul to the body.[2] The human community was not divided into two spheres, its body ruled by the human law rising from the people, its soul by pontifical law descending from God: such a dualism was not even applied to the individual, for a man was one thing, not two.

He generally used *jus* and *lex* as interchangeable terms, a hint that legalism should follow the grain of reality and that continuity between implanted right and enacted law should be kept. Whereas the jurists generally spoke of *jus naturae* and the theologians of *lex naturalis* he was inclined to reverse the usage, preferring *lex* in his judicial treatise and *jus* in his theological treatise on the cardinal virtue of justice.[3] The point, otherwise of no great moment, indicated a refusal to separate nature and art, that is, the fundamental rights we did not ourselves create and the regulations we framed in order to protect them. He adopted the two recognized etymologies of *lex*, *a ligando* to show that it constrained, *a legendo* to show that it was rationally apprehended.[4] *Lex* was not *jus* precisely, but in some manner its rational expression. *Jus* also was brought into our mental activity: originally it signified an objective quality and then by derivation the art which recognized it.[5]

---

[1] 2a–2ae. xliii, 8, *sed contra*.
[2] W. Ullmann. *Medieval Papalism*, vi. 'Pope and Emperor'.
[3] On law, 1a–2ae. xc–cxiii. On justice, 2a–2ae. lvii–cxxii.
[4] 1a–2ae. cv, 2, *ad* 3.
[5] 2a–2ae. lvii, 1, *ad* 1, 2.

St Isidore (*Etymologies*, v, 2, 3, 4), better at repeating phrases than relating them, was not helpful in the matter of terminology. Though he said that *jus* was human *lex*, he seemed to treat *jus* as a generic term, of which *lex* was a written enactment. *Mos*, or custom approved by antiquity, was unwritten law. Human law was based on custom, divine law on nature. Divine law was called *fas*.

He identified the Glossator's *jus* with Aristotle's *justum* or *dikaion*. At the same time he noted a contrast, *contrarietas*, for whereas the jurists put *jus civile* under positive law (which was set against *jus naturale*) and so heightened the contrast between the civil or political on one side and the natural on the other, the philosophers, with whom he sided, took the *justum politicum* or *civile* to be partly *justum naturale* and partly *justum legale*, and so combined the natural and the legal within the same political order. There was here a difference of approach, one positivist, the other teleological. As the theologians looked askance at the canonists so, lower down in the scale, philosophers were pleased to put the civil lawyers in their place—a belated come-back after the closing of the Athenian Schools by Justinian in 529. The jurists treated laws and institutions as existing social artefacts, he observed, for they have to keep to facts, and define the political or civil in terms of the constitution actually in force. The philosophers, on the other hand, looked rather to the whole purpose of the organized community in the light of its natural origins and purposes. They judged how these were served by social institutions, and so considered the reasons of law rather than legal terms. They defined the political or civil by what was beneficial to the citizens, not by what was officially commended or permitted.

The theory that Natural Law underlaid political association was strongly in evidence. Political justice was part natural and part legal; *utuntur enim cives et justo eo quod natura menti humanae indidit et eo quod est positum lege*.[1] In this context the *legal* was contrasted with the *natural*; elsewhere it could bear two other senses. It was applied to justice, and legal justice then meant that general justice which, like law itself, served the common good and was distinct from the particular justice of one individual towards another.[2] It could also mean the legalism or code-justice which stuck to the letter of the law and was thereby contrasted with equity.[3]

Similarly, justice itself, the specific human virtue corresponding to *jus* and *lex*, had varying meanings treated precisely in

---

[1] *V Ethics, lect.* 12 (*Ethics* v, 7. 1134 b 19).
[2] 2a-2ae. lviii, 5. See below, Chapter VII, 3.
[3] 2a-2ae. cxx, 2. See below, Chapter VIII, 5.

the appropriate settings of the *Summa Theologica*.[1] On occasion St Thomas adopted its generic meaning of *righteousness*, used by the Scriptures and the Fathers, thus when treating of *justitia originalis*, the right state in which human nature was created, and of the justification of the sinner.[2] He also admitted the related sense it had for Plato, Cicero and Macrobius, namely, that poise and adjustment in social comportment on every occasion which was a general condition of all virtue.[3] So by analogy he spoke of God's justice.[4] Normally, however, he kept to its narrow sense, which signified the moral virtue, specifically distinct from the others, which paid what was owing and established the right balance in external affairs.

The spirit of fairness and plain dealing discovered in the *Ethics*, was linked with Ulpian's celebrated definition, that justice is the lasting and unwavering will of rendering each man his due, *perpetua et constans voluntas jus suum unicuique tribuendi*.[5] Characteristically he combined the Latin and Greek concepts, for *jus* was given its Roman meaning of objective right set forth by law, and *voluntas* was interpreted according to Aristotle's psychologico-moral teaching on the virtues. Virtue was a settled quality which made the possessor good in himself and in what he did. There was nothing stilted about it, for good here meant more than the state of being acceptable to the legislator or of being on the safe side of the law. It was not merely imputed righteousness, but signified real completeness and worth.[6]

Whether he was referring back to the biological origins of law or considering the psychological poise produced by virtue, the fact that justice squared a man with the world about him, or explaining the rational content of law or the moral value and godliness of virtue, St Thomas wrote as one studying a single evolutionary process ever ascending by divine causality but not, as it were, jerked up or interrupted by factors which invade it from without. Law, virtue, justice—they were rooted

---

[1] 2a–2ae. lxi, lxxix, lxxx.
[2] 1a–2ae. lxxxii, 3. cxiii, 1.
[3] 2a–2ae. lviii, 1, *ad* 3, 5, 6. 12. lix, 1. lxxix, 1. *III Sentences* xxxiii, 1, 1, *iii, ad* 3.
[4] 1a–2ae. lxi, 5. 1a. xxi, 1, 2, 4.
[5] 2a–2ae. lviii, 1.
[6] 1a–2ae. xlix–liv.

like plants not stuck in the ground like lamp-posts, and they grew because they were alive.

2. *The Concept of Law*

An empirical and historical method which records merely what in fact has been laid down or enforced as law leaves unsettled what communicates to a command its specifically legal character. The upshot is the sort of definition travestied by Bentham, 'a rule of conduct for those who are to observe it, prescribed by those who prescribe it, commanding what it commands and forbidding what it forbids'—not that when he recognized the need for a science about the assumptions of law he was out to defend the existence of Natural Law. Reflections on the nature of law, set off when Roman jurists and statesmen encountered the customs of non-Roman people which seemed to derive from a natural order of things, led to conclusions about the *jus gentium* which were framed in semi-philosophical terms.

The medieval thinkers were more speculative. Influenced partly by scientific theology and partly by a renewed Greek philosophy, they attempted to expose the fundamental principles behind all the laws with which they had some acquaintance—the Roman Law both civil and canonical, Lombard Law, national traditions, the miscellaneous statutes of kingdoms and cities, the accumulations of custom and Divine Law itself. Thereby they opened up questions which belonged to political science. 'The philosophic analysis and definition of law,' wrote Pollock and Maitland, 'belong to the theoretic part of politics.'[1] They did not stop short at certifying what had been historically enacted or at describing what would work for the benefit of the community. They looked for a general idea, not limited to one culture or civilizaiton or set of positive laws, which would serve as the essential criterion for juridical obligation.

Peter Lombard did not broach the subject but merely discussed the relationship of the Decalogue to the two Gospel precepts of charity.[2] Of the surviving 252 questions of Stephen Langton one only relates to natural law and another to the *potentia gubernandi*. The early and middle thirteenth-century

---

[1] *History of English Law, before the Time of Edward I*, Introduction, p. xxiii. Cambridge, 1898.
[2] *III Sentences*, XXXVII.

summists advanced little farther. William of Auxerre, who was familiar with the *Ethica Vetus* and quoted from the *de Anima*, the *Physics* and the *Metaphysics*, proposed some of the rudiments for a coherent theory: his *Summa Aurea* may have influenced Alexander of Hales and St Albert. The earliest systematic exposition seems to have been attempted in the Franciscan treatise, *de legibus et praeceptis*, composed probably by John of Rochelle and used as a source by St Thomas.[1] Vincent of Beauvais in the *Speculum Naturale* did not linger over the impression of the Eternal Law on man's mind and will; he was more leisurely in the *Speculum Doctrinale* where after citing various descriptions of law from classical authors known at his time he offered his own definition, *recta ratio imperandi et prohibendi*, the rightful reason for commanding and forbidding.[2] The important element of reasonableness was there, but the definition remained incomplete, since it applied to the just precepts of any private authority, of an abbot or baron, for instance, and these were not laws. The concluding section of St Albert's *Summa de Bono* was devoted to justice; there he attempted to clear the notions of *jus* and *lex*, but found himself tangled with the four laws enumerated in the *Glossa Ordinaria* once attributed to Walafrid Strabo—the Natural Law, the Mosaic Law, the Law of Grace, and the Pauline Law in our members. Another treatise on law, attributed more surely now than heretofore to Peter of Tarentaise, a colleague of St Thomas and afterwards Pope Innocent V, written about this time, fared no better.[3]

St Thomas seems to have been the first to put forward *ex professo* a full definition of law by its fundamental properties followed by a balanced division of its types. After sketching several parts of law in his early works, the *Commentary on the Sentences* and the *Summa Contra Gentes*,[4] he arrived at his con-

---

[1] O. Lottin. *Psychologie et Morale au XIIe et XIIIe siècles*, ii, pp. 20, 64.

[2] xxix, 72. iv, 61.

[3] P. Glorieux. *La littérature quodlibetique.* ii, p. 90. Paris, 1935.

[4] *III Sentences*, XXXVII, 1, on the decalogue and the advantages of a written code. IV Sentences XXXIII, i and ii, on monogamy and divorce. III *Contra Gentes*, 113, 114, on the reasonableness of Law. The doctrine of *Lex Aeterna* pervaded his writing at this period, though the term does not often occur, see V *de Veritate*, 1, ad 1. III *Contra Gentes*, 54–113, on Providence. III *Contra Gentes*, 114–130, on Divine Law. Before he wrote the *Prima Secundae* he described sin as *contra legem Dei*, not as *contra legem aeternam*.

sidered definition towards the end of his life and devoted a
whole question of the *Summa Theologica* to its explanation.[1] Law
was an ordinance of reason, directed to the common good,
issued by the authority in charge of the political community,
and promulgated to its subjects: *quaedam rationis ordinatio ad
bonum commune et ab eo qui curam communitatis habet promulgata.*[2]
Each of the four elements of the definition was discussed in a
separate article; the divisions of law were treated in the
questions that followed.

The formula was reached less by analysis of the notion of law
conducted within the medium of strictly legal science than by
a synthesis of the findings of moral science, itself a part of the
philosophical reading of our environment. A particular science
assumes its own premises without demonstrating them;
jurisprudence is no exception. To what extent the science of
law derives from the science of politics, and the science of
politics from other historical and philosophical sciences will be
touched on later. Law was obviously a versatile notion, but no
deep separation, still less antagonism, between morality and
legality was supposed; the definition was intended to cover
both Natural Law and Positive Law. The authorities cited—
Aristotle, St Paul, Cicero, Justinian's *Digest*, Isidore, Gratian,
and Peter Lombard—offer a cross-section of the construction
from Greek, Jewish, Roman and Germanic elements. Yet when
the whole treatise was finished, its end being protracted with a
lengthy examination of the Mosaic legislation, the measures of
legality were seen for what they were worth, worthy of obedience but not of utter devotion. The system of reason was
thrown open to the Gospel law of love. Regulations were all
very well up to a point and conformity to social patterns was a
duty, but the spirit bloweth where it listeth.[3]

Let us consider in turn the four clauses of the definition. The
first declared that law was an ordinance of reason, *ordinatio
rationis.* Commanding and forbidding were its evident function,
for law does more than persuade; it is ready to enforce. Where

---

[1] 1a–2ae. xc.
[2] 1a–2ae. xc, 4.
  G. Granieris. *Contributi tomistici alla filosofia del diritto.* Turin, 1949.
[3] 1a–2ae. xcviii–cv, on the Old Law. cvi–cviii, on the New Law.

St Thomas differed from scholastics of the 'voluntarist' school was in teaching that law was elicited by mind, not by will, that is by the practical reason, *intellectus practicus*. This was not a faculty separate from the theoretical reason, *intellectus speculativus*, since where truly human outgoing activity was concerned thought and action were not specifically distinct.[1] Action was contemplation turned to doing and making. *Virtus intellectiva de se est ordinativa et regitiva*—the emphasis on the ruling power of mind accorded with his general dynamic psychology.[2] The moment of final happiness was constituted in the intellect, for vision, not delight, was the *formale in beatitudine*; and beforehand, in the development of a typical human act, the *imperium*, or final effort leading immediately to its attempted performance, belonged more directly to cognition than to appetition.[3] His analysis of free-will, *liberum arbitrium*, fastened on the play of reason and deliberation, not on executive spontaneity.[4]

He held that law should make sense, and the principle *lex plus laudatur quando ratione probatur* was honoured throughout his social theory. The domination of power was not accepted unless charged with evidence for assent and blind or capricious force was granted no authority as such. It was admitted that we live in a world of compulsions, nevertheless one man can rightfully control another only by showing reason for his power: even omnipotence cannot break the order of truth.[5] It was not surprising, then, that he required an ordinance to manifest intelligible goodness, the honesty of virtue and the integrity of decorum; this was the first condition of lawfulness.[6] Reason went before the ability to enforce. Not that a logic of necessity had to be disclosed in every case, since human laws worked in a world of contingent events, but that appropriateness to the situation had to be sufficiently evident. Legislation was a part of the practical wisdom of governing the community,

---

[1] 1a. lxxix, 11. III *de Veritate*, 3. *III de Anima, lect.* 15.
   For a comparison with the teaching of Scotus, see G. Budzik. *de Conceptu Legis ad mentem Joannis Duns Scoti.* Burlington, Wis., 1954.
[2] III *Contra Gentes*, 78.
[3] 1a–2ae. iii, 4. xvii, 1.
[4] 1a. lxxxiii 3, 4. IV *de Malo*, 1. XXIV *de Veritate*, 4, 5, 6.
[5] 1a. XXV, 3, 4, 5. I *de Potentia*, 4–7.
[6] 2a–2ae. cxlv, 1, 2.

prudentia regnativa, a species of prudence, the intellectual and moral virtue of which the principal act was to command, *praecipere*.[1]

The jurists were more concerned than the theologians with the fact of law and less with its reason, still less with its exemplar in the mind of God.[2] It is true they had welcomed the *Corpus Juris* because of its rational elegance and superiority to tribal laws, not out of deference to existing authority—for the Emperor of the West governed by custom and consecration by the Church while as for the Emperor of the East, who governed by the Roman Law, he was a remote figure. Nevertheless many of them soon began to look to the sovereign will of the ruler as the source of law. A scrap from Justinian's *Lex Regia* was alleged in support, that the pleasure of the prince has the force of law, *quod principi placuit legis habet vigorem*.

The phrase, part of a text dealing with the act of alienation in the people's contract of subjection to the Emperor, was rejected by St Thomas because it would make for wickedness, *magis esset iniquitas quam lex*.[3] Bracton declared that there was no king where the will and not the law had dominion; if the king be without a bridle, they ought to put a bridle upon him. Both spoke for the same theological tradition. Deriving from the Stoic teaching of reason immanent in nature, which had been supplemented by St Augustine's theology of the Eternal Law in the mind of God imparting what justice there was in temporal laws, it was confirmed when men learnt from Plato and Aristotle that mind ruled will and directed all arrangements of heterogeneous parts. Seneca and St Augustine had been haunted by the sway of forces exempt from the control of reason, the *mors lex*, *tributum*, *officium mortalium*, the compulsions of concupiscence and corruption. St Paul, too, *found another law warring against the law* of my mind.[4] St Thomas was easier with this *impetus sensualitatis* than St Augustine had been; it was not necessarily sinful and penal, a kind of caricature of law, for its

---

[1] 2a–2ae. xlvii, 8. l. 1.

   For a study of the 'intellectualism' of St Thomas compared with the 'voluntarism' of Henry of Ghent, see T. E. Davitt, *The Nature of Law*. St Louis, 1951.

[2] 1a–2ae. lxxi, 2, *ad* 4. xciii, 3, 4. 1a. xv, 2, 3. xxxiv, 3.

[3] 1a–2ae. xc, *ad* 3. *Digest*, i, 4. *Institutes*, 1, 2, 6.

[4] Romans, vii, 23.

essential propensity, *inclinatic propria*, was to the common good and could be controlled by intelligence.

The second clause of the definition committed law to the service of the Common Good.[2] Government for the sake of the governor had never been defended, nor had decrees designed for his private convenience to the detriment of the body politic: what was new was that henceforth law was reserved to general rulings affecting the community as a whole. Enjoining or forbidding kinds or types of social action was not directly concerned with particular occasions, hence law was more sweeping than a precept, *praeceptum*, which might be issued by any superior or parent about an individual act or course of conduct.[3] Laws also were wider than privileges, *privilegia*, which were like private laws, or than *sententialia* which were judicial decisions on determinate cases which might bind in law.[4] An ordinance serving a sectional interest was not a law in the full technical sense, though it might rightly claim obedience. Not every precept was law, therefore, though every law was precept—the difference was like that between a law passed by Parliament and an order made by a Government department on the authority of a regulation allowed under an Act of Parliament.[5]

To discuss the *bonum universale*, the full and final social good as St Thomas conceived it, would take us far afield from political theory, yet since it gave both moral dignity and character to the partial and penultimate general welfare which was the immediate purpose of law and political action, it must be at least saluted in passing.[6] It was not a collective-value, the greatest good of the greatest number, the welfare of the whole considered as a mass-effect, but the personal good of each and all which ultimately implied the vision of God and the lasting companionship of friends. It was held in an act of mind—for St Thomas's intellectualism descended from high theology to social philosophy—yet it was no abstraction. The *bonum com-*

---

[1] 1a–2ae. xci, 6. *ad* 3.

[2] 1a–2ae. xc, 2.

[3] 1a–2ae. xc, 2, *ad* 2.

[4] 1a–2ae. xcvi, 1, *ad* 1.

[5] See *Falmouth Boat Construction v. Howell*. Court of Appeal. *The Times*, 10 February 1950.

[6] T. Gilby. *Between Community and Society*, pp. 194–6, 211–3. See below pp. 236–49.

mune was not *bonum in communi* or goodness in general, it was *the* Good Thing embracing all that was good and real. The possession of God, who is the Whole who creates the universe, was more than the answer to a question; it was the end of desire.

Theology outspread social philosophy and obviously the Common Good so conceived went far beyond the public benefit or *res publica* of Roman jurisprudence; similarly the laws of the City of God transcended the legal and political categories of the earthly city. The Beatitudes, or the lessons of the Sermon on the Mount were promises of happiness, but their merit and reward were not achieved in the practices of good citizenship, which did not require us to be humble of heart or to mourn or to endure persecution. For the common good of the political community was a humbler affair altogether. It was sufficient if the social decencies were observed. As we shall see later, when discussing the limits of legalism and the relations between citizenship and eccentricity, St Thomas would not have our rulers take too much on themselves. They were guardians of the peace, not spiritual directors. The body politic may be compared to the individual body: the physician may regret a moral disorder yet be content to prescribe only for psychological and physiological health. So also the State, while it should impede no human decency, lacks the ability to promote every virtue. Its duty is restricted to that outward justice without which social life would be impossible. At least let it regulate the economic provisions for physical and mental health, and inculcate fair-dealing; for the rest it will serve moral health best by protecting freedom.

Nevertheless subjects are immortal persons who are not good unless they are being prepared for a life beyond that in the State. Let the ruler listen to the Sermon on the Mount for the Beatitudes already begin in this life.[1] Sovereign rights in the complete hierarchy of means and ends are subordinate to the ultimate purpose of human life. This is the *primum principium* in everything we do, and especially in the making of laws which are meant to be guides and conveyances to heaven.[2] St Thomas quoted Aristotle, that those laws are just that tend to produce

---

[1] 1a–2ae. lxix, 2.
[2] 1a–2ae. xc. 2.

and preserve happiness and its components.[1] He recognized that tensions are likely to be set up between the claims of personal friendship, which is the long-term purpose of law, and of normal observance, which is its immediate object.[2] Whereas St Augustine left the virtue in political power at least cloudy, for our true city lay beyond this world, and Aristotle scarcely envisaged any human nobility that was not of service to the community, St Thomas characteristically reversed their roles, and summoned St Augustine to support reverence for civil authority and Aristotle to support extra-political virtue.

The idea of the Common Good was a Greek preoccupation. The public interest was not clearly defined by the Romans from the legal point of view; to them origins were clearer than ends. They were concerned with the source of law, with the *Populus* and *Princeps*. The third clause of the definition, that law should be pronounced by authority, raised the question, Who was the legislative sovereign?[3]

The question was not sharply defined, for in medieval days the notion of sovereignty was at once vaguer and less ambitious than it became afterwards. Except for some canonists, nobody thought of a visible authority which claimed complete *imperium*, or which stood supreme, without partner, peer or competitor, free from limitations of prescription: not even the Pope was generally regarded as omnipotent by himself within the Church.

Power implied responsibility in a moral setting, and since law was for the welfare of the whole people, it followed that the power of making law belonged to the power able to promote the common good. This power, under God, resided in the people themselves or in their guardian, since no alternative organ had been appointed, or detailed political instrument revealed. The argument was brief; such questions of the legal authority of God in the Mosaic community, or the supreme authority within the Church, or the ineradicable right of the paterfamilias (who issued precepts, not laws) lay outside its scope. It did not decide where this underlying authority should

---

[1] *Ethics*, v, 1. 1129 b 17. *IX Ethics, lect.* 9. *de Regimine Principum*, i, 14. 1a–2ae. xciv, 1.

[2] See 1a–2ae. xcvi, 1, 6.

[3] 1a–2ae. xc, 3. For *dominium* see 2a–2ae. lxvi, 1, 2.

in practice be located, or adjudicate between monarchic, aristo-cratic, and democratic regimes. Though the argument held that supreme power should in some manner be representative, the constitutional character of the ruler was left unsettled—a theologian, unlike a jurist, is more concerned with the exercise and purpose of civil authority than with its titles, hence the Church is usually prepared to work with any government which does not violate the decencies, however illegitimate its origins.

As the Common Good in the philosophical and theological senses of the term was wider than the *res publica*, since it com-prised relationships beyond the reach of legal guarantees, so the supreme authority in the commonwealth was not so exactly defined as the *persona publica* of the jurists. The social theologians did not investigate the hypothesis of the historical legal act which might be presumed to have determined the seat of sovereignty; the related question whether the prince's position depended on the continued consent of his subjects came up only in passing. That St Thomas's own sympathies lay with the old doctrine, that the ruler spoke with the agreement of the whole people and observed an unwritten constitution, and not with the new theory of the lawyers, that he enjoyed absolute power which nobody could impugn, can be argued from references elsewhere in the *Summa Theologica*. Thus he advocated a wide-spread political prudence through popular participation in the business of legislation and government, and taught that obe-dience was owing to a superior only within warranted limits. Nevertheless as he grew older he seemed to harden against the deposing power of the people. The classical expositors of his social thought in the changed conditions of the sixteenth century did not consider that the people's viceregent was no more than the channel of their power; he was a representative with initia-tive and responsibility of his own, not merely a delegate pre-viously committed to a detailed policy and responsive to every mood and whim of his supporters.[1]

---

[1] See Thomas de Vio Cajetan (d. 1534). *de Auctoritate Papae et Concilii Commentaria in Summam Theologiae S. Thomae* (*in* 2am–2ae, i, 10).

Francis de Vitoria (d. 1546). *Relectiones de Potestate Ecclesiae prior et posterior, de Potestate Civili, de Potestate Papae et Concilii*.

Dominic de Soto (d. 1560). *de Justitia et Jure*.

Francis Suarez (d. 1617). *de Legibus*.

Cicero's contention that liberty implied some share in the conduct of State affairs accorded with the antique tradition that the people were the source of power; indeed the legal scores of the Roman Empire were a palimpsest underneath which could be discerned the principles of Roman republicanism. It was confirmed in the thirteenth century when men read in Aristotle that the deliberative power was sovereign, and ratified what was initiated by the magistrates.[1] Moreover, the policies of the Church did not favour the separation of princely power from popular approval. A favourite quotation from St Isidore, used by St Thomas and Gratian before him, was that law was an ordinance of the people whereby something is sanctioned by the elders together with the commonalty.[2]

St Thomas preferred the customs of free people to the prince's initiative as the origin of legislation: better, he thought, when men can prompt laws for themselves instead of having to be looked after with laws made for them. In a free community, *libera multitudo*, the people's consent was more important than the prince's authority, for he could make laws only as 'impersonating' them. Only in the case of a nation under tutelage was he the source of law, and, even so, popular customs had the force of law as long as they were tolerated or tacitly approved.[3] These principles were used alike by the Spanish Thomists in their not unsuccessful attempt to mitigate the exploitation of the American Indians and by the League of Nations in dealing with mandated territories.

The *populus* in this context meant the whole group of citizens, *universitas civium*. A *civis* was a male adult who practised political prudence and took part in public affairs. Women, children, and perhaps resident foreigners were not included; serfs and dependents tied to the land were more like the *perioikoi* than the *douloi* in Aristotle's *polis*. St Thomas never referred to the Emperor as a force to be reckoned with, nor identified him with the *Princeps* of the law-books. He cherished no mysticism about the origins of the Western Empire. Nor was he haunted by the shadowy *Populus Romanus* of medieval Roman juris-

---

[1] E. Barker. *The Politics of Aristotle.* 'Notes on the Vocabulary,' p. xvii. Oxford, 1948.
[2] 1a–2ae. xc, 3 *sed contra. Etymologies*, v, 10. PL lxxxii, p. 200 *Decretum* I, i, 1.
[3] 1a–2ae. xcvii, 3, *ad* 3.

prudence, to which Frederick II appealed when he crossed the
Alps to assume the imperial dignity—the democratic sincerity
may be doubted but not the advantage of appealing over the
heads of the Pope and German princes. 'Theoretically the name
might denote anything from the whole assemblage of peoples
within the unity of *Latinitas* to the degenerate inhabitants of
Rome, who occasionally amused themselves with reviving the
Senate and other republican dreams. In effect it meant nothing
at all, or nothing that had any genuine connection with Rome.
If the Roman Emperor was a fiction, the *populus Romanus* was a
myth.'[1]

The fourth and final clause of the definition, that law needs
to be promulgated, was introduced by the Canonists. It was a
commonplace that laws should be brought to the minds of
subjects. A *summula* of Bulgarus started off, Inasmuch as laws
should be known and understood by all, *Quia leges ab omnibus
sciri debent et intelligi*. Gratian, however, seems to have been the
first to bring out the importance of promulgation: laws are
instituted when they are promulgated, *leges instituuntur cum
promulgantur*.[2] St Thomas acknowledged his source and confirmed the meaning from one of St Isidore's etymologies, *lex a
legendo vocata est*.[3]

The gist of the argument was that law had to be reasonably
received as well as reasonably enunciated. It should be proposed
without undue technicality in a manner clear and intelligible
to persons of ordinary understanding. That it was beneficial had
to be commended, for who will obey unmeaning regulations?
This was of a piece with the rule that it was not enough for
justice to be done, but that justice should be seen to be done.
Unlike Natural Law, which, in theory at least, was a body of
commands and prohibitions discoverable by unaided reason,
the Positive Law was not bound to be what it was from the

---

[1] W. H. V. Reade. 'Political Theory to c. 1300.' *Cambridge Mediaeval History* vi,
p. 620.

[2] Printed by H. Kantorowicz. *Glossators*, p. 244.

[3] 1a–2ae, xc, 4. *Etymologies*, xi, 10. PL lxxxii, 130. *Decretum* I. 4. 3. S. Kuttner.
Kanonistische Schuldlehre von Gratian bis auf die Dekretalen Gregors IX, xii, pp. 153–
75. Vatican City, 1935.

necessity of things; it could be otherwise. Consequently the fact of its institution had to be published and brought to the minds of men whom it proposed to rule. Natural right was not created by the written code which contains it; its force came from nature, not from human legislation. Positive right, *jus positivum*, on the other hand, was both contained and created by the code which gave it the *robur auctoritatis*.[1]

The leading principle was that nobody is bound to what he does not know about, *nullus ligatus nisi mediante scientia*.[2] Ignorance which was not wilful, either by choice or from negligence, always excused. The distinction between ignorance of the law, *ignorantia juris*, and ignorance that an action here and now was covered by the law, *ignorantia facti*, appeared in the writings of canonists such as Roland Bandinelli and Stephen of Tournay (d. 1203) and of theologians such as Roland of Cremona and Hugh of St Cher. St Thomas made it equivalent to Aristotle's distinction between *ignorantia universalis*, lack of moral science, and *ignorantia particularis*, a mistaken judgment about a contingent case.[3]

To summarize this section on the four elements in St Thomas's conception of law. First, it was a rational ordinance, for though the legislator should be backed by the ability to enforce his ordinance the initial condition for its acceptance was that it placed a meaning in our social conduct. We were obedient to it in a manner different from our submission to the force of fire and water or to any mere might we could not resist. Secondly, its meaning lay in its reference to purpose. Why should we obey? Because of the Common Good. Again an object which required intelligence to perceive. Thirdly, this purpose could be envisaged only by the commonalty in theory and by its representative in practice. Fourthly, it must be brought to the rational acceptance of its subjects. Law could not bind unless promulgated, and on this head the moralists

---

[1] 2a–2ae. lx, 5.

[2] XVII *de Veritate* 3.

[3] J. F. von Schulte. *Die Summa des Stephanus Tornacensis*. Giessen, 1891. 1a–2ae, vi, 8. 1 *Quodlibets*, 19. *III Ethics, lect.* 3. 11. 1110 b 18, 1113 b 30.

O. Lottin. 'Le problème de l'*ignorantia juris* de Gratien à saint Thomas d'Aquin.' *RTAM*, v, p. 345. Louvain, 1937.

debated how far subjects were excused from its observance by the accidents of ignorance.

3. *Types of Law*

Proceeding from definition to division and drawing on the treatise *de Legibus et Praeceptis*, probably by John of Rochelle, the *Summa Theologica* sorted out the various sets of laws.[1] They had been muddled by theologians suspicious of physical motions, by exegetes treating the substance of the Decalogue as divine revelation, by writers on jurisprudence uneasily combining opposed texts from Gaius and Ulpian and by canonists prepared to claim that theirs was the law of the Gospel.[2] Eight types of law were currently received—the Eternal Law, the Natural Law, the Divine Law, Positive Law, the Mosaic Old Law, the New Law of the Gospel, the *Jus Gentium*, and the *Lex Fomitis*. It will be apparent at once that the term *law* was flexible or, as the Scholastics would say, analogical. Our main interest is the distinction between Natural Law and Positive Law, also the character of the *Jus Gentium* which shared in the characteristics of both. However it will be useful to glance at the others, if only to appreciate the surroundings of St Thomas's social science.

The Eternal Law in the mind of God was the first exemplar of all law and government.[3] Transcending all legal categories, it descended into created minds and was there partially expressed in two ways, directly through the biddings of natural and gracious reason towards such and such types of action, indirectly through an act of human will which determined certain supplementary regulations. The first was Natural Law, the second Positive Law.[4] A similar distinction appeared in higher primitive cultures between the laws 'written in the hearts of men' and those 'decreed by the chieftains', and was implied in Antigone's defiance of King Creon, 'as if you, a mortal, could overrule the sure unwritten laws of the Gods'.

---

[1] 1a–2ae. xci.

[2] 1a–2ae. xciv, 4 *ad* 1.
   W. Ullmann. *Medieval Papalism*, pp. 42–6.

[3] 1a–2ae. xciii, 3.

[4] A. Rohner. 'Naturrecht und positives Recht.' *Divus Thomas*, xii, pp. 59–83. Fribourg, 1934.

Natural Law was present from the beginning of human activity, for the mind was set towards right by an inborn habit, called *synderesis*.[1] It was apprehended almost instinctively; indeed, Ulpian described it as basically animal. Nevertheless human activity, properly speaking, was reasoned, and so was the human response to law. At this level certain common standards were recognized, and the fact gave rise to Gaius's conception of Natural Law, namely that its precepts were universally respected by all peoples.

Variations were admitted and though no systematic code of the Natural Law was written down, parts of it from the time of Roland of Cremona were ranked into primary and secondary precepts according to their closeness to the first principles of morality: some followed swiftly as conclusions, others called for a longer process of reasoning before they could be admitted. Telling the truth, for instance, was a primary imperative, despite the embarrassments of application to certain cases, as, for instance when a 'white lie' was convenient; monogamy was secondary, certainly desirable but less fundamental. Some truths were universal—fire burns the same in Greece and in Persia, remarked Aristotle—and the first principles, *communia principia*, of natural morality were everywhere known. Yet its implications, *propriae conclusiones*, were unequally drawn. Accordingly Natural Law was not evenly developed or observed in every region or period. At one stage its development might stop short, thus Julius Caesar noticed that robbery was not condemned by the Germans though in fact it was against the order of natural justice.[2]

Moreover, moral practice dealt with contingent matters in which a deal of latitude had to be allowed for. Difference of physical condition affected judgments especially with regard to social morality. The sugar-intake of the medievals through their ordinary diet was less than ours; their drinking, and therefore their drunkenness, had a different quality about it. Their psychology of sex, to judge from the moralists, seems to have been more directly genital and less influenced by romantic

---

[1] 1a. lxxix, 12. 1a–2ae. xciv, 1, *ad* 2.

[2] *V Ethics, lect.* 12. 1134 b–35 a. 1a. 2ae. xciv, 4. 2a–2ae. lvii, 2, *ad* 1.

literature. Their response to physical suffering and death was hardier.[1] There were other variations, too, which should prevent our too flatly transferring judgments from one culture to another.

The Gospel Law, which marked an evolution from within the Old Testament dispensation, brought in because of transgression, to a freer life of personal conscience, was a spirit not a code, a promise not a coercive dictate, an invitation to love God above all and our neighbour as ourself.[2] The Sermon on the Mount was the proclamation of a moral ideal, not the promulgation of a moral system. The New Law imparted life, and was not a bondage—such was the argument of the Epistle to the Galatians. It was concerned not only that we should do virtuous deeds but that we should do them virtuously, and act not as slaves but as the children and friends of God. It followed from the constitution of human nature in a condition of grace: that this was entirely of God's bounty and beyond our deserts did not mean that the appropriate operations were forced or arbitrary. On the contrary, as we have already noticed, they proceeded from us naturally and congenially and were directed to ends which met our abilities raised to the highest power. We shall come back to this Law of Liberty, but in the meantime let us pause on the concept of Positive Law.

Institution by an act of will which could have settled the matter otherwise was the essential feature of Positive Law. What it commanded was right because commanded, what it forbade was wrong because forbidden, unlike Natural Law where deeds were right and therefore commanded, or wrong and therefore forbidden. Its decree—for instance, the forbidding of murder— might coincide with an ordinance of Natural Law, and a sin thereby be turned into a crime as well, but its scope was restricted to the temporal well-being of the community. Some things it should leave well alone; some virtues were not matters of civil or ecclesiastical duty and some vices were not matters

---

[1] See 2a–2ae. cl, cliii, clvi, clix.

L. Brandl. *Die Sexualethik des hl. Albertus Magnus*. Regensberg, 1955.

[2] 1a–2ae, cvi, 1.

T. Gilby. *Between Community and Society*, pp. 165–70, 176–83, 194–200, 329–32.

C. Spicq. 'La Conscience dans le Nouveau Testament.' *Revue Biblique*, 1938, pp. 50–80. Paris.

for prosecution.[1] Then again, Positive Law could be repealed, Natural Law never.

In practice Positive Law could be equated with human law— we shall presently touch on the concept of Positive Divine Law. The two types of human law were the Civil Law of the State (which included what is now called Criminal Law) and the Canon Law of the Church. In between lay an area ruled by a kind of condominium of the spiritual and temporal powers through ecclesiastical laws which affected, for example, the ownership and management of religious foundations, or the civil obligations of clerics.

Finally it remains to notice the *Lex Fomitis* and the Positive Divine Law, notably as expressed in the Old Law, *Lex Vetus*, in order to fill in the background, psycho-biological and historical, to medieval political theory.

Opposed to the law of liberty St Paul wrote of 'another law in my members warring against the law of my mind, and bringing me into captivity to the law of sin which is in my members.'[2] This agony within human nature redeemed but not yet restored, described in the literature of conversion, rose partly from those animal drives which according to Ulpian entered into Natural Law. But human nature was fallen, and these were corrupted by Original Sin. The Stoics had preached a passionless virtue, and the Christian moralists deprecated any disturbance of reason. The Augustinians lamented lust or con-cupiscence springing from the loins of sin. There was a depravity about any emotional impulse, *secundum impetum sensualitatis*; it lit the kindling of sin, the *fomes peccati*, or *inclinatio sensualis appetitus in id quod est contra rationem*.[3] This sort of com-pulsion within our unregenerate nature was named by Peter Lombard the *lex fomitis*—that *lex* should be used in such a context shows how ambiguous the term was.

St Thomas agreed that any lapse from the order of reason into the sway of irrational forces was a penalty of Original Sin; so too was the physical subjection implied in mass-compulsions,

---

[1] 1a–2ae. xciv, 3. xcvi, 2, 3.

[2] Romans, vii, 23. 1a–2ae. xc, 1, *ad* 1. xci, 5.

[3] See 1a–2ae. lxxiv, 3, 4. lxxxii, 3. lxxxiii, 1. 1a–2ae. xci, 6. 3a. xv, 2.

obsessive sexuality, disease and death. Nevertheless, human motions which issue from sub-rational depths were not obscene in themselves but healthy: even jungle-law was adjusted to the balance of nature and to the preservation of species and individuals.[1] Sensuality, or the *voluntas sensualitatis*, was accepted without protest—indeed it was present in Christ.[2] In the *Summa Theologica* the term *concupiscentia* sometimes kept its conventional sense and signified wrongful lust, but it also recovered a cleaner sense, and stood for the response of the *appetitus concupiscibilis*—according to the pain-pleasure principle —or for innocent straightforward desire working even in the highest virtue, and notably in the theological virtue of hope.[3] The *lex fomitis*, which held no important place in St Thomas's divisions of law, was treated more cursorily in the *Summa Theologica* than in the *Commentary on the Sentences*.

Similarly the special concept of the Positive Divine Law calls for but brief delay. The terms *lex divina* or *jus divinum* were used loosely sometimes for the ultimate backing of all laws, particularly the precepts of morality and religion. More particularly they referred to God's entrance into history as a legislator; the consequent prescriptions were to be found in the Scriptures and the documents of the Christian Church. Some, like the Ten Commandments, were articles of natural morality, theoretically within human competence to discover and keep, which, by analogy with the truths of natural religion, had been divinely revealed and promulgated, since Providence does not expect the plain man to bear the burden of his nature unaided.[4] Others were supernatural; the Old Testament was prophetic and directed men to ends beyond reason, and the call of grace rose clearer in the New Testament.[5] The *Summa Theologica* devoted a lengthy and detailed study to the Mosaic Law, which comprised moral, ceremonial, and judicial ordinances for the Jewish politico-religious community; its

---

[1] 1a–2ae. xci, 6. c *& ad* 3.

[2] 3a. xviii, 2.

[3] 2a–2ae. xvii, 8.

[4] 1a–2ae. xci, 4. c, 1. 2a–2ae. ii, 4. I *Contra Gentes*, 4.

[5] 1a–2ae. xci, 4, 5.

theme was Messianic, and it was accordingly treated as a historical prelude to the Gospel.[1]

The special juridico-theological importance of Positive Divine Law was bound up with the divine constitution of the Church; thus the prerogatives of the Apostolic See and the Episcopate were *ex divina institutione* and *ex jure divino*.[2] So also was the sacramental economy. No wonder medieval authors extended the Positive Divine Law to details of Church discipline. If some took the Natural Law into the Divine Law, others, one might say, merged the Divine Law with the Canon Law. Huguccio, the canon lawyer who may have provided Innocent III with his juristic equipment, identified the Law of the Old and New Testaments with the law of nature, because the *summa natura, id est Deus* has delivered it to us through prophets and evangelists; playing on the scriptural word *canon*, he concluded that Divine Law could also be called the Canon Law. To show the danger of simplification which might lead us to believe he was a political Canonist, it was Huguccio also who formulated the dictum that he who was chosen by the Electoral Princes is the true Emperor even before he was confirmed by the Pope; this reflected the process of historical development and the claims of the prince to rule by right of conquest and sanction of civil law.

There is no evidence that St Thomas ever thought of a régime of which God was legal sovereign or regarded the Christian Church as the legatee of the political prerogatives of the Jewish Church. The *Summa Decretalium* (1210–15) of Damasus clearly distinguished Natural Law and Positive Law, which last included Canon Law: *est autem jus positivum sive expositum ab homine, ut sunt leges saeculares et constitutiones ecclesiasticae*.[3] If the opinion that Canon Law was a kind of human law was only rarely expressed by the Church authors of the time, it should be remembered that when early decretalists, such as Rufinus, Faventinus and Stephen of Tournay, wrote of the Canon Law as *jus divinum* they were merely contrasting

---

[1] 1a–2ae. xcviii–cv.

   D. Daube. *Studies in Biblical Law*. Cambridge, 1947.

[2] 2a–2ae. lvii, 2, *ad* 3.

[3] See W. Ullmann. *Medieval Papalism*, pp. 40, 43, 72.

it with *jus civile* and *jus humanum*, which they took to be synony-
mous. The term *jus divinum* went out of fashion, and so did
jus sacrum, to be succeeded by *jus pontificium* (in contrast to *jus
caesareum, jus imperiale, jus regium*) and *jus ecclesiasticum*. The final
approved technical term was *jus canonicum*.[1]

St Thomas thought that purely ecclesiastical institutions and
domestic legislation belonged to human law, and therefore,
unlike the divine and Natural Law, were under the dispensing
power of the Pope.[2] Canonical legislation was rooted in historical custom and past enactments, yet possessed a peculiar
character and status; the modern *Codex Juris Canonici*, promulgated by Benedict XV, regards its own specific ordinances as
distinct from any others as well as from custom.[3] Certainly it
was well both for the clarity of law and for religious devotion
that Canon Law was never officially identified with the Gospel
Law.

4. *The* Jus Gentium

To medieval jurisprudence the *Jus Gentium* might signify
anything between the developed Natural Law and a kind of
universally recognized Positive Law.[4] The ambiguity was
reflected in the *Summa Theologica*. Whereas the *Prima Secundae*,
while allowing that the precepts of the *Jus Gentium* were
inferred like conclusions not very remote from the principles of
the Natural Law, was inclined to treat them as belonging to
Positive Law, *humanitus posita*, the *Secunda Secundae*, while
emphasizing that they expressed a more deliberate judgment
than the instinctive adaptations of the Natural Law as described
by Ulpian, ranged them under the Natural Law as described
by Gaius and reflected that they needed no legislative enactment since nature has instituted them.[5]

Historically the *Jus Gentium* was originally that part of the
Roman system which had grown partly from the edicts of
magistrates charged with jurisdiction over strangers and partly
from the studies of jurists who sought to accommodate the

---

[1] G. Michiels. *Normae Generales Juris Canonici*, i, pp. 7–14. Lublin, 1929.
[2] IV *Quodlibets*, viii, 13. 2a–2ae. cxlvii, 3.
[3] See can. 27, 100, 107, 196, 219, 329, 727, 1016, 1060, 1068, 1110, 1139, 1405,
1495, 1509, 1513, 1539, 2198.
[4] G. Lombardi. *Ricerche in tema di Jus Gentium*. Milan, 1946.
[5] 1a–2ae. xcv, 2, 4, *c* & *ad* 1. 2a–2ae. lvii, 3, *c* & *ad* 3.

relations of persons of different nationality. It derived both from the *Jus Civile* and from tribal usage, but was figured in form and spirit according to Roman ideas of justice. All subjects of the Empire fell under the *Jus Gentium* as well as the *Jus Civile* when the largess of Caracalla extended citizenship to peregrins in 212. Since much of it owed more to custom than to positive legislation and showed what could be produced beyond the pale of Roman civilization, it engaged the interest and approbation of the philosophically-minded jurists. Here was a law more universal than the *jus proprium Romanorum*. Here, thought Ulpian, was a law more rational than the demands of animal life.[1]

The medievals lacked the learning to appreciate its history; in any case their habit was to read the past from the present. To them it was a category of juridico-moral science to be inserted somewhere between the general law of nature and any given system of human law. From the twelfth century onwards the jurists, and especially the decretalists, concentrated more and more on the rational character of Natural Law. Ulpian's inclusion of animal motions was felt to be embarrassing. Rufinus, who died after 1180, and Faventinus—John of Faenza—who died about 1220, preferred to describe it in more specific terms, *de eo juxta quod humano generi ascribitur*.[2]

The theologians agreed. St Albert equated it with rational law, the *Contra Gentes* developed its character as a personal participation in divine law and the sketch of law in St Thomas's *Commentary on the Sentences* was filled in about fourteen years later by the *Prima Secundae* (1269) with the same emphasis. Law properly so called was an affair of reason, *aliquid rationis*.[3] The teaching of his friend, Peter of Tarentaise, that *lex naturalis* was a *habitus* was criticized.[4] As might be expected, the authority of

---

[1] F. Senn. *De la justice et du droit*. Explication de la définition traditionelle de la justice, suivi d'une étude sur la distinction du *jus naturale* et du *jus gentium*. Paris, 1927.

[2] *Summa Rufini, ad Dist.* I. *Glossa Ordinaria* (Faventini), *ad Dist.* 2. *cap.* 7.

H. Singer. *Die Summa Decretorum des Magister Rufinus*. Paderborn, 1902.

J. Juncker. *Summen und Glossen*. Zeitschrift der Savigny-Stiftung für Rechtsgeschichte Kanonistische, xxv, pp. 462–71. Berlin, 1925.

[3] III *Contra Gentes*, 111–8. *III Sentences* XXXVII, 2, 3, 4. *IV Sentences* XXXIII, i, 1. 1a–2ae. xci, 2, *ad* 3.

[4] 1a–2ae. xciv, 1.

Gaius was prominent throughout this treatment he incidentally did not speak of Natural Law but of *ratio naturalis.*[1] Cicero, also, was appealed to. Hence the *Jus Gentium* came to be regarded as retaining much of the vigour of the principles of Natural Law, principles from which it developed some conclusions. Articulated in universal custom and recognized by the test of general acceptance, they provided guides to right conduct discoverable by the reason without the intervention of positive legislation.

The greater prestige of Aristotle then began to exert its influence. St Thomas's commentary on the *Ethics* dated from about the same time as the *Prima Secundae*; there he mentioned jurists who took Natural Law as a postulate of animal nature, whereas he himself preferred to follow Aristotle to whom it was a human and reasonable standard.[2] But the *logos* or reason Aristotle stressed was not quite the same as that of the Roman Stoics and jurists; it was more a meaning embodied in a process, a teleological striving, than a *ratio* fixed in a scheme conceived almost as a set piece composed by art. The *Prima Secundae* observed how law rationalized what had started at the lowest levels, and built up from the blind appetites for self-preservation and from animal instincts—Ulpian was here echoed without acknowledgment—to the specifically human demands of social life.[3] The stages might be distinguished, but they were not exclusive: *communicant in una radice.*[4] Primitive and civilized functions were rooted in the same thing, one single human substance manifesting itself in different ways; there was no abrupt break between the *impetus* of nature and the *industria* of civilization, the natural expression of feeling and speech.[5]

That may help to explain why, less than a year later when he came to treat *jus* and *justitia* in the *Secunda Secundae* (1270) he left Gaius and reverted to the lesser legal authority of Ulpian,

---

[1] *Institutes*, i, 1. *Digest*, i, 1, 9.
  F. de Zulueta. *The Institutes of Gaius*, i. Text with Critical Notes and Translation. Oxford, 1946.
[2] *V Ethics, lect.* 12.
[3] 1a–2ae. xciv, 2. xcv. 4, *ad* 1.
[4] *Ibid. ad* 2.
[5] 1a. lxxxvi, 3, 4, 6, 8. lxxvii, 1–6. *I Politics, lect.* 1.

and to the fragment of his teaching that Natural Law was
common to men and animals—Ulpian himself had not restricted natural law to the quasi-instinctive adaptations of sex
and parenthood.[1] This was awkward from a legal point of view.
The theologians had found it manageable only when they were
contrasting primitive rights and civilized adjustments, so,
although St Thomas dismissed the difference between the two
jurisconsults as mainly a matter of words, it was strange that
he should hark back to Ulpian. His name and doctrine may
have been running through his head that week when writing,
for the next article was to treat of the non-political and non-
reasoned quality of patriarchal, slave-owning and domestic rule
(*justum paternum, justum dominativum, justum oeconomicum*), and the
next question was to analyse and expand Ulpian's celebrated
definition of justice—*perpetua et constans voluntas jus suum
unicuique tribuendi*.[2] Perhaps it was a clue to how close he would
keep legality to human biology. It was certainly in keeping
with the movement of his ideas, which were taking on a more
Ionian complexion as he accepted more profoundly the reality
of material objects and the naturalness of the human community in the fullest physical sense of the word.

Whether natural rights were taken in their animal rudiments
or in their reasonable codification, or whether or not the *Jus
Gentium* were reckoned to belong to that, all agreed that a body
of law preceded the making of positive law. Human legislation
had to work on that datum. For the protection of its citizens
the State's function was twofold: first, to set forth and enforce,
according to circumstances, those of the principles and conclusions of the natural moral law which were necessary for
organized social life; secondly, to go farther and add detailed
provisions, *dispositiones particulares*, not of themselves implied in
the moral law, but imposed in order to ensure uniformity and
public convenience.[3] These were the ordinances purely of
Positive Law, which all subjects were bound in conscience to
obey.[4] In themselves they could be otherwise: they derived

---

[1] *Digest*, i, 1, 3, 4. 2a–2ae. lvii, 3.

[2] 2a–2ae. lvii, 4. lviii, 1–4, 8–11.

[3] 1a–2ae. xcv, 2.

[4] 1a–2ae. xcvi, 4, 5.

their force not from their inner morality, but from the fact of their enactment by lawful authority—like traffic regulations, which are reasonable, not because there is no alternative, but because all must keep the same rule of the road.

This capital distinction between the rational evolution of Natural Law and these artificial supplements of the Civil Law prescribed by the State will be discussed in the next chapter. Both classes entered into the civilized community. Part of political justice, Aristotle noted, was natural, part legal—natural, that which everywhere has the same force and does not exist by people's thinking this or that; legal, that which is originally indifferent, but when laid down is so no longer.[1] Civil laws alone, and no others, were generated by the State. Even there some ordinances proceeded from the agreement of citizens among themselves and from their consent to custom; they were not initiated by the Prince.[2] Customary laws, said Aristotle, have more weight and relate to more important matters than written laws; a man may be a safer ruler than a code, but not safer than custom.[3] The stability of the State depended on custom rather than on the art of the legislator.[4] The two however were related, and our next step must be to consider the status of the legal sovereign with respect to the natural needs of the political community.

5. *Dominion a Natural Condition*

A. J. Carlyle wondered how the curiously unhistoric reading that political authority was founded on sin could have replaced Aristotle's sane and searching analysis.[5] We may wonder, too, how it became too firmly fixed in the theological tradition for the weight of St Thomas's authority to shake it. Not that he was a mundane moralist disposed to exalt the earthly city. The *bonum commune sensibile et terrentum* was below the *bonum intelligibile et coeleste*. It was like the Old Jerusalem, not like Babylon, in relation to the New Jerusalem.[6] Political life and institutions

---

[1] *Ethics*, v, 7. 1134 b 18–22. St Thomas, *lect*. 12.
[2] 1a–2ae. xcvii, 3, *ad* 3.
[3] *Politics*, iii, 16. 1287 b 5–7.
[4] 1a–2ae. xcvii, 2, *ad* 1.
[5] *History of Medieval Political Theory*, v, p. 6.
[6] 1a–2ae. xci, 5.

rose from natural rightful needs, and public authority was therefore the object and not merely the occasion of rational and Christian virtue.

He was the first of the great Latin divines whose outward deference to the powers that be was not more or less tacitly accompanied with reserve, and even cynicism. They moved in this world somewhat like Cardinal Consalvi at the Congress of Vienna, courteous to the diplomats, loyal to engagements, concerned mainly to preserve the freedom of organized religion by reaching practical accommodations to existing forces, but unimpressed by the improving and solemn rhetoric with which politicians clothe their actions. A concordat might be hoped for, and if struck would be observed, but such prelates were not seriously convinced that the secular power possessed the intrinsic power to promote virtue, let alone the inclination. When religion was socially powerful the State could be harnessed and prelates could curb potentates, but when secular policies became ends in themselves and the means to implement them lay handy, religion became a private association; its activity retreated more and more into the domestic enclosure of the Church and the inner fastnesses of the soul.

The apostolic injunction, *submit yourselves to every ordinance of man for the Lord's sake*[1] which had always been preached and obeyed except by visionaries for whom Rome was Anti-Christ, could appear grudging when Europe was Christendom and political power was consecrated. No persecution of religion as such was likely to arise, despite conflicts between ecclesiastical and civil magnates. Still the old theory persisted, that men were divided between two opposed cities, the earthly and the heavenly, and that the earthly city, while necessary to ensure public security, was not charged with justice in the fullest sense of the word. It offered a tarnished sort of good, but good enough to go on with. St Augustine had not expected righteousness and the true worship of God from civil government as such, and Vincent of Beauvais, an older contemporary of St Thomas, echoed the dualism. Political power, he said, was different in Christians and in infidels for without the righteousness of grace there was no true *res publica*. He allowed that pagan rule could

---

[1] I Peter, ii, 13.

compose a *concordia* which was a social benefit in the *civitas terrena* and worthy of respect; laws not conflicting with religion were common to both pagan and Christian realms, yet there were no full legal rights apart from Christian titles to them.[1]

The Sicilian law book, the *Liber Augustialis*, foreshadowed the change that was to be brought about from the reception of Aristotle's political teaching; there Frederick II cleared his title to rule away from any dependence on ecclesiastical ratification or argument that sin must be remedied. He claimed a stainless power which issued from the necessity of things and was as needful as marriage for the continuance of the race. St Thomas, born in his realm and from a family distinguished in his service, extended this claim to political authority as such. It was more than an attempt to remedy a failure in the past, it was a corollary of social human nature; it was not merely an interim arrangement to mitigate the effects of sin or a police-threat to potential criminals. The political order was beautiful and worthy for its own sake. It was the opportunity, not the trial, to Christian virtue, a means of grace as well as a civilized convention. Its power was educational and health-giving, like that of a teacher or doctor, and though it should be modest about its ability to improve human character and should consequently restrict itself to outward social justice, few Aristoteleans would have agreed with John Stuart Mill that religion was outside its sphere. Integration in the political community was a condition of full virtue.[2] At the root of this difference from many of his contemporaries lay St Thomas's doctrine of Original Sin; he did not think that actual or 'wounded' human nature was profoundly unlike 'pure' human nature—had it ever existed.[3]

His early writings showed traces of the Augustinist persuasion that secular authority was a substitute for lost innocence; his later writings were, as might be expected, more definitely Aristotelean. Let us compare some texts, from the *Commentary on*

---

[1] *Speculum Doctrinale*, vii, 3, 7.

[2] 1a–2ae. lxxii, 4. xcii, 1.

[3] J. B. Kors. *La justice primitive et le péché originel d'après saint Thomas.* Paris, 1930.
R. M. Martin. *La controverse sur le peché originel au début du XIVe siècle.* Louvain, 1930.

the Sentences (1253-5) and on *St Matthew's Gospel* (1256-9) of his early period, and from the *Summa Theologica* (1266-73) and the *Commentary on the Epistle to the Romans* (1272-3) of his maturity.

His exegesis of the text, *Render unto Caesar the things that are Caesar's and to God the things that are God's* started with the literal sense.[1] A coin was produced: *Whose image and superscription is this?* asked our Lord, as though to say that what you are and what you use are God's and Caesar's, for natural riches, such as bread and wine, are from God and to be offered to Him, while artificial wealth, such as money, is from Caesar who must be given his due. He then turned to the allegorical sense. Our soul is made to God's image and must be rendered to him, yet the world puts its stamp on us, and we must accept it peaceably. Even holy men lifted above mundane cares, he added, have to mix with their fellows and *pray for the life of Nabuchodonosor the king of Babylon and for the life of Balthasar his son, that their days may be upon earth as the days of heaven.*[2]

The *Commentary on the Sentences* cited the same text to support civil obediance to properly constituted authority and adduced another.[3] *What thinkest thou, Simon? of whom do the kings of the earth take tribute? of their own children or of strangers? Peter saith to him, Of strangers. Jesus saith unto him, Then are the children free.*[4] Was this a suggestion of the existence of two classes of men, the ordinary run of Christians tributary by birth to the secular power and an élite exempt by reason of their apostolic life, who were neither slaves subject to service nor owners with possessions liable to taxation? *Nothwithstanding,* the passage continues, *lest we should offend them, go thou to the sea, and cast an hook, and take up the fish that first cometh up; and when thou hast opened his mouth, thou shalt find a piece of money: that take, and give unto them for me and thee.*[5] The irony was not lost on the Augustinist theologians. Civil power was artificial like money, reflected St Thomas, and notwithstanding the fact that some compromises were unavoidable, men were freed from its exactions to the extent that they embraced the life of perfection.

---

[1] Matt. xxii, 21. *In Evangelium Lectura,* xxii (b).
[2] Baruch, i, 11.
[3] *II Sent.* XLIV, ii, 2, *ad* 1.
[4] Matt. xvii, 25-6.
[5] Matt, xvii, 27.

Dare any of you, wrote St Paul, *having a matter against another, go to law before the unjust, and not before the saints?*[1] More had been read into the text than the simple advice to avoid civil litigation. Did it not question the foundations of earthly power? St Thomas for his part was content with the pragmatic reasons which prompted it. If the faithful submitted their secular concerns to infidel authority unsanctified by the sacraments of the faith, then Christian authority and the dignity of Christian men would be impugned, religion itself brought into disrepute, and occasion offered for calumny and persecution. Noting St Peter's injunction to the faithful *to submit themselves to every ordinance of man for the Lord's sake,*[2] he concluded that St Paul was not disapproving of obedience when summoned to appear before a secular non-Christian court, but of voluntary recourse and submission to it.

Nevertheless the treatment of civil obedience in the *Commentary on the Sentences,* included in the section significantly entitled *de potentia peccandi* by Peter Lombard, freed its essential character from involvement with sin. Would lordship have existed in a state of innocence? The answer drew a distinction between two modes of rule, one well disciplined, *praelationis modus ad regimen ordinatus,* the other domineering, *ad dominandum.*[3] Rule for the profit of the ruler was well enough when exercised over animals—incidentally it was held that the Fall has weakened our mastery there—but thoroughly evil when men were concerned. A political tyrant was like a slave-owner.[4] Rule for the profit of the ruled was justifiable, however, and for three reasons; firstly, *ad dirigendum subditos in his quae agenda sunt,* in order that people might live together in well-ordered and disciplined agreement; second, *ad supplendum defectus,* that they might be defended by the prince; third, *ad corrigendum mores,* that wrongdoers might be forced to behave decently. The second and third reasons supposed the fact of sin, but the first, based on congenital inequality, carried on Plato's and Aristotle's thought, that wisdom should be the ruling force and that

---

[1] I Cor.; vi, 1.
[2] I Peter, ii, 13.
[3] *II Sentences.* XLIV, i, 3.
[4] *Ethics,* viii, 10. 1160 b 30. St Thomas, *lect.* 10.

its possession brought the responsibility of governing others not so well endowed, *secundum quod unus alio munere sapientiae et majori lumini intellectus praeditus fuisset.*

Soon he was to begin the *Summa contra Gentes* (1259), of which the second book pictured a hierarchic universe composed of things diversified in kind and degree, beautiful *modo, specie et ordine.*[1] Men also were born unequal; their inequality was not caused solely by environmental factors originating from sin. It was not as the Augustinists thought, so in a sense foreshadowing in social theory the biology of Lysenko, that conditioning is what chiefly matters; on the contrary, human beings were not all entirely composed of the same homogeneous stuff which could be fashioned to this style or that—or victimized in this way or that—by outward circumstances which sufficed to explain their differences. Their social aptitudes were innately various. Qualities of leadership were uneven, and here temperament counted for much. Political subordination, therefore, was not based only on historico-theological accidents, but also on the social nature of dissimilar human beings; hence the moral right to rule could be ascribed to secular power as such and, at least in the abstract, be examined without reference either to the Christian theology of the Fall or to the existing system of Western Christendom in which could be found only the rudiments of State authority as we know it.

The changing situation brought the matter to a head. Christian men were faced with what for them were new problems. Abroad they were falling under non-Christian sway, and it was asked, Were they religiously bound to obey? At home Church and State were slowly becoming more separate, and it was asked, To what extent did the secular ruler enjoy rights which were properly his own?

Eastern territories long Christian had been taken by Moslems, and their rule was sometimes tolerant and—more so in the case of the Arabs than of the Turks—enlightened. Did their subjects owe them allegiance? It was a practical issue. Hostiensis took the line that since the coming of Christ all principality and jurisdiction had in principle been taken from infidels and

---

[1] *On the Truth of the Catholic Faith.* Book II: 'Creation.' Tr. J. F. Anderson. New York, 1956.

handed to the faithful; he admitted, that in practice it might be prudent to let sleeping dogs lie. Giles of Rome contended that infidels had no legitimate title to their possessions. For clerics to hold that you were not bound to keep faith with Saracens was current form. Yet the inhabitants on the spot could not afford such detachment, and the Latin States in Palestine, despite chronic war and frequent treachery, and the Eastern Empire itself were often on courteous terms with their neighbours. Christians did not hold aloof from them: as the *Acta* for his canonization bear witness, St Dominic was very much at ease with Moors and Jews in all human relationships. The missionary friars, penetrating through the belt of Islam, acknowledged the rights of rulers among the Mongol and other peoples they hoped to convert or turn into allies. This deference was less noticeable in Spain and the Baltic lands where Christendom was expanding, the scenes of wars of religion where the rights of Christian conquest were taken for granted and without the scruples which theologians expressed two or three centuries later during the colonization of Central and South America.

Nearer home within Christendom itself the secular power was emerging complete with its own proper claims. When asked from whom he held the Empire if not from the Pope, Barbarossa replied, 'From God alone.' He was not to make good his claim during his own lifetime, but before the end of the conflict between Pope and Emperor, the clerical arguments that all authority was subject to ecclesiastical control were counter-attacked by the argument that the secular order possessed its own inalienable power, responsible to God's judgment and its own laws, but not to priests. The movement was successful even in those countries where the Papacy had acquired special rights by agreement, as indeed in two of the most politically advanced realms in Christendom, namely Sicily where the king acknowledged the Pope as his suzerain and was his *legatus natus*, and England which John had surrendered in 1213 and then received back from the Roman Church as a feudal dependent. These transactions had been clothed in religious terms but were not generally treated as belonging to divine law.

The claims of the political Canonists grew more extravagant as their effective power waned outside the Church; they were defeated by events as much as by a rival philosophy. Once the Nation States had succeeded the Holy Roman Empire and the Holy See was felt to be Italian in its personnel and policies, the tide of events flowed against them. Then, too, although they may have claimed that their utterances were semi-inspired by the Pontifical Court, they lacked the solid support of the theologians of the centre who were not inclined to grant unlimited earthly dominion to the Pope. Christ himself who was the king of everything and possessed the *universalis judiciaria potestas* had not subjected all human affairs to it *quantum ad executionem*.[1]

Innocent IV, a moderate when he argued for the supremacy of the spiritual power, had disavowed any intention of disturbing existing rights fairly established though without recourse to Church ratification. St Thomas clearly laid down that grace offered no violence to the order of nature; consequently true human rights constituted apart from official religion were to be respected, though the Church should not allow infidels to acquire dominion over Christian men, and possessed the power of releasing slaves on their conversion to the Christian faith.[2] When he spoke in passing of kings being the *vassalli Ecclesiae* he either had in mind certain special cases or used the word in an untechnical sense in contrast to the days of persecution *quando astiterunt reges adversus Christum*.[3] The *enfant terrible* of the Dominicans, Durand of St Pourcain (d. 1332), usually so critical of him was his ally here, and agreed that legitimate power could be vested in non-Christian rulers and should be accordingly maintained.

That political authority was grounded on the social nature of man appeared more emphatically in his later writings. There also the dignity of power was enhanced. The *Summa Theologica* repeated the question, put forward in the *Commentary on the Sentences*, Whether in a state of innocence man would have been

---

[1] 3a. lix, 4, *ad* 2.

[2] 2a–2ae. x, 10.

[3] *XII Quodlibets*, xiii, 19, *ad* 2.

subject to human power?[1] The same distinction was drawn
between the government of slaves for the benefit of the governor
and the government of freeman for the benefit of the governed.
It was developed in the *de Regimine Principum*.[2] For a man to
cede his freedom and the disposing of what is his own was
grievous, *contristabile*; that could only be penal and the result
of sin. But that he should be politically subordinate, for his own
sake and that of the common good, was no derogation from
his dignity. At first sight this may seem rather tame, an
obedience to an enlightened and benevolent prince far removed
from a critical and sturdy radicalism. From a closer reading of
the texts, however, it is clear that the subordination to the
common good did not spell subservience to a group but
personal and responsible sharing in social purposes and
decisions.

These transcended private interests, which would still have
had to be controlled even were there no disorder due to sin.
Neither self-interest nor the profit motive was inherently
vicious. It was in the nature of things that private advantage
might be a public danger that could be accepted with
equanimity and then controlled. The reverse was also true,
according to the motto on the common seal of the Stockton and
Darlington Railway, *periculum privatum utilitas publica*. Stresses
were inevitable in any community composed of heterogeneous
parts. One man was endowed with knowledge and public zeal
superior to that of his fellows and it would be awkward, St
Thomas remarked, if he did not use his abilities for the benefit
of others. He quoted St Peter's advice, that we should be *good
stewards of the manifold grace of God, ministering the same one to
another*; then, characteristically pillaging the Egyptians, he took
St Augustine's saying, Not lust of power moves the great man,
but the office of counsel, thus has nature's order prescribed,
and man by God was thus established.[3]

Such was the argument of the *Prima Pars*. Two years later
when the *Secunda Secundae* turned to domestic life and private
property it recognized that physical compulsions inflicted and

---

[1] 1a, xcvi, 4.
[2] ii, 9. iii, 19.
[3] I Peter, iv, 10. *de Civitate Dei*, xix, 15.

endured were penalties of the Fall. That the man must sweat at the unfruitful soil, the woman labour to deliver a child and put up with the moods of the husband, all these were curses and the consequences of sin. Nevertheless at a deeper level human nature as such was essentially committed to and engaged with the powers of the material world: sick pain was one thing, physical effort another. Man's dignity as a maker demanded that he should be a worker—this was his title to be a property-owner. Similarly it was a woman's dignity to be a mother and obedient to her husband. Child-bearing, St Thomas guessed, would have been painless and domestic intercourse 'polite' in a state of innocence, but he did not share Alcuin's opinion that no thorns would have grown then, but thought there would have been wild flowers but no weeds, that is, plants where they were not wanted.[1]

The same distinction, between an essential condition and a particular mode of it due to sin, entered his inquiry on private property. As political power had acquired a coercive character so private property had acquired a certain exclusiveness; social institutions had come to terms with selfishness. Moreover, positive laws have rightly determined detailed arrangements for the transmission and retention of property, leaving intact the principle that the root of human ownership lay deeper and grew from man's need and duty to assume responsibility. Man was an artist made to God's image, and, though he cannot create in the strict sense of the word, he was called to make things grow through his own initiative. Some kind of right to property resided in the individual not granted by the organized group, and here some anticipation may be detected of Locke's teaching of the pre-social and inalienable right of freeholders. Its extent, here more here less, was to be settled by social authority.

Less academically communist than those divines who saw behind the present city the image of a classless community where everything was shared in common, St Thomas's prescriptions were neither so deep nor so far ranging as were

---

[1] 2a–2ae. clxiv, 2. *c* & *ad* 1.

For the *subjectio civilis* of woman to man, the *caput* and *gubernator* see 1a. xcii, 1, *ad* 2. xciii, 4, *ad* 1. 2a–2ae. lxxvii, 2.

For women's exclusion from civil and political office, see *IV Sentences* XXV, ii, 1. 1a–2ae. cv, 3, *ad* 1.

those of some of the Franciscans. Vowed poverty was a counsel of religious perfection and communism was a good system for specially dedicated groups to choose. The value of personal administration, *potestas procurandi et dispensandi* was insisted on, yet the enjoyment of the fruits of the earth should be for all. He shocked some of his contemporaries by maintaining that a man in dire necessity did not steal who helped himself from another's goods.[1]

The same paradox appeared when slavery was the topic. With Aristotle he calmly accepted the fact that men were born socially unequal in their abilities, opportunities, and vocation. That followed because psychological qualities were so closely bound up with organic conditions.[2] One might there expect him to have been rather more tolerant than an Augustinist about slavery: after all did not its origins lie in the nature of things and was not sin responsible only for its cruelty and incidental abuses? On the contrary, he was less inclined than the Fathers to excuse its continuance.[3] Some things are best tackled when you enter into their strength and not let them pass. Social theology is like politics, it needs men who will wrestle with the here and now and not escape into the hereafter. One weakness of 'other worldly' schools of theology is to discourage the spirit of social reform by assenting too easily to bad social conditions on the grounds that the city of this world is anyhow a compromise with evil, and that there is little to be done about it except to keep oneself uncontaminated. Passive non-approval easily turns to condonation.

St Thomas inherited the temper of the early Middle Ages. Disobedience was the right answer to the precepts of wicked power. Towards the end of his life he seemed to grow more guarded against the least hint favourable to rebellion, without however approaching Cranmer's position, that if the prince be wrong then it is for God alone to punish him. The Lutheran

---

[1] 2a-2ae. lxvi, 2, *c* & *ad* 1. 7. xxxii, 5, *ad* 2. lvii, 3. *II Politics*, *lect.* 2, 4.

A. Horvath. *Eigentumsrecht nach den hl. Thomas von Aquin*. Graz, 1929.

C. Spicq. 'La notion analogique de dominium et le droit de propriété.' *RSPT*, 1931, pp. 52-76.

[2] 1a. lxxxv, 7.

[3] 1a. xcvi, 4. 1a-2ae. xciv. 5, *ad* 3. 2a-2ae. x, 10. lvii, 3, *ad* 2. civ, 5. clxiv, 2. *II Sentences*, XLIV, i, 3. For slavery and marriage, *IV Sentences* XXXVI, i, 1-3.

doctrines of submission to the powers that be and the denial of
the Church's power to judge the actions of the earthly sovereign
would have appeared to him strange. Usurped authority or
unjust decrees deserved no obedience, except *per accidens*, in
order to avoid scandal or the danger of worse happening.[1] For
it was wrong to bring the principle of civil authority into
disrepute, and wrong also, though not technically the sin of
sedition, to overthrow a tyrant if the people were likely to suffer
more from the consequent disturbance than from his misrule.[2]

His last passage on civil dominion appears in the exposition
of the *Epistle to the Romans* written towards the end of his life.
*Let every soul be subject unto the higher powers. For there is no power
but of God: the powers that be are ordained of God. Whosoever
resisteth the power, resisteth the ordinance of God: and they that resist
shall receive to themselves damnation.*[3] Some early Christians, he
commented, urged that they were not subject to earthly power
because of the liberty Christ had brought them. They were
mistaken, however, for this liberty was of the spirit, a freedom
from the law of sin and death. Our flesh was still in subjection;
we can but await a freedom both of spirit and body, *when Christ
shall have delivered all the kingdoms to God the Father, when he shall
have brought to nought all principality and power.*[4] Until then, so long
as we are clothed with corruptible flesh we must submit to bodily
masters: *servants, be obedient to them that are your lords according to
the flesh.*[5] The 'higher powers' of the text were men constituted
in power to whom we should be subject according to the order
of justice. St Paul spoke without qualification—the term higher
should be taken unrestrictedly, and he meant that we were
their subjects because of their high office, even if they were
evil. Hence St Peter said, *Servants, be subject to your masters, not
only to the good and gentle, but also to the forward.*[6] For all power
was from God, even as our Lord reminded Pilate, *Thou couldest
have no power against me, unless it were given thee from above.*[7]

The words of the prophet, *They have reigned but not by me; they
have been princes and I knew not,*[8] were no rebuttal of this teaching,
he went on to say. For there were three ingredients in the

---

[1] 2a–2ae. civ, 6, *ad* 3.   [4] I Cor., xc, 24.   [7] John, xix, 11.
[2] 2a–2ae. xlii, 2.   [5] Ephesians, vi, 5.   [8] Hosea, viii, 4.
[3] Romans, xiii, 1–2.   [6] I Peter, ii, 18.

power of a prince, or of any dignitary: the power itself, which
was from God; the mode of acquiring it, which was from God
when it was obtained in due form, but not otherwise; its exercise, which was from God when the precepts of divine justice
were observed, but not otherwise. The subordination of lower to
higher was permeated with divine purpose. Hence to resist
proper authority was against virtue, and obedience and submission were necessary both for decency and for salvation.[1]

Little room for civil disobedience was allowed by such
doctrine. Two theories on the origin of sovereignty which have
been held by followers of St Thomas help to illustrate the shift
of emphasis between his early and his late writings. According
to the sixteenth-century 'Translation Theory', expounded by
Cajetan, Vitoria and Dominic Soto, the right to govern was
transmitted to and vested in a ruler by the explicit choice or
tacit consent of the people, who must then obey so long as his
power was not forfeited by breach of contract and violation of
the constitutional laws. Suarez, too, was of this opinion, though
his studies served as a bridge to the nineteenth-century
'Designation Theory' put forward by Thomists of the revival
inaugurated by Leo XIII. To such writers as Liberatore,
Zigliara, Cathrein, Schwalm and Billot the people's choice did
not of itself constitute that form of government called democracy, which, therefore, was no essential part of Natural Law.
The government originally established by a kind of election
might take other forms, and was henceforth to be obeyed even
though it might not be representative according to formal
suffrage or even when it appeared unpopular.[2]

Both sides have appealed to St Thomas for support, the first
probably on better grounds. His convictions have to be construed, for he was confronted with the doctrine neither of the
Divine Right of Kings nor of the Sovereign People. The
sentiments they have evoked are not easily run into his political
scheme of things.[3]

---

[1] *Expositio in Romanos*, xiii, *lect*. 1.

[2] G. Bowe. *The Origin of Political Authority*. Dublin, 1955.

[3] 1a–2ae. xc, 3. xcvii, 3, *ad* 3. *de Regimine Principum*, i, 6. Y. R. Simon. 'The
Doctrinal Issue between the Church and Democracy.' *The Catholic Church in
World Affairs*. Ed. W. Gurian. Notre Dame, 1954.

VI

A DRAFT FOR THE JURISTS

LEGAL or positive right was based on natural right. Cicero was quoted to this effect by the thirteenth-century writers.[1] All belonged to the 'Natural Law School', not that they necessarily held that the Natural Law was an organic system of legislation to which Positive Law could be compared as inferior to superior, as tactical plan to strategical design. But they required human legislation to respect lawful values which it did not itself create. These were the social premises of the good life, emanating from God's Eternal Law, discovered in nature and confirmed and heightened by Revelation. The Natural Law taken alone scarcely composed an effective corpus of precepts. Do to others as you would be done to yourself—the maxim did not take you very far. Its negative variant, do not do to others what you would not have done to yourself, adopted in King Alfred's code, was sharper and more effective.

General moral principles and goodwill were too shapeless to give bone for the moral life either of the individual or of the group. Definite conclusions and decisions had to be come to about theft, for instance, or sexuality outside marriage. These constituted a set of derivative precepts of which the human reason had no original intuition and to which the human will had no instinctive bent. They were reached only by deliberation and effort not by *inclinatio naturalis*, and held only by instructed good-sense. Such were the judicious ordinances which held a community together, the social contrivances or *utilia ad bene vivendum*.[2]

Furthermore, merely as statements even these remained academic so long as they were not carried into practice. Thereupon they, like the rules of statesmanship, were involved with contingency and contrariness. Enlightened doctrines may produce conflicting policies, as happened to the British between the two World Wars when they supported self-determination

---

[1] See *V Ethics, lect.* 12. 1a–2ae. xci, 3. xciv, 2.
[2] 1a–2ae. xciv, 3.

for the Arabs and a national home for the Jews and ended by losing control of the Suez Canal. The application of social morality varied according to circumstances. Alternative ways of implementing its purposes could also present themselves. Granted that men should be responsible owners and masters of their life, several methods lay open for regulating the acquisition and exploitation of property; in order to ensure conformity in the group, legislation was necessary which enacted the form, or forms, to be accepted by all.

At this stage entered a special act of legislative and political will. Its precept was not drawn from the resources of the Natural Law but superimposed on them. From the point of view of moral science it was not a conclusion but an addition. It was like a work of art, justified more by its success than by the evidence of ethical principles. Of course as a practical measure it was expected not to thwart ultimate moral purposes, for what is the use of anything that does not conduct us to happiness? To this extent moral science and religious belief should exercise a negative control over law-making and politics. Yet neither could provide the immediate and pragmatic tests, neither was so on the spot that it could tell us what laws should be enacted and what policies pursued in order that the population should be at once secure and mettlesome, contented and honourable, neither over-disciplined nor lacking in public spirit.

Customs and fundamental laws were woven into the social fabric. They had to be preserved were the community to keep its traditional identity and inherited way of life. But they did not serve to meet every new circumstance. Adaptations, alterations and additions were called for, and it was in the deliberate framing of these by statute and in the execution of the improvisations necessary for the needs of the State that our governors needed a special technique, *ars*, and practical wisdom, *prudentia*. Here their decisions are their own, and they must have the courage of them.

Talk is not enough, nor high-minded protestations, nor gestures expressing the national spirit. Only the functions of *making* and *doing*, as opposed to *demonstrating* what is right and patriotic, take us into the proper field of human law and politics. St Thomas seems to have been the first Christian moralist who appreciated the fact. Let us consider then his grant of limited autonomy to juridical and political action, and first with respect to the positive lawyers.[1]

The threat of too much law, of which he was well aware, arose in his day less perhaps from the Civilians than from the Canonico-Moralists who, like modern Welfare-State officials, already disclosed their addiction to nagging. The entrance of more and more legal forms into theology, particularly into moral theology, served many good purposes, but when too many came crowding in theology itself scarcely had room to breathe. His dislike for the intrusion of Decretalism into theology has already been noted,[2] also his detachment from the ambitions of the political Canonists, though he was high in the counsels of the *Curia*. The two Popes he served and with whom he was familiar, Urban IV and Clement IV, were both French administrators of great experience who had made their reputations outside the Court of Rome; Clement had been a civil lawyer, adviser to St Louis of France and a married man before embracing the clerical state.

From the nature of his writings he had more frequent occasion to appeal to the Canon Law than to the Civil Law, but it was usually on minor points. The *Summa Theologica* and *Contra Gentes* between them contain 193 references to Gratian's *Decretum* and sixty-one to Justinian's *Institutes*, seventeen to the *Digest*, thirteen to the *Codex*, and none to the *Novellae*. His entire works include but 155 references to the *Corpus Juris Civilis*. While he maintained the dignity of the Roman juridical order, he used its Law mainly as a practical system of reference. Some of its notions were worked into his synthesis, for instance, *servitus*, *status*, *legimatio*, and *adoptio*.[3] But so also he borrowed from the Lombard Law. The influence on him of the Roman Law was not to be compared with that of Aristotle.

Without descending to details we may observe the general bearing on social morality of the Roman Law taken in both its

---

[1] F. Olgiati. *Il concetto di giuridicità in San Tommano d'Aquino*. Milan, 1944.

L. Lachance. *Le concept de droit selon Aristote et saint Thomas d'Aquin*. Ottawa, 1948.

P. M. van Overbeke. *De relatione inter ordinem juridicum et moralem*. Louvain, 1934.

[2] *Contra Retrahentes*, 13. 2a–2ae. lxxxviii, 11. XI *Quodlibets*, 9, *ad* 1.

[3] J. M. Aubert. *Le droit romain dans l'oeuvre de saint Thomas*. Paris, 1955.

versions, the Canon Law and the Civil Law. Each should be looked at rather as a new work of art than as developed from the medieval deposit of morals and custom. Here again we recall that the original distinction between them was not that between the codes of two separate bodies, namely Church and State, the first concerned with the spiritual and the other with the material organization of social life, but that between the disciplines of two different interests within one single community, namely the Christian Commonwealth. Its life was not split into two halves, one given to the sacred and the other to the profane. Two social purposes were not divided as they were by Dante, the *duo ultima* of the *Monarchia* corresponding to the two beatitudes, heavenly and earthly, described in the *Convivio*.[1] Such dualism was not to the mind of St Thomas whose repetition of St Augustine's doctrine of the two cities was merely reminiscent and rhetorical. All duties, contractual or communal, public and private, civil and ecclesiastical, were performed from the motion of grace in human nature; all shared the same intent, to take us to our single end, the face-to-face vision of God.

1. *Law-Making as Art*

The lawyers were grumbled at for going their own way. There was nothing new in that. They were the experts whom ordinary men had perforce to employ. True, there were safeguards, and some of their entanglements could be broken through by a public opinion formed by a strong sense of religion and custom. As the thirteenth century drew on so laws tended to become additions to, rather than adaptations of, the familiar social structure. The academic lawyers themselves were no longer mainly commentators and interpreters, for the Post-Glossators, joined by the new statesmen who had digested the lessons of the *Politics*, were shaping Roman laws into instruments of government in the Nation-States then separating out from feudal Christendom. Legal and political disciplines began to acquire a privileged status, which put them beyond the reach of theology and folk-custom.

---

[1] *Monarchia*, iii, 16. *Convivio*, iii, 4, 6, 13, 15. iv, 13, 17, 22.
  A. P. D'Entrèves. *Dante as a Political Thinker*.

The process can be described according to a current technical vocabulary adopted from Aristotle. His philosophy encouraged the close analysis and detailed classification of parts in individual and social psychology. The responses of organisms to their environment were not left undifferentiated but were apportioned to their various active powers, abilities, propensities; *potentiae*, *facultates*, *aptitudines*. Sensation, for example, was not identified with emotion nor seeing with touching.[1] Furthermore, the higher cognitive and affective abilities were not altogether instinctive but allowed for some free play; they could be trained in one direction rather than in another by supervening qualities called habits, *habitus*.[2]

It was not enough to record that an activity was performed. There were questions to be pressed. From what power was it elicited? What was its condition? Scientific treatment of individual and social behaviour demanded nothing less. Hence the inquiries of the Aristotelean Summists into the virtues, or good habits of activity.[3] Instead of describing, in the manner of St Gregory, the components and general conditions of virtues so that they shaded off into another one, they set themselves to define the peculiarities of each special type. The classical achievement of this method is found in the *Secunda Secundae*, where, without an exaggerated faculty-psychology or losing sight of the unity of the human substance and its all-round activity or treating virtues as little entities separate from one another, more than ninety distinct species were exactly classified. The basis was laid down in Aristotle's *de Anima* and *Ethics*, and amplified in the *Prima Pars* and *Prima Secundae*. The working principle of the classification was that different objective targets or 'formal objects' in our surroundings diversified our activities about them, and therefore the appropriate habits and abilities.

The theoretical and practical reasons were not regarded as distinct abilities or faculties. The human mind was single; one and the same power looked into eternity and accommodated itself to time, asked questions about its environment and sought

---

[1] 1a. lxxvii, 1, 2, 3, 5, 6.
[2] 1a–2ae. xlix, 1, 3, 4. l, 3, 4, 5. li, 1.
[3] 1a–2ae. lv, 2, 3.

to change it.[1] Nevertheless a twofold function was engaged, contemplative and active. The mind may remain a spectator—we speak of philosophical contemplation, for religious contemplation is another matter. It may observe the world and develop the implications of what it sees, yet while enunciating truths not do anything more about them or put anything into effect. It may stop short at theory and speculation. Or it may go on to be active and practical by planning and directing other psychological powers, by shaping conduct and exploiting the world and by turning things to advantage.

For both pursuits the mind could acquire or be endowed with certain good habits. Leaving aside those qualities of character called the moral virtues, five qualities of mind or intellectual virtues were enumerated by Aristotle and taken over by St Thomas, namely intuitive reason, scientific knowledge, wisdom, practical wisdom, and art.[2] Of these we reserve attention to scientific knowledge, *scientia*, a virtue of the theoretical mind, *ratio speculativa*, and to practical wisdom, *prudentia*, and art, *ars*, both of which were virtues of the practical mind, *ratio practica*.

Scientia meant demonstrated knowledge, the result of the kinds of proof described in the *Posterior Analytics*. Observing the logical proprieties, it arrived at conclusions which could be shown to be inevitable, given assent to the premisses and patience. The discourse was deductive. Yet such scientific knowledge had its limitations. It might grasp reasons embodied in the outside world, but these were abstract and general whereas material beings were concrete and individual. It might understand types, perhaps even examples; it could not comprehend things. Here, in brief, was the cause of the profound uneasiness in the strictly scientific reading of the world on the Aristotelean theory of knowledge; here the perennial problem of the gap between notional essence and real existence—hang up philosophy if it cannot make a Juliet!

Aristotle and St Thomas set themselves to close it by bringing the mind into contact with individual facts. It must suffer a

---

[1] 1a. lxxix, 9, 10. 1a–2ae. iii, 5.

[2] *Ethics*, vi, 3. 1139 b 16. 1a–2ae. lvii, 2, 3, 4.

real experience of the outside world.[1] This could take place in several ways. We may notice two. First, if reason were fused with sensation and emotion then such 'imaginative' knowledge could reach nearer to an individual thing than could a convergence of general ideas. Secondly, and this is relevant to our present discourse on social and political theory, if it entered physical process by doing or making something then it could be occupied, as we say, 'with real things'.

We need not delay on the distinction between *doing* and *making*. The first, a dynamic condition relating immediately to the agent, is the affair of prudence defined as *recta ratio agibilium*, which can be rendered as right reason in human activity. The second, which relates to the external effect, is the affair of art, *recta ratio factibilium*, which can be rendered as right reason in the product.[2] Obviously the two are closely connected, and their distinction needs to be elaborated when discussing the relations of morals and aesthetics.

For the present it is enough to notice how both differ from *scientia* in that they are directly engaged with concrete situations. For though sound learning is a moral discipline, scientific knowledge does not ensure that we shall act aright or make things well; a good scientist is not *ipso facto* an admirable character or a sound practitioner. Science, as we know, gives power, but it is power for good and ill. It is morally neutral. It is also, as such, ineffective. Renoir said that no beautiful picture is made by theories. They may provide the recipe, but not the know-how. Conversely, the judgments of prudence and art cannot be taken back entirely to theory. Nor can they expect to enjoy scientific certitude, but only the practical confidence to be gained by careful calculation, reliable information, courage to commit oneself and stamina.[3] So much must be said if we are to appreciate what was meant when lawmaking and statesmanship were described in terms of prudence and art.

Both addressed themselves to the practicable here-and-now

---

[1] T. Gilby. *Poetic Experience: An Introduction to Thomist Aesthetic.* London, 1934.

[2] 1a–2ae. lvii, 4.

J. Maritain. *Art and Scholasticism.* Tr. J. F. Scanlan. London, 1939.

[3] 2a–2ae. xlvii, 9, *ad* 2. *II Ethics, lect.* 2. *VI lect.* 6.

without ambition about the far and abiding values. They dealt with the useful, *bonum utile*, rather than with the worthy, *bonum honestum*, and their immediate social purpose correspondingly was to promote team-work and cooperation, *amicitia utilis*, rather than deeper ease and intimacy, *amicitia honesta*.[1] Their temper was pragmatic, ready to chop and change according to circumstances, to lay down a ruling here, to take advantage of an opening there: they were content with limited gains. Such was practical wisdom—for a large problem, atomic armament let us say, may be insoluble as it stands, and yet be broken into parts on some of which effective agreement may be reached. It was not low cunning, it was better than the *Klugheit* of Kant, it was virtue being shrewd.

The Low-Latin term *positivus* signified what was accidental and imposed as against what was essential and inherent, hence Positive Law as such meant a practical ordering of issues in themselves neither right nor wrong, not a deduction from ethical principles. Statesmanship, too, meant the businesslike employment of existing facts for the welfare of the community, more immediately concerned to secure *concordia* or unanimity in the conduct of affairs than to ensure the inner peace which was the fruit of virtue.[2] We may question the definition which says that politics is the art of translating moral principles into institutions, certainly if that signifies merely the extension of ethics to community-processes. For these are directed into certain arbitrary courses by human law and politics, neither of which looks to pure theory for its authoritativeness. Part of the evidence for what they do is simply that they do it.[3]

Again, a certain pliancy is called for if law and politics are to make the adaptations necessary for the well-being of the State. To be oversensitive to the charge of trimming, that is less of a weakness in moral theologians than in legislators and statesmen who should practice compromise and pragmatism, and be paragons like Talleyrand, of whom it is said that the sense of proportion and the sense of occasion transcended

---

[1] 1a. v, 1. 2a–2ae. xxiii, 3, *ad* 1. *V Ethics*, lect. 12. *VIII*, lect. 2, 3.

[2] 2a–2ae. xxix, 1.

[3] J. Dabin. *La philosophie de l'ordre juridique positif.* Paris, 1929.

opportunism, but amounted to genius.[1] Of course a social
doctrine must be present if community-life is to have meaning
and ultimate purpose and there are enduring principles for
political as for military art, yet they have to be constantly
rethought, restated, and applied analogically in no hard and
fast manner: thus command of the sea should not be pinned to
surface-warships. Past prestige is dangerous if it leads to repeti-
tions of what was appropriate once but is no longer applicable
to reach a world which has moved on. James I has been criticized for seeing himself as the schoolmaster of his realm, and
indeed rulers should be practitioners rather than men of theory
for on them lies the responsibility of getting things done and
making them work. Hence they should respond to the play of
changing forces.

The conduct of affairs may go case-hardened because of a
tradition of success or by the action of conservative sectional
forces. A State too largely controlled by moralists and legalists
stiff on detail is particularly exposed to this danger: perhaps
an inflexible pedantry of government contributed as much
as anything to the decline of the Spanish Empire from the
seventeenth century onwards. Clericalist polities have also
been liable to lose touch with actual conditions, and have
failed, not because they were corrupt, but because they represented the specialist preoccupations of a class—the clericals
have not always been priests and their supporters, for liberals,
and communists too, can count their doctrinaires who failed in
the business of government by sticking too closely to formulas.

Now it was recognized by the Scholastics that the precepts of
the Natural Law, indeed of all moral laws, were in themselves
statements of a theory or doctrine although they were about
what we should do. They told us which types of action were to
be done and which to be avoided. It was left to the individual
to apply these abstractions to the particular occasions of his
conduct. He did this by a judgment of conscience—preferably
informed by prudence—which bade him do what he should do
here and now.[2] Similarly the community applied moral social
principles through the political wisdom, *prudentia politica*, of its

---

[1] H. Nicolson *The Congress of Vienna*, x, 2. London, 1947.
[2] 1a. lxxix, 13. 1a–2ae. xix, 3 (*ad* 2), 4, 5.

rulers and citizens.[1] What kind of conscience a man possessed largely determined what kind of man he was. So also a country's political good sense manifested in repeated acts throughout its history went to build up the national character and stamp the quality of the laws and constitution. Prudence was not only an intellectual virtue which dealt with ways and means on the presupposition of certain principles and ends, it was a moral virtue as well and without it there could be no true moderation, courage, or justice.[2]

Doctrine and realism went together, the theory which gazed at ends and the practice which adapted means to ends. The first was the business of the social philosopher; left to himself he tended to simplify situations since principles were his interest, not the multiple and variety of individual cases. The second was the affair of the lawyers and statesmen—practical men whose talents were with facts and who consequently tended to dismiss philosophical questions as being academic. Both were distinct and complementary.

That bad morals made bad law might be true, also that no lasting political advantage followed from wrong conduct. Conversely, bad laws and policies hindered good morals. Good laws and policies rendered it easier for a man to be a good citizen, and so helped him to be a good man. But the converse did not follow, for excellent moral doctrine and moral dispositions could not of themselves produce beneficial legislation and successful statemanship. The reason for this, one of the ironies of history, was found in the analysis we have just conducted.

These considerations may now be applied more closely to Positive Law, bearing in mind a distinction drawn by St Thomas. Decisions, he said, may be derived from the Natural Law in two ways, either as conclusions from premises or as applications of abstractions, *sicut determinationes quaedam aliquorum communium*.[3] The first was the method employed by science when one truth was proved from another: thus when the

---

[1] 2a–2ae. xlcii, 10, 11, 12.

[2] 1a–2ae. lxvi, 3 *ad* 3. 2a–2ae. xlvii, 6, 7.
Also 1a–2ae. lxvi, 3 *ad* 5. lviii, 4, 5. lxv, 1, *ad* 3, 4.

[3] 1a–2ae. xcv, 2. *V Ethics, lect.* 12. 1a–2ae. xciv, 5. 2a–2ae. lvii, 2, 3. lxvi, 2, *ad* 1.

precept, thou shalt not murder, was seen to be implied in the Natural Law principle that wrongful harm was not to be inflicted on anybody. The second was the method employed by art when general ideas, *formae communes*, were made concrete, *determinantur ad laiquod speciale*: thus when from the Natural Law principle, that crime should be punished, the legislator proceeded to enact what kind of punishment shall be inflicted. He might try to make the punishment fit the crime, yet his business was not with poetic justice and, except in some cases of compensation, there was an arbitrary quality about the sentence he passed. A human penal code, unlike divine justice, could not pursue the interior connection between human acts and their effects, but had to be content to attach certain deterrent or remedial consequences to some outward acts which disturbed the community.

It was in the second manner of derivation that purely political decisions were arrived at and positive laws enacted. They were expected not to contravene the principles and conclusions of morality but they were not implied in them. Right or wrong was not the only question, or indeed the decisive one. What was feasible and advantageous, that was the point, and moral theory could not settle it. It could no more achieve a prudent political course or a good piece of lawmaking than an elaboration of the theory of building will make a man a good architect, for the general idea of a house had to be shaped in all manner of ways, and what served for one was no use for another; *artifex formam communem domus necesse est quod determinet ad hanc vel illam domus figuram.*[1] The medievals had no methods of mass-production except for such things as coins.

Pragmatism determined every case, for, as Aristotle taught, meanings were expressed in general terms, but actions and facts were particular instances. A scientist—we use the word in its Scholastic sense—was not as such an artist, nor even a prudent man. His function was not to intrude himself into his subject-matter and to let the evidence speak for itself, whereas prudence was responsible for what was done and art entered into its material and contributed to the result. In other words, the

---

[1] 1a–2ae. xcv, 2.

sort of detachment proper to the theoretical reason was not to be looked for in the practical reason.

The Natural Law itself was no less elastic than the human lives it measured; the history of human laws witnessed to the variations they have allowed. Yet schools of professionals may become too stereotyped in their methods—it has happened to painters, poets, literary critics, philosophers and football-teams. Politico-legists are no exception. When Aristotle criticized Phaleas of Chalcedon and Hippodamus of Miletus, both of them doctrinaire town-planners, he noticed that Nature itself was less rigid than the schemes imposed on her—easier to set bounds to property, he remarked, than to control the birth-rate.[1]

Not that he advocated that human legislation and political action should be modified according to every shift of circumstance, for, as he also pointed out, tinkering with the operation of a law was not like altering the technique of an art, since its authority to instil obedience came from habit formed by the passage of time. Consequently he deprecated changing laws too lightly.[2] All the same, if citizens would know where they stood and statesmen pursue fairly undeviating courses, it still remained true that positive legislation and acts of State policy were largely responses to present and future opportunity, not to a past doctrine. Though respectful of history and custom, they had in them an element of innovation.[3]

The corollary of this teaching, that to this extent the legislating and political organs of authority acted of their own right, met the growing lay sentiment of the late thirteenth century. The Roman Law itself, so admired for its geometrical elegance, had in fact been a political instrument, not least when Justinian modified its severity under the influence of Christianity. When mastered by the medievals it was not long before they too began to adapt it to the conditions of their period.

Law, then, was the art of framing and directing social life, *quaedam ars humanae vitae instituendae vel ordinandae.* Even *jus* itself came to signify the technical ability of discerning what was

---

[1] *Politics,* ii, 7, 8. 1269 a 11–24.

[2] *Politics,* ii, 8. 1269 a 13–24.

[3] 1a–2ae. xcvii, 1, 2.

right under the circumstances.[1] To determine the official
measures which protected the factors of social cohesion in the
developing life of the community was the work of lawyers. To
see they were supported by public opinion was the work of
statesmen. The relationship of the laws to religion entered
when they were being deliberated on—hence the importance of
the Lords Spiritual in Parliament—but to speak precisely of
Positive Laws as such, laws, that is, which did more than
reinforce a precept of morality, expediency was the ground on
which they were settled. They then became what has been in
fact enacted, what should be accepted, and what will be enforced. They bound in conscience, not because they were
logically implied in the moral law, but because they have been
prudentially added and willed by just authority. Only in that
sense were they 'irradiations' of the Eternal Law—a condition
of all lawfulness to medieval thinkers. The obligation was
bound up with the duty of living in agreement with one's
group and of obeying the *dictamen* of its legislative and political
head about what was *utile*.[2]

That an article of Positive Law was good because commanded had long been recognized. Both Aristotle and Cicero
had noted its difference from natural law on this count.[3]
What St Thomas brought out was that legislators were practical
contrivers, not scientists; they were *sicut architectores in artificiali-
bus*.[4] Hitherto law had not been classed as an art except in so
far as training for litigation had been included in rhetoric. Now
lawyers began to claim their independence. The freedom of
law from morals, however, was less that of a separate and
systematic body of ideas than of a collection of judgments about
particulars which no theory could comprehend. Law was free
in the sense that history was free, because its material escaped
definition and facts were intractable to generalization, not in
the sense that mathematics was free, because its own proper
theoretical object could be developed in isolation from everything else.

---

[1] 1a–2ae. civ, 4. 2a–2ae. lvii, 1, *ad* 1.
[2] 1a–2ae. xcii, 1. *V Ethics, lect.* 12.
[3] *Ethics*, v, 7. 1134 b 20.
[4] *VI Ethics, lect.* 7.

Law and politics accordingly were social arts which pre-served the continuity of tradition and at the same time adapted the life of the community to fresh conditions. Vain to expect them to build up a system of consistent propositions. The construction was haphazard. Like the English Common Law, they were worked up more by judges, practitioners and men of affairs than by academic teachers. The *sententialia justa* were not the enunciation of rules but the discernment of living meaning and its application to particular cases.[1] Civil laws and political institutions grew by experience and improvisation, rather than by logic and theorems. The English jury, for example, works on the antique prescription that twelve men must digest the evidence and be unanimous in their findings; that it was devised by a scientific legislator is inconceivable, so also that it could be tolerated by a tyrant.[2]

Some of the most successful civil growths have little to recom-mend them in pure theory; some, like flogging, may even have moral sentiment against them. Of course in a Christian com-munity a specifically Christian view will be taken of them. Moreover, both jurisprudence and political theory can also be taken as normative sciences, in which case they will have some-thing to say about what kind of relations should prevail in the State and the manner in which they should be conducted.

Theology pressed on medieval conduct and nobody, not even the Civilians, whether teachers or practitioners, imagined that positive law could enjoin a course of action repugnant to natural justice.[3] Rulers swore acceptance of treaties in church. The criterion of authority was right, not might. Laws were binding only when given a moral reference. This began to change from the thirteenth century onwards, though for a long time the laws were enacted against a background of religion and a theological doctrine was present in official action as a theory of perspective was present in landscape-painting. The reference to morality, however, gradually became more indirect in the case of human legislation and political action on matters about which the moral law was silent.

---

[1] *V Ethics, lect.* 12.
[2] P. Devlin. *The English Jury.* Hamlyn Lecture 1. *The Times,* 15 November 1956.
[3] 2a–2ae. lvii, 2, *ad* 2.

Hence law and politics could not be wholly interpreted by ethical principles; they were no more branches of moral science than military art was a branch of geography because its manoeuvres complied with topography. They were subaltern disciplines, and some of their character was quite their own, not borrowed from elsewhere. So much was granted, not freedom to do what they liked: for if they were not contained in moral science they were still to be regulated by its precepts. It was not until the fifteenth century that *raison d'état* emerged as an independent interest, and not until the sixteenth century that diplomacy became a specialized profession, the practices of which were difficult to reconcile with older standards of honour and decency, and not until much later was it held that ordinances could be legal and yet violate the principles of morality.[1]

Whereas early medieval law had been the declaration of custom, discovered perhaps by itinerant justices or settled by consultation with the magnates, and the purpose of legislation had been to expand and reinforce what had been implicitly present from of old, after the thirteenth century a sovereign body began slowly to emerge as the master, not the creature of law. New law was made, the force of which did not lie in its moral cogency or conformity with ancient usage, but in the fact and threat of enactment and enforcement. Hence law came to mean statute, and custom sank to an inferior condition; it almost possessed the force of law, but existed on sufferance according to the goodwill of the prince. An analogy may be found here with medieval land-law corresponding to the upper and lower social strata: bookright was the law administered in the Royal Courts, folkright the customs operative in the daily life of the rural population.[2]

St Thomas himself considered custom superior to statute because it regulated men's conduct by their own habits of mind, and there was less compulsion about it from outside authority. All the same even he quoted the *Digest*, that explanation cannot be offered for everything our betters lay down, and Aristotle too, that we ought to attend to the undemonstrated

---

[1] G. Mattingly. *Renaissance Diplomacy.* London, 1955.
[2] P. Vinogradoff. 'Customary Law.' *LMA*, p. 302.

statements and opinions of older and more experienced people
not less than to proofs.[1]

Any theory of State absolutism was quite strange to medieval
thought, though, in one sense, not altogether inconsistent with
one strain in Augustinism. For what public power can be pitted
against Leviathan? If political authority were not inherently
committed to true justice, as when it arose outside the Christian
scene, but formed by toughs ganging up for their own
immediate advantage, and, if it had the monopoly of worldly
power, could it not then dare anyone to declare its commands
illegal however much the private conscience condemned them
as vicious?[2] On the Thomist theory, however, that political
authority rose from the needs of human nature, it followed
that the natural justice with which it was charged, though not
necessarily subjected to ecclesiastical tests, could be subsumed
by Christian righteousness. Moreover, reason, not will, sounded
the first note of law; authority was made evident by an appeal
to the mind and not by the threat of force. It was a dictate of
governing reason.[3] Might must show its right: this was a
condition of its validity. Then also in the Middle Ages the
sheer power of the ruler, limited in any case by the primitive
mechanics of government and the strength of regional feeling,
was mitigated by the general preference for government by
custom as against government by edict, for tested and stable
institutions as against new fangled devices and innovations likely
to unsettle the people.[4]

All the same, new ideas were already beginning to ferment.
One of them concerned the power of the prince to make new
law, which the growth of a centralized bureaucracy made
more forceful. Another was his more formal augustness and
legal sovereignty. We have already noticed how St Thomas's
later writings seemed to enhance the prestige of existing
authority: the violent deaths in his own family during the
troubles that marked the end of the Hohenstaufen added
poignancy to his condemnation of rebellion. He required better

---

[1] 1a–2ae. xcvii, 3. 1a–2ae. xcv, 2, 2, *ad* 4. *Ethics*, vi, 11. 1143 b 11.

[2] J. N. Figgis. *The Political Aspect of St Augustine's City of God*, p. 64.
    C. H. McIlwain. *The Growth of Political Thought in the West*, pp. 155–60.

[3] 1a–2ae. xcii, 1.

[4] *de Regimine Judaeorum*, i.

warrant than the moralists of an earlier age for any attempt to disturb the civil order. He was less downright than John of Salisbury in defending tyrannicide, for he admitted a kind of law even in unjust rule. More to the point, however, was his admission that the offices of legislators and statesmen were exercised in a proper medium. A positive law was a moral imperative specifically by the fact that it has been laid down, not by its content. In this sense he was against the moralization of all legality. Now let us consider his more clearly marked opposition to the legalization of all morality.

2. *The Limits to Legalism*

Positive Law formed a code of injunctions and restraints additional to those of the moral law, and it was largely determined by the history, genius, national character and constitutional structure of the State.[1] If, as in the Middle Ages, it was not all-inclusive but restricted to bodily and temporal arrangements within the wider eternal and spiritual community served by religion, then only limited sovereignty could be claimed and in fact self-denying ordinances were implicit in legislation. Even the Church, as Innocent III acknowledged, did not judge of hidden matters—an impressive admission from so commanding a pontiff.

The Treatises in the *Summa Theologica* on Civil Law and on the Jewish Law, the only code examined in detail, were at pains to hedge-in the field of legality: St Thomas was certainly among those who hold that the science of human law is but part of social science. While he recognized the majesty of law, his attitude to the legislature was not unlike that of a Victorian property-holder to the police—they exist to safeguard the liberties of the subject and are answerable to the public. He was closer to the English constitutional principle, that the law allows what it does not specifically forbid, than to the opposite assumption of Imperial Rome, that a citizen might have to produce a law authorizing what he wanted to do, otherwise he might suffer from the *coercitio* of the magistrates.[2]

---

[1] *V Ethics, lect.* 2.

[2] A. V. Dicey. *Introduction to the Study of the Law of the Constitution.* 9th ed. p. 202. London, 1939.

E. G. Hardy. *Studies in Roman History*, p. 37. London, 1906.

Still, law did not solicit, but commanded and engendered an obligation to make a right actual. Hence it dealt with what is possible and keyed with non-legal and non-moral processes of life; the human response to it was a judgment of fact as well as of value. It bound in conscience to its performance, not merely to the penalty for its infringement, for though St Thomas was familiar with rules not binding under sin, since the Dominicans themselves lived under them, such ordinances lacked the scope and majesty of law, and he did not entertain the notion of a purely *penal law*.[1] This says, in effect, that you may obey or disobey on condition that you accept the sanction—take your chance but do not complain if you have to pay the price.

Though every matter of law was a matter of conscience, the converse was not true, for not every matter of conscience could be made a matter of law. Not all moral precepts were to be enforced, but those only directly affecting public order, *pertinentia ad bonam disciplinam*.[2] In other words, every crime might be a sin, but not every sin was a crime. It was not that the dynamism of law stopped short of virtue, but that those charged with its making and maintenance should not assume responsibility for what lay beyond being law-abiding.

Though the Canonists claimed jurisdiction over many extra-religious cases because sin was involved—clerical tribunals were later restricted to *crimen ecclesiasticum*, a crime touching religion—both they and the Civilians were beginning to perceive, if not always to practise, the economy proper to their disciplines and to confine themselves to breaches in the outward order which was their concern.[3] Like Queen Elizabeth later, they refused 'to make windows into men's souls'. The early texts, it is true, did not clearly discriminate between *crimen* and *peccatum*: this however was not without advantage, for the

---

[1] 1a–2ae. xciv, 4. xcv, 3. 2a–2ae. lxii, 3.

J. Tonneau. 'Les lois purement pénales et la morale de l'obligation.' *RSPT*. xxxvi, pp. 30–51. Paris, 1952.

[2] 1a–2ae. xcvi, 3.

[3] W. Ullmann. *Medieval Papalism*, p. 103.

S. Kuttner. *Kanonistische Schuldlehre von Gratian bis auf die Dekretalen Gregors IX*, pp. 2–22.

F. Russo. 'Pénitence et excommunication. Etude historique sur les rapports entre le théologie et le droit canonique dans le domaine pénitentiel du IXe au XIIIe siècle.' *Recherches des sciences religeuses*, xxxviii, pp. 257–79. Paris, 1947.

analysis of circumstances conducted by Penitentialists and
Casuists, and their insistence on the importance of intention
when assessing responsibility, provided models for the investigations of secular criminal lawyers.

The cause of civil and ecclesiastical liberty was advanced
when it was established that immorality as such was not
illegality, and, on the other hand, that some acts might be
frowned on without fault being imputed. A cleric who killed a
man in legitimate self-defence might incur a penalty, but no
blame. It meant, among other things, that the governing
officials of the organized community, whether of Church or
State, were halted before they could invade the individual
conscience. There God was the sole judge. The law's business
was with deeds and intents outwardly expressed, not with
thoughts and private motives. That at least was the theory,
and modern techniques of 'brain-washing' were not available to tempt rulers to do more. Of course, then as now,
there were fanatical improvers who would if they could have
exacted total conformity, in the name more often of a quasi-
religious doctrine than of good citizenship. The distinction
between fault and irregularity may later have induced a state
of mind to which laws were merely penal or to be discreetly
evaded on condition that you were ready to pay the price if
detected, but this has been outweighed by the advantage that
superiors have been prevented from laying intolerable moral
burdens on their subjects.

Doing your duty and enjoying yourself could coincide—St
Thomas was no puritan. He supposed no conflict between law
and liberty—the virtuous were never coerced, for they were the
free and lawful men, prompt to render the justice of obedience.[1]
Positive Laws as such did not contain explicitly moral values;
they were observed because put forward by legitimate authority
for the sake of community ease and agreement, and perhaps to
safeguard some social decencies. The proper response to them
in the normal course of things was provided by ordinary
legalist justice.

On occasion, however, justice had to go beyond the letter of
a law to its meaning and spirit; it was then called equity,

[1] 1a–2ae. xcvi, 5. 2a–2ae. civ, 1, 2, 5, 6.

epieikeia—epicheia in scholastic spelling.[1] Dutifulness and emancipation were not contrasted after the fashion of some canonico-moralists, as though rival virtues were at work, legalist justice standing strictly for the code, equity making exceptions. Rather they were different intensities within one and the same justice which began on set forms yet was already in sympathy with a fairness transcending them. All the same, as appeared in his comparison of Mosaic and Gospel Law, a tension was recognized between the legal pattern and the Christian project: legality was external, approximate, pragmatic, and, by implication, coercive: equity was spiritual, confident, categoric and impelled by charity.[2]

A positive law, which could take into account only what should happen in the majority of cases, attempted to be as constant and complete as may be, and its broad effect disregarded what was rare and exceptional.[3] Now *jus* itself, embodied in individual things, was modulated according to circumstances and could never be wholly explicated in general propositions. Aristotle's lesson had been well learnt, that the individual could not be reduced to scientific rule: *scientia non est de singulari*.[3] The moralists were well aware of this, and the lawyers supported their own distrust of abstract formulae with the maxim *omnis definitio in jure civili periculosa*.

Moreover, effective law operated through a judiciary. Not only had a multitude of contingent events to be grouped under a general heading by a legislature when it formulated what types of action were to be prescribed or forbidden, but these abstractions had to be brought to bear on special cases as they arose. The number of factors irreducible to theory was thereby increased. Unlike the philosophical reason which dwelt largely in the world of lucid meanings, the practical reason had to cope with acts to be done and things to be made, *operabilia* and *opera*, all of which were singular and escaped simplification, and some of which were paradoxical. You could not squeeze more

---

[1] 2a–2ae. cxx, 1. 1a–2ae. xcvi, 6. 2a–2ae. lx, 1, 4, 5.

[2] 1a–2ae. cvii, 1, 2, 4.

[3] 1a–2ae. xcvi, 1.

[3] 1a–2ae. xci, 3, *ad* 1, and *passim*.

rational evidence out of a subject than it will yield.[1] Hence the verdicts of human law could not aspire to the certitude proper to demonstrated conclusions, but must make do with practical or moral certitude, sometimes called *certitudo probabilis*. Judgment on mere suspicion was ruled out.[2] Modern usage makes a similar distinction, for a balance of probability is enough to decide a civil case whereas proof beyond reasonable doubt is required for a criminal case.

Laws and rules of policy were not like mechanisms the automatic application of which could dispense with human discernment, adjustment and tact. How impracticable was the canonical prohibition of money loans at interest when the economic structure of Europe changed after the Middle Ages— the question is at least arguable. A written code amounted to no more than a net of approximate rules, and though some of the cases that escaped its meshes might be met by unwritten and case law and by the *responsa prudentum*, the process of law could not work fairly unless inspired by a justice beyond legality. Modestinus was cited, to the effect that recourse to equity must be made when the mere application of the code would prove unjust; then the judge must put the better construction on doubtful cases.[3] Note that equity was not regarded as one department of justice, still less a subsidiary one at that: rather it was the virtue of supreme justice.[4] St Thomas sided with the 'Equity Wing' among the lawyers, the *Gosiani* or followers of Martinus Gosia, described by Hostiensis as a spiritual man for his period—the mid-twelfth century—who had a sense of the Divine Law and softened the rigour of the Civil Law.[5]

When he echoed the 'Police Theory', that secular laws operated to suppress crime rather than to promote virtue, it was in no mood of pessimism, as if the typical subject were the froward man or the potential criminal not the free and lawful person,

---

[1] 2a–2ae. lx, 3, *c*. & *ad* 1. 1a–2ae. xcvi, 1, *ad* 3.
   I Ethics, lect. 3, 11.

[2] 1a–2ae. xci, 3, *ad* 3. xcvi, 1, *ad* 2, 3. 2a–2ae. lx, 3, 4.

[3] 1a–2ae. xcvi, 4.

[4] 2a–2ae. lx, 4, 5, *ad* 2. cxx, 1, 2.

[5] *Lectura in Decretale Gregorii IX*, i, 43. Quoted by H. Kantorowicz, *Glossators*, p. 91.

but in order to show their inherent limitations.[1] The echo was faint, for even coercion was meant to bring its subjects to a better mind. Human laws worked within a pale smaller than the full domain of social virtue; they did not touch all the relations of justice of men among themselves, let alone those of the other virtues; they did not make men good but rather established the outward conditions in which a good life can be lived.[2] Hence the preliminary definition adopted at the beginning of his treatise in the *Summa Theologica*, that law was the rule and measure whereby a person was induced to or restrained from certain acts, *regula et mensura actuum secundum quam inducitur aliquis ad agendum vel ab agendo retrahitur*, better expressed its external character than the popular definition given by Alexander of Hales, that law is a holy sanction, commanding decency, forbidding the contrary, *sanctio sancta, jubens honesta, prohibens contraria*.[3] Bracton, more lawyerlike, substituted *justa* for *sancta*, and St Albert ascribed a similar definition to Cicero.

The curbing of over-legal zeal appeared also in the principle that an authority could legislate and pronounce sentence only where it was competent to judge. God alone searched the heart and the reins, he alone knew the secrets of hearts. We saw what was externally manifested, and our inferences from them to what has really gone on inside a man were often guesswork, and could never be infallible.[4] Our praise and blame were approximate. Consequently there was a great difference between divine and human law regarding the ability to assess the presence or absence of the three conditions of virtuous activity indicated by Aristotle, namely that it should be done knowingly, willingly, and in a right frame of mind.[5]

To assess the degrees of guilty knowledge in order to convict for a crime was difficult; all the same a human court could go sufficiently far in the case of statutory offences.[6] Perhaps we

---

[1] 1a–2ae. xci, 1–5. xcii, 1, 2. xciii, 1–4. xcv, 1, 2, 4, 6. xcvii, 1, 3. 2a–2ae. lvii, 1. lviii, 1, 2, 8, 11. lix, 1.

[2] 1a–2ae. xcii, 1.

[3] 1a–2ae. xc, 1. *Summa Theologiae*, III, xxvi, 4.

[4] 1a–2ae. xci, 4. *IV Sentences*, XVIII, ii, 2.

[5] *Ethics*, ii, 4. 1105 a 31. 1a–2ae. c, 9.

[6] J. Ll. Edwards. *Mens Rea in Statutory Offences*. London, 1956.

cannot improve on the McNaughton Rules. We can ask simply whether by ordinary standards a man knew what he was doing and whether he knew that it was wrong, without penetrating to the springs of human conduct. Torture and trial by ordeal were attempts to supply human defects of knowledge.[1] Yet it was a step forward in civilization when these strained attempts to get at the truth were superseded by the uninspired processes of rational inquiry, even though they lead to a middling sort of justice.

Moralists and psychologists are uneasy—and rightly according to their lights—about the workings of courts where attention is paid more to types of action and inherent purposes of action than to idiosyncracies of character and the peculiar circumstances of a crime. Nevertheless the acceptance of a norm, which carries with it a limitation, is a condition of the stability of law, and, on analysis, of the freedom of the subject.[2] For once the administration of justice is swayed by purely personal factors then it must judge on them, and where it may judge there it may go on to enforce. A code for common civil conduct might be replaced by a set of psychological case histories, and the legal profession, instead of keeping us in our appointed places within the community, will write our biographies. Canon Law can regulate the time when an obligation can be undertaken; it cannot determine when a subject begins to exercise the use of reason.[3] Similarly, Civil Law can ask what a reasonable man might be expected to do, not what an individual of nonnormal mentality could do under the circumstances.[4] Systems of Positive Law do not set up courts of morals or psychological boards, but confine themselves to certain rules of normal behaviour, departures from which are condemned according to formal procedures which are not allowed to stray outside the strictly juridical evidence.[5]

The element of will was even more difficult to decide. How far was any particular act free from compulsion? God knows.

---

[1] *Expositio in Job X, lect.* 1.
[2] 1a–2ae. xcvi, 1.
[3] *Contra Retrahentes,* 12.
[4] *See Regina v. Ward.* Court of Criminal Appeal. *The Times,* 12 Jan. 1956.
[5] 2a–2ae. lxvii, 2.

Here again a limitation must be accepted. Unlike Divine Law, which could judge the interior motions of the will, human law did not punish a man who has not carried into execution the murder harboured in his heart. As for virtuous dispositions, there it had nothing to say, for not even Divine Law punished as a transgressor of its precepts a man who did his duty to his parents without, however, possessing the virtue of piety towards them.[1] The penalties of human law fell on crime, not sin. And even there, as was inevitable if a pity all the same, a court was directly concerned with a criminal act, not with a habit of criminality. The law comes down more heavily on one unfortunate lapse than on the disposition never to be anything but a burden to the community: an honest man who has committed an act of murder will . . . may be tried and condemned, whereas a man habitually murderous in his heart may well escape the law.

Furthermore human laws were framed to fit men in a given system of reference, *in ordine ad tale regimen*.[2] What was to the public benefit, *utile communitati*, varied according to the type of constitution: a good monarchy man was not necessarily a good whig, nor a good whig a good democrat. Human law operated to make men good subjects, not necessarily good men—the two were not irreconcilable, and Aristotle, for instance, unlike the early Christians, would scarcely have envisaged a conflict between good citizenship and personal integrity.[3] We can imagine, too, St Thomas wanting to qualify Newman's contrast —of 'the beggar-woman, lazy, ragged, filthy, not over-scrupulous of truth, but if she is chaste, and sober and cheerful, and goes to her religious duties, she will, in the eyes of the Church, have a prospect of Heaven, quite closed and refused to the State's pattern-man'. But then his times were not so respectability-ridden.

The citizen of a State regulated by divine justice will be a virtuous man through obedience to the laws. Nevertheless, their immediate business was not his eternal salvation but to ensure public tranquillity and safety. Over and above this a good

---

[1] 1a-2ae. c, 9.
[2] 1a-2ae. xcii, 1. *III Politics, lect. 3. V Ethics, lect.* 2.
[3] 1a-2ae. xcii, 1, *ad* 2. *Politics*, iii, 2. 1277 a 20.

man had much else to supply. For the laws did not command all the virtues, nor was perfect virtue a legal obligation. Even though the legislator's motive might be to direct men to virtue, it was the law itself that was of precept, not its purpose, *finis praecepti non cadit sub lege*.[1] On the other hand, a moral duty did not constitute a legal right. The government's control was limited to public affairs; there it should be content with obedience, preferably good-humoured, and demand neither obsequiousness nor enthusiasm.

All supposed that the cause of law was the cause of freedom; few medievals laboured the fact that every positive law was a restriction of liberty. The Dark Ages and invasions of the North-men were near enough for men not to know that the law was their protection against barbarism; the revival of Hellenism confirmed their objections to capricious power. Yet legality was not elevated into an object of awe. It was respected, but as an instrument well under control, the purpose of which was *utilitas hominum, sicut etiam Jurisperitus dicit*.[2] It was limited to what was expedient for the political community, that is to the outward acts of certain virtues. The prince could make sure that justice was done, but not that it was done justly, for the mode of virtue lay outside the scope of positive law. Some plain needs made its operation irrelevant, since necessity knew no law: thus a starving man could help himself to food so long as he did no harm and acted without contempt of civil authority.[3]

Prepared to tolerate a lesser evil lest the alternative be worse, not impatient with common weaknesses, restrained in moral indignation, the ruler should accept human nature as it is, knowing that people's habits cannot suddenly be changed by legislation, no more than a spirit of co-operation and sharing can be induced by the nationalization of the means of production.[4] To take one instance. Usury was hateful to the medieval temper, as Dante's scorching words bear witness; it stood condemned by economics, the scriptures and the law— Canonists and Civilians agreed on this point. Moral philosophy

---

[1] *III Sentences XXXVII*,i ii, 2, *l. See* ii, 4. 1a–2ae. xcii, 2, *ad* 2. xcvi, 3.
[2] 1a–2ae. xcv, 3.
[3] 1a–2ae. xcvi, 6. xcv, 3, *ad* 2.
[4] 1a–2ae. xcvi, 2, *c.* & *ad* 2. ci. 3, *ad* 2. III *Contra Gentes*, 71. 2a–2ae. lxix, 2, *ad* 1.

14

went farther, and condemned interest on a money loan as such, not merely an exorbitant rate of interest. The Arab and Jewish casuists were no less disapproving. It was energetically denounced by Popes, and by General Councils from the Third Lateran (1179) to Vienne (1311). Nevertheless to destroy a practice to which clerics themselves and ecclesiastical institutions were committed proved impracticable. Churches, then as now, were built on loans. The most that could be done was to confine the activities of usurers, and even commands to this effect became muted when the growth of commerce and Capitalism changed conceptions about the function of money and the social doctrine of Christianity.[1]

Then also ordinances should be reserved to matters where sanctions could be effectively applied. No law should be passed which cannot be enforced, since no bill of rights could go beyond what the State could guarantee. The power to punish went with the power to make laws, *huiusmodi disciplina cogens metu est disciplina legum*[2] Men of goodwill were not intimidated, but criminals were kept from evildoing; in this sense 'the law is not made for the righteous man, but for the lawless and disobedient'.[3] The hope was, of course, that fear would lead to love. In the meantime right should be backed by might and the State should inspire healthy respect by ensuring that the consequences of crime were painful and inescapable.

St Thomas sought some correspondence between crime and punishment, yet, while he allowed for 'poetic justice' in the expression of corporate disapprobation, he did not admit a vengeful spirit in human law which demanded an eye for an eye and a tooth for a tooth. Naked vindication belonged to divine law alone where, but for the intervention of mercy, the penalty followed inevitably from the nature of the deed, and

---

[1] *In erno*, xvii.

2a–2ae. lxxviii, 1–4. Disputations, XIII *de Malo*, 4.

A. Bernard. 'La formation de la doctrine ecclésiastique sur l'usure.' *DTC*, fasc. cxliv–cxlv, 2316–36. Paris, 1948.

G. le Bras. 'La doctrine ecclésiastique de l'usure à l'époque classique (XIIe–XVe siècles)' *Ibid.* 2336–72.

H. du Passage. 'La doctrine à partir du XVIe siècle.' *Ibid.* 2372–90.

[2] 1a–2ae. cv, 4, *ad* 5. xcv, 1. xcvi, 5. *X Ethics, lect.* 14, 15. (1180 a).

[3] I Timothy, i, 9.

was not arbitrarily imposed.[1] Evil was chosen, evil will be found; God was not chosen, the sinner will lose him.

Human authority could pronounce no such tragic doom. The reasons for the penalties it inflicted were utilitarian. Unless they could be shown to be reformative or protective they could not be justified. Punishment was prospective, that is, it sought a future good effect, whether considered as a piece of surgery which amputates a corruptive member from the community, or as healthy medicine to rehabilitate the offender, or as a deterrent and warning to others. The idea of reformative punishment is of course a dangerous one, though it looks humanitarian: imprisonment for instance, originally preventive by segregation of the offender, turns into solitary confinement or special treatment under isolation so that the offender may come to a better mind. In the Ages of Faith the death-penalty itself was reformative, and a Christian prison-chaplain may say that it still is, since the wrongdoer has the opportunity to face God's judgment prepared.

The *Codex Juris Canonici* acknowledges that its laws look to the future, not the past, except to serve as a warning.[2] And so it is with all human codes, the punishment inflicted should not be retrospective. Its designation and execution should not be the making of gestures about what has happened, for then execration would be no worthier than the venting of spleen. The purpose of the penalty is to promote the observance of law; if it cannot hope to prevent a man from being a misery to himself, it can yet act to prevent him from being a danger to others. Thirteenth-century penology was moving away from retaliation and mass-effects. Innocent IV forbade corporate excommunication, and St Thomas attacked the idea of indiscriminate punishment. The parable of the cockle suffered to grow in the wheat was cited. The purport of excommunication was revised, and in part restricted to the outward order, the *consortium Ecclesiae militantis* where *jurisdictio in foro causarum* could operate.[3]

The more law there is the less it will be respected, and

---

[1] 2a–2ae. lxviii, 1. xcix, 4. lxi, 4. *V Ethics, lect.* 8. 1a–2ae. xxi, 3. xlvi, 7. xlv, 3.

For *vindicatio, severitas*, and *clementia* see 2a–2ae. cvii, clvii. Also 2a–2ae. lxvii, 4.
[2] Canon 10.
[3] 1a–2ae. lxxxvii, 7, 8. 2a–2ae. lxiv, 2. lxvii, 4. lxviii, i. cviii, 1, 3. xlvii, 1, 2. clix, 1, 2. 1a. xxi, 3, 4. *IV Sentences*, XVIII, ii, 3, *ii*. XIX, i, 1, *iii*.

therefore economy should be practised.[1] Otherwise occasions of sin will be multiplied. The impulse to make laws has to be checked by wider social considerations, historical, psychological, moral and theological. 'We cannot go on legislating for ever', Palmerston remarked to Goschen—one of those touches which endeared him to ordinary folk, who ruefully feel that more laws are passed than are repealed. The danger is the greater when laws are not so much the organic development of community-sentiments as the manifestations of the improving zeal of official planners—or of their desire to justify their existence. Art is more unregulated than nature. As the avarice for artificial wealth is more unbounded than natural lusts, since these are self-limiting, so arbitrary enactments are more likely than the commands of natural reason to go on piling up, particularly in the hands of technicians.[2] The more impressive the instrument the greater the threat of over-organization.

Government is like a machine which tends to take charge even of the governors, and to attack those very human values it was invented to serve. A living theology and liturgy can be clogged by legalism and rubrics. Devotion itself can be lost in elaboration. Civilization can be overdone. The Eighth Army fought better after it had burnt its paper. Regulations should be kept to the minimum consonant with good administration. Criminal law should be reserved for criminals. Already in the Middle Ages men lamented too great a growth of discipline; centuries later the process came to a head when the Civil Law, instead of promoting the dispensation of justice, became a technical system for the creation of costs, and government officials who would otherwise be under-employed used the State for the creation of jobs. Such search for occupation does not make for a happy and efficient political community.

Legal reforms are usually inspired from outside the legal system. Perhaps it is too much to expect the law to remedy the very conditions it sets up. All the same it can recognize its own bounds, as when a court, deeming it inexpedient to inflict

---

[1] 1a-2ae. xcvi, 2, *ad* 2.

[2] 1a-2ae. ii, 1, *ad* 3.

punishment not fixed by statute, allows an absolute discharge of a person found guilty of a crime. What is required above all is a sense of proportion which appreciates that the system is open to pre-legal and post-legal influences, or that human law should take human nature as it is and consult a superior moral order. From this may follow a lively sense of equity. Obedience will be no less prompt, but happier, when it is felt that there are limits to government and that the administration of law is humane and fraught with fair dealing. It was in this temper, common to the English Common Law and the *Summa Theologica*, that equity was enthroned as the highest justice.[1] Equity was a virtue all good citizens should share. It was not a special legal department, nor the power of dispensation, nor the ameliorative interpretation of burdensome laws allowed by juridical experts.[2]

The legal machine of Church and State had not reached such a size in the thirteenth century that St Thomas felt compelled to build up works of defensive engineering in the style of later moralists. There was some humour in their proceedings, for, like the old soldier who scrounges from the quartermaster's stores, they sought to mitigate the law by legal maxims, for instance, that a doubtful law does not oblige, that positive law does not oblige to grave detriment, that a trespass must be proved not assumed, and that some laws are merely penal and not binding in conscience.[3]

3. *Legality and Politics*

The State means different things to men at different times. Juridical and political doctrines vary with their historical, geographical, and religious backgrounds. The Nazis had their own ideas about the nature of law and the American and Rus-

---

[1] 2a–2ae. cxx, 2. See below pp. 300–12.
[2] 2a–2ae. cxx, 1. li, 4. lx, 1, 5. lxvii, 2. *V. Ethics, lect.* 16.
  T. Gilby. *Between Community and Society*, xx, 3. 'Equity'.
[3] Disputations, XVII *de Veritate*, 3. II *Quodlibets*, 7, 8. VIII, 13. IX, 5.
  1a–2ae. xcvi, 4, 6. 2a. 2ae. lxii, 3. lxxix, 2, *ad* 2. cxlvii, 4, *ad* 3.
    A van. Hove. *de Legibus Ecclesiasticis*. vi, 3. '*de epikeia et aequitate.*' pp. 274–304. Malines, 1930.
  T. Deman. 'Probabilisme.' *DTC* xiii, 2. 417–619. Paris, 1936.
  H. Davis. *Moral and Pastoral Theology*, i, pp. 80–115.

188 LEGALITY AND POLITICS

sian conceptions of politics are based on opposed theories about what human nature is or should be, whether these be clearly stated as reasoned convictions or vaguely held as inherited or injected prejudices.[1] With respect to social deportment, the forms it will take in the good citizen, 'the State's pattern-man' as Newman called him, are stamped on him by the laws and are configurated in miniature to the larger shape of his community. The same lines will not be drawn under competitive and planned economies.

Now the factors which go to make up the constitutional physique, temperament, and character of the State may be summarized under two headings. The first includes all manner of social forces, both pre-political and post-political; they range from the physical impulse to huddle to the desire for the highest spiritual intercourse. All these offer the living material presupposed to political science, which, said Aristotle, does not make men but takes them from nature.[2]

Under the second heading are ranged specifically political forces.[3] They are those directly and immediately concerned to produce and foster that state of social order which is called civilization, that is to say, a stable arrangement of rational beings so communicating in a common purpose that they agree on the rules they will keep and are prepared to back them. Much lay outside this 'polite conversation', much more in the Middle Ages than in classical Greece, when the *polis* was well nigh all-inclusive. St Thomas pictured the political order as a community within the larger communities of the race and the City of God; it rose from the first, aspired to the second, and was responsive to the conditions of both. Hence he had to call on two adjectives, *animal sociale et politicum*, in order to translate Aristotle's one, *zöon politikon*.[4]

A further narrowing of the term *politicum* should be noticed. Of course it was never given its modern party-sense, as when it is said, for instance, that the President of the United States 'is

[1] *II Politics, lect.* I.
[2] *Politics*, i, 10. 1258 a 21.
[3] *VI Ethics, lect.* 7; *I. lect.* 2.
[4] Occasionally he used the term, *animal civile*, also *animal domesticum et civile.* St Albert spoke of *animal conjugale et civile. Animal sociale* came from Seneca.

meant to be a national but strictly non-political figure'.[1]
Politics covered the whole business of civil government, and all
agreed that it must be founded on *jus* expressed in laws.[2] But
whereas the philosophers brought in terms of social psychology
and considered what was advantageous, the jurists treated the
subject in terms of positive law and considered what had been
enacted.[3] The distinction may appear in judgments on world
affairs, where a country may be a real aggressor even when no
infringement of International Law can be proved, while on the
other hand a country may offend the United Nations yet be
acting only in legitimate self-defence.

St Thomas was a philosopher rather than a jurist, nevertheless he could not but accept the legal cast to politics which
had been copied from Rome. He was faced with a social
organization in which juridical forms and institutions were
more dominant than they had been in Greece and more deeply
affected conduct. And so his social thought differed from Aristotle's not only because he allowed for a wider city, both earthly
and heavenly, enfolding the *polis*, but also because he read there
the influence of Positive Laws in shaping the constitution and
determining the virtuous pattern of life.

The political community was knit both by natural and
artificial bonds. Thus sedition, the sin which strikes at its unity,
was wrong because it was both anti-social and illegal.[4] For the
people were not any sort of gathering of the multitude, so St
Augustine echoed Cicero, but an association united for common welfare and in one consent of law.[5] *Utilitatis communione*
and *juris consensu*—the two phrases corresponded respectively
to the two sides of the commonwealth, the political *bonum
commune* and the more legal *res publica*, or, let us say, the country,
and the State. That the State was the government, in other
words that the constitution was identified with its ruling part,
is a proposition more likely to arise from a reading of Aristotle
than of St Thomas, for whom the action of the power in office

---

[1] *The Times*, 13 Sept. 1949.
[2] *III Politics*, lect. 7. *V Ethics*, lect. 8.
    L. Lachance. *Le concept de Droit selon Aristote et S. Thomas*. Montreal, 1933.
[3] *V Ethics*, lect. 12.
[4] 2a–2ae. xlii, 2.
[5] *de Civitate Dei*, ii, 21. xix. 21.

was limited by customary and constitutional law, and who had not to face the problem of political continuity beneath the alternations of tyranny, aristocracy and democracy.

Consequently apart from the Common Good taken in the widest sense—namely the universal good shared by all who live with God, a theological value which moralists expected to be upheld, or at least not to be attacked, whatever the system of government—two lesser and more local conceptions began to be distinguished. One was Greek in inspiration, the social health of the whole community translated as the *bonum commune* or *communis utilitas*; the other was more legal and Roman, the *res publica* or *unitas juris*. The Common Good was served by *justitia generalis*, the public order by *justitia legalis*—two terms which brought out different aspects of one and the same virtue serving the commonwealth.[1] It may be noted in passing that the State was interpreted to begin with as a partnership and afterwards as a legal corporation; the notion of community-service was older than that of legal due.

Thus three conceptions, theological, political and juridical, could be disengaged when the best form of constitution was discussed. So long as moral virtue was safeguarded the theologian was not disposed to be engaged with the ways and means of politics. To him they offered choices between morally permissibles. Should the State be monarchic, aristocratic, or democratic? These were questions of secondary importance. As a political philosopher St Thomas preferred, for the sake of the *communis utilitas*, a constitution which showed a balanced mixture of all three. The proportion should vary according to circumstances. The legal pattern of the State, however, was less fluid, for laws are bound to be more frozen than social and political purposes. Unlike articles of experimental science or of art, they could not be changed to match every variation in the situation, though judges should be responsive to the climate of public opinion in enforcing them. Revision of the laws, however, supposed judgments of equity and political good sense which referred to values outside the system of positive

[1] 2a–2ae. lviii, 5. See below Ch. VII, 3.
E. Barker. Introduction to Gierke's *Natural Law and the Theory of Society, 1500 to 1800*, pp. xxi–xxiii. Cambridge, 1934.

law. These three phases, the theological universal good, the political common good, and the juridical public good respectively correspond to the distinctions between the good man, the good citizen, and the good subject obedient to law.

One effect of the entrance of legal studies into social thought was to congeal political forms and purposes. As we have said, St Thomas was a philosopher rather than a jurist, and he scarcely discussed the legal foundation of sovereignty. Nevertheless a combination of the social teleology of Aristotle with the stylized order of the Roman Law can be discerned in his thought. He stood midway between the old and the new in the movement which was marked in civil government by the substitution of official edict for folk-custom, and in ecclesiastical government by the substitution of the elective chapter for the acclaim of clergy and people.[1] And, we may add, in the theology of the Fall by the transition from the notion of racial guilt to that of corporate delict. Twenty years after his death legality was seen to menace the *lex perfecta juxta vias philosophiae*, as Roger Bacon put it; he burst out with the reflection that there was more worth in a few chapters of Aristotle than in the entire *Corpus Juris*.[2] So also Giles of Rome, though a Canonist himself, called the legists *ydiote politice*.[3]

4. *Legal Supremacy*

Common speech, customs, and traditions all went to unify people who dwelt in the same territory; it was their home country to which they owe service.[4] There they were rooted. The fact constituted a fundamental right, and the mass deportations of modern times have done violence to natural morality. Geographical and political unity were not identical. The medieval theologians never subscribed to a principle of nationality such as would demand that by Natural Law all the people of the same race in the same area should belong to the same State—they might have criticized the border between the Five Counties and the rest of Ireland, but not because it was

---

[1] F. M. Powicke. *Stephen Langton*, p. 80. Oxford, 1928.
[2] *Compendium Studii Philosophiae*. ed. J. S. Brewer. pp. 420–2. London, 1859.
[3] *de Regimine Principum*, ii, 2.
[4] *II Politics*, lect. 1. *III. lect.* 2. 2a–2ae. ci, 1, 2, *ad* 3.

against a primary precept of morality.[1] Nor would they have
maintained that no restrictions could be put upon what a
State did with its own territory.

The essential factor of unity was an acknowledged ruler who
directed the entire community effectively and exercised its
power to defend itself even to the extremity of inflicting the
death penalty and waging war.[2] Otherwise, as Metternich said
of Italy, the country was but a geographical expression. The
supreme power was currently expressed in the making and
applying of laws. He was sovereign who pronounced law.[3]
What was the sovereign power?—the political complexion of
the State was determined by the reply to the question. In the
thirteenth century it was certainly not answered in terms which
suggested that any authority existed in this world free from all
restraints of morals, religion, custom and prescription.

Everybody agreed that government should serve the common
interest and not merely sectional advantage. That moral right
and duty being supposed, more specifically political inquiries
began into the origins and purposes of political institutions.[4]
Here, as we have noticed, St Thomas entered midway between
two conceptions—informal politico-cultural and codified
politico-legal—of the State. The first belonged to the immemorial tradition that a folk accommodated itself to changes
in environment of its own consent and from its own resources;
the ruler, a trustee and interpreter for the group, came to
decisions only after a *colloquium*, or talking things over with the
notabilities. The second rose from the revised ideal of the
Princeps in the light of the Roman Law. He could invent new
ordinances, and the State he governed was the multitude
formed into a juridical association by virtue of a deed called a
constitution.

If sovereignty meant absolute power and the State were
sovereign in that sense then it could not at the same time be
subject to law. So much was recognized. Hence the State was not
granted unlimited liberty of action against which there was no

---

[1] M. Sheehy. *Divided We Stand: A Study of Partition.* London, 1955.

[2] 2a–2ae. lxiv, 3.lxvii 1. xl, 1.

[3] 2a–2ae. l, 1, *ad* 3. lx, 6.

[4] Y. Simon. *Nature and Functions of Authority.* Milwaukee, 1940. *Philosophy of Democratic Government.* Chicago, 1951.

appeal. The deified Emperor of the Old Empire had long been eclipsed.[1] In the East the Empire was Christian, and the religious honours shown to the *Basileus* were not debased by Statolatry. In the West, despite its high pretences, the imperialist cause ineffectively wrestled with a loose unity of duchies, ecclesiastical principalities, and merchant-cities, which according to shifts of policy might support one claimant or another to the crown. The Christian ideal of Empire was a powerful force in the Middle Ages, but it cannot be identified with the historical Empire of the West which by the time of St Thomas was but one State among others with no higher effective rights than its neighbours. The office of Caesar was hawked about and eventually under Papal patronage became hereditary in the House of Habsburg, and it was round the rulers of other realms and republics, not round the person of the Emperor, that the idea of the State gathered strength.

While the power of commanding others had not perplexed the Greeks since *kurion* was a straightforward need which called for no apology, *dominatio* seemed to the early Latin Christian social writers to be flawed with sin. This theological prepossession, which, in theory at any rate, checked undue awe for earthly authority, was not shared by the Aristotelean schoolmen. They considered that ruling-power, which would have existed in a state of innocence, was rooted in inequalities not wholly caused by sin. Not all were equal in the eyes of God, for some were holier than others, and it was divine election which made the difference.[2] Nature, too, showed its favouritism; that men should be born with different aptitudes was part of the essential course of things.

Since their endowments were different there was no reason to suppose that they should strive to live at the same social level, quite the contrary, for their common life should display an hierarchical order. As Chrysippus drily said, some seats at the theatre are always better than others. It was desirable that all should be equal before its laws, for that ensured civic liberty and the maintenance of contracts—the notion of liberty was not unlike that of John Stuart Mill, a man might do anything that

---

[1] T. P. Parker. *Christianity and the State in the Light of History.* ch. ii–v.
[2] 1a. xx, 3.

did not restrict the freedom of others.[1] Slavery, they held, was a consequence of the Fall, and not to be countenanced, because repugnant to the human decencies and a bar to widespread political responsibility.[2] But the power of command was another question. No blame attached to its possession, and that all were not equally wise was not anybody's fault. Consequently those who prevail in understanding should wield authority.[3] It was their responsibility, and the theme, *sapientis est ordinare*, often recurred in St Thomas's writings; he belonged to an order which granted consultative and special electoral status to Masters in Theology.

The organ of government or the effective sovereign with large communities cannot consist in the assembly of the people. How was it constituted? We must return to the distinction between political morals and political legality in order to understand the situation as it appeared to the medieval Scholastics. The Greeks were not preoccupied with the legal titles to supreme power. The State was a *polis*, *civitas*; its responsible parts were *polites*, *cives*; its constitution a *politeia*, *politia*, out of which developed the *politeuma*, the *maxime principatus* or the supreme governing power. The constitution, the arrangement of magistracies in the political community, was in fact the government; it was everywhere the sovereign, and determined the State's identity.[4]

The problem, how this could persist beneath the fluctuations of parties and laws, was not discussed. It did not arise, any more than it does in the United Kingdom to-day, where continuity and conformity are ensured because of the monarchy, a permanent civil service and a judiciary independent of party-politics; it may be added that organic principles are largely uncodified and unwritten, and that reliance has to be placed on extra-legal assents and traditional loyalties.[5] But given a break with the past, as has happened elsewhere, then the strict

---

[1] *II Sentences* XLIV, i, 3, *ad* 1. 1a. xcii, 1. xciv, 4. III *Contra Gentes*. 81.

[2] 1a–2ae. xciv, 5. 1. 2. 2a–2ae. lvii, 4.

[3] *I Politics*, *lect*. 1. (i, 2. 1252 a 31).

[4] *III Politics*, *lect*. 2. (iii, 6. 1278 b 9). *III lect*. 6. Moerbeke, *dominans quidem ubique est politeuma civitatis*. St Thomas comments: *talis impositio ordinis est ipsa respublica*.

[5] J. W. Gough. *Fundamental Law in English Constitutional History*. Oxford, 1955.

legality of the office and exercise of acts of sovereignty will be more searchingly scrutinized. To take such examples as the unification of Italy, the formation of Yugoslavia and the partition of British India, once the changes of sovereignty were successfully effected then the legal principles governing them became matters of great moment.[1]

Aristotle was no more troubled about preserving the continuity of the State under changes of regime than were the citizens of medieval Italian cities, where opponents were banished or killed and the populace sided with the faction in power. It is true that he assumed that the magistrates would be of Hellenic race, but what he was attending to was the government considered less as a juridical form than as a power shared in by all. It was this which shaped the whole of social life and which settled what manner of man the citizen should be.[2] Ideas of political right and obligation according to a legal charter were of later dáte and came from the Roman lawyers, civil and canonical. The Greeks were content with the theory and informal practice of a common good secured by a working *politeuma*, though Aristotle, no legalist himself, opened the way for the lawyers when he affirmed that the deliberative body was the supreme organ in the State.[3] St Thomas, true to his habit of running Greek notions into Latin words, treated the *politeuma* as the *res publica*. Yet, as we shall see, he had little to say about the juridical foundations of supreme power.[4]

The Roman effort to justify legal dominion became in effect the search for the source of law. A special problem was encountered when law was conceived as the bond of political partnership, *civilis societatis vinculum*. St Augustine had taught that where there was no *jus* there was no *populus*, and if this were taken to mean that the authority of a people was caused by some sort of legal deed, not by some pre-legal principle, men might well ask, What legalized the original act of legislation? What made the first law lawful? Moreover, if this *vinculum juris* were supposed to arise originally from consent and to be sealed

---

[1] See D. P. O'Connell. *The Law of State Succession*. Cambridge, 1956.

[2] *III Politics, lect.* 6.

[3] *Politics*, iv, 14. 1299 a 2.

 J. W. Jones. *The Law and Legal Theory of the Greeks*. Oxford, 1956.

[4] *III Politics, lect.* 5.

by some kind of compact, and there emerged the figure of the *persona publica* who 'impersonated' the State and protected and promoted the *res publica*, then it might well be an urgent matter to challenge his legal warrant, especially when he took on the airs of an official proprietor.[1]

The inquiry was conducted less on a moral than on legal grounds. To an Aristotelean the State was an organic order which responded to men's social needs and limits them in pursuit of a common object. To a jurist it was a legal system founded on convention, entered into by the people. Few thought that the prince was directly appointed by God or that he was sacrosanct whatever he did. St Thomas's contribution was slight. He referred, somewhat vaguely, to the power of deposing a tyrant when the ability is present, *cum facultas adest*.[2]

This *facultas* was the problem. Was it a legal power? He raised the point in considering the extinct Jewish constitution, *qualiter debeat institui supremus princeps*, but only to disappoint us.[3] He was meeting the criticism that no provision was made for sovereign authority although detailed instructions were issued about subordinate offices, and that, consequently, the Mosaic system did not amount to a political constitution. He pointed out that the Jewish State was a theocracy where God reserved to himself the appointment of the legal head of the community. Then, as though aware that this language was over-juridical and anachronistic, he added that the power in question was charismatical rather than constitutional, since the chosen people needed saviours and deliverers on whom the spirit of the Lord descended, and their epic and prophetic vocation called for measures surpassing the rational forms of Graeco-Roman thought. The kingdoms of Israel and Juda held the interest of historical theology not because they were models of government but because they symbolized the Church married to the Lord; like Hosea's wanton wife, their courses were not those of law but of the drama of unfaithfulness yielding to the strategems of divine patience and mercy.

---

[1] *de Civitate Dei*, xix, 21. Cicero, *de Re Publica*, i, 26, 28, 32. ii, 43, 44.
   C. H. McIlwain. *The Growth of Political Thought in the West.* pp. 116–118.
[2] *II Sentences*. XLIV, ii, 2.
[3] 1a–2ae. cv, 1, *obj.* 1 & *resp.*

His predecessors and contemporaries were interested more in the legal functioning than in the legal origins of authority.[1] Things were taken as they were, without overmuch inquiry into their past. The main question concerned actual jurisdiction. The State was treated *in facto esse*, not *in fieri*. Existing institutions were accepted so long as they were not manifestly illegal or immoral. The theory of the origin of power scarcely strayed outside theology. All power was of God, and coercive power was a consequence of sin.[2] There was some talk of the hypothetical surrender which was supposed to have given Caesar his original sovereignty; the discussion was on surer historical ground when it moved to the consecration of the Holy Roman Emperor by the Church. The theory of a transference of power from the people and the fact of this blessing was extended to all independent princes. On occasion the legitimacy of particular rulers might be disputed or denied, nevertheless, the legality of sovereignty as such was not taken as a special question and threshed out. The persistence of feudal principles was partly the reason, for positive law was considered as the consequence not the cause of the community, from which it issued in the shape first of custom and afterwards of ordinances conformable to custom. Statutes were still tested by the stock of immemorial habits, and respected Natural Law and Christian teaching.

This may go to explain the indifference of the moralists to the State's particular constitution. Whether the government was controlled by one, or few or many, determined whether the laws were conceived monarchically, aristocratically or democratically; what was much more important, they held, was the effectiveness of laws for promoting the Common Good. The term *politia* was generally applied to all just constitutions, thus St Albert, *omnis politia est ad commune bonum et nulla ad privatum*.[3] St Thomas sometimes spoke of monarchy, aristocracy and democracy as three kinds of *politia*, and sometimes expressed his own preference and contrasted *principatus regalis* with *principatus politicus*, reserving the last for a mixed and balanced

---

[1] *III Politics*, cap. 4.
[2] A. J. Carlyle. *A History of Mediaeval Political Theory*, i, p. 11.
[3] *II Sentences* XLIV, i. 2.

constitution which combined unified rule and the service of an élite with popular participation in the business of government: then only were human relations truly 'polite' or 'civil'.[1]

Supreme dominion might be effectively possessed by one man, or a council, or a parliament or even theoretically by the assembly of the whole people. Even so the same question arose, What was the act investing the sovereign with the right to rule? The moralist's preliminary answer was bald. The right lay in a relationship to the common good, and this was a moral value to be evaluated by philosophy and theology, not by law.[2] It was true that Civil Law touched its outward conditions, namely the public security or *tranquillitas* of the present city, and this, unless it were a mere agreement of people to work together in concord, perhaps for wickedness, was a preparation for virtue, while virtue itself was a preparation for a vision and fruition of God.[3] Law to be law must fit in with this high purpose, or at least on the most pessimistic reading not impede the peace of the *Civitas Dei*, which St Augustine called a most orderly coherence and fruition of God and of one another.[4] No lesser order was the ideal of the Scholastics. Whatever the constitutional shape of the State, obedience could be morally commanded only when government on the whole was for the common good taken up into this highest good, and not merely for the interests of a section. Hence tyranny, self-seeking plutocracy, and mob-rule lacked the moral right to rule because of their defective teleology.

So much for the final cause or purpose of Law. Now for its efficient cause, producer, or *agens*. St Thomas instituted no historical investigation into the origins of legislative authority, but was led by a process of deduction to place it in the people. He was—if we may employ a term apart from its history— what may be called a liberal constitutionalist, who maintained the moral excellence of a régime where political prudence was widespread and as many citizens as possible assumed responsi-

---

[1] *III Politics, lect.* 5, 6. *I, lect.* 10. *Politia* was sometimes translated simply as *civitas*.

[2] 1a–2ae. xc, 3. xcvii, 3. 1a. cv, 1. 2a–2ae. lx, 6.

[3] 2a–2ae. clxxx, 2.

[4] *de Civitate Dei*, xix, 13.

bility for political decisions under a common law.[1] Not only should the government be directed to the common good, it should also in some manner proceed from the common will of the people, since, apart from the direct intervention of the divine will, no lesser and sectional competence was commensurate with such a wide purpose: the dialectic followed his usual method of determining *potentia* from *actus*, and ability from proper object.

If this were thought of as a kind of 'general will' it was neither interpreted as the corporate appetite of a group which constituted an entity over and above its members nor was it in theory committed to a majority vote—though in practice there might be no alternative means of ascertaining what it was.[2] It was the responsible resolve of free men enlightened by counsel and desiring the common good. In this sense the Scholastics, in accordance with custom and Roman Law, treated the people as the source of sovereignty.[3] While they skated lightly over any suggestion of a primitive bargain or social contract, whereby the people have given their services in exchange for the prince's protection, they spoke of, and more frequently implied, the need of popular consent and collaboration in the business of government. The thirteenth century appreciated that the magnates tended to represent only themselves. 'Then why not call in the lesser gentry and the burgesses? They are always used in local matters. Why not use them in national concerns? Bring them up to Westminster, two gentlemen from every shire, two tradesmen from every borough.'[4]

The *populus* no more meant the populace than a *civis* meant anybody in the community. If we see here the affirmation of what is now called popular sovereignty we should recall that it may have meant nothing more than the denial that the prince held power of his own right and as a personal possession. St Thomas was clear that the status of the people, considered as a political group and not merely as a mass, was not conceded by the prince; the reverse is true, the prince

---

[1] *I Politics, lect.* 1, 2.

[2] T. Gilby. *Between Community and Society*, pp. 114, 196, 249.

[3] 1a–2ae. xc, 3. 2a–2ae. lvii, 2.

[4] Winston S. Churchill. *A History of the English-Speaking People*. i, p. xv. London, 1956.

depended on the people. He adopted Aristotle's division between natural and conventional rights within the political order,
and supposed the existence of rights in the people antecedent to,
and immune from interference by, the legal organ of sovereignty. In addition he spoke of positive rights arising from
ordinary consent between persons within the political community and from public compact based on common agreement,
which were besides those ordained by the prince who was the
people's guardian and acted in their person.[1]

Et ejus personam gerit—here was the crux of the matter. All
agreed that public authority was originally vested in the
people, and most that it was not possessed by such a title as
inheritance, which sufficed for private ownership. It is remarkable how strongly the old classical republicanism lingered on,
and what advantage it was to the Papalists in their disputes with
the Imperialists, though Frederick II showed that both sides
could play at the game when to spite Gregory IX he flattered
the people and senate of Rome.

The phrases which refer to sovereign power, *condere legem vel
pertinet ad totam multitudinem vel pertinet ad personam publicam quae
totum multitudinis curam habet*, and again, *vel totum multitudinis vel
alicujus gerentis vicem*,[2] suggest that the prince's office was to
represent. However, a representative was not merely a delegate
and, unlike some Papalists, St Thomas did not argue that the
secular prince was merely the vicar of the people in the sense
that he was a mere channel of their voice, a stately demagogue
existing on sufferance. The concept of authority responsive to
some kind of general will lay deep in the Canonical Tradition,
and more than a hundred years later, during the attempts to
heal the Papal schism, those Canonists who supported the
Conciliar Theory were to contend that the Pope's right to rule
was conferred by the *congregatio fidelium* which could not irrevocably alienate its own authority.[3]

The Canonists generally had a keen sense of the rights of
an 'ordinary'. They were familiar with the concept of an office
which, although derivative, carried its own proper responsibili-

---

[1] 2a–2ae. lvii, 2.
[2] 1a–2ae. xc, 3. xcvii, 3. See 2a–2ae. lx, 6. 1a–2ae. cv, i. *II Sentences* XLIV, i, 3.
[3] B. Tierney. *Foundations of the Conciliar Theory*.

ties. Dominican philosophers, too, were at ease with that seeming contradiction in terms, a secondary principal cause. It entered into the relations of beneficial clerks to bishops, and of bishops to the Pope. Bulgarus had pointed out that each and every man cannot do what is permitted to his *universitas* or to him who holds the place of the *universitas*, that is the people. Some jurists held that supreme authority still resided in the people, others, perhaps the majority of the Civilians, that it had been irrevocably transferred to the *persona publica* who thereafter required no consent or confirmation for his authority. The doctrine of the Divine Right of Kings was foreshadowed by this doctrine that power had been alienated from the people and that the prince was secured by divine ordinance from any attack on his prerogatives.

St Thomas cannot be cited in support of this act of abdication. His immediately political test for legitimacy was the consent of the community. His followers shaded off into two schools, neither of which allowed the ruler to run out of control. On one side it was maintained that political authority primordially lodged in the people still remained there, and while for convenience it had been *translated* to the ruler, the form of government was, as we should say nowadays, democratic. On the other side it was maintained that Natural Law was silent about popular sovereignty, but that historically a government was *designated*, and henceforth, democratic or not, possessed authority so long as it enabled people to live decently together.[1]

His own political preference was for some sort of government by the people, at least when they act as *cives*, not *subditi*, free because conscious of themselves, or as Kant said, as authors of the laws they obey. Even so, he was silent about the political instrument or quasi-legal intervention which set up sovereignty. Was it really strange that he should never refer to the general teaching of the jurists that the people had conferred legislative authority on the prince, though he was well acquainted with their writings? Was it not in keeping with his concentration on philosophical politics rather than on legal politics? Because of his nonchalance about the legal fashions of his time he avoided

---

[1] L. Billot. *de Ecclesia Christi*, i, pp. 511–513. Rome, 1927.

the anachronism of transferring the attributes of Justinian's Prince to the medieval ruler, and the incongruity of tracing the political ancestry of the Orsini and Colonna factions and the Aventine rabble from the *Senatus Populusque Romanus*.

VII

CITIZENSHIP AND ECCENTRICITY

SHARING on one side, solitude on the other, both are human needs. A struggle goes on between the attraction of the group, in which the individual can be merged and find security, and the impulse to be separate and express personality. To be committed or free? It was a major question and not to be avoided when we leave academic ideas and consider St Thomas's response to the culture and ethos of his historical environment. It went with a profoundly religious unrest, for the Patristic Age had revealed the stresses between the institutional and pneumatological conceptions of the Christian fellowship, stresses which were complicated by rigorists on one side and trimmers on the other.[1] They grew stronger when Christianity set up a design for social living as well as throwing down a challenge to what this world stood for, and the Church advanced claims not only as a religious but also as an economic and political power of great importance.

Public service and private freedom began to manifest themselves in new ways during the thirteenth century when social life was assuming a more compact political form. Royal officials had a conception of office which was not that of feudal lords, and friars bore witness to the Kingdom of God in a manner strange and even scandalous to the monks. Yet as we shall see, despite the new ideals developed from Aristotle and the Roman Law, the old ideals of personal integrity remained strong and St Thomas recalled the loyalties and traditional observances of the twelfth century no less than he foretold the juridical institutions of the fourteenth.[2]

During his lifetime the settlement of natural rights and duties by personal arrangement between individuals was being superseded by the more impersonal action of the State.[3] The area of

---

[1] K. E. Kirk. *The Vision of God: The Christian Doctrine of the* Summum Bonum. London, 1931.
  R. A. Knox. *Enthusiasm.* Oxford, 1950.
[2] J. Maritain. *Man and the State.* Chicago, 1951.
[3] 2a–2ae. lviii, 8. *V Ethics, lect.* 3.

private contract was being invaded by public control. The figure of the Crown Prosecutor was entering Civil Law, and proceedings against a plaintiff could dispense with a defendant. No representation, no taxation; the principle was there in embryo, but consent to a tax did not mean that it was a free engagement, to which one man could agree and another refuse. Again, despite the preaching of the Waldenses, which reappeared with Wycliffe a century later, that the validity of status depended on righteousness, the distinction between person and office was made more clear-cut; divines and jurists alike recognized that dominion was founded on legal possession, not grace. Title mattered more than worth when justice was formalized. It was inevitable, and the effect was not without its social compensations of security. Men knew where they stood.

Partly due to Romanizing influences a written code weakened the archaic force of custom; partly due to political centralization the enactments displaced the less official agreements produced by the play of individuals and associations among themselves. The power of the ruler solidified. *Caesar lex viva*—he was no longer the guardian of custom and the avenger of violations of the common law, but the fount of justice and the chief of a State-machine of which the administrative officers became more important than the landowners. Bishops, too, were in a parallel case, and might wonder how they stood to the Roman Court. A similar opposition grew between the *Curia* and the bishops. The sovereign stood complete in his own right, almost as it were apart from the commonalty. His was a *potestas rotunda*, rounded off from all others.

The development of the interior organization of the State was partly repeating, though on a smaller scale, the history of the three centuries from Augustus to Diocletian. Despite many differences of property arrangement, there was a similar movement towards a money-economy and the officialdom of a salaried bureaucracy and away from local self-government, and some repetition, too, of the process whereby municipal councils lost their administrative functions and were changed into bodies responsible for the payment of taxes. Absorption was resisted, and with some success, by the powerful merchant-cities which were in a position to control supplies.

The political situation was paralleled in the University of Paris when an oath of obedience to the Rector was added to the oath to obey the liberties and honest customs of the Faculties.[1] A similar issue was raised later during the Conciliar disputes about the Pope's position as *caput Ecclesiae*. Gradually the functions of government evolved according to State-needs away from the principles of personal morality. Such at least was the tendency; not for centuries was the process complete, though then as now rulers might compensate themselves for private maladjustment by public aggression. Political amorality was neither defended nor legal unconcern with natural rights professed.

St Thomas was of the old persuasion that the sovereign will manifested by custom is more deep-seated than that manifested by new decree. On this account he disapproved of the making up of laws as the community goes along, as though law worked in the provisional manner of an empirical science and ever sought to improve itself from every chance occasion.[2] But since Positive Law derived from an act of quasi-autonomous human will, to that extent it was set apart from the unfoldings of moral precepts and immemorial custom and moved on its own proper course. The immunity of lawyers and politicians to checks from outside was to be pushed later to the extreme; in the thirteenth century, however, the claims of the moral law were still paramount, and they were supported by the spirit of feudalism, above all by the conviction that no man however exalted could shuffle off the responsibility for what he did.

The notion had not yet arisen of the State as a *persona* making its own demands which could sweep aside private decencies, or of a public justice which could overrule private justice between individuals. 'I'd sue the country,' said the American soldier surveying the ruins of Hiroshima, a statement his Japanese guide found incomprehensible. He spoke in the tradition of the Middle Ages. But this was weakening, for as the social and economic organization grew more complex so the personal touch counted for less: even the Cistercians, instead of directly farming their demesnes, changed to an economy of rents and

---

[1] H. Rashdall. *The Universities of Europe in the Middle Ages.* i, p. 329.
[2] 1a-2ae. xcvii, 2, 3, *c* & *ad* 2, 3.

leases, and our pious hopes are the only evidence that they proved kindlier landlords than other anonymous business concerns.

The fame and honour of the medieval ruler depended on a dignity and delicacy, an *honestas* and *verecundia* which to the Stoics were ingredients of virtue. The *Summa Theologica* restated these sentiments in the specialized terms of Aristotle's logical and moral science, and set them in the economy of grace.[1] *Prudentia militaris*, good soldiering, was transferred from art to the virtue of prudence, but in a subordinate capacity.[2] St Thomas was civilian-minded. Roman virtue and early medieval chivalry were grafted on the magnanimous man of the *Ethics*, and the composite type was lifted up by the law of the Gospel, which was a challenge addressed to the personal conscience.[3] In brief, the Christian prince and his servants were answerable to God as individual men. There was no evasion, and they could not cloak their disgrace under an impersonal and official justice or allege that they acted merely as instruments of State policy.

Another effect of centralization was to emphasize the strangeness of bodies of men—the medieval community was composed of groups rather than of individuals—which renounced property and its obligations and were not constrained by the observances of ordinary ways of life and sometimes not restrained in attacking them. Enthusiasm more readily ran to anarchism as the organization of Church and State became tighter and more uniform. By comparison with earlier times when discipline was more informal, some of the inspiration and easy confidence had gone out. Later religious revivals were not like the Great Alleluia of North Italy in 1233 when the friars were in their Pentecostal period; it was a time of peace and quiet, wrote Salimbene, of merriment and gladness, of praise and rejoicing. The legalism which by forcing a stilted style on moral theology was sometimes to cramp the life of the spirit, and by subjecting the citizen to a complicated code was to embarrass his freedom, had also the effect of making the community less tolerant of

---

[1] 2a–2ae. cxliv–cxlv. 1a–2ae. ii, 2, 5, 6.
[2] 2a–2ae. l, 4.
[3] 2a–2ae. lx, 4. cxxix, 2–4, cxxxii, 4. *IV Ethics, lect.* 10.

minorities. They were either absorbed or went eccentric and nonconformist, and so were persecuted. Movements previously humoured were now becoming outcast and disreputable.

The Abbot Joachim of Fiore, a respected figure of a century before, had allegorized the scriptures: the Old Testament of the Father prefigured the Gospel of the Son, and this prefigured the new Age of the Spirit. St Thomas spoke of him with gentle disparagement.[1] Yet soon the historical symbolism was turned into a social cause by men discontented with the rule of law. The apocalyptic stream was swollen by friars unable to reconcile evangelical poverty with a status in the official structure of the Church. The new era never dawned, and the zeal went to waste in the bitter troubles of the Spirituals and Fraticelli, described by Angelo de Clareno in his *Historia Septem Tribulationum Ordinis Minorum*.[2] Even the Dominicans, aloof from the extravagances of revivalism by their essentially clerical profession and rationalist temper, came under fire from the entrenched clergy, secular and monastic. Mistrusted as a para-ecclesiastical formation, a kind of private army, they were saved by establishing themselves in the universities and in the counsels of the Pontifical Court. The Franciscans followed their example and, under the generalship of St Bonaventure and with the support of Nicholas III, secured a similar position.

Official orthodoxy grew more formal, its discourse arid, its justice repressive. Underneath lurked a morbidness of which some symptoms were the whispering campaign which led to the suppression of the Templars and the mass-hysteria of the flagellants. Theology lost the grace of literature. The spirit of Arcady flourished only in the arts which sang a fresh awareness of natural beauty, transferred light to paint, and drew out the resources of the vernacular in novel and poem.[3] There were poets and singers among the Aquino family. The first sonnet ever composed came from Frederick II's Court. The Rinaldo d'Aquino, who was the author of the tender lament on the

---

[1] *Expositio in Secundam Decretalem. IV Sentences* XLIII, i, 3. 1a. xxxix, 5. 1a–2ae. cvi, 4.

P. Fournier. *Etudes sur Joachim de Flore et ses doctrines*. Paris, 1909.

[2] D. Douie. *The Nature and Effect of the Heresy of the Fraticelli*. Manchester, 1932.

[3] See K. Clark. *Landscape into Art*, i. 'The Landscape of Symbols.' pp. 1–15. London, 1949.

departure of a lover for the Crusades, *Giammai non mi conforto*, if not the elder brother who hired a courtesan to put St Thomas off the Dominicans, was a close kinsman.[1]

A defence of the lonely and lyrical virtues, truer to the heart than to the civic reason, was all the more important because its author was a cleric and a theologian committed to the cause that political association and authority were natural and rightful. Free from the endemic religious pessimism which set little store on social institutions, except as checks to sin, St Thomas brought out the dignity of law and the majesty of the sovereign without thereby dulling the play of personal freedom. He never explicitly considered the romantic love of the poets and so did not condemn it; he was aware, however, of a springing purpose in friendship which preceded and surpassed the reasonable order of law and social good manners.

1. *Justice within the Official Community*

Feudalism may be pictured pyramidally with the king at the apex. In practice the structure was loose. For if in England his power was maintained in royal courts, exercised through sheriffs and extended by royal writs, so that a crime anywhere was a breach of the king's peace, elsewhere the system was less tightly held together from the top. Power was so spread out that its application usually lay between an immediate superior and his subordinate within an arrangement of mutual relationships affecting protection and service. Political apparatus was rudimentary, communications were slow and difficult, and government departments, such as they were, lacked trained staffs with long traditions of service.

Hence the pressure of the whole acting through an effective organ of sovereignty was not easily concentrated against one part of the community. Feudal domains such as Normandy, Flanders, Anjou, Blois, Champagne and Burgundy 'in the eleventh and twelfth centuries played a similar part to that of the Greek city states in antiquity, or to that of the Italian municipalities in the Renaissance'.[2] Power could be controlled,

---

[1] F. Brittain. *The Medieval Latin and Romance Lyric to A.D.* 1300, pp. 200–202. Cambridge, 1951.

[2] C. Dawson. *Religion and the Rise of Western Culture.* p. 169. London, 1950.

for its instrument was not enormous, its effects not remote; it could be clearly attributed to its holder as a personal responsibility. It was not anonymous. An official was a trustee, and what was done could be brought home to the individual person. Christianity inculcated the lesson that rulers were answerable to God for their actions. Churchmen, who lacked neither the spirit to speak out nor the temporal means to enforce their disapproval, were not at all inclined to be onlookers when common morality was abused or the rights of religion impugned. St Hugh of Lincoln elbowed his way without ceremony into the circle of courtiers round Henry II.

No detailed theory of contract had yet emerged, and the essential condition of equality between the partners was not present in a feudal engagement. For all that, social life was covered by a network of personal associations freely accepted if not freely entered into, which supposed that trust would be honoured. There was little call for State-intervention. Most of what now falls under public service and is governed by public law was then an affair more of private law between master and man, performed in a system of personal rights and duties based on faithfulness and loyalty. A feudal suzerain was no imperator, nor was the ideal of the Christian prince that of the *Princeps* of the law-books. The transition from one to another appears when St Louis is compared with his grandson, Philip the Fair.[1] It was slow, for examples from the past continued to be evoked and admired well into the period of the humanism which perished at the Reformation; such men as Erasmus and More, writing later than Machiavelli, refused to allow rightful conflict between private and public morality, and More died for his conviction.

Aristotelean social philosophy and Roman jurisprudence were like marginal comments on the text of history written by economics and sociology. A State was being superimposed on the old feudal community. The king, once the war-leader of a tribe and still at the head when it had reached agricultural stability, wielded a power that devolved through many inter-

---

[1] H. Dupin. *Le Courtéoisie au moyen âge, d'après les textes du XIIe et du XIIIe siècles.* v, 'La loyauté et la fidelité.' Paris, 1931.

Jean de Joinville. *Le livre des saints paroles et des bon faits de nôtre saint roi Louis* (1309). Transl. and ed. R. Hague, *The Life of St Louis.* London, 1955.

mediaries and rarely was brought directly to bear. With the
expansion of trade, the growth of towns, the increased efficiency
of the machinery of government and the rise of a class from
which permanent officials could be recruited, the central
authority was able to take more on itself. Supported by the
middle-class of burgesses and merchants, it could find the money
to pay for the professional troops against which the feudal levies
could not stand. The proportion of direct royal vassals increased.
Before long the nobles were deprived of their private armies,
and the palatines became in effect anachronisms. The great
offices of State were filled, not by feudal magnates with a stake
in the land, but by officials who might be, like Henry III's
Poitevins, strangers to the country.

Already under Henry II, when the Judiciary and Exchequer
tightened the administrative and financial organization of the
English Realm, the beginning of the process could be seen.[1]
There however the influence of the Roman Law was limited
and indirect, and the supreme organ of the State never became
formidably formal until the reign of the Tudors. But elsewhere
the reception of the Roman Law hastened the process. The
Post-Glossators dwelt on the sovereign power of the Nation-
State, the *universitas superiorem non recognoscens*, more than on
other attributes, such as the unification of a people within a
determinate territory.[2] The claims of the political community
to self-sufficiency described by Aristotle were sharpened; its
power gradually closed in on itself and rejected any public
authority from outside its own organic structure. The ruler, the
dread sovereign and *persona publica* who gathered to himself the
might of the community, tended to become more and more
exempt from personal moral judgments in the exercise of his
official functions. When Charles I left Strafford to his fate he
was advised that his conscience as a king could be separated
from his conscience as a man.

Supreme power, moreover, was specialized in one organ;
indeed both in Church and State later polemics produced the
image of a head able to act without a body. The theory of some

---

[1] T. F. Tout. *Chapters in the Administrative History of Mediaeval England*. Manchester,
1920.

[2] G. de Lagarde. *Naissance de l'esprit laïque au déclin du moyen âge.* i. 9. *Le Droit
romain et la théorie de l'Etat.* pp. 144–165.

Papalists during and after the Conciliar Movement ran parallel to the Regalism of the civil lawyers; publicists on both sides prompted the ideals of autocephalous absolutism. I, declared Louis XIV, am the State, and Pius IX was supposed to be speaking in much the same sense when he remarked that he was Tradition. In effect sovereign authority was stylized, and, to speak only of the State, it assumed a special kind of activity which seemed different in kind from the pooled activity of all its members. It was a political engine created with purposes not precisely those of the men who drove it, purposes which might override their private wills.

Whether the constitution was monarchic—the typical form in the Middle Ages—or aristocratic or even democratic, the idea of the trustee-ruler was losing ground and it was easier for the government to run out of control. It was the law, it claimed, not merely the guardian of law. It performed functions which could not be resolved into the responses of honour and conscience. It acquired mannerisms which were not those of individual persons. It sucked policy-making into the recesses of government offices. Even now we have yet to relearn from Tocqueville's admiration for English ways that a strong government does not necessarily spell a highly centralized administration.

St Thomas played some part in this movement inasmuch as he treated all human law as public law, enacted by the legal sovereign for the common good; he also allowed political authority the freedom of acting like an artist. All the same he praised political discipline for its ability to control community-action. He insisted that a ruler was personally responsible when he applied the State's power; any wrong he did was aggravated by the exalted office entrusted to him by God, and if the harm exceeded his culpability, well that was the penalty of his dignity and he must take the consequences, like the captain whose ship has grounded through the navigator's error. He was the administrator of the commonwealth, not the owner. In short, the action of the whole on the part was a matter of particular and personal justice.[1] Nobody thought that human

---

[1] Commentary on the *Politics*, Prologue. *de Regimine Principum*, i, 12. 2a–2ae. lviii, 7 lxi, 1, 2.

power could be constituted apart from the decisions of human persons. Leviathan had not yet emerged.

Resistance in the past to any pretensions to impersonal and active power had been based on feudal usage. While it is true that popular liberties and representative democracy as we know them were unknown and that Magna Charta, for instance, protected the interests of the baronial class, the ideal of government responsible to the people was nothing novel. It was now reinforced by the draft of citizenship set forth in the *Ethics* and *Politics*, and taking on a new colour from the rising middle-class. The pattern-man was a figure in a rational programme, not in a heroic legend or moral story; the token of his dealings was the just price, not knightly honour. The new man's greed was less for spreading territorial possessions than for gold. Make a profit in this world, save your soul in the next, that was his sentiment.[1]

Chivalry was becoming a court luxury and literary cult; like Romance in the cinema, the glamour shed on it was a sign that it had been tamed. Henceforth when it came to resisting the Prince it is to a secular individualism we must look rather than to a gentility with its sword at the service of the Church and the poor. Great nobles might still fire the imagination, but the new magnates were the merchants together with the civil lawyers who served their interests: these were the men of power, if not of panache. At first the Crusades had been undertaken by straggling marches across the Balkans and Asia Minor, but later they were carried and supplied by sea-power and their course was decided more in the counting-houses of Genoa and Venice than in the castles of warrior-lords.

The civil lawyers entered into this rising lay and mercantile movement which was irked by canonical restrictions. Romanists were not welcomed at the Inns of Court, and it was not altogether because they stood for something alien. The competitive system of sixteenth-century Capitalism was to break the planned economy of the medieval clerics, and those governments not in alliance with the movement went down like the

---

[1] I. Origo. *The Merchant of Prato: Francesco di Marco Datini*. London, 1957.

J. Hagenauer. *Das justum pretium bei Thomas von Aquin*. Stuttgart, 1931.

For fraud, a special injustice in buying and selling, see 2a–2ae, lxxvi.

Cavaliers before the New Model Army. In England an aristocracy, marrying into trade and popular with the crown, defeated
the policies of the Bourbon courts, and Acton and others have
discerned some of their Grand Whiggery in St Thomas.

He mingled patrician and radical sentiments. His family was
governing-class, more notable as soldiers and administrators in
the royal and imperial than service for their feudal holdings: an
uncle was Viceregent for Frederick II in Jerusalem. Sensitive
to honour, he praised a delicacy and tenderness not found in
the philosophical ideal of the magnanimous man though his
references to women were lacking in gallantry. Money-changing
he found distasteful—*quamdam turpitudinem habet*—and like most
contemporaries he abhorred usury.[1] He admired the soldierly
virtues, and added to Aristotle's moral categories the special
virtue of military prudence.[2] His own Order was closely
associated with the Military Orders, not always without injury
to its own genius during the period of its collaboration with the
Teutonic Knights. Yet the Dominicans in East Prussia, as in
Wales and Ireland, if they came in with the conqueror were
soon identified with native interests: the English found Anian
of Nannau no tractable nominee as Bishop of St Asaph.[3] Most
of the Dominicans were also urban in outlook, and, on the
whole, his ethical and political philosophy may fairly be called
middle-class: the ideal type was not the fighting man or landed
paterfamilias, but the good citizen, the reasonable man in a
polity, the maker and keeper of contracts.

One effect of the growth of medieval town-life, an important
contribution to the history of law, was connected with the
development of the theory and practice of Contract.[4] The
transactions of the free associations, religious, academic,
professional and mercantile—examples of the *amicitia utilis*
described in the *Ethics*—were governed by private law.[5] The
Roman Law supplied the concepts of the *societas* or business
partnership, and the *universitas* or legal corporation. Gierke,

---

[1] 2a–2ae. lxxvii, 4. lxxviii, 1, 2, 3, 4.
[2] 2a–2ae. l, 4.
[3] R. Easterling. *Flints Historical Society Journal*, i, 1915. DNB under 'Schonau'.
[4] P. Vinogradoff. *Customary Law*. LMA. p. 311.
[5] *VIII Ethics, lect.* 3, 4, 13. *IX lect.* 6, 12. *Contra Impugnantes*, 3.

with his feeling for the State as an organism, regretted that the medieval lawyers did not keep the two distinct. The political theorists, who gathered many of their ideas from the Roman lawyers, when they came to deal with the origin of the State, 'borrowed the contract of partnership rather than the apparently far more appropriate act of incorporation.'[1] Consequently they were disposed to consider political union as a partnership of citizens arising from some sort of social contract.

Casting farther back than any pact, convention or covenant, St Thomas declared that the political community rose from the pre-contractual conditions of natural impulses. Nevertheless its actual constitution should be markedly contractual. For the *justum simpliciter*, the unqualified right observed by ordinary justice, was a matter lying between two distinct and equal parties. Consequently, like Aristotle and unlike Plato, he favoured a pluralist order for the State in which free associations were not merely agencies of supreme authority, and persons could deal with one another not merely under licence from the top.[2] For equality was not present between part and whole but only between part and part, and this partnership was dissolved when an individual 'belonged' or was 'incorporated'. He concluded accordingly that the *justum politicum simpliciter* demanded that citizens should stand on their own, free and equal under the law.[3]

2. *Private and Public*

The *Commentary on Job*, composed by St Thomas between 1261 and 1264, enlarged on the comfort of Eliphaz the Themanite; retribution was exacted for sins committed by men, not merely as private persons, but also as rulers, *peccata pertinentia ad principatum*.[4] Violence in obtaining power, capricious might in exercising it, failure to render subjects their due or to protect the weak against oppression, none of these would God's

[1] Maitland-Gierke, p. 89. Barker-Gierke, p. lvii.
   J. W. Gough. *The Social Contract: A Critical Study of its Development*. 2nd ed. Oxford, 1957.
[2] 2a–2ae. lvii, 4.
[3] *V Ethics*, lect. 11.
[4] *in Job expositio, xxii*, lect. 1.

judgment overlook at the Great Assize. The theologians were unanimous that princes were not exempt in the name of public necessity from the rules of justice obtaining between ordinary men, and on this charge would be judged before the divine tribunal. No use to say, How doth God know? can he judge through the dark cloud? for his justice, though patient, is not to be escaped.[1]

Responsibility could be more easily assigned when the community was politically amorphous, a *familia* governed by the private justice of *scientia oeconomica*, not a *civitas* governed by the public justice of *scientia politica*. The State had not yet developed its own legal personality, or a special morality which might cover the deeds of its officials. Now justice was the virtue of rendering others their due, and these 'others' were no other than living persons. The notion of service due to the group as such was not distinguished from the notion of duties to our neighbour. Taxation itself was paid as a kind of rent. But with the reception of Aristotle's political philosophy and of legal doctrines of incorporation, the *bonum commune* and *res publica* appeared to be more than the sum of the particular goods within the community. Public authority accordingly made claims which could not be broken down to the private rights of men among themselves. Between the *jus* of the *princeps* and the *jus* of the *dominus* or *paterfamilias* lay a difference of kind.

Previously the moralists were not exercised by the problem of reconciling two goods, namely the rights of the whole, personified in the *Princeps*, and the rights of its parts, existing in people. Social issues were tested by the plain question of right and wrong, and that was addressed to the individual mind and will. Responsibility lay there, and nowhere else. The notion that the civil community had an independent personality or a will over and above the wills of individuals, had never struck them; if it had they would have rejected it. It was not a natural body born of mass needs and embodying a group-instinct but a legal entity constituted by a convention of men among themselves under divine Providence, a tolerable compromise to check the effects of sin. The right of the organized community, both civil and ecclesiastical, to oversee private

---

[1] *Job*, xxii, 13.

transactions was admitted; sumptuary regulations were a case in point, also the office of the *fiscus*. Those institutions, however, which modern lawyers would class as part of public law were permeated by principles governing the relations of one person to another, and the forms of private law served most political functions. When John of Salisbury described the commonwealth as if it were a living creature, he was speaking in metaphors and not teaching that the State was really an organism with a life of its own.

On the other hand, the earthly group was no longer reproached for being gathered together in the power of the Prince of this World, since kingship was now consecrated by religion, although the suspicion still lingered that secular dominion was tainted at its source—as were ownership and sex—and its sacrifice was admired. Medieval denunciations of rulers centred on their abuse of power, for the practice of social morality was perhaps no better than then now. That was a difficulty, but not the problem expressed in Cavour's reflection: 'If we did for ourselves what we did for our country, what rascals we should be.' Nobody held that it was allowable for the group to act through its officers in a manner contrary to the ordinary laws of decency which all could recognize. Some, thinking of the history of John of England—though perhaps he was not so black as he was painted by Victorian histories—would not have disagreed with Mandeville's paradox that private vices could make for public benefits. High position, of course, laid a man open to special temptations, and his sins might be tolerated with indulgence—just as a court chaplain might condone his royal master's mistresses.

Machiavelli's observation, that those princes who have achieved great things have held good faith of little account, led him to reflect that while it may be beneficial to appear merciful, humane, religious and upright, it may be injurious to the State to act accordingly and not craftily. This was certainly contrary to the convictions of the thirteenth century. Everybody, however exalted, was judged by the same standard of virtue. Everybody was responsible for what he did, and nobody could shuffle off the onus on the plea of public necessity. The State had no other life than that of the men composing it; they had no other life than that lived according to justice. If the group were moved to injustice, then moral judgment was passed according to the rules governing *co-operatio ad malum* or co-operative injustice, and the participants condemned and bound to restitution according to their degree of fault.[1] Group-responsibility for wrong was broken up into its parts. The matter was handled in law as a criminal conspiracy, in which individuals combined to break the law and had implicated others.

This is not to assume that public injustice was in fact consistently checked, despite the steady intervention of the Church, or that whole towns were not razed and countrysides devastated by private ruffians or public tyrants, but merely that convictions were operative which later found expression in the Nuremberg Trials. Some deeds were abominable and admitted no excuse of an anonymous will or higher orders. When Innocent IV decided against mass-excommunication, which punished the innocent with the guilty, he seems to have regarded a people much as English law does a firm, namely as a collective name for the partners.[2] He was in agreement with the prevailing feeling, that responsibility should be brought home to particular persons. This could be done more readily when the individual was not swallowed in the community. That was before the State was credited with a movement of its own, to which ordinary men contributed as subjects rather than as partners, and superiors led a double life, as men and as rulers.

St Thomas lived when a political community in which sovereign rights were seen as the culmination of the personal rights of its members was becoming one where rights descended from the top to the bottom—the simplification may be allowed to stand in order to typify the transition. Occasionally he referred to law as an instrument of co-ordination, a contractual bond between citizens, yet in general his treatise conceived law rather as an instrument of subordination of individuals to the common welfare. His approach was in the spirit more of a social moralist than of a jurist, his interest was the *bonum commune* rather than the *res publica*, and the discussion hinged

---

[1] 2a–2ae. lxii, 7. *IV* Sentences, XV, i, 5, *iii*.
[2] Decretal, *Romana Ecclesia*, 21 April 1246. See *IV Sentences*, XVIII, ii, 3, *ii*.

rather on the Aristotelean notions of general justice towards the State and particular justice towards the individual than on the notions of public and private law.[1]

True, he allowed that *jus positivum* might be set up *per aliquod privatum condictum*, a contract between private persons, as well as *ex condicto publico*, when the whole people agreed that such shall be the law, or when the prince, who guards the people and acts in their person, so ordained.[2] The rights of free associations within the public constitution of the commonwealth were also entertained.[3] There was no clear separation of *public* and *private* and the two notions ran into one another. The first represented the community, the second the condition of a human person apart from his office in that community. 'If I may speak broadly,' said Vincent of Beauvais, 'private persons are those who are not constituted in some dignity.'[4]

Since all law was conceived as directed to the common good, how was it possible in theory to draw a hard and fast distinction between Public Law and Private Law? Although the welfare of the State might appear to be engaged more immediately in some cases than in others, was not the purpose of every law a public affair, as was shown by the State's readiness to enforce it? In practice, however, Public Law was restricted to those actions in which the *Princeps* was a party. This supposed that an ordinary person could be pitted, as it were, against the person who represented the power of the State. On analysis this came back to Private Law, for it revealed a situation in which one party within the community was conducting an action against another; it was not a relationship of part to whole.[5] Note with regard to Criminal Law that the wrongdoer who was a diseased and dangerous member, the *homo periculosus communitati et corruptivus ipsius propter aliquod peccatum*, was not reckoned a true part of the living body politic and could be treated accordingly.[6] At the same time his condemnation was

---

[1] *V Ethics, lect.* 2. *VIII, lect.* 10, 11.
  I Politics, lect. 1, 4. *III lect.* 6.
[2] 2a–2ae. lvii, 2.
[3] *Contra Impugnantes*, 3.
[4] *Speculum Doctrinale*, vii, 77.
[5] J. T. Delos. *La société et les principes du droit publique.* Paris, 1929.
[6] 2a–2ae. lxiv, 2, 6.

governed by personal morality, a judicial sentence being a matter of commutative justice, that is, lying between person and person.[1] Consequently any unjust penalty inflicted carried an obligation to make restitution.[2]

The Romans had investigated the notions of the *imperium* of the State and the *dominium* of the citizens, but their working practice allowed private rights little weight when they conflicted with State-interest. Matters were otherwise in the thirteenth century, when the State had not yet appeared with its own ponderous personality and all community-policies were subordinate to moral and religious values, of which the Church was the effective guardian. There was then no acceptance of State omnicompetence, no religious resignation or passive resistance; instead Christian men felt they had the duty of fighting tyrannical laws with all apt weapons at their disposal. The sovereign was the creature, not the creator of law.

The State, such as it was, possessed no paramount rights over every social interest. Nobody reckoned that it was inclusive with a *potestas plena atque rotunda*; nobody credited it with sovereignty in the modern sense of the word. It could be described as an association the rights of which were still private when set against the general and public background of Christendom. An analogy may be sought from the present condition of International Law, which still remains a system of Private Law inasmuch as nations deal together as if they were individuals, with the awkward thought that each of them will claim to do exactly as it pleases within the territory it controls, until such time as an effective supra-national court is set up to which individuals may appeal against their States.[3] Then International Law may achieve some of the dignity held by the virtual embodiment of some Natural Law principles in the public ordinances of Western Christendom during the Middle Ages.

3. *Individual and Social Justice*

Justice put a man in his due place in the universe and set him interacting properly with others. It looked outwardly to

[1] 2a–2ae. lxxx, 1, *ad* 1.
[2] 2a–2ae. lxii, 1, 2, 4, 7.
[3] H. Lauterpacht. *International Law and Human Rights*. London, 1950.

objective things and so was wider, as it were, than the virtues of fortitude or temperance which composed his individual emotions. The *Commentary on the Sentences* applied the term *general* to justice, first, because a certain measured fairness was an integral part of every virtue, hence righteousness itself was called *justitia*, and second, because all virtues were commanded by some law, human or divine, and therefore as *legal* were matters of justice.[1] The *Summa Theologica* gave more precise attention to the idea of general justice.[2] There justice was discussed according to its specific meaning as one of the four moral virtues—a virtue of the will rendering to others their due and keeping the balance between rights and duties. In classifying its types or species both sides were taken into account, namely the object claiming a service or invested with a right and the subject duly rendering it.

Consider first who had the right to receive justice in the broadest sense. That was either the community at large or a person—real or legal—within it. Immediately the distinction arose between *General Justice* which directly served the common good of the whole community, and *Particular Justice* which directly safeguarded the rights of an individual or an association of individuals. All moral virtue was political virtue in some manner since man was a social animal and all he was and did had an effect on his community, and therefore should be pervaded by duties towards it—duties perhaps less pressing in the medieval *universitas* than in the tighter Aristotelean *polis*. But in addition there were occasions when a man stood in a special relationship to the group, and owed it a determinate duty, for instance, of paying his taxes or doing his military service. These were covered by a special type of justice, called *General Justice* because it subordinated our deeds to the general welfare, and *Legal Justice* because such was the purpose of law.

Two notes were sounded here, of the Common Good and its legal form; their relations vary with the extremes of biological and juridical social theory. Which is emphasized will depend

---

[1] *III Sentences, XXXIII*, i, 1, iii, *ad* 3.

[2] 2a–2ae. lviii, 5, 6. lix, 1. *V Ethics, lect.* 1, 2, 3.
   1a–2ae. lv, 4, *ad* 4. c, 2 *ad* 2. cxiii, 1.
   H. M. Hering. *de Justitia Legali*. Fribourg, 1944.
   J. Newman. *Foundations of Justice*. Cork, 1954.

on whether the community is taken teleologically in a Greek temper as promising the ends and amenities of the good life or more statically in a Roman frame of mind as a *respublica* or State which establishes a system of rights: a similar oscillation appears in theological discussions about the structure of the Church. *Justitia legalis*, usually taken to stand for all community service, could be narrowed to the observance of the letter of the law and so came to signify legalistic justice as opposed to equity.[1]

Marking that justice was therefore an analogical term, we pass now from the object to the subject who rendered what is due, namely the individual person. St Thomas never paused on the idea that the community as such had a duty towards the individual: the obligation resided in its responsible ministers. What nowadays is called Social Justice was ascribed to persons, either to private citizens in their dealings with their group, or to public officers of State in dispensing the advantages arising from community life. The subject of such justice was a personal will, its object a personal right, not the welfare of the whole community, which was already the object of general justice.[2]

In other words it was a special and *particular justice* governing fair dealing with our fellows within the social order, but considered in themselves rather than as parts of the community. Unlike General Justice, it did not subordinate us to the whole, but co-ordinated us among ourselves.[3] The whole field of morality was not covered by this particular justice. It was a special and localized virtue, not engaged on every virtuous occasion. But it maintained a measure in external actions and things without which civilized life was impossible. A man who paid his debts grumpily could not be accused of injustice on this head, though he might be illiberal, unfriendly and mean; indeed there were many grave sins which broke no strict obligation in particular justice—among them despair, pride and secret hate.[4]

The first division of Particular Justice lay between *justitia commutativa*, a fair give-and-take in mutual exchanges between

---

[1] 2a–2ae. cxx, 2.
[2] 2a–2ae. lviii, 7.
[3] 2a–2ae. lviii, 8.
[4] 2a–2ae. cxiv, cxvii, cxviii, cxxxv.

persons, and *justitia distributiva*, a fair allotment of what could be dispensed from the credit of the community. Both directly served the interests of individual persons and were, therefore, kinds of particular justice; both were elicited by an individual will.[1] But whereas Commutative Justice was exercised in the engagements of real or legal persons among themselves, usually according to contractual obligations, Distributive Justice was administered by our public representatives in apportioning benefits and honours from the community surplus.

Both types of Particular Justice gave what was proportional to the recipient, but in different manners.[2] Commutative Justice proceeded according to fixed rule and arithmetical proportion; so much was promised and so much must be repaid, no more no less, irrespective of the condition of the parties. On this score a magnate must discharge his debts exactly like an ordinary man. It implied a relationship between equals, and any failure to render the *quid pro quo* incurred the obligation of restitution. Distributive Justice, on the other hand, was not egalitarian in this sense, but aristocratic, for it bestowed wealth, honours and jobs in alterable proportions according to merit, whether that was measured by initiative, ownership, or excellence of character.[3] Justice here meant dealing unequally with unequal men; it allowed, as we say nowadays, for differentials. It was open to the abuse called favouritism, *acceptio personarum*, against which remedies might exist, although in strict justice—though not perhaps in decency—the party with a grievance possessed no strict right to receive compensation.[4] Some wrong deeds, remember, are not specifically unjust.

The State was not merely the individual multiplied.[5] Nor were its functionaries merely people of more than ordinary importance. Hence Distributive Justice was not Commutative

---

[1] 2a–2ae. lxi, 1, *c* & *ad* 4.
[2] *Ethics*, v, 3, 4. 1131 a 10–1132 b 20. St Thomas, *lect*. 5, 6, 7.
[3] 2a–2ae. lxi, 2, 3.
    A. J. Faidherbe. *La justice distributive*. Paris, 1934.
    M. L. Martinez. 'Distributive Justice according to St Thomas.' *The Modern Schoolman*, xxiv, pp. 208–223. St Louis, 1947.
[4] 2a–2ae. lxiii, 1, 3, 4, *ad* 1.
[5] 2a–2ae. lviii, 7, *ad* 2.

Justice quantitatively increased, but a special kind of justice, more flexible and applied less evenly. What one person, real or legal, owed another according to commutative justice could be isolated, often in the light of a contract, without consulting wider considerations. The sentence and verdict on a breach of Commutative Justice could be passed without considerations of class: in this sense, all citizens of a polity were equal under the law. But given a heterogenous structure of the political community, grants were conferred not in equal measure but in proportions graduated to the merit or status of the recipient— a ship's company shares the prize money according to length of service and rank, the army officer wins the DSO, his runner the DCM.

Hence it may be suggested that whereas the claims of Commutative Justice should be pressed to the hilt, since literal observance of engagements is essential to civilized intercourse, the claims of a person in the community, or of a section in it, to special State-benefits according to Distributive Justice should safeguard the balance of the commonwealth and be tempered by opportunity. Let justice be done though the heavens fall; this is true of straightforward rights, not of favours. A Trades Union may bargain with private employers according to Commutative Justice, but when an industry is nationalized and preferential treatment is demanded by its workers—like the workers in the vineyard who came before the eleventh hour— then another kind of justice is brought into play. Note that Distributive Justice does not deal with the elementary decencies, such as a living-wage and tolerable conditions, but rather with rewards where fair shares have to be assigned according to a sliding-scale adjusted by the ruler of the commonwealth.

The three distinct types of justice—General, Commutative, Distributive—were not exclusive but complementary duties. General Justice and Distributive Justice governed the basic order beneath the particular exchanges regulated by Commutative Justice.[1] Let us consider them as they affected sovereign and official authority.

---

[1] P. D. Dognin. 'La justice distributive.' *RSPT*, xxxix, pp. 18–37. Paris, 1949.
   P. O'Donoghue. 'The Scope of Distributive Justice.' *Irish Theological Quarterly* xxii, pp. 291–317. Dublin, 1954.

General Justice was at its highest pitch in the *persona publica* who was the guardian of the whole community: *est in principe principaliter et quasi architectonice.*[1] For rulers were expected to act for the commonweal, more so than subjects were. Self-seeking perverted democracy into mob-rule, aristocracy into oligarchy, monarchy into tyranny.[2] To the sovereign power belonged the making of law; it was *legis positiva* and regulated the common exchanges within the political community.[3] To it belonged the exercise of equity when judgment must transcend the code in the name of general justice.[4] Also the reaching of decisions from the highest political prudence, *prudentia regnativa.*[5]

Now this official power was not pictured as acting in an impersonal situation which allowed for no play of character. Particular justice was involved on both sides, of the giver and of the receiver of orders. The *praeses* could not divest himself of personal responsibility when discharging his public functions.[6] The people have recourse to a judge, said St Albert, as to the *jus animatum.*[7] The business of the judiciary, which applied law in the courts, was to see that particular justice was done, and commutative justice at that.[8] Were unjust damage inflicted or rights denied then an obligation of making restitution might be incurred.[9] The living law, the *jus dicens* and *interpres justitiae* was found in human agents who must act according to their conscience, although their acts have an essentially official and public character, notably in sentencing to punishment; judges, counsel, jury and witnesses, all have to answer for their share in the verdict and sentence.[10]

One embarrassment was that judicial procedure had to be conducted according to the evidence submitted in court since a case was not to be settled by private certitudes. The English

---

[1] 2a-2ae. lviii, 6.

[2] *Politics*, iii, 7. 1279 b 5. *de Regimine Principum*, i, 3. *VIII Ethics, lect.* 10. 1a-2ae. cv, 1.

[3] 2a-2ae. lxxx, 1, *ad* 4. lviii, 5.

[4] 2a-2ae. lxxx, 1, *ad* 5.

[5] 2a-2ae. l. 1.

[6] 2a-2ae. lxi, 1, *ad* 3.

[7] Commentary, *I Politics, cap.* 14.

[8] 2a-2ae. lxvii, *Prologue.*

[9] 2a-2ae. lxii, 1, 2, 6, 7.

[10] 2a-2ae. lx, 1. lxvii, 3. lxxx, i, *ad* 1. lxvii, lxviii, lxx, lxxi.

Common Law and the *Summa Theologica* here agreed; a judge was an umpire, not an inquisitor, not even a benign one. He must avoid the *judicium temerarium* of his secret heart, and confine himself to what was set forth before him, though perhaps its course might run counter to his own unofficial conviction.[1] Even so, the very purpose of this teaching was to protect the private rights of individuals by maintaining a stable system of law. Justice should not only be done, but shown to be done according to manifest outward form not secret information. The judiciary was not the instrument of the executive acting *ad hoc*, at its best to protect every delicate individual cause, at its worst to push government advantage; its duty was to uphold the laws of the country. Hard cases, it is said, make bad law; hence remedy for grievance arising must be sought by appealing to a higher court of equity or to the prerogative of mercy.

The prince and his servants were required to observe particular justice with respect to the individual rights of citizens. Unjust extortion amounted to plain theft; the sovereign must punish the officials responsible and compel them to make restitution, and could not himself profit from their malpractices with an easy conscience.[2] Their public standing did not destroy their liability as ordinary persons, and they might be summoned by common law. It may be noted that modern codes of military law, not least in Germany, have come round to the principle that subordinates are not to obey 'criminal orders'.

An unresolved problem remained none the less. Perhaps State needs could override individual rights, not because these were not recognized, as in totalitarian theory, but because there were occasions, perhaps rare, when between the whole and a part the conflict was between two goods? A case in point was a condemnation which was just according to the show of legal evidence though actually the accused was innocent. Here there was a clash of principle, on one side that law should follow constant rules, on the other that nobody should be punished except for guilt. That was an extreme instance, but there were many other rubs. They seemed inevitable since no political community could mirror the complete rights of all its

---

[1] 2a–2ae. lxvii, 2. lx, 2, *ad* 1.

[2] *Regimine Judaeorum*, vii. 22ae. lxi, 1, *ad* 5.

persons or reproduce within itself all the justice of personal relationships—that was reserved for the perfect society of the Kingdom of God.[1] Not even within the Church itself was the tension between the *congregatio fidelium* and the juridical institute perfectly resolved.

The State had its own proper character and could not be treated, except by rhetoric, as the human individual or family writ large.[2] Nor could its public acts be stripped down to the elements of personal acts or be completely judged by the standards which suffice for the intercourse of men among themselves. Inasmuch as the State's dealing was for and from the whole and not between equal parties its justice was said to be metaphorical.[3] The most that could be hoped was that official depersonalization was kept to the minimum required by any complicated community. As far as possible personal responsibility should be always brought home, for if ordinary people sometimes had to suffer for the advantages of belonging to a State why should its dignitaries be immune? No excuse of superior orders nor of official capacity should be accepted for a breach of common morality.

Correspondingly the non-ruling parts of the political community should demonstrate by their bearing that mere civic obedience was not enough for virtue. Good citizenship itself was not merely being a good subject who carried out the commands of the executive. Social life demanded more than keeping on the right side of the law, and personal honour demanded more still: non-criminality was but an accommodation to an external measure. Were public injustice flagrant then it might be dealt with, but the underlying problem remained, inherent in the very nature of human group-life. The official action of the State was sometimes bound to be clumsy with personal values. Then the good of the actually working community was at variance with the immediate good of the individual, and the power of the whole might even be mounted against the right of a part. How St Thomas appreciated the

---

[1] 1a–2ae. xcvi, 1. 2a–2ae. lviii, 2.

[2] *I Politics, lect.* 1, 5.

[3] *Ethics*, v, 11. 1138 b 5. St Thomas, *lect.* 17. 2a–2ae. lviii, 2.

problem will appear from his teaching of the Common Good
and the Corporate Personality of the State.[1]

4. *Politics and Morals*

Early in the *Ethics* Aristotle argued that moral character built
up from within was proof against misfortune from without.[2] So
also the conditions of political morality were regarded as
within our power to bring about: national honour could ride
misfortune. Whatever the reason was able to control was an
affair for moral virtue, and men were not at the mercy of the
instruments they contrived and were held responsible for the
effects of their operation.[3] No individual person should be
caught up and carried away helplessly by the flood of governmental power.

St Thomas held no brief for the State being allowed to run
out of hand. He agreed with Aristotle that politics was a
practical science, because its objects were practicable; he would
have agreed with Marx that it was a method not only of
interpreting social conditions but also of changing them.
Political prudence was part of prudence—the charioteer of the
other virtues—which commands means to good ends. To that
extent it was a category of morality: good morals meant human
activity keyed to true happiness, discovered by experiment,
reflection and inference, not by an unearthly intuition of right for
right's sake.[4] Right and wrong in human acts, he said, should
be discussed in the same temper as good and bad in things.[5]

Moral science was divided into three departments: the first
dealt with personal conduct, the second with the management
of a household, the third with the government of the city or
realm. Correspondingly three types of prudence were enumerated: personal prudence, *prudentia simpliciter dicta* sometimes
called *prudentia monastica*, domestic prudence, *prudentia oeconomica*,
and political prudence, *prudentia politica*. The last was like

---

[1] See below pp. 237–262.
[2] *Ethics*, i, 11. 1100 a 10–1101 a 21. St Thomas, *lect.* 15, 16.
[3] 2a–2ae. lviii, 8. *I Politics*, *lect.* 1.
[4] 1a–2ae. i, 3, 7. ii, 7, 8. iii, 3, 4, 5. xviii, 2, 4, 6, 7.
  A. Mansion. 'L'eudémonisme aristotélicien et la morale thomiste.' *Xenia
  Thomistica*, i, pp. 435–41. Rome, 1925.
[5] 1a–2ae. xviii, 1.

General or Legal Justice in that it dealt directly with the common welfare.[1]

The complete subordination of political morals to personal morals was not thereby argued, such as would require a Chancellor of the Exchequer to conduct the nation's financial policy according to the rules governing private business and to declare in advance his intentions regarding taxation or currency valuation. Nevertheless, the plea of office was not taken to excuse a man from breaches of the code of personal morality in civic affairs—if it is doubtful whether the sort of moral indignation could have been roused in the Middle Ages which brought down Dilke and Parnell, there was quick sensitiveness to official contempt for law and custom. State action never became so impersonal that nobody was held responsible. Medieval sentiment would have agreed with President Wilson's demand that corporations should deal with one another after the fashion expected of individual men among themselves. Even International Law, it seems, must be treated as a species of private law until a supra-national tribunal is constituted to sit on State rights and limit sovereignty.[2]

The problem does not concern purely political decisions, that is, when principles of decency are not engaged, for these are not regarded as ethical judgments at all. When a man states that he is against proportional representation he does not expect his words to carry the same force as when he states that he is against compulsory euthanasia. The problem arises when political action involves right and wrong, and especially when it involves right and wrong, and especially when it involves a conflict of rights between the just claims of the State and those of the individual. How then to relate personal and group morality and preserve honour while providing for the needs of the community? Where are the rights when the police prevent parents making a private deal and paying the ransom to the kidnappers of their child?

The question was more embarrassing for the Aristoteleans than for those Augustinists who, after all, expected the secular

---

[1] L. E. Palacios. *La prudencia politica*. Madrid, 1946.

[2] J. T. Delos. 'La sociologie de saint Thomas et le fondement du droit international.' *Angelicum*. xxii, pp. 3–16. Rome, 1945.

State to betray a certain injustice. After all, since its authority
did not derive from true religion, some injustices were inevitable
and to be tolerated by a Christian so far as he could without
compromising himself. It was as if provisional accommodations
were made to its power, not profoundly moral assents. To
Aristoteleans, however, it was natural and just. They also
admitted that State-action was not entirely reducible to the
acts of individual men. Hence political science was different
from the science of personal morality, because its activity was
not the activity of one man or many men but of the group
they composed. The same discipline, St Thomas remarked, did
not consider the behaviour of parts when they were together if
the whole they made up was not a substantial unity but an
arrangement of separate things.[1]

Thus a distinction was allowed between individual psychology and group psychology, as there was between the
personal reminiscences of a soldier and the military science
which studied the campaign of his army. Thus also, the
distinction between the single good of a person and the common
good of his group was not merely of degree but also of kind;
non secundum multum et paucum sed secundum formalem differentiam.[2]
Consequently a State was not to be reckoned just like many
people multiplied a thousandfold; its claims and duties were
extensions neither of individual moral imperatives nor of private
law. This is indicated by special qualities of the public criminal
law which are unlike those of private arrangements: for instance,
its habits of not reversing a process or compounding a felony.

Aristotle taught that man's highest powers were brought out
by life in the political community, and that politics was the
most comprehensive part of morals. In his rôle of commentator
St Thomas did not disagree that all social relations were
conducted within the State: *omnes communicationes continentur sub
politica.*[3] He added the proviso, however, that the supremacy
was not absolute but relative to the other practical disciplines
which served the civilized life, for above political ends rose the
higher and ampler ends considered by theology.[4] No Dominican

---

[1] *I Ethics, lect.* 1.
[2] *I Ethics, lect.* 2. 1a. lviii, 7, *ad* 2. 1a–2ae. xc, 2. 2a–2ae. lviii, 7, *ad* 2.
[3] *VIII Ethics, lect.* 9.
[4] *I Ethics, lect.* 2.

was likely to forget the need of theory behind practice. That contemplation fed action was the principle of his life—as Hugh of St Cher said, 'The bow is bent in study, the arrow let fly in preaching.' Aristotle also, it should be remembered, had been convinced of the supremacy of the contemplative life over the active life, that is, life as lived in the State, and was understood to suggest that the highest contemplation in which our true happiness lay was out of this world altogether.[1]

Certainly the political order manifested a true value not inherently compromised by sin and was, within limits, an end in itself, *bonum honestum*, not merely a means to something else, *bonum utile*; so much so that serving it was to the social philosopher the noblest and most important of human activities.[2] Still it was only one city or realm within the wider and more ultimate order of the City of God; the common good it proposed was more confined than the universal good which was man's whole happiness and was confined to a temporal tranquillity, a *pax civitatis*.[3]

Furthermore, this social security which was the prime purpose of government was itself only a postulate and no more to be questioned by political science than health by medical science.[4] Was it worth having? How and where might it be found? What were its conditions? These were questions for other sciences, anthopological, psychological, moral and theological, which entered more deeply into the nature of man and things. Some of these had to be opened out before political inquiry could profitably begin.

Hence the medieval writers treated politics as a subordinate study and properly to be approached with prepossessions. The same was true of moral science itself, for happiness explained right conduct, not right conduct happiness. As moral science, having accepted the notion of human happiness from elsewhere, mainly from philosophical psychology and theology, then proceeded to discuss the kinds of action conducive to it, allow-

---

[1] 1a–2ae. iii, 5, 6, 7, 8.
[2] 1a. xcvi, 4. *X Ethics, lect.* 11. *de Regimine Principum*, i, 12. 1a–2ae. lxvi, 4. 2a–2ae. l, 2, *ad* 2. lviii, 12.
[3] 1a–2ae. lxxii, 4. 1a–2ae. xcvii, 1, *ad* 3. xcvi, 6, ad 2. xcvii, 1. xcv, 1.
[4] *de Regimine Principum*, i, 2.

ances being made for circumstances and motives, and as psychology in its turn consulted physiology, and as economics itself did not produce the goods whose disposal it arranged, so politics assumed, but did not prove, that the civilized order was a true and practicable value, and then set out to explore and supply the means to it.[1]

In other words political discipline did not work in a vacuum. In order to keep its rightful character and to be successful, anyhow as a long-term affair, it must appreciate what human nature is in the individual and in the group, how men will react to a given set of social circumstances, and, ultimately, what they want from life and what they are for. And if then the reading of human nature is cynical and conjectures about its destiny are pessimistic, is not that better than the inconsequential opportunism of pure politics?

Hitler was not the only one who has shown what disastrous policies issue from bad philosophy and theology: false theological beliefs, and not merely insults to established worship, were crimes against the social order, according to Plato's *Laws*, and therefore to be repressed. Not that good philosophy and theology offer any guarantee of good government —otherwise the Papal States might well have been a model realm. The art of government is for experts and politics form a special discipline, distinct in that they have their own proper medium, but not self-sufficient because they should respond to the conditions set by wider interests.

The point is not merely of academic interest, for it marks the difference between those who recognize inalienable human rights and social values antecedent to legal or political action and those who believe such rights and values relative to the historical development of the community at any given stage. Also the difference between those who would check the power of the executive by customary or constitutional law and those who would commit themselves to the sovereignty of an emergent will—or the improvisations of ambitious politicians.

Subordination, however, does not spell subservience. For not every secondary cause is merely an instrument of the first cause, not every intermediate end merely a means to the ultimate end.

[1] *I Politics, lect.* 8. i, 10. 1258 a 21.

A pluralist philosophy rejoices in a world of many principals and purposes, indeed of many substances, and welcomes a hierarchy of sciences, each independent within its own field. The Scholastics reckoned that subordination was of two kinds, strait and easy. The distinction roughly corresponded to that between implicit and virtual content, or that between analytic and synthetic inference. By *subalternatio propria* the premisses of a derivative science were the conclusions of another and schematically higher science; so optics could be ranged under geometry, and so also a special section of a science fell under its general treatment of metaphysics and optics under geometry. Politics was not thus contained under ethics. By *subalternatio impropria* one science was either governed in practice by another—so military science was dependent on political science and all sciences were guided by logic—or in theory was related to it as a species to a more generic science of which it observed the findings when working with its own special procedure and data—so psychology depended for its material on physiology and music came under arithmetic.[1] After this fashion political science was checked by ethics and accepted ethical data; it was not thereby merely a department of ethics any more than the species *man* was merely a branch of the genus *animal*. As we have seen, personal goodness of character will no more of itself produce a good statesman than muscle or nerve will sense or think, or mathematical numbers will sing.

Circumstances in some countries have thrust on Catholics the need of forming their own political parties for good and sufficient reasons; the situation is now changing with respect to confessional membership. The effect has sometimes been to entangle religion and morality with lesser matters and to commit them to answers on open questions. For a political party is bound to take a line in debates such as those on the Navy Bills in Hohenzollern Germany or on colonial expansion under the Third Republic or on the break-up of large estates in Southern Italy: even in municipal politics a clerical party has to come to a decision about the contract for the sewerage works. The project of Catholic Action launched by Pius XI was misunderstood in quarters not sympathetic to the concept of

---

[1] See *de Trinitate*, v, 1, *ad* 5, 6. 1a, i, 2.

political action descending hierarchically from above though executed by laymen. But whatever the arrangement, the effective maintenance of the Church's duty to speak on social questions always involves the possibility of a clash with the civil power. This can be avoided only if the Church swallows the State, or if Christians, resigning themselves to the condition of passive onlookers, agree that religion is a private and other-worldly matter. Neither alternative is acceptable to Catholics, and the second was never even contemplated by the men of the Middle Ages—they would have wondered how the priest's right to speak on politics could ever be questioned.

All the same St Thomas never considered that theological science was ever a substitute for statesmanship. He avoided alike the philosophism of making the natural sciences so many branches of metaphysics and the moralism of deriving political science from the principles of Natural Law. To say that morality should never be outraged did not imply that politics came under moral condescension. As Richelieu said, none is more dangerous to the State than he who would govern by maxims drawn from books. Moral precepts provided few clues to what was politically advantageous.[1]

Similarly he was free from clericalism, another name for government for sectional benefit condemned in the *Ethics*. He held that the political discourse could proceed without arguing from ecclesiastical prescriptions. The division of two castes, the clerical and the lay, called by Stephen of Tournay (d. 1203) the *duo populi*, went deep into social life. St Thomas relegated to an appendix this jurisdictional and largely canonical division of the Church considered as an integral and functional whole, an institute which worked through various states and offices.[2] To be a cleric or a vowed religious was only supplementary to the common purpose of all Christians, the life of friendship with God through Christ.[3] All in this sense were ministers of Christ, but not all were accredited ministers in the juridical

---

[1] *V Ethics*, lect. 2. *VII*, lect. 7. *de Trinitate*, v, 1, 2. Disputations, I *de Potentia*, 4. *I Posterior Analytics*, lect. 21. *Metaphysics*, Prologue. IV *Metaphysics*, lect. 6. *de Divinis Nominibus*, i, lect. 2.

[2] 2a–2ae. lcxxxiii, 2.

[3] 1a–2ae. lxxi, 2. xcviii, 5. 2a–2ae. xl, 2. lxx, 1, 2. lxxxvii, 4. clxxxiv, 3. clxxxv, 6. clxxxix, 8. *de Perfectione Vitae Spiritualis*, 1, 2, 7, 8, 10, 11.

Church founded by Christ—both senses were found in St Paul.

Politics was not restricted to demonstrations; it must have elbow-room because much of it dealt with shifting evidences about the ways people behave in groups. Aristotle warned us that relativity always entered genuine discourse about what was practical. If this were true of morals it was even more true of politics. Its methods, determined not only by what should work in theory but also by what does work in fact, were those of art which makes up as it goes along without casting back to the evidence of its principles. Otherwise, like Lot's wife, it became petrified. Guides to practice were not like abstract judgments which were indubitably certain. There was no Chinese immobility about the Greek *polis* or the medieval *civitas*: neither was the product of theory. A good constitution and government was no more brought about by right views, good will and general friendliness than a thirteenth-century cathedral by an upsurging of religious aspiration; both were the work of artists applying the proper geometry, using the proper engines and ready to compromise, improvise and invent.

In this sense the statesman must be a politician, even in the modern and derogatory sense of the term. They call Adenauer an old fox—is that so bad? Let the *politicus virtuosus* be a match for the children of this world. Why should he not be secret, put a twist on things, display masterly inactivity and sometimes make a deal with successful enemies rather than with unsuccessful friends? Political business is not usually conducted in an atmosphere of kindly sentiment. There comes a point where an evil must be tolerated lest its removal be worse, as Newman saw in preferring Conservatism to subversion—and was thereby criticized by Acton for divorcing politics from morals.[1]

St Thomas was not high-minded to the extent of disdaining material considerations or being squeamish about bringing force to bear. Right was built on good, and good was built on physical facts. In the order of time lower good came before higher good, *non prius quod spirituale est, sed quod animale*—you must eat before you philosophize.[2] He would not have disagreed with Marx, that the political understructure determined the over-

---

[1] *Letters to Mr Gladstone*, p. 181. London, 1913.
[2] 1a–2ae. cv, 3.

structure. Political discipline must inevitably include the *ars subministrativa* of economics, or the art of acquiring property, the *chrematistic* of Aristotle, the *possessiva* or *pecuniativa* of Moerbeke and Albert.[1] All the same the proper business of politics is disengaged only when economic arrangements have been satisfactorily settled. Thus it has been argued that Socialism, for instance, can set about its real civilized mission only now that the Welfare State is as established as taxation can make it.[2]

Artificial wealth was suspected because the lust for it knew no limits.[3] The financiers came in for strong criticism—St Thomas called the spivs and money-lenders the Cahorsins—it is surprising that he branded the men of Cahors for a business mainly conducted from Northern Italy, the Florentines being most powerful in the century from 1250.[4] Real wealth, however, was not despised and search for it, the profit-motive, held a proper place in moral and political science. 'Virtue' says Cardinal Newman, 'is the child of knowledge: Vice of Ignorance, therefore education, periodical literature, railroad travelling, ventilation, drainage, and the arts of life, when fully carried out, serve to make a population moral and happy.'[5]

Similarly politics consulted geography. Thus the city should not be low down nor in a place subject to fog or frosts nor near to marshes but open to the skies and temperate breezes.[6] How blessed his own University of Paris has been by its climate. On the other hand a programme that mistook sanitation for health or fancied that economic arrangements could supply for a lack of political order incurred the criticism levelled against Phaleas of Chalcedon: he missed the heart of the matter, *insufficienter de substantia ordinavit*.[7] It may be that the predominance of economic interests in a civilization is not the least factor in its disintegration.

The general field—or in scholastic language the material

---

[1] *Politics*, i, 4. 1253 b 23. i, 8–11. 1256 a 1–1259 b 35.
[2] C. A. R. Crosland. *The Future of Socialism*. London, 1956.
[3] *I Politics*, lect. 7.
[4] J. H. Clapham. 'Commerce and Industry in the Middle Ages.' *Cambridge Medieval History*, v, p. 486. 1929.
[5] *Apologia pro Vita Sua*. Note A. ed. 1886.
[6] *de Regimine Principum* ii, 2, 3.
[7] *II Politics*, lect. 9. (ii, 7).

object—of political science was covered by a mesh of relationships caused by human beings living together. They produced needs and opportunities which exceeded the sum of their personal wants and contributions. At the same time they could never abrogate their personal responsibilities with respect to the moral law. Within this field a special aspect—or formal object—was studied: this was the right and practicable arrangement of means to the common security based on laws which could be enforced by earthly sovereignty.

Two conditions were presupposed to this pattern of a civilization formed within a wider cultural and religious pattern. First, that physical and psychological needs antecedent to politics were fulfilled and that the decencies demanded in the name of divine and natural law were observed. Second, that political art was allowed sufficiently free play to shape the social material confronting it.

The first had long been appreciated, but the second, on which the practice of statesmanship principally centres, was not explored until the thirteenth century. Then it was recogmized that civil legislation and political decisions were more than functions of morality. The practical rule, *go to war only when you think you can win*, is a case in point. History is full of the misfortunes of policies inspired by religious or moral indignation without the strength to back them up. That under some circumstances war is permissible is an ethical judgment. That here and now it should be declared is a political judgment, and a more problematical and reluctant one, calling for the consideration of many factors outside the field of moral science. By war, of course, is meant the classical *bellum*, an extension of a policy seeking eventual peace and agreement, not destruction seeking unconditional surrender. Even so it is a clumsy instrument to adopt for it deprives the statesman of control. Bismarck, a master of the art of limiting an objective, declared that the Balkans were not worth the bones of a Pomeranian grenadier.[1]

Indeed utilitarianism is nobler than it sounds. It is surprising that a generation which had learnt from Aristotle could have been in a mood to support the attempt of the Joachimites and Spirituals to establish an anarchy of pure love out of due time,

---

[1] A. J. P. Taylor. *Bismarck: The Man and the Statesman*. London, 1955.

though to some extent the secularists and *fraticelli* were brought together by their common hatred of an ecclesiastical power which took its temporal responsibilities seriously, perhaps some may think too seriously. Twenty years after St Thomas died, a mingling of religious enthusiasm and weariness with political churchmanship, as much for its gloss as for its corruption, was to elect a bewildered hermit to the Papacy. Celestine V was to fumble dangerously with the machinery of government for a few weeks before he resigned. The experiment was never repeated.

5. *Personal and Common Good*

For all his careful arranging of abstract types, each holding its appointed place in the scheme or moving from essential principles to general ends, an advertence that every act was an individual event and a solicitude for singular substances ran constant through the moral writings of St Thomas. He was not so scholastic as to forget that the Christian religion was a response to the *gesta Dei* or to imagine that living it was the same as exhibiting a stock of reasons or deferring to a list of obediences. Perhaps also, like other philosophers, he sought a metaphysical ground for an historical experience, for his times were favourable to a sense of the individual and, particularly in Northern Italy, to the need for political freedom.

Furthermore he thought of the single human substance not merely as an individual, a numerical unit to be determined by location in a quantitative field of reference, but also as a person, the *thing* divinely created however else some elements were formed, the ultimate rational substance, the centre of free activity, able to know and love God in himself and not only in his effects. If *individual* was a term of natural philosophy, *person* belonged to metaphysical and moral philosophy, and above all to theology.[1]

The term *persona* originally meant the part of a man played on the stage, the face, or mask, he showed the world, the figure he cut, the personage he appeared: thus Sabellius said that the

---

[1] ia. viii, 3. xii, 4. xix, 4. xxix, 1. xliii, 3. IV *Contra Gentes*, 15. V *Metaphysics*, *lect.* 8. *I Physics*, *lect.* 1.

E. Kurz. *Individuum und Gemainschaft beim hl. Thomas von Aquin*. Munich, 1932.

J. Maritain. *The Person and the Common Good*. New York, 1941.

Person of the Father was the Son in that he was born of Mary, and the Holy Ghost in that he sanctifies us.[1] Afterwards it acquired a legal sense and indicated free status, the man *sui juris et non alieni* or of official standing, thus the *persona publica*.[2] Then during the Trinitarian and Christological controversies of the early General Councils it became philosophically charged; the definition of Boethius—the individual substance of rational nature—was expanded, and person signified the intimate reality and inalienable value of a human being which could not be merged into anything else, the very substance or hypostasis, *sui juris et alteri incommunicabilis*.[3] *Acceptio personarum* was the sin of choosing a man for office for purely private connections and not on grounds of his public fitness; the phrase in the Epistles, that God is no respecter of persons, meant something rather different, namely that divine grace was not deferential towards differences of status, profession, nationality, or sex but regarded only inner worth.[4]

Theologians enriched the legacy left by St Augustine, the doctrine of the person, the noblest thing in nature, who was made to the image of God, who actively participated in the Eternal Law and the work of Providence, and, though called to be engaged in a doctrinal, sacramental and jurisdictional system, reached out to God himself without the interposition of human authority.[5] Faith assented in a darkness doctrinal exposition could not illumine; charity was deeper than profit, well-wishing and serving; the presence of God in the soul was unmediated by thoughts about him.[6]

On the other hand this ideal of extra-political perfection had to be reconciled with integration in the life of the group. Had not Aristotle taught that all virtue was political virtue? St

---

[1] H. C. Dowdall. 'The Word "Person".' *The Times Literary Supplement*, 8th May, 1948. 1a. xxvii, 1.

[2] 2a-2ae. clxxxiii, 1. 1a-2ae. xc, 3.

[3] Boethius, *Contra Eutychen. PL* lxiv, 1343. 1a. xxix, 1, 2. xxx, 1. 3a. ii, 2, 3. Disputations, IX *de Potentia*, 4.

[4] 2a-2ae. lxiii, 1. Commentaries, *Job, lect.* 1. *Romans*, ii, *lect.* 2. See Ephesians vi, 9. I Peter i, 17.

[5] Disputations, X *de Veritate*, 1, 2, 7. 1a. xxix, 3. 2a-2ae. ii, 3. 1a-2ae. xcix, 3. c, 2. *III Sentences*, X, ii, 7, iii. IV *Contra Gentes*, 22.

[6] 2a-2ae. i, 1, 2, 4. vi, 1. xxiii, 1. xxiv, 2. 1a. viii, 3.

A. Gardeil. *La structure de l'âme et l'expérience mystique*. Paris, 1927.

Thomas followed him closely enough to agree that the good life was subordinate to an immediate project, namely the civilized social community, outside of which it cannot be found, and that self-damage and suicide were unjust because they injured the State.[1] Moreover the political virtues were the noblest and most beautiful of all the moral virtues.[2] The claims of the person and of the group which enter into the fundamental social debate of our time, how to plan for freedom, cannot perhaps be altogether harmonized. At least the nature of the tension was not unappreciated in the thirteenth century.

No steady advance towards its resolution can be recorded. The *Prima Secundae* (1269) declared that the human person was not entirely enclosed in the political community, *homo non ordinatur ad communitatem politicam secundum se totum et secundum omnia sua*.[3] Just over a year later the *Secunda Secundae* talked in a different tone of the whole person ordained to the service of the whole community, *ipse totus homo ordinatur ut ad finem ad totam communitatem*.[4] If the contexts dispel the contradiction, there is at least a contrast of tone. As the Aristoteleanism deepened so a City was presented which possessed a more fundamental justice than the patristic commonwealth and which spoke in more stately and commanding terms. At the same time the exaltation of community-power was qualified by polemics on behalf of men who were vowed to live as poor wanderers, or, their enemies would say, as parasites on the body ecclesiastic and politic.

When the University Professors of Divinity attacked the friars the paradox was that they themselves were Augustinists and therefore disposed, theoretically at least, to exalt personal worth above integration in any governmental scheme, while some of their chief opponents were Aristoteleans with a growing sense of the organic quality of the group. It was heightened by the fact that social authority could be represented as possessing little more than a conventional title on *Propter Peccatum* premis-

---

[1] 2a–2ae. lxiv, 5. lxv, 1. *Ethics* v, 11. 1138 a 10.
[2] X *Ethics*, lect. 11. I de Regimine Principum, 12.
[3] 1a–2ae. xxi, 4, *ad* 3.
[4] 2a–2ae. lxv, 1.

I. T. Eschmann. '*Bonum commune melius est quam bonum unius*. Eine Studie uber den Wertvorrang des Personalen bei Thomas Aquinas.' *MS*. vi, pp. 62–120. Toronto, 1944.

ses, whereas to the Aristoteleans it sprang from the very
constitution of social human nature. On this score the Paris
Masters and not the Dominicans should have been the
defenders of extra-civic virtue. They were entrenched, however,
in a system of benefices against intrusion, and the established
order counted more than ideas did.

Between the lines of the controversy can be read the theme
that a life of political usefulness could not easily be combined
with the 'folly' of perfection. Though he would have had legal
justice control all moral virtue, St Thomas limited the field of
positive law and was not over-confident about the State's
improving rôle.[1] He stressed the reasoned mode of virtue, yet
adopted the passages in the *Liber de Bona Fortuna* on the fortu-
nate man to illustrate the 'enthusiasm' of the Gifts of the Holy
Ghost.[2] Nobody was exempt from duties to the group, but
justice ended where mystery began. His ideal of the free and
lawful man, not entirely possessed by the political virtue of the
Greek or sobered by the gravity of the Roman, was touched by
the heroism of the Gospel, the genius of the eccentric and the
virtue of the anchorite living apart not because he was brutal
and could not endure his fellows, but because he would cleave
wholly to divine things.[3]

Here were ends strange to social reform, and he welcomed
them; he allowed for the enemy harboured in the human heart
to any order short of the final order and for a disquiet with any
knowledge short of vision. Forms of theory and practice,
rational meanings and precepts, indeed any social organization
scheme, even the most sacred, are means not ends, and only the
sight of the living God beyond them all will still human
restlessness.[4] The Spirituals exercised no great influence on the
universities. His longing for the perfect liberty of the sons of
God in the Christian Society was not weaker than theirs. But if

---

[1] *V Ethics*, lect. 2. 1a–2a. xcvi, 2, 3. xcii 1.

[2] 1a–2ae. lv, 4. lvi, 3. lviii, 4. lxiv, 2. lxv, 1. lxviii, 1. The *Liber de Bona Fortuna*,
a medieval compilation from the *Magna Moralia*, ii, 8. and the *Eudemian
Ethics*, vii, 14. St George Stock, *Magna Moralia, Ethica Eudemia, de Virtutibus
et Vitiis*. Introduction. Oxford, 1915.
T. Gilby. *Poetic Experience: An Introduction to Thomist Aesthetic*. London, 1934.

[3] 1a–2ae. lxi, 5. 2a–2ae. clxxxviii, 8.

[4] 1a–2ae. ii, 8. iii, 1, 6, 7, 8.

anarchism was an aspiration it was not a doctrine, still less a programme. He never expected such an outpouring of the spirit as would set up the rule of the saints and do away with the political institutions of Church or State.[1]

It might be argued that he spoke in two parts, as a theologian for the supremacy of the person, as a social philosopher for the supremacy of the community. Certainly he brought out the extra-political character of perfection when he wrote on such topics as sanctifying grace, the theological virtues of faith, hope, and charity, and the contemplative life. For sanctifying grace marked a personal quality and friend-relationship rather than a place or status in an organization.[2] Divine faith laid the mind open to ultimate reality, *prima veritas*, and did not, as it were, cage it in a system of propositions.[3] The theological virtues soared beyond all reasonable regulations to God himself who was not enclosed in the scheme of things. Not the common good but the supreme good was the object of charity.[4] The contemplative life directly served no good outside itself.[5]

All these were of immense value to social health. For if Christianity promised no short-cuts by which you could avoid having to work hard with natural rights, St Thomas echoed the experience of Christian spokesmen, that the precepts of justice were not enough for happy human relationships. True peace was more profound than concord or mere absence of strife; it was a blessing which followed only from charity.[6]

He drew some sort of distinction between the Christian and the purely ethical man; thus he referred to sin as an offence both against God and against reasonable living.[7] Nevertheless his social teaching is misrepresented if the simplification and separation of Nature and Grace are pressed, for he never thought that men lived under two contrary dispensations, one natural, the other supernatural. Nor did he think of them as

---

[1] 1a–2ae. cvi, 4.

[2] *VII Quodlibets*, 17. III *Contra Gentes*, 136. 1a–2ae. xciii, 9 *ad* 2.

[3] 2a–2ae. i, 1, 2, 6, 9.

[4] Disputations, *de Caritate*, 5, *ad* 4. 1a–2ae. lxii, 1, 2.

[5] 2a–2ae. clxxxii, 1. 3a. xl, 1. *de Hebdomadibus*, Prologue.

[6] III *Contra Gentes*, 130. 1a–2ae. lxix, 1, 3. 2a–2ae. xxix, 1, 3, 4.
E. Bezzina. *de valore sociali caritatis secundum principia S. Thomae Aquinatis*. Naples, 1952.

[7] 1a–2ae. lxxxi, 6, *ad* 5.

parallel—and not really meeting. He took them together, as they have been lived in history. Grace has always been on the scene, either accepted or rejected, explicitly or implicitly. The purely natural man and the City of Reason are fictions— scientific abstractions only partially corresponding to concrete historical things and situations. All the same they are useful pieces of methodology when we investigate how human nature ought to act when left to itself, and what natural decencies ought to persist through the highest operations of religion.

In truth the issue between community-service and self-expression lay elsewhere. It was not pitched between the natural and the supernatural. The tensions were found within both orders, though they would have made no more sense to Aristotle than they do a juridically-minded Roman theologian. Social philosophy recognized how they spread into justice itself; there, as we have noticed, legal justice and particular justice may set up pulls in different directions, and equity has to absorb the pressure of legalism. High theology, too, recognizes the polarity of authority and freedom, of disciplined obedience and conscience. Macrobius spoke of the virtues of the soul in purgatory, a state of other-worldly purification, present when we break out of the conditions of group-life.[1] This was no academic abstraction but could present a practical problem. What about the early Christian solitaries of Egypt and Syria who deliberately cut themselves off even from the sacramental life of the Church? The inevitable friction in the working of any organization does not necessarily argue injustice or abuse of power. A sacred group is no less subject to them than a secular group, and probably more so, not only because the contenders are higher and the struggle deeper, but also because the issue is more delicate. St Thomas noted that the ecclesiastical hierarchy imperfectly matches the angelic hierarchy, for often those closest to God are not highest in office.[2]

Bonum commune was the key-term, and its ambiguity confused the issue. *Bonum in communi* was an abstract generalization, namely goodness in general. The common good could also be taken as a collective total, the sum of the purposes at work

---

[1] 1a–2ae. lxi, 5.
[2] 1a–2ae. cvi, 3, *ad* 1.

within the group. But it could also stand for a universal value neither increased nor diminished by the number of the things which share in it, and at least once it was identified with God himself.[1] One may say roughly that *bonum commune* represented a collective idea when men were treated as individual units enclosed within the whole community—as, for instance, when it was said that a criminal, having lost his human dignity, could be excised from the body politic to which he was a danger.[2] It represented a more open and universal idea when they were treated as persons, actively co-operating in a shared purpose not merely numbers in a crowd. What was this shared purpose but the *bonum commune*, transcending the sum of all single goods and the collectivity they compose, which was the outside principle and end of all striving?[3] It was in the mind which stood apart from the process, like the idea of an ordered army in the mind of the commander: it was the *bonum separatum* introduced towards the end of the *Metaphysics*—the supreme Good, separate from the world yet no absentee, the total cause of every being and activity, the meaning of all goodness, subsistent and completely real, *ipsum bonum subsistens*.[4]

Since God was the happiness of all creatures, and, in a special manner, of rational creatures, theologians were led to reflect on the nature of union with him. Men were citizens of this world and partners with Providence, and it was noticed that when they entered into things by knowledge and love no absorption or destruction was implied and no third entity or compound was generated as in physical processes.[5] The metaphysics of cognition and appetition and the mystical theology of association in the life of the persons of the Blessed Trinity were the undercurrent of St Thomas's political doctrine, which drew more deeply from the *de Trinitate* of St Augustine than from the

---

[1] 1a–2ae. x, 1. 1a. xxxi, 1, *ad* 2. lxv, 2. ciii, 2, *ad* 3. lx, 5, *c*, & *ad* 5.
See T. Gilby. *Between Community and Society*. xiv, 1, 2. xv, 3.
[2] 2a–2ae. lxiv, 2.
[3] 1a–2ae. xc, 2, *ad* 2, 3.
III *Contra Gentes*, 17. I *Quodlibet*, iv, 8. *de Perfectione vitae spiritualis*, 13. 1a. xlvii, 1. 1a–2ae. xix, 10. xxi, 4. cix, 3.
[4] *Metaphysics*, xii, 10, 1075 a 11. *St Thomas*, lect 12. 1a. vi, 2, 4.
[5] III *de Anima*, lect. 24. 1a. vii, 2, *ad* 2. xxx, 1, *ad* 4. lxv, 2. lxxxi, 1. xciii, 2. 1a–2ae. ii, 3. lxxix, 2.

de Civitate Dei. Every human grouping, however humble, reflected the exemplars of divine association. The political community was no exception; friendship was its greatest blessing and the aim of its legislation. It sought to be an ordered whole of which the well-being was never really promoted by violence done to any of its parts.

Given such a theology of the *bonum commune*, it was clear that virtues, however dutiful their air, could never be confined within a closed system. If they were able to move into a world beyond the cosmos, the *universitas creaturarum*, they were certainly not to be confined to the *polis*—and still less to the *res publica*, an arrangement of offices rather than a way of life, the geographically wider but socially narrower and more legal structure the Romans made of the Greek State. Not until Christianity is obliterated from memory will political subordination be made the test of all virtue, or the State appear as completely self-contained and offering the satisfaction of every human want. To many liberals and humanists the Church no longer appears an effective society, yet they invoke its likeness when they appeal over the head of the government to a tradition of human decency and Natural Law.

Let us now turn to the historical succession of St Thomas's ideas and discover if the emphasis was shifted in the relations of the person and the group. In 1256, soon after he had finished the *Commentary on the Sentences*, he wrote the first of his polemical tracts in support of the friars, entitled *Contra Impugnantes Dei cultum et religionem.* St Bonaventure's *de Paupertate Christi* appeared about the same time. Both were defending their brethren against the philistinism, *astutia philistinorum*,[1] of William of St Amour, whose *de Periculis Novissimorum Temporum* accused the Dominicans and Franciscans of not undertaking social responsibilities and leading a life contrary to morality and religion. This was a resumé of another broadside *de Antichristo et ejusdem ministris*, aimed at the Dominicans.

The nerve of the controversy, touched by Matthew Paris, was constitutional and concerned the rights of the mendicants to set up chairs of theology in the University, but the struggle ranged far and wide over the whole field of property and

[1] *Contra Impugnantes*, Prologue.

poverty.[1] On the somewhat rambling arguments of the *Contra Impugnantes* in favour of the free-lance work of economically unproductive and non-beneficed groups, vowed to poverty but not to stability, we need not delay since they were set forth more systematically many years later in two works, the *de perfectione vitae spiritualis* (1269) and the *Contra pestiferam doctrinam retrahentium homines a religionis ingressu* (1270), written when the offensive against the friars was renewed.

The *Summa contra Gentes*, begun in 1259, reached its third book two or three years later. This was a defence of the traditional doctrine of a particular Providence against the inroads of the Averroist doctrine of a single World-Mind which dealt only with broad effects. It showed that God was not remote and uncaring. His causality did not leave secondary causes to work out the details; his knowledge and love entered into every minute particular. A reference occurs to the collective good of the community as being more godlike, *divinius*, than any particular good, that is, it better represents God's goodness.[2] But the burden of the discourse was to show that the individual was more important than the race. Human persons were not utilities, pawns in a game, but ends in their own right, responsible agents who could consort with God and share his mind.[2] The very argument that a part is subordinate to the whole was bent to prove the supremacy of the person, for a personal mind could possess all being and so, a microcosm, as such was no longer a subservient component but itself an open and generous whole.[4]

Next, the Disputations *de Spiritualibus Creaturis* (1266-8) lifted from Aristotle's *Metaphysics* the idea of a twofold order in the universe: one the general arrangement or common good intrinsic to the group and constituted by the co-ordination of the parts themselves within the whole—this, on a smaller scale, was the common good of a political community—the other the plan and purpose outside the scheme conceived in the mind and

---

[1] *Chronica Majora*, v. (ed. H. R. Luard. Rolls Series. 7 vols. 1872-80).
See H. Rashdall. *The Universities of Europe in the Middle Ages*. i, pp. 344-97. 'The Mendicants and the University.'
[2] III *Contra Gentes*, 64.
[3] III *Contra Gentes*, 111-5, 128.
[4] III *Contra Gentes*, 112.

will of its maker. The first, the *finis intra* or *bonus intrinsecum*, was compared to an army's organized array, the second, the *finis separatus* or *bonum extrinsecum*, to the general on an eminence commanding his troops on the battlefield whose will makes the victory—the picture was like that of Blenheim or Waterloo, not of soldiers' battles such as Albuera or Inkerman.[1] The comparison illustrated how purposes could work to an end not contained within their own immediate system—St Thomas's political philosophy followed his natural and metaphysical philosophy in not adopting closed systems except as useful hypotheses for specialized and departmental investigation.

The attack on the friars flared up again in 1269. It was led by Gerard of Abbeville, a cooler and deadlier opponent than William of St Amour. St Thomas, who had been rushed back from Italy to Paris by the authorities of his Order, countered the *Geraldini* with the two works de *Perfectione* and *Contra Retrahentes*, of which the first was the more important. St Bonaventure's *Apologia Pauperum* also belonged to this period.[2]

Nicholas of Lisieux, one of the chief critics, reckoned that the *de Perfectione* was subversive of the Church's discipline, *libellus in quo sacrosancta subvertitur hierarchia*. Unusual among St Thomas's works in that Aristotle was not quoted, it has become the classical exposition of what constitutes the life of religious perfection. Charity and nothing else was the heart of the matter; men were good and perfect by observing the two great precepts of the Gospel, not by their rank in an organized body; holiness admitted no professional caste system within itself. The 'state of perfection'—a technical phrase—was constituted by religious vows by which a person was fixed, committed and dedicated to special means to holiness, ratified by the Church as juridical obligations. Vowed poverty, chastity and obedience were classical methods to free the spirit—there were others. In the thirteenth century religious Orders were founded, for instance, the Mercedarians under Dominican auspices, the members of which bound themselves to release captives from the

---

[1] *de Spiritualibus Creaturis*, 8. *Metaphysics*, xii, 10.
  XII Metaphysics, *lect.* 12.
[2] P. Glorieux. 'Les polemiques contra Geraldinos'. *RTAM* vi, pp. 5–41. Louvain, 1934. vii, pp. 129–157. 1935. ix, pp. 56–84. 1937.

Moors by offering themselves in ransom—yet their profession was secondary and instrumental to the play of the moral and theological virtues, above all of charity.[1] Their purpose was nothing more extraordinary than a good Christian life.

This also was the message of the spirited tractate, *Contra Retrahentes* (1270), written in a style unusually informal. Skilful appeal was made to the Fathers and the Canons to defend the friars against the criticism that they were untraditional and not integrated in the propertied establishment of the Church. Beginning with a manifesto against secular business, since Christ himself, *auctor fidei et consummator*, was born in lowly Bethlehem of a virgin who knew not man and who lived in poverty and refused power, it went on to argue that there was nothing queer or esoteric about the ideal set by the friars.

They were not enthusiasts who despised plain morality, for you could keep the Gospel precepts without the counsels, but not the counsels without the precepts. Nor were they types of special calibre nor spiritual athletes who flattered themselves they had mastered the practices of virtue and could now dispense with them and go on to something better: this was a necessary reassurance in view of the contemporary fears of antinomianism. They were men like other men and their religious state could be tackled without elaborate preparation, even in the case of the young or recent converts from error or sin.[2] Of course their life was a folly, but after all the Gospel had something to say about that. St Paul had gloried in preaching Christ crucified, a stumbling-block to the Jews and foolishness to the Greeks. To condemn it out of hand was to fall foul not only of the authority of holy doctors but also of the teachings of psychology, *sed etiam physicis documentis*, since Aristotle in a chapter entitled *de Bona Fortuna* admired those who are moved by an instinct better and more divine than human calculation. Let a man blush who calls himself a Catholic yet displays more worldliness than a pagan philosopher.[3]

The disputations *de Caritate* (1269–72) again picked out the

---

[1] *de Perfectione*, 1, 2. 2a–2ae. clxxxiv, 1, 2, 3, 4.

[2] *Contra Retrahentes*, 1, 3, 4, 5, 8.

[3] Ibid. 9. See 1a–2ae. lxviii, 1. Commentary, *St Matthew*, v, *lect.* 2.

idea of a social love going beyond the group.[1] Aristotle had said that if men were to be good citizens they should be trained to love the common interest and act well as parts of the State to which they belong.[2] Now by divine grace men were admitted to the heavenly happiness of seeing and enjoying God; they were enrolled as partners and companions of that blessed society called the heavenly Jerusalem: *you are fellow-citizens with the saints, and of the household of God*.[3] To this end were they trained and equipped and were they to play a worthy part they should have the welfare of their company entirely at heart. What was this but God's own goodness? *Bonum divinum prout est beatitudinis objectum*, that was the cause of eternal joy in friendship.

But, the argument went on, the common interest might be loved in two ways, as something to be possessed and as something to be cherished. To love the common good for what you get out of it did not make for political virtue; even a tyrant acted like that since it was to his advantage to command a well-run State. To love the common good more than oneself, however, to such an extent that death was risked and private advantage thrown away for its safety and increase, that was virtuous patriotism and love of the commonwealth. To be devoted to the good in which the blessed share, not merely in order to possess it oneself, for so even wicked men desire heaven, but also for its own sake, that the Kingdom of God should spread and be strong and safe from attack, that was the true virtue of men who belong to the society of the blessed, that was charity which loves God for himself and our neighbour as ourself.

In other words the notion of the Common Good in the argument was not that of a well-ordered mass of citizens composing an order within themselves, nor even, from a religious point of view, the *urbs Jerusalem beata vivis ex lapidibus*, but an end outside the group, so beloved that men will suffer deprivation and death rather than disown it. The transcendence was more evident a quality of the *bonum divinum* than of the *bonum civitatis*, and it is not difficult to appreciate why it was spoken of in more elevated

---

[1] *de Caritate*, 2. See 7, *ad* 5.
[2] *Politica*, viii, 1. 1337 a 20.
[3] Ephesians, ii, 19.

tones in the disputations *de Caritate* than in the contemporaneous commentaries on the *Ethics* and *Politics*, which were more concerned to interpret Aristotle than to put him in a Christian setting.

The introduction to the *Ethics* repeated without disapproval and in language Siger of Brabant might have used, Aristotle's remark that the purpose of the State was greater and fuller than that of any single man; the inference was drawn that the science which investigated it, namely politics, therefore took all other human interests in its stride. The introduction to the *Politics*, too, agreed that the State contained all other communities as a house included its walls.[1] Yet the non-utilitarian elements of Aristotle's thought were also brought out and they were reinforced by lessons learnt from St Augustine. Politics was supreme only in the domain of practice, which did not enclose all the things which were ours to contemplate and enjoy. Prudence was surpassed by wisdom as the *bonum utile* was surpassed by the *bonum honestum et delectabile*. The test of success might apply to what we produced and how we conducted ourselves, but there were higher objects and ends outside the reach of pragmatism.

The mature judgment of the *Summa Theologica* combined both strains of thought, namely, that a man must act for ends lying beyond the *civitas* and the *universitas creaturarum*, and that he must be integrated in the political community. Dedicated virginity was defended, though its social benefits were difficult to certificate.[2] The common good was regarded as a true human value only when it was grasped by personal mind.[3] The very co-ordination of parts within the universe existed for a *finis ulterior* outside them; God, *ipse Deus*, not the well-being of the whole, was man's ultimate end.[4] The *Summa Theologica* agreed with the *Ethics* in rejecting health, wealth, pleasure and power as the highest aims of human activity; at the same time it noted the inadequacy of the felicity in the philosophical contemplation of the whole universe and its parts.[5] Beatitude

---

[1] *I Ethics, lect.* 1. *I Politics, lect,* 1.

[2] 2a–2ae. clii, 4, *ad* 3.

[3] 1a–2ae. ii, 1, 8.

[4] 1a–2ae. ii, 8, *ad* 2.

[5] 1a–2ae. ii, 1, 2, 4, 6. iii, 6, 7. iv, 1 2.

was nothing less than the face to face vision of God and enjoy-ment of his friendship.[1] The political community existed to promote social virtue, but even moral virtue, noble though it be, was not its own reward, for it opened out to an object outside itself.[2]

On the other hand the present city was more consolidated in the *Summa Theologica* than in the earlier writings. It was the complete community to which the individual past was sub-ordinated as imperfect to perfect. Its well-being was the purpose of law: *cum comnis pars ordinetur ad totum, sicut imperfectum ad perfectum, unus autem homo est pars communitatis perfectae, necesse est quod lex proprie respiciat ordinem ad felicitatem communem.*[3] The doctrine hardened against rebellion and grudged the subject's right to remove a tyrant, yet not the State's right to cut out a diseased and criminal member of the community. Clerics, however, were to stand apart from the proceedings.[4] Like St Augustine who did not shrink from the harsh beauty of good edged by pain, the argument at times seemed more sensitive to the spectacle of the justice of a whole order than to the ease of any part.[5] St Thomas's successors were inclined to strengthen the might of the community, perhaps to be less tender towards the victimization of individuals which might arise. When a man fitted in with the State then he lived according to reason, *cum vivit secundum rempublicam operatur secundum rationem*, wrote Peter of Auvergne, the continuator of the *Commentary on the Politics*.[6] And Remigio de Girolami, who had followed St Thomas's lectures in Paris and was Dante's master, appealing at Santa Maria Novella for concord among his fellow-citizens, told them that otherwise they would ruin the city and themselves: then will you be not a Florentine, *forentinus*, but a weeper, *flerentinus*, and if not a citizen then not a man, *si non es civis non es homo.*[7]

---

[1] 1a–2ae. iii, 8.

[2] 1a–2ae. iv, 4. v, 4, 7. xix, 2. xxi, 1. lv, 2, 4.

[3] 1a–2ae. xc, 2.

[4] 2a–2ae. xlii, 2, *c* & *ad* 3. lxiv, 2, 3, 4. lxvi, 1. civ, 5.

[5] See 1a. xlix, 2. xxxiii, 5, *ad* 3. xlviii, 2. 1a–2ae. lxxxvii, 3, *ad* 3.

[6] *V Politics*, *lect.* 7. St Thomas's commentary ends III, *lect.* 7.

[7] G. de Lagarde. *Naissance de l'esprit laïque au déclin du moyen âge.* iii, 5. 'Les succes-seurs de Saint Thomas, 1270–1300.'

6. *The Corporate Group*

Corporate property was managed according to thirteenth-century jurisprudence as if it were a matter of joint ownership; the rights of the whole were bound up with the rights of the men comprising it, and the rights of the members were asserted by actual enjoyment of their common possession.[1] A human group was not yet credited by political and legal theory with a kind of soul of its own. The political community formed a whole, *quoddam totum*, to which the attributes of a body might be ascribed—the body politic of the State, the mystical body of the Church—and afterwards those also of a person.[2] First, then, let us consider the group as corporate; next, the nature of group-personality.

Extremes of political theory have offered opposite interpretations. On one side the State may be represented as a legal artifice or as a mechanism made by individuals for their own convenience, which, though it may gather its own impetus, should always be kept under control. On the other side it may be represented as an organism with its proper life, over and above and absorbing the lives of its members. The distinction corresponds roughly to St Thomas's first classification of wholes, namely single objects which somehow contain different parts,[3] into logical whole and real wholes.

The political group was certainly at least a logical whole, that is to say, an object expressed by a single concept and term. A generalization made by the mind to cover many things was sometimes called a *communitas*.[4] It might be used as a collective term, in which many things are bracketed together and for convenience of speech assume a group individuality indicated by the grammar of giving them a singular verb.[5] It might also refer to a distributive general idea when many objects shared in one nature. Thus in speaking of *all* as a single idea we might

---

[1] J. W. Jones. *Historical Introduction to the Theory of Law.* p. 75.

[2] *III Politics*, lect. 1.
  B. Tierney. *Foundations of the Conciliar Theory.* ii. 'The Structure of a Medieval Ecclesiastical Corporation.' iii. 'The Whole Church as a Corporation.' pp. 106–53.

[3] 1a. lxxv, 8.

[4] *I Sentences*, XXV, i, 3.

[5] 1a. xxxi, 1, *ad* 2.

be taking the term either collectively—all together and only together—or distributively—all together and each alone.[1] The logic could be applied to general justice, which might be represented as a *bloc* notion, an overall attribute produced by the State to which all partially conspired. But, more profoundly, it was a personal virtue in which all fully shared, in the sense that the justice of all was the justice of each.[2] Our present inquiry is whether St Thomas, and if so, to what extent, treated the State as a real whole.

A real whole, that is to say an actual reality not merely a verbal heading which covers many items, could be of several kinds. If its parts were incomplete realities so coalesced that one single subsisting thing was formed, then a *substantial whole* was the result. This was subdivided: it was called an *essential whole, totum essentiale*, with respect to any components of its very nature—thus man was composed of body and soul; an integral whole, *totum integrale*, with respect to any quantitative parts, thus a man's body was composed of its bodily members; a functional whole, *totum potestativum*, with respect to diverse abilities in the same subject—thus a man could be treated as a complexus of abilities, intellect, will, senses and emotional powers.[3] When, however, the parts in question remained complete things and were not assimilated in a higher substance, the result was an *accidental whole*, so called because the union was constituted by their relation of order among themselves, and *relation* fell into the category of accident, not substance.[4] This also was subdivided, into a *natural group*, when the things were conjoined in pursuit of their innate and proper purposes, thus a family or swarm of bees; an *artificial whole*, when they were assembled by human planning, thus a machine or a sporting club; a *chance whole* when the collection was haphazard, thus a drift of leaves or a random mob.

Now to apply these divisions to the political community. At once we can rule out the likelihood that medieval writers of the European tradition considered that any group of men, however

---

[1] *II Politics, lect.* 2.

[2] 2a–2ae. lviii, 6.

[3] 3a. ii, 1. *I Sentences*, XIX, iv, 1. 1a. lxxvi, 8. lxxvii, 1, *ad* 1. 1a–2ae. lvii, 2, *ad* 2. 2a–2ae. xlviii, 1.

[4] 3a. ii, 6.

compact, could compose a substantial whole; they had no hankering after or even notion of a State Absolute. The Aristoteleans among them were firm that individual things were the first substances and the real subjects of existence. They defined the person as the ultimate unassimilable, *incommunicabilis*. To Christians it was the centre of responsible activity. The universe itself, supposedly forming a greater unity than any city, was not a higher substance containing lower individual substances: its unity was not that of a single substance, but of the positioning and ordering of many parts which remained themselves without being absorbed in the whole, *unum positione vel ordinem cujus plurimae partes non sunt assumptibiles*.[1] Hence at the beginning of his *Commentary on the Ethics*, where various types of combination were reviewed, St Thomas expressly rejected any theory of incorporation which implied that the political community was a single thing or substance.[2]

It was not even to be compared to one large household, for he agreed with Aristotle that if you strain for too close a unity you destroy the proper character of the State and level it down to a more primitive condition: 'it is like forcing harmony to unison'.[3] For a truly political whole kept its parts intact, unlike Plato's State in which lesser groups were mere agencies completely controlled by the highest power.[4]

Moreover, justice without qualification, the justice which serves the *jus politicum* was essentially a matter between two quite distinct parties: *simpliciter est ad alterum sicut ad quod est omnino distinctum*. When one was somehow not entirely his own but the other's, as when children or slaves were dealt with by father or master, then the justice engaged fell short of full justice. For this required that individual right-givers and right-takers were balanced in agreed opposition, as appeared when two parties were equal before the law which adjudicated between them and neither was in the other's power though both were subjects of the same civil authority: *sicut apparet in*

---

[1] 3a. iv, 1, *ad* 4.
[2] *I Ethics, lect.* 1.
[3] Politics, ii, 2. 1261 a 16. Also ii, 5. 1263 b 30.
[4] J. J. Navone. 'Division of Parts in Society—Plato and Aristotle'. *Philosophical Studies*, vi, pp. 113–22. Maynooth, 1956.

duobus hominibus quorum unus non est sub altero, sed ambo sunt sub uno principe civitatis, et inter tales secundum Philisophum est simpliciter justum.[1]

Allowances should be made for the metaphorical description of the State as a body. Then it appeared either as an integral whole, when it was set forth as a group of people arranged according to status, or as a functional whole when it was set forth as an ordered system of offices.[2] Allowances also should be made for the social biology and psychology which might discover a herd instinct among animals, treat it as an entity and extend it to human groups. Notwithstanding such figures of speech, individual human beings were always considered to be the prime realities. Gierke was probably right in his contention that the medieval idea of a corporation, in which the principle of unity resided in the members who came together in order to achieve an end determined by themselves, was transformed by the Canonists into the idea of an institution of which the principle of unity was imposed from outside and above. It seems strange, however, that he should have thought that the thirteenth-century schoolmen encouraged an organic theory of the State, or allowed that a human group-reality could be a real thing distinct from the men and women composing it.[3] The political community was not a substance, but a collection, order or arrangement of substances, *compositio vel ordo vel figura*, an accidental group in the sense already defined.[4]

It did not follow that the political community was therefore merely a chance aggregation, a number of human beings who happened to live together with little sense and less service of common purposes: a mass of people enclosed within a wall may be a nation, but not a State. 'Like this, we may say, was Babylon.'[5] No more was it only a vast *artificium juris*, an artificial group set up by convention and edict, a juridical corporation

---

[1] 2a–2ae. lvii, 4. *V Ethics, lect.* 11 v, 6. 1134 a 16.
[2] For the differences of 'states' and 'offices', see 2a–2ae. clxxxiii, 1, 3.
[3] O. von Gierke. *Political Theories of the Middle Ages.* Transl. F. W. Maitland. Cambridge, 1900.
    E. Lewis. 'Organic Tendencies in Medieval Political Thought'. *American Political Science Review*, xxxii, pp. 849–76. 1938.
[4] *I Ethics, lect.* 1.
[5] *Politics*, iii, 3. 1276 a 27. See iii, 9. 1280 b 12.

which pursued legal ends through official means. If it might be presented as such according to an Augustinist antithesis of nature and convention, to the Aristoteleans it was a natural combination, partly instinctive and partly deliberate, rooted in preconventional rights, a 'mystery' embodied in folk-lore and custom, and which, through an enhancement rather than a cession of individual freedom, promoted the decencies and virtues of human, that is social, life.

Cicero had spoken of the *totum corpus rei publicae*.[1] The term *body* was used to designate any organized structure, thus *corpus civile* or *corpus ecclesiasticum*, or a systematized collection of articles, thus *corpus juris*. The *body politic* was a classical phrase, and it was a favourite practice of writers on social morality, such as John of Salisbury, Vincent of Beauvais, and Ptolemy of Lucca, to draw out its allegorical senses.[2] The comparison occurred to St Thomas, but not frequently; thus a criminal was likened to a diseased member of an organism, and the inference was drawn that through his own fault he had lost his personal rights and lapsed into the condition of an individual part, which could be surgically removed if dangerous to the health of the whole.[3]

That the usage was metaphorical appeared when he discussed the mystical body of the Church; there the cohesion was certainly more intimate than in any State. He was aware of the anthropomorphism and, while admitting its propriety as a figure of speech, would not have the Church's physical unity pressed too literally. Of the individuals composing a human group he said cautiously, *reputantur quasi unum corpus*, and of the Church, *dicitur unum corpus mysticum per similtudinem ad corpus naturale*.[4] So also he spoke about the Church as a building, *ad aedificationem Ecclesiae*.[5] His reserve may also be usefully repeated

---

[1] *de Officiis*, i, 25, 85.
[2] *Policraticus* iv, 2, 3. v, 2.
   Speculum Doctrinale, vii, 8.
   de Regimine Principum, iv, 3.
[3] 2a–2ae. lxiv, 2, 3.
[4] 1a–2ae. lxxxi, 1. 3a. viii, 1, *c* & *ad* 2.
   See 1a. lxxv, 1. 1a–2ae. xci, 2, 3, 4. 2a–2ae. lvii, 7. clxxxiii, 2. *Romans*, xii, *lect.* 2. I *Corinthians*, xii, *lect.* 3.
[5] 2a–2ae. clxxi, 1. clxxxii, 2, 3.

with regard to tropes such as the Bride of Christ or Mother Church, lest theology match an uncritical fashion in social philosophy, which lifts a social organism from biology or a Mass-Will from psychology, or in foreign history which treats the John Bull or Uncle Sam of the cartoonist as real figures. The rhetoric may be more genial, the logic is no less invalid.

7. *State Personality*

The attribution of personality is no less tricky. Activities issue from a human group different in kind from the activities of its constitituents clubbed together; similarly the difference between a heterogeneous whole and its parts taken together is not just one of degree or size.[1] Previously treated rather as partnerships, associations from the thirteenth century onwards were coming to be treated more as corporations. The Canonists naturally responded to the institutional continuity of the Church and saw there a principle of corporate permanence underlying the successive changes of individual life. The Civilians borrowed the notion of a *corporation sole* from ecclesiastical law.[2] Gradually the State itself was portrayed less as a family or a number of individuals in partnership together than as a living thing with a personality of its own.

The discourse was muddled by the double meaning of *person*, legal and philosophical or theological. The term could stand either for a subject possessing a histrionic, public, and juridical character, and acting in that capacity, or alternatively for the single private rational substance who was the subject of moral responsibility. The two were distinct, for one real person could be several legal persons, for instance, a citizen, a magistrate, a university elector, whereas one legal person could be composed of many real persons, for instance, a religious foundation or a college.

At the outset the lawyers were not occupied with the philosophical overtones of the term, but—the Canonists especially—

---

[1] 2a–2ae. xlvii, 10, 11. l,1.

[2] F. W. Maitland, *Collected Papers*, ed. H. A. L. Fisher, iii, p. 245. Cambridge, 1911.
   F. Pollock and F. W. Maitland. *History of English Law*, i, pp. 486–511.
   W. S. Holdsworth. *History of English Law*, iii, pp. 469–490. London, 1923.

with problems of corporation law arising from litigation undertaken by bishoprics, religious orders, abbeys, priories, colleges,
chantries, guilds, confraternities and other institutional bodies,
greater and lesser, within the embracing *universitas* of the
Church. All they were attempting was to explain certain
technical rules which for certain acts treated a group enjoying
rights recognized by the law as if it were one person, and,
following the example of Innocent IV, the reputed father of
the notion, they were content to regard such a personality as a
fictitious entity.[1] It was not due to them, but to those political
publicists and philosophers who were over-impressed by the
organic character of the State, that group-personality was
blown out into a quasi-metaphysical object.

The theologians on their side were exercised about the
moral personality and responsibility of groups. They had to
cope with the major problem of the collective guilt of Original
Sin. Here was a fault of the whole human race, not confined to
the doings of one local corporation.[2] Everybody born into the
world incurred the penalty, and also, which was more embarrassing, the guilt of a sin not committed by any personal act of
their own. In what sense could the whole of humanity be
blamed? How could Original Sin really be called sin at all?

It was true, of course, that innocents suffered through
another's fault, that was the way things worked, as when
parents neglected their children or a careless driver let his
wagon run away—in those days instruments were not so lethal
as they are now, and one slip did not have such far-reaching
effects. On the other hand it was a principle of justice that
penalties should not be inflicted when no crime or fault had
been committed; only for the wrong a man himself did should
he be punished as a criminal, *quia actus pecati aliquid personale est*.[3]

The problem of Original Sin was more profound than the
legal difficulty of punishing collective guilt. That arose when
many persons, each and all, were accused in varying degrees of

---

[1] I. T. Eschmann. 'St Thomas and the Decretal of Innocent IV. Romana Ecclesia.,'
    MS, viii, p. 33.
    P. Gillet. *La personalité juridique en droit ecclesiastique*, Malines, 1927.
[2] I. T. Eschmann. 'Thomistic Social Philosophy and the Theology of Original
    Sin.' *MS* ix, pp. 19–55. Toronto, 1947.
[3] 1a–2ae. lxxxvii, 7, 8. *II Sentences*, XXXVII, i, 4.

co-operating criminally to abuse the specific means offered by their community-organization. The more humane jurists sought to exclude the innocent from the penalty; for this reason Innocent IV abolished the practice of mass-excommunication.[1] It was appreciated that sin was an ambiguous term when applied to a fault of the race and a fault of the person. All the same, was not Original Sin indiscriminate in its effects—even more so than the hydrogen bomb? The tentative solutions proposed—for even the scholastic theologians recollected that they were addressing themselves to a mystery—took two different lines; one may be called biological, the other juridical.[2]

Along the first the human race was approached as a single descent-group. The hereditary infection which was seen to run through it from its origins provoked reflections in various moods. The lust which bore us from the loins of Adam might be lamented or the inevitable consequences of belonging to the physical world of predatory natures might be more dispassionately assessed. Whether it occasioned revulsion or resignation Original Sin was seen as a flaw transmitted to all who are generated from the same origins and belong to the same mass. The streak ran through the entire *corpus malorum*, and therefore through us all. If you inquire, Vincent of Beauvais remarked, whether it be contracted by violence or by will or by nature, then we reply by nature, and by corrupt nature at that, though by previous just secret judgment of God.[3]

Along the second line of argument the problem of our solidarity in sin moved in a more legal setting; the human race was treated as a single constitutional association which fell from original justice in the person of its first representative formally appointed by divine Providence, and so was continued throughout posterity, disinherited and deprived of its titles to happiness.

Both themes appeared in St Thomas. He sought analogies

[1] See *IV Sentences*, XVIII, ii, 3, *ii*.
[2] J. B. Kors. *La justice primitive et le péché originel d'après saint Thomas.*
R. Bernard. *Somme Théologique. Le Péché*, i, Appendice 2. Paris, 1931.
For some of the background difference see E. Gilson. 'Pourquoi saint Thomas a critiqué saint Augustin.' *AHDL*, i, pp. 5–127. Paris, 1926–7.
[3] *Speculum Naturale*, xxix, 98.

from medicine, physiology, psychology, logic and law to try to
explain why the tragedy should have spread. At first he took
Original Sin as a racial defect, without labouring the point of
individual involvement.[1] He observed the point of law, that a
child is *res patris*, the fact that a family sank to poverty as a
result of the parents' fault and that disease can be inherited,
although as in the case of the man born blind, it was idle to
track down the blame.[2] He also scouted in Porphyry's logic, on
the common sharing of individuals in the species, to see if he
could find some clue there to explain the notion of a general
sin.[3]

His final thought revolved round two arguments. The first
compared the human race to a single organism, in which all
individual parts were moved by a common will, and conceived
Original Sin as a *peccatum naturae*; the second compared it to
a single community put to trial and found guilty in the person
of its representative, and compared Original Sin to a *delictum
universitatis*. We were responsible for what our rulers did, *quod
princeps civitatis facit dicitur civitas facere*.[4] Their contrast of the
two arguments was sharpened by the disputes of two Dominican
theologians, Dominic Soto and Ambrose Caterini, at the
Council of Trent.

Less involved in natural philosophy than the medieval
authors and affected by the Roman theory of corporations, the
theologians of the Baroque enlarged on the attributes of legal
personality attaching to sovereignty. Stressing the second
argument, they put Adam in the position of the *princeps* of the
civitas humana which by divine covenant had been given a grant
of corporateness. The first argument, less juridical and closer to
racial sources and instinctive motions, has been revived in
recent years: anthropology has discovered how widespread is
the figure of the public scapegoat, who acts as a vehicle to
draw off the evils which afflict a whole people.[5] We are the

---

[1] *II Sentences*, XXX, i, 1, 2.
[2] *II Sentences*, XXXIII, i, 2, ad 3, 4, 5. Commentary, *St John*, ix, *lect.* 1.
[3] *IV Contra Gentes*, 50, 52.
[4] Disputations, IV *de Malo*, 1. Commentary, *Romans*, v, lect. 3. *Compendium Theologiae*, 196. 1a–2ae. lxxx, 1.
[5] J. G. Frazer. *The Golden Bough: A Study in Magic and Religion*. Abridged ed.
lvii, lviii. New York, 1945.

seed of Adam; he is less our prince than our begetter. There is a kind of will, *voluntas totius humanae naturae*, primarily in the head and consequently in the members, which descends to each of us from our natural origin. From the failure of this will we are weakened in body and soul, vulnerable and exposed to destructive forces.[1] A *vis praeditiva* now roves through the *universitas humana* as it does through the *universitas politica*.[2]

The corporate sin of mankind cast but the faintest shadow of a 'Race-Soul' theory to the eyes of the medievals. Yet they might have found something suggestive in the notion of a collective unconscious, the repository of ancient and dynamic images, called archetypes by Professor C. G. Jung, which may represent past stages of development.[3] And why not also of past lapse? As it may go to explain the sense of 'God-almightiness' which is the heritage of some peoples—'we don't do that sort of thing in the Buffs'—so may it serve for the awareness of lack of integrity widespread in the entire human race.

The Aristoteleans, however, would have recollected that symbolism was one discipline and rational metaphysics another, and to the latter there was no such thing as a human group possessing substantial identity. The ascription of corporateness and personality was guarded—*omnes homines possunt considerari ut unus homo, reputatur communitas quasi unus homo*.[4] A quasi-personality was granted, inasmuch as the organized group was bent on an end which was not the sum of the personal purposes of its components, and for this reason the science which studied it, namely political philosophy, was not resolved in the ethics of personal activity.

The common good was different in kind, not merely in number and degree, from the total of single goods.[5] Emergent characteristics are disclosed by the group which are not those of its members; thus the first Lord Halifax noted an accumulative cruelty in a number of men though none in particular are ill-natured. It is shown in the jeers hurled at the referee during

[1] 1a. lxxxii, 4. lxxxi, 3, *ad* 2. 1a–2ae. lxxxii, 1, *ad* 1, 3.
[2] See *I Politics*, lect. 6.
[3] N. P. Williams, *The Ideas of the Fall and of Original Sin*. p. 528. London, 1927.
   V. White. *God and the Unconscious*. London, 1952.
[4] 1a–2ae. lxxxi, 1.
[5] 2a–2ae. lviii, 7, ad 2. *I Ethics*, lect. 1. *I Politics*, lect. 1.

a professional soccer-match. Mass-hysteria is another case in point, and, of greater dignity, the majestic tread and devastating volleys of the Fusiliers at Albuera. On more humdrum occasions too, it is evident how business done through groups of people acting collectively as committees differs from the conduct of single individuals.[1]

8. A Note on Terminology

Here and there these pages have suggested that St Thomas allowed for two extreme types of human conjunction. One corresponded to the material cause or stuff of civilized association: it was the mass into which a man was born or otherwise incorporated, and to which he belonged as a part subordinate to the whole, a unit in a scheme, an instrument for an overriding community purpose. The other corresponded to the final cause or purpose: it was a communication of minds and wills through contemplation and charity, a society which involved no surrender of identity or of proper interests and was loaded with no burden of duties and rights, though these may be embraced.[2] Between these extremes was placed a combination, namely the political community which rose from the first and aspired to the second—a mixed type and, like a mongrel, all the tougher for not being of one strain. The nature of a group was determined by what sort of things composed it—hence the difference between a producer-consumer in a community, a friend in a society, and a citizen in a State.[3]

St Thomas's political philosophy can be accordingly presented as a dialectic based on these three abstract types, the pure community, the pure society and the society-community.[4] His terminology, however, followed no consistent usage and sometimes was indiscriminate. His general heading was *communitas*, the equivalent of Aristotle's *koinonia*, an analogical term which included logical and real wholes or groups of every

---

[1] K. C. Wheare. *Government by Committee*. Oxford, 1955.
[2] III *Contra Gentes*, 158. 1a–2ae. lxxxvii, 7. 3a. xlviii, 2, *ad* 1.
[3] III *Politics*, lect. 1.
[4] See T. Gilby. *Between Community and Society*.
   I. T. Eschmann. *Studies on the Notion of Society in St Thomas Aquinas*. MS, viii, pp. 1–42. 1946.

kind. It could stand for a generalized classification, a mass, a household, a city, a fellowship, a partnership, a commonalty, the universe itself. *Universitas* was a synonym, usually taken by St Thomas in its widest sense—as by Cicero, thus *in universitate rerum*, or *in universitate generis humani*—was coming to have a narrower juridical meaning and signify a set of men joined together for some particular project, who possessed a common property, undertook lawsuits, decided policy by a majority vote and who had been granted by higher authority the *privilegium universitatis*. Such a group might be called a *collegium*.[1]

Groups approximating to the condition of the pure community might be indicated by such terms as *genus humanum*, *gens*, *natio*, *familia*, *patria*; associations which were like the pure society by *amicitia*, *conversatio*, and *communicatio spiritualis*; while for the intermediate group we have *communitas societatis*, also *congregatio*—thus *congregatio corporis mystici*.[2] It is interesting that *communitas* was used for sacramental unity, but *societas* for fellowship in what the sacraments signify, the *res sacramenti*.[3] The terminology was not altogether consistent, for St Thomas also spoke of a *mercationum societas* and *societas oeconomica*.[4]

The political group, *communitas civitatis*, was commonly called the *civitas*: the Aristotelean *polis*, the community in which everything sufficient for life can be found, was extended to the size of a realm or *regnum*.[5] *The* Kingdom in the thirteenth century was not the *Regnum Italicum*, nominally part of the Empire though the field of contention between communes and feudal lords, but St Thomas's own country of Sicily and Naples; the Dominicans in those parts were divided from the *Provincia Romana* to form the *Provincia Regni* (1294), the older Province in North Italy being entitled the *Provincia Lombardiae*. The city was not a place, *urbs*, but the people, *civitas vel populus*; it was

---

[1] *Contra Impugnantes*, 3.
[2] 2a–2ae. ci, 1. 1a–2ae. iii, 2, *ad* 3. 2a–2ae. xxiii, 5.
Disputations, *de Caritate, VIII Ethics, lect.* 9. 2a–2ae. xxiii, 1, *ad* 1.
3a. lxv, 1. *IV Sentences*, XV, i, 5. *iv, ad* 3.
Vincent of Beauvais, *Speculum Doctrinale*, vii, 6.
[3] 3a. lxv, 1. lxxiii, 3.
[4] *Contra Impugnantes*, 3. Note the distinction between *auxilium amicorum* and *societas amicorum*, 1a–2ae. iv, 8.
[5] Disputations, *VII de Veritate*, 1. *de Regno* was the alternative title of the *de Regimine Principum. I Politics, lect.* 2.

the *multitudo*, and to be precise, the ordered multitude, *multitudo ordinata*, which functioned as a *coetus* or *collegium populorum*.[1]

He did not echo those Glossators who likened European communities to the municipalities of the classical texts, and which enjoyed no rights as against the *Populus* who had conferred power on the *Princeps* whose successor was the Holy Roman Empire. Instead there is nothing in his writings against a sentiment not uncommon among the Dominicans who came after him, that the rulers of independent States possessed the old imperial prerogatives within their own territories. At the time of Philip the Fair it was said, 'le roi de France est emperour dans son royaume'.

Different nations might own the same political allegiance or one nation might be governed by different rulers, for nation was a term which stood for a geographical grouping. The French Nation at Paris University included the Mediterranean peoples, and the English Nation the Flemings and peoples from across the Rhine and North Sea. Oxford men were divided by the Trent into *Australes* and *Boreales*; the differences between southerners and north-countrymen were composed in 1274, and the term *nations* ceased to be used, 'a symbol,' says Rashdall, 'of that complete national unity which England was the first of the European kingdoms to affirm'.[2]

None of the three main groups as such, the mass or pure community, the political community, and the pure society—certainly not the two extremes—should be imagined to represent complete concrete situations sealed off in different compartments. The historical dialectic proceeded with an intermingling of all three types. Even in the wide world itself, the *universitas rerum*, the perfection of each part derived from its communion in the common good.[3] Hence it was called a commonalty ordered by law.[4] Intelligent creatures made it their own.[5] They

---

[1] 1a–2ae. xcvii, 3, *ad* 3. xcviii, 6, *ad* 2. cv, 3, *ad* 2.
2a–2ae. xcii, 2. c, 6, *ad* 4. 1a. xxxix, 3. 3a. lxxxi, 2.
IV Sentences, XL, i, 1. *Contra Impugnantes*, 7.
[2] *Medieval Universities*, iii, p. 58.
P. Kibre. *The Nations in the Mediaeval Universities*. Mediaeval Academy of America, 49. Cambridge (Mass.), 1948.
[3] 1a. xliv, 4. III *Contra Gentes*, 19–21, 24.
[4] 1a. lxxxix, 5. ciii, 1. 1a–2ae. xix, 3, 8, *c* & *ad* 2. xxi, 4, *ad* 3.
[5] 1a–2ae. iv, 8. v, 1, 5, *ad* 1. 2a–2ae. ii, 3.

became partners with God, and enjoyed the intercourse of persons with persons.[1] Companionship above all, for, though justice needed friendship, friendship could dispense with justice.[2]

[1] 1a. ciii, 5, *ad* 3. 1a–2ae. xci, 2. xcix, 3. c, 2, 3.

[2] *VIII Ethics, lect.* 1.

VIII

THE RECEPTION OF ARISTOTLE

THERE seems to have been no period of his life when St Thomas did not write as an Aristotelean, even when he had not yet discovered Aristotle's mind on an issue. Nevertheless he was no mere repeater of another man's arguments. For one thing he was not equipped to set them in their historical context, for another he was not always in possession of a clear and authentic text. In any case he held that argument from human authority held the lowest place in science—the point is not, who said it? but, is it true?[1] Respect for the Philosopher nowhere implied that his patronage was a substitute for hard thinking, and St Albert made mock of the awe which regarded Aristotle as a god.[2] Many quotations were in effect free adaptations, many conclusions exceeded the range of Greek speculation.

When St Thomas was a student and young lecturer at Paris the Masters of the Arts Faculty had not yet declared that Aristotle's philosophy was equivalent to philosophy itself, and the troubles of the Double-Truth Theory—that truths of reason could contradict truths of faith yet both be professed—were yet to come. The Franciscans refused to separate, in St Bonaventure's phrase, the water of philosophy from the wine of the Scriptures; the Dominicans of the period legislated against profane novelties—so much philosophy was allowed, but not too much. The brethren were not to address themselves to the secular sciences and liberal arts, nor to study books of pagan philosophy, though they might dip in them for an hour or so—the 'hour' was a concession soon stretched. In comment-

---

[1] 1a. i, 8. *de Coelo et Mundo*, i, *lect.* 22.

[2] *VIII Physics, cap.* i,

ing on the *Sentences* St Albert used the great seventh book of the *Ethics* on justice; St Bonaventure ignored it.[1]

During the decade following his death St Thomas was episcopally condemned at Paris and Oxford; the Franciscans maintained their hostility to his teaching much longer.[2] His Scholastic opponents were no obscurantists. They esteemed Aristotle, blended Avicennism with their Augustianism, and were ardent and exacting scientific investigators. What they feared was the establishment of a self-contained world of human values owing nothing to revealed religion, and their fears were largely borne out by the later development of scientific and political thought in the West. The reaction of the divines against lay-minded philosophy and law was prompt and the interdictions of Aristotle in 1215 and 1231 were recalled. No wonder the rising young Dominicans soon after the middle of the century were accused of naturalism and worse for espousing so whole-heartedly the new cause—St Albert sometimes irascibly, St Thomas always composedly.[3]

Both possessed the complete texts of Aristotle's two main works on social philosophy, the *Nichomachean Ethics* and the *Politics*. The two books of the *Economics*, by an early Peripatetic, mentioned three times by St Albert but never by St Thomas,

---

[1] B. M. Reichert. *Acta Capitulorum Generalium Ordinis Praedicatorum* 1220–1303. Monumenta Historica, iii. Rome–Stuttgart, 1898.

B. M. Reichert. *Litterae Encyclicae Magistrorum Generalium*, 1223–1376. Monumenta Historica, v. Rome-Stuttgart, 1900.

M. D. Chenu. 'The Revolutionary Intellectualism of St Albert.' *Blackfriars*, January, 1938. Oxford.

Humbert of Romans. *Opera de vita regulari*. Ed. J. J. Berthier. Rome, 1888.

[2] M. Burbach. 'Early Dominican and Franciscan Legislation regarding St Thomas.' *MS*. iv. Toronto, 1942.

P. Glorieux. 'Comment les thèses thomistes furent proscrites à Oxford (1284–86).' *Revue Thomiste*, xxxiii, pp. 259–91. St Maximin. 1928.

E. Gilson. *History of Christian Philosophy in the Middle Ages*. pp. 387–427. 'The Condemnation of 1277.'

[3] M. Grabmann. *Mitteralterliches Geistesleben, Band II*. xiv, xvi, xvii. Munich 1936.

E. Gilson. 'Les sources Gréco-Arabes de l'augustinisme avicennisant.' *AHDL*, iv. pp. 142–9. Paris, 1930.

R. de Vaux. 'La première entrée d'Averroès chez les Latins.' *RSPT*, xxii, pp. 193–243. Paris, 1933.

D. Salman. 'Albert le Grand et l'averroisme latin.' *RSPT*, xxiv, pp. 38–64. Paris, 1935.

may have been translated by William of Moerbeke.[1] The *Ethics* were more freely quoted by St Thomas than any other of Aristotle's works, at first in the Latin version preceding that of William of Moerbeke.[2] Before 1269, when he embarked on the *Secunda Pars* of the *Summa Theologica*, he had completely analysed Moerbeke's text: a comparison of the techniques of his moral science before and after shows a decided advance. As for the *Politics*, his commentary, started some years later, probably in 1269, reached only into the third book.[3] Important as this portion is, especially for its firm assertion of the inherent excellence of political institutions and the naturalness of civilization, the political teaching of the commentary on the *Ethics* is more considerable. The suggestion is unfounded that economic and political questions are omitted: you have only to look at the treatment of general justice in the fifth book, of political prudence in the sixth, of friendship in the eighth and of conventional law in the concluding chapter.[4] Moreover personal virtue was an essential theme in his social morality.

1. *The Commentaries on the* Ethics *and* Politics

Usually when St Thomas's first systematic work, the *Commentary on the Sentences* (1254–6) appealed to the *Nicomachean Ethics*—in Grosseteste's translation—it was rather to drive home a point than to explain an argument. His last systematic work, the *Summa Theologica* (1266–73), was technically more accomplished and more familiar with Aristotle's thought. Its moral part (*Prima Secundae*, 1269–70, and *Secunda Secundae*, 1271–2) was based on his careful and detailed study of Moerbeke's revision of Grosseteste's version of the *Ethics* divided into *lectiones*. The date of this commentary, *in X libros Ethicorum Expositio*, has been moved back by recent research from 1269 to 1266, and it may have been composed in 1264 when the *Contra Gentes* was

---

[1] *Œconomica.* Translated and Edited by E. S. Foster. Oxford, 1921.
   P. Mandonnet. 'Guillaume de Moerbeke, traducteur des Economiques. Albert le Grand et les Economiques.' *AHDL*, viii, pp. 9–35. Paris, 1933.
[2] Thus, in 1256, *the Contra Impugnantes*, 6, *ad* 9, and 7, *ad* 2, referred to *Ethics* ii on the virtuous man, and to iv on the magnanimous and liberal man.
[3] To *III Politics, lect.* 7 inclusively, (1280 a 7).
[4] A. M. Pirotta. Preface, p. xiii. *In decem libros Ethicorum Aristotelis ad Nicomachum expositio.* Turin, 1934.

finished, or even earlier.[1] The witness of Ptolemy of Lucca is not clear on the point in his *Historia Ecclesiastica*.

On the first reading it appears a disappointing document, a mere paraphrase of Moerbeke's text, lacking the reflectiveness of his other commentaries, notably on the *Metaphysics* and *Physics*, and even on the *de Anima*. It marked, however, a decided advance towards the scientific moral doctrine of the *Summa Theologica*. Here was a human morality which was to be sublimated in a theology of grace. From a consideration of the Good to which everything tends, of the End which is the *beatitudo* of rational creatures and of the facts of life, the possible means of achieving happiness were systematically set forth. They are the co-ordinated human acts which proceed from appropriate abilities and habits in response to right objects and ends within the unity of the human organism. The dynamism was exactly analyzed on a scientific classification of kinds and types of activity, but the importance of personal motives and special circumstances was allowed for.[2] The study of human group-activity was set in this context.

Nor is the *Politicorum Expositio* (1269) taken alone more rewarding.[3] Begun too late to affect his thought profoundly, it stopped at the eighth chapter of the third book, the remainder being continued by Peter of Auvergne with a greater bias towards a self-contained rational community than St Thomas

---

[1] P. Mandonnet. *Des écrits authentiques de saint Thomas d'Aquin*. Fribourg, 1910.

M. Grabmann. *Die Werke des hl. Thomas von Aquin*. 3rd ed. p. 284. Munster, 1949.

L. W. Keller. 'The Vulgate text of St Thomas's Commentary on the Ethics.' *Gregorianum*, xvii, p. 434. Rome, 1933.

E. Franceschini. 'S. Tommaso e l'etica nicomachea.' *Rivista di Filosofia Neo-Scholastica*, xxviii, p. 328. Milan, 1936.

G. Verbeke. 'La date du commentaire de saint Thomas sur l'Ethique.' *Revue Philosophique*, xlvii, p. 203. Louvain, 1949.

R. A. Gaulthier. 'La date du commentaire de saint Thomas sur l'Ethique à Nicomaque.' *RTAM*, xviii, pp. 66–105. Louvain, 1951.

[2] 1a–2ae. xviii, 1, 2, 3, 8, 9.

H. Y. Jaffa, *Thomism and Aristoteleanism: A Study of the Commentary by Thomas Aquinas on the Nicomachean Ethics*. Chicago, 1952.

[3] *In VIII Libros Politicorum Expositio, seu de Rebus Civilibus*. Vol. xxi of the Parma *Opera Omnia*, p. 364–466. Paris, 1966.

A. O'Rahilly. 'Notes on St Thomas: II, The Commentary on the Politics.' *Irish Ecclesiastical Record*, xxx, pp. 614–622. Dublin, 1948.

perhaps would have shown. However he seems to have been acquainted with the whole of the *Politics*—he quoted the eighth book. At the beginning of his commentary on the third book he surveyed topics raised in the fourth and seventh books, though he made no detailed examination of the separation of governmental powers.[1] To the 104 references to the *Politics* in the *Summa Theologica*, of which twelve are to texts outside his commentary, there are but three references in the *Contra Gentes*. The *Ethics*, which was cited much more frequently, played a preponderant part in the formation of his social theory.

St Albert's study of the *Politics* appeared about the same time.[2] The two Dominicans were the first Latin expositors of a work which, with Plato's *Republic* and *Laws*, is the chief contribution of Greece to Western political theory. A comparison is interesting. Both commentaries were running explanations of a Latin word-for-word translation from the Greek. They divided and sub-divided every phrase of Aristotle's argument step by step. Both authors may be assumed to approve the doctrine they are elucidating unless the contrary clearly appears, but their intention was rather to present an impartial exposition than to express their own personal views; these were to be found elsewhere in their *quaestiones* and *summae*.

Neither was aware that the text was a mosaic and that the traditional order of the books needs to be re-arranged.[3] They knew nothing about Aristotle's own *Constitution of Athens*, and little about the cultural background to social and political patterns of classical times. They did not appreciate that the Greeks themselves were heirs to the mature civilizations of Troy, or that Mycenae and Crete were matrices of both. But then they were not undertaking the sort of criticism for which they were not qualified, and their occasional touches of historical information come almost as a surprise, as when the importance of sea-power to Athens was noted, or the fact that cattle-raising preceded crop-growing in the history of culture.[4]

---

[1] *Politics*, vii, 12–14.
[2] *Opera Omnia*. Ed. A. Borgnet, viii, Paris, 1891.
[3] W. Jaeger. *Aristotle, Fundamentals of the History of his Development*. Transl. K. Robinson. Oxford, 1934. The books of the *Politics* are set out in this chronological order—ii, iii, vii, iv, v, vi, i.
[4] *I Politics*, lect. 2. 1a–2ae. xciv, 2. *in Job, i, lect.* 1.

Despite minor misreadings on points of detail, for instance on slavery,[1] they showed a remarkable sympathy with and understanding of Aristotle's discourse isolated from its historical context—it was as if they were explaining a contemporary. They referred to his Greek interpreters, Alexander of Aphrodisias, Porphyry, Themistius and Simplicius, and were familiar with Jewish and Arab thought; their religious bent was towards Avicenna, yet their respect for Averroes, if critical, was generously acknowledged.

St Albert's style was vivid, rather uncouth; he was inclined to be wild with his etymologies and to guess at a meaning, like a cockney explaining the Elephant and Castle without a nod towards the Infanta of Castille. He took *Rhetora* as the proper name of a writer on jurisprudence, and, confusing timocracy and democracy, remarked *demos enim divites sunt. Dike*, he also construed, *civilis communicatio est.*[2] He professed to restrain himself to the plain exposition of the text, *nunquam de me dixi aliquid, sed opiniones peripateticorum quanto fidelius potui exponi*;[3] in fact here, as in his other commentaries, he could not resist a fling at his fellow divines for obstructing the advance of science and philosophy. St Thomas, more self-effacing, wrote more drily and with fewer digressions. His divisions were neater; he made less parade of authorities from Greek and Latin literature, and was quicker to suggest the Christian setting of a topic; he spoke of marrying where St Albert spoke of mating. His information was not so extensive and possibly he touched contemporary life at fewer points, but he was the more careful and synthetical thinker, and the greater theologian.

The *Summa Theologica* and the *Contra Gentes* made forty-three references to the *Timaeus*, twenty each to the *Phaedo* and the *Phaedrus*, nine to the *Republic*, eight to the *Parmenides*, five to the *Theaetetus*, four to the *Alcibiades* (authenticity doubtful) and to the *Meno*, three to the *Philebus* and to the *Laws*. The communism of the *Republic* criticized by Aristotle was mentioned by Moerbeke as occurring in some sort of way in Plato's political thought

---

[1] *Politics*, i, 6.
[2] *I Politics, cap.* 4, 3, 2.
[3] *Epilogue*, Ed. Borgnet, viii, p. 803. F. Pelster. *Kritische Studien zum Leben und zu den Schriften Alberts des Grossen*. Freiburg. 1920.

—*quemadmodum in politia Platonis.*[1] The locus according to St
Albert was the second part of a book called the *Timaeus*, which
he described as a treatise on positive justice and the ordering
of cities, adding that such a treatise was not a common Latin
interest, *quas apud Latinos rara est, quamvis habeatur a quibusdam.*
St Thomas was no less perfunctory.[2] Where Aristotle admired
the originality and inquiring spirit of Plato's writings and
warned us that perfection is not to be expected everywhere,
Moerbeke mistranslated and presented Socrates' talk as
redundant, trifling, immature and querulous, *superfluum quidem
habent omnes Socratis sermones et leve et nobum et quaestionum plenum.*[3]
St Albert and St Thomas were little more considerate. How could
they have been otherwise?

2. *The Brief Neo-Hellenism*

Susemihl, the first editor of Moerbeke's translation of the
Politics, praised him for his faithfulness and for reproducing the
curtness of the original.[4] It must be confessed, however, that
the medieval Latin versions of Aristotle are crabbed documents,
and insertions from Arabic authors do not make for easier
reading. The look of whole paragraphs and *lectiones* is unin-
viting, though occasional phrases are telling. No considerations
of literary style deterred the later Scholastics from tying and
untying the knots of close argument.

Whatever the reason—the growth of analytic specialization
or of the apparatus for government or too rich an experience
for the academics to assimilate—the fact was that as the thirteenth century wore on so the jargon of experts increased at the
expense of graciousness. Their terminology may have achieved
exact description, but it was not communicative except to
people in the know, as happens when specialists lack a general
education. The clichés of Scholasticism were not even in plain
wording. The poets, historians and orators of ancient Rome
were omitted from the Arts curriculum of Paris; grammar

---

[1] *Politics* ii, 1. 1261 a 5 (Republic IV, 421c–427b, 457b).

[2] *I Politics, cap.* 1 & *lect.* 1.

[3] *Politics* ii, 6. 1265a 10. St Albert. *cap.* 3. St Thomas, *lect.* 6.

[4] *Aristotelis Politicorum libri octo cum vetusta translatione Gulielmi de Moerbeka.* Leipzig,
1872.

drove out literature and cramming from set books replaced browsing on the classics.[1] Even for Orleans, where the tradition of Chartres lingered longer than in other French universities, there is scant documentary evidence that a regular Faculty of Arts existed after the end of the century. It is not much of an exaggeration to say that the fertile deposits from twelfth-century humanism were blown into dust, the racy allegories of the biblical theologians were left brittle by the logicians, and the rich humours of custom were dried under the legists.[2]

Music and mathematics were sisters, but philosophy was forgetting how to sing. The schoolmen disputed about abstract truths; they did not show us their hearts. Lengthy passages of analysis in rough logical notation were unrelieved by description. A few intermittent prose lyrics relieved the *Summa Theologica* but the work was less eloquent than the *Contra Gentes*, and neither could compare with the best work of earlier divines. Chartres was no longer a school; only its cathedral survived to manifest the marriage of the perfect ratios of Pythagoras with the philosophy of light.[3] Theologians left the gardens and fields to the painters and profane poets. To the philosophers they were but an occasion for a treatise on vegetables. It is is strange that an intellectual conviction of the real and not merely symbolical value of the sensible world should have waxed with a decay of style in declaring its beauty.

Such however was the effect of Latin Aristoteleanism, except in the theology of the devout life.[4] Even there Petrarch deplored the professionalism it engendered, and spiritual writers preferred a *docta ignorantia*. Symbolism turned on ecclesiastical ornamentation, natural science failed to live up to its promise at the time of Grosseteste, the full empirical method practised by St Albert, particularly in zoology, relapsed into the hearsay

---

[1] H. Denifle and E. Chatelain. *Chartularium Universitatis Parisiensis*, i, 228, 278; ii, 678; iii, 145. Paris, 1889–97.

[2] E. Faval. *Les arts poétiques de XIIe et XIIIe siècles*. Paris, 1933.
  H. Waddell. *The Wandering Scholars*. v, 'Humanism in the first half of the Twelfth Century.'
  E. Gilson. 'Le moyen âge et le naturalisme antique.' *AHDL*, viii. Paris, 1932.

[3] O. von Simson. *The Gothic Cathedral: The Origins of Gothic Architecture and the Medieval Concept of Order*. London, 1956.
  K. Clark. *Landscape into Art*, i, 'The Landscape of Symbols'. London, 1949.

[4] H. Grundmann. *Religiöse Bewegungen im Mittelalter*. Berlin, 1935.

of the medieval bestiaries, philosophy was lost in nominalism. Not surprisingly fables abounded and the world seemed composed less of objects of fresh observation, experiment, and research, than of hackneyed allegories with a moral—the pelican in its piety, the viper a warning to frigid women.[1] If the humanities languished under Scholasticism and an earlier warmth and colour were dispelled, still the arts and philosophy had not altogether drifted apart in the thirteenth century. Men were at least trying to argue with a real Aristotle, not to exhibit a dummy dressed up in scholastic orthodoxy. The sap of humanism still flowed beneath the wrinkled integument.

On occasion St Thomas could write with elegance and feeling, as some of his prologues and his liturgical poems bear witness. Cicero and Seneca were quoted, the poets too, Horace, Ovid and Terence, the historians Julius Caesar and Livy, the geographer Strabo. Macrobius was used and, on points of political doctrine, the anecdotes of Valerius Maximus. Sallust was often referred to in the *de Regimine Principum*. The military text of Vegetius—Marlborough's favourite reading—sprang to his mind on points of Scripture.[2] Like other medievals he had learnt from the *Timaeus* the justice of the world-order, and an early fourteenth-century fresco by Triani at Pisa portrays him seated between Plato and Aristotle who offer him their books. Quotations from most authors were usually at second-hand. Polybius was not consulted, Cassiodorus was known only for his exposition of the Psalter. It is said, however, that he possessed a wider knowledge of Greek patristic literature than most of his immediate predecessors and contemporaries.[3]

His workaday prose, terse and laconic of phrase, repetitive of commonplace analogies and monotonous in syntax, was sufficiently functional and sometimes revealed a certain spare beauty undecorated by imagery: usually he composed by

---

[1] *The Book of Beasts*. Edited by T. H. White. London, 1954.
  A. C. Crombie. 'Grosseteste's Position in the History of Science.' *Robert Grosseteste, Scholar and Bishop*. Ed. D. A. Callus. Oxford, 1955.

[2] *de Factis Dictisque Memorabilibus Libri IX. Rei Militaris Instituta.*
  1a-2ae. xl, 5. 2a-2ae. cxiii, 1, *ad* 2. cliii, 5, *ad* 2.

[3] I. Backes. *Die Christologie des hl. Thomas von Aquin und die griechischen Kirchenvater.* Paderborn, 1931.

dictation to a secretary.[1] The fixtures of his social and
political theory may look like law-words and logic-words, and
the mechanics of their combination may conceal the lope, one
may well say, the leap of his argument. Latin terms which
came trailing a long history in Roman jurisprudence were
newly inflected from Greek thought and breathed an ampler
air than the categories of law, thus, for example, *consensus, usus,
imperium, ratio, dominium, naturale, jus, societas, judicium, mos* and
aequitas. The Roman *dos* was heightened to signify the lissome-
ness, glow and other qualities of human bodies after the Resurrection.[2] Later Scholasticism scarcely sustained the freshness
and naturalism.

Few writers of the thirteenth century were well-versed in
Greek. *Politica vero a polis, quod est pluralitas*, hazarded Vincent
of Beauvais.[3] Roger Bacon was scathing about 'inexpert boys
who were made Masters before they were fit to be scholars'.
Yet he also referred to men well able to work from Greek texts.[4]
They were to be found in the circles in which St Thomas
moved—William Moerbeke was a conspicuous example—and
the scraps of Greek in his commentaries were lifted from
Grosseteste. Interpretations of Aristotle were more confident
when dealing with ideas, as in the first book of the *Politics*,
than with Greek history, as in the second book. His insight into
Aristotle's mind was remarkable, especially when it is remembered how easily he could have been distracted by the Neo-
Platonists and the Arab Aristoteleans. A genuine Hellenism
was recaptured: a pity it was lost so soon. Perhaps a genuinely
philosophical discourse which corresponded to the Greek City
could not answer to the new Nation-States or manage the
apparatus of Roman Law taken over from the Late Empire
and furbished by the Glossators.

Then also he met and lived with other Dominicans, either
attached to the *Provincia Graeciae*, the thirteenth foundation of
the Order (1228), in whose territory the still unruined Parthe-
non was a Christian temple, or working in the Near and Middle

---

[1] A. Dondaine. *Secrétaires de Saint Thomas*. Rome, 1956.
[2] *Supplementum*, lxxxii–lxxxv.
[3] *Speculum Doctrinale*, iv, 2.
[4] *Opus Minus*, 7. Opus Tertium, xxv.

East. His *de Regimine Principum* was dedicated to the King of Cyprus; in return a chapel was dedicated to him after his death in the Cathedral of Nicosia. Though most of the friars were Westerners, mistrusted by the Greeks as intruders and chaplains to the Frankish aggressors or to the Genoese and Venetian traders, others were true Hellenists, acquainted with the literature of the men with whom they debated. If Greek was taken into Latin so was Latin into Greek—the translation might even be of the Latin version of a Greek Father.[1]

The commerce of ideas between West and East matched the trade exchange of woollens, salted fish and ironmongery for silks, spices and precious stones. Both were paralleled by the attempt to impose Western political forms and ecclesiastical discipline and ritual on the occupied territories of the Eastern Empire. The Byzantines were proud of their culture and disposed to dismiss Latin theology as crude because of the alleged poverty of its language. Though the title of Romans adhered, as Gibbon said, to the last fragments of the Empire of Constantinople, the name of Frank and Latin had acquired an equal signification and extent and the Latin tongue had fallen into gradual oblivion since the reign of Justinian.[2]

The split between the Western and Eastern Churches was now beyond human repair; the crucial date was not 1054 under the Patriarch Michael Cerularius, but 1204, when the behaviour of the Latins during the Fourth Crusade brought to a head the resentment the Greeks had long felt about the establishment of the Frankish and German Empires, their apprehensions of designs on the Balkans by the Normans who had conquered Byzantine Italy and their disapproval of the Hildebrandine reforms which had made the Pope his own Emperor.[3] From fear of the Turk the schism was temporarily healed—it was the main business of the Council of Lyons to which St Thomas was travelling when he died—but the fundamental differences of ideology, liturgy and discipline were not composed, and Constantinople was nervous about the ambitions of the dour

[1] R. Loernetz. *Autour du traité de fr. Barthelmy de Constantinople contre les Grecs.* AFP vi, pp. 267–311, 361–71. Rome, 1036.

[2] *Decline and Fall of the Roman Empire*, ch. liii.

[3] S. Runciman. *The Eastern Schism: A Study of the Papacy and the Eastern Churches during the XIth and XIIth Centuries.* Oxford, 1956.

king at Naples, Charles of Anjou, brother to St Louis and friend of the Dominicans—though rumour passed into legend that he was reputed to have poisoned St Thomas.

The Western Church was never quite able to forget that its first language was Greek. Nevertheless its adoption of Latin, the language of a long tradition of law and administration, brought its own subtle dangers to philosophical and religious thinking especially when it became a kind of *lingua franca*, a medium between peoples with their own different and racier vernaculars, and relapsed into a condition like that of pidgin English, useful for business transactions but not for the communication of imaginative and abstruse conceptions. The ordinary people were unable to enter into its discourse, and it became a class-language for schoolmen. It served for clerics in the Canon Law and professionals in the Civil Law; it invested the forms of religion itself so that many became matters of sectional interest, unlike the great days of Eastern Christianity, when speculation and the liturgy were conducted in a language generally understood and an educated body of laymen threw itself into theological debates.

The grave genius of Latinity fitted the disputation when terms—and ideas—were cut and polished as if they were stones. In the hands of many of his successors, trained in canonical legalism, St Thomas's moral science took on a hard glitter and his dialectic lost its suppleness. The response of the single human substance to the living God was analysed into a set of abstract items, which were isolated and made to look like granulated particles within a system of regulations mechanically adjusted to a hairsbreadth. Whereas he had recognized an inner finality in law, even in its sanctions, and had related the idea of power to ultimate felicity, later social theologians had the air of insisting on the *status quo*.[1] Whereas he had taken *imperium* as the expression of practical wisdom charging a right human act at the moment of performance, they transformed it into the dictate of governing will.[2] Whereas he had treated right as the

---

[1] 1a–2ae. ii, 4. xc, 3, *ad* 2. 2a–2ae. lxvii, 1.
  V Metaphysics, lect, 1. *I Politics, lect*. 1–5.

[2] 1a–2ae. xvii, 1–9. *III Ethics, lect*. 1. *VI, lect*. 9. *III de Anima, lect*. 15. Disputations, XVII *de Veritate*, 3.

dikaion of the Greeks and the equity of the Roman Stoics, for them it was the less elastic *jus* of the legalists.[1] Whereas he acknowledged the spiritual freedom of the person talking with God beyond the scheme of creatures, their notion was less versatile.[2] The freeman became merely the possessor of such rights which the ruler allowed as not detrimental to the State and which were accordingly guaranteed against violation or trespass by another private person, and of a capacity for originating such action as belongs to the scheme of law. The process had been at work in the life of the Western Church since the beginning of the Middle Ages. A position for every clerk in the hierarchy of jurisdiction was defined; there was no ordination without a title, and this was provided by the benefice, or permanent endowment for the office.[3]

The ideal of the *civitas*, a harmonious common life, gained in clearness but lost in richness when it was legalized as a *vinculum sociale* engendering an obligation, and that, according to juridical theologians, *ex delicto*, for human nature was criminal, they thought, and unless prevented by law man will prey on man. To St Thomas, on the other hand, citizenship was an active partnership, a sharing in a social process, as well as the possession of certain legally guaranteed rights. A *politia* was a living association adapting itself to people's various and changing needs as well as a legal and immobile setting, or *Status*, established once for all.[4] The common good was more embracing and generous than the public good. Social life had not yet been tidied up by the detailed legislating of a central authority; there was more of a sprawl about it than a political planner would like, and also a profounder *pietas* and religion.

The *multitudo ordinata* was peopled with persons striving for their proper ends rather than with individuals set in their proper places. 'Reason', according to St Thomas, was less the

---

[1] *I Metaphysics, lect.* 3. (i, 2, 982 b 25).

[2] *de Hebdomadibus*, Prologue. *III Sentences*, X,ii,2, iii. I *de Potentia*. 1. X *de Veritate*, 2, *ad* 5.

[3] G. le Bas. 'Canon Law'. *LMA* p. 330–1.

[4] 2a–2ae. clxxxiii, 1, 2.

A. E. Zimmern. *The Greek Commonwealth: Politics and Economics in Fifth-Century Athens.* Oxford, 1922.

Latin *ratio* than the Greek *logos*. In a sense he had to wrestle
with unyielding terms; his achievement may be compared with
the effect of Rubens on previous Flemish mannerisms. It will
pass unnoticed unless his constant use of analogy is appreciated
and the variations he played on the meaning of terms. The
law-words he used in social philosophy should not be taken in
an unequivocal sense. His use of contrasting forms in a single
situation is coarsened when treated as the shaking of lumps in a
deposit; thus his teaching on the so-called 'mixed life' of
perfection was later rendered as if it demanded periods of
contemplation interspersed with bouts of activity.[1] Greek
modulations also should relax Latin words in the context of
ownership, of law and of obedience. *Superior* and *praelatus* kept
their sense of high place and preference, but *auctoritas* recovered
its old sense of *fontalitas*; ruling meant pasturing, and principality proclaimed origin rather than self-assertiveness.[2]

Let us not exaggerate the inflexibility of contemporary
Latin. In the thirteenth century it was not yet a dead language,
and accent and assonance, which disregarded the quantities of
literary Latin, were telling effects in expository treatises and
chancery documents as well as in poetry. St Jerome's Vulgate,
as Dean Milman said, had almost created a new language,
pliant and expansive, naturalizing Eastern imagery, modes of
expression and religious notions, yet retaining much of its own
peculiar strength and solidity. Later came rhyme, then new
rhythms from the vernacular. Hymnody borrowed from the
secular lyric, and the Goliards who parodied liturgical pieces
were merely reversing the process; in those days the partition
was thin between the sacred and the profane.[3] Some things are
better said *in romana*, said Hugh of St Victor. St Thomas
preached in the Neapolitan, but the tang of romance in his

---

[1] 2a–2ae. clxxxviii, 6.

[2] *I Sentences*, XXIX, i, 1. 1a. xxxiii, 4, *ad* 1. 3a. xvi, 11. lv, 5. lxiv, 6. 2a–2ae.
lxxiv, 1. xcviii, 3.
Commentary, *Psalms*, xxii, 1.
T. Roberts. *Black Popes: Authority, its Use and Abuse.* London, 1954.

[3] See S. Gaselee. *The Transition from the Late Latin Lyric to the Medieval Love Poem.*
Cambridge, 1931.
F. J. E. Raby. *History of Christian-Latin Poetry from the beginnings to the Close of the
Middle Ages.* Oxford, 1927.
F. Brittain. *The Medieval Latin and Romance Lyric to A.D.* 1300.

writings, blended with Hellenism, evaporated too soon and there was little trace of it in his followers.

One does not have to read between the lines of his scholastic arguments to perceive that humane intercourses were accounted more important than official transactions. He did what Sir Ernest Barker requires for an appreciation of Aristotle's thought: unhooking the word *nature* from the Latin *natura*, with its suggestion of *nativitas*, birth and the primitive, he hitched it to the Greek *phusis*, with its suggestion of growing up and the civilized.[1] *Natura finis est*, translated Moerbeke, *finis rerum naturalium est natura ipsarum*, commented St Thomas.[2] His teleology was less concerned to accumulate external purposes for happenings than to discover the inherent drives at work.[3] The political virtues disposed from within themselves to contemplation.[4] In other words, the present city and the City of God were stages in a single process. By serving our country we may help save our souls and the sword should not sleep in our hand till we have built Jerusalem in a green and pleasant land.

3. *Political Method*

Scholasticism has been compared to Cobdenism or Marxism for its habit of meeting changed circumstances with doctrinaire rigidity, as for example with its allegedly obsolete condemnation of usury. Certainly many social theologians and philosophers of its tradition only grudgingly reconciled themselves to the creation of credit by a paper entry, and never to industrial Capitalism. Perhaps they did not altogether avoid what Lord Salisbury called the commonest error—of sticking to the carcasses of dead policies.

The *a priori* temper of the schoolmen of the high Middle Ages has been exaggerated. They sought everywhere for reasons, some of which appeared far-fetched and empty when the early impulse of Aristotelean empiricism had died out. The later Scholastics, the nominalists included, would have been the

---

[1] *The Politics of Aristotle.* 'Notes on the Vocabulary', p. xxiii.
[2] *Politics*, i, 2. 1252 b 27.
[3] *III Contra Gentes*, 14.
[4] 2a–2ae. clxxx, 2.

better for a dose of positivism. During the thirteenth century, however, it was well recognized that induction was indispensable to sound reasoning and that *a priori* proof was but one half of deduction, and the second half at that. St Thomas's own argumentation never pretended to arrive at facts from principles, rather the reverse, for it was by *a posteriori* deduction that it interpreted the findings of induction from sense-data.[1] His reason was not cold, his metaphysics did not dwell in a lunar landscape of meanings seen in a reflected light. His political theory took account of the variety of social experience, offered no ready-made orthodoxy, and recommended no single line of action from which Utopia would result.

His learning did not comprehend economic history, the comparative study of cultures, or the sociological investigation of human behaviour as affected by the social structure. If he appreciated, which is doubtful, that the distinction between warriors and food-producers was taken for granted by the Greeks and was the foundation of their communities, he himself did not restrict citizenship to an élite living on a tributary population. As we have noticed, his was a civilian, not a military, conception of the State. Then also he belonged to a world-religion with a universal doctrine and law. Consequently the frontiers of his political community were more open than those of the Greeks. Intermarriage between subjects of different City-States was abnormal according to Aristotle; it was not frowned on by the Church's law which then, as now, strove to break down barriers of race, prejudice and accident.

There is little to suggest that the medieval writers ever thought that their plan, still less the accomplishment, of the *civitas* or *regnum* was a reconstruction of antique models. They themselves, the largest body of writers to attract palaeographers, had no knowledge of palaeography. They may appear to us to have been conscienceless about the falsification of facts, yet with respect to history it was their powers of criticism that were deficient rather than their sympathy. They felt the dramatic strength of the Bible and never doubted that it was the authentic word of God, but it was a widespread habit to use the factual

---

[1] T. Gilby, *Barbara Celarent: A Description of Scholastic Dialectic*, xxvii, xxviii. London, 1949.

details chiefly as textual ornamentations to an argument.

When they did not treat history as theology or literature or, as Bolingbroke said, as 'philosophy teaching by examples', they manipulated it as an art rather than a science, and when, for instance, they appealed to such titles as the Donation of Constantine and the Translation of the Empire, their success in shaping the future by their version of the past anticipated the Whig interpretation of Magna Charta or the derogatory picture of Toryism between the two World Wars drawn by Labour publicists.[1] Although they stretched points of history it was not with the passion of later controversialist: the age was not one of confessional conflict like that which produced the *Magdeburg Centuries* or the *Ecclesiastical Annals* of Baronius.

Mythical and real characters were spoken of in the same breath—Aeneas, Trajan, King Arthur, King Alfred, and the Cid Campeador, all were equally real. Alexander the Great was at once a historical figure and the dream-symbol of Daniel's prophecy; he was regarded sometimes as an instrument of God and sometimes as a manifestation of the devil.[2] The medievals were not historicists who felt that an accumulation of events of themselves disclosed meanings; they saw themselves caught up in a living drama of which the acts were the great events of the Redemption played in the soul of Everyman. They had an eye for detail, a taste for anecdote, a keen sense of precedent, and they produced many chroniclers, but history, they thought, was as universal as Divine Providence. They found it in the Bible and the Lives of the Saints. They saw it painted on the broad canvas of St Augustine's *de Civitate Dei*. Their religion was grounded on the deeds of God still made manifest, not on a stock of reasons. History was the record of a world-process which began with the Creation, was centred in Christ and his Church, and culminated in the Judgment. It was not the record of events which stretched into endless future series or ever repetitively circled back.[3]

Their interest was not in pure history. Committed to a

---

[1] See *Deliberatio Domini Papae Innocentii super factum imperii de tribus electis.* PL, ccvi, 1025.

[2] G. Cary. *The Medieval Alexander.* Cambridge, 1956.

[3] J. Baillie. *The Belief in Progress.* London, 1950.

cause, they would have appreciated the bias of a Droysen or Treitschke, but not the detachment of a Ranke. With this difference, however, in the case of the Aristoteleans among them, namely that their dialectic was not an idealism which imagined that ideas could produce facts, or that any abstraction, or accumulations of abstractions, could adequately express real things. Despite his skill with analysis, classification, and synthesis, St Thomas never reckoned, as the Averroists did, that singular substances were trivial because they could not entirely be stated as formal types or schematized.[1] Truth was the uttering of what exists, not the understanding of a bodiless essence, and what exists first of all for the human mind was an individual material thing. Every true statement we made came back to a judgment about the physical world. The mind was in touch with this environment through *ratio particularis*, that is through the experience and experiment of intelligent sensation.[2] Hence natural philosophy, to which moral and political science were were committed, if it were to remain natural must preserve the movement and sensibility of our surroundings and resist the temptation of transferring its conclusions wholly into mathematical notation.[3]

The world was like a woman then, not quite tractable by cold argument. Moreover politics was a discipline which dealt with the practicable in a workaday world. Its proper material was much more contingent than that of natural philosophy. Hence it was not really an exact science. As Clausewitz said of the art of war, that while it must adhere to the capital maxim, maintenance of object, for the rest it operates in the province of chance, for the intrusion of which it must leave a great margin.

Nevertheless its method combined insight into ideas with an examination of facts and decisions about them. If some of its rules were merely the result of digested experience, others were conclusions of higher sciences. For it was not practical to take means and let those ends follow which might. For means were determined by ends, and ends as such were objects of theory.

---

[1] Disputations, *de Caritate*, 2.
[2] *XV de Veritate*, 2. ad 3. 1a. lxxviii, 4. *II de Anima, lect.* 13.
[3] *I Physics, lect.* 1. *de Trinitate*, vi, 1, 2.

Thus prudence applied theory to contingent events.[1] Thus meanings lay behind the technique of politics. That didactic moral generalizations were none of its business might well be granted. Nevertheless if it were to be really practical, as Clarendon recognized, it must allow for transcendental notions, such as Divine Providence working through history and the suprarational character of social happiness, and not reduce itself to the positivism of Hobbes' *Leviathan*.[2]

The Roman Law itself was not developed by mere practitioners but by lawyers who reflected on *ratio naturalis* and its implications. They were rarely so empirical as to be wary about philosophizing. The theoretic apparatus provided by the Byzantine academics was influenced by Christian values. It played an important part in shaping the imperial jurisprudence, as did instruction in the texts of Justinian in reviving it. Yet when all is said and done, politics is specifically empirical and practical.

'Observation shows us that—' this phrase, which began the *Politics*, was sustained throughout. The first disciples of Aristotle in the West were neither exclusively *a priori* in their discourse, nor even deductive, but thoroughly involved in the play of events.[3] They were not political puritans who suffered an abstract principle to override the feelings, desires, hopes and fears of ordinary human beings. They were not so preoccupied with an allegedly divine design as to be forgetful of experience. They were well aware that political science operated in a mutable medium, *in materia variabili et contingenti*, where even justice varied according to differing conditions.[4] Their judgments were not distilled in a vacuum but were in touch with the way things worked. They remembered familiar custom, turned to experience and argued by induction.[5] If they were rationalists their mood was not that of the Enlightenment and French Revolution. If they showed an improving spirit their schemes were not imposed in defiance of the past.

---

[1] *VI Ethics, lect.* 7.
[2] B. H. G. Wormald. *Clarendon.* p. 237, Cambridge, 1951.
[3] R. Linhardt. *Die Sozialprinzipen des hl. Thomas von Aquin.* Freiburg, 1932.
[4] *V. Ethics, lect.* 2, 12. *I, lect.* 3. VI lect. 9. 2a–2ae. xlvii, 3, 6, 7.
[5] *I Ethics*, lect. 11. *II Posterior Analytics*, lect. 20. *II Sentences*, XXV, ii, 2.

Legal science was expected to consult the *sententialia* of judges and limit its precepts to what was practicable. Similarly politics should know that the practicable is not the same as the everything possible. Let it imitate the House of Savoy taking Italy leaf by leaf like an artichoke. Then a disciplined order may be achieved, in which men are content with sufficient justice, suspicious of fanaticism, unsubmissive to a martinet conscience and prepared, like Sir Robert Walpole, to let sleeping dogs lie.

A favourite comparison likened the well-ordered city to the balanced personality composed of different powers, intellectual, volitional, sensitive and emotional.[1] He was not a doctrinaire or an ascetic who attempted to live by will-power alone. He was neither fanatical nor finical. He suffered no part of himself to tyrannize over the rest. He was reasonable, dutiful and sufficiently sensual. He fitted his skin. And so the science which treats of such a political community will not demand abstract demonstration on points of fact: from past experience and present inclination it will distrust a lofty moral tone. It will not be tyrannized over by ideas, still less by incantations, such as equality and colonialism. To use the words of St Thomas More, it will not be the philosophy 'that makes everything to be alike fitting at all times', but 'another philosophy that is more pliable, that knows its own proper scenes, and accommodates itself'; it will recognize that human affirmations or negation do not change the natural course of events.[2] Perhaps political good sense thrives best in a temperate zone. *Est igitur eligenda regio temperata ad institutionem civitatis vel regni.*[3] History bears out the reflection that representative institutions formed in a empirical, sceptical and tolerant atmosphere hardly bear transplanting to a hotter climate.

4. *The Polity*

Let the ruler be the servant of his subjects—the pride and pomp of power may have prevented compliance with this injunction

[1] 1a–2ae. lviii, 2. *V Ethics, lect.* 17. 1a. lxxxi, 3, *ad* 2.
[2] *I Perihermeneias, lect.* 14.
[3] *de Regimine Principum,* ii, 1.

of which a prince was reminded by the ceremonies of Maundy Thursday. He may have been a rough master, but there were many such moments when the Church recalled him to pity and even tenderness. During the thirteenth century it was the general conviction that the realm was preserved by customary and constitutional law. The king was a kind of trustee whose duty it was to safeguard the laws. There was scarcely any important statute in which he omitted to claim that he had consulted advice and received assent, in other words, that he was in agreement with the legal convictions of the community.[1] Powerful interests jealously watched for a breach of promise on his part, and this might well provoke appeal to ecclesiastical authority.

The Church's own government was theocratic not democratic in that authority descended from top to bottom, and the action of the popes was directed towards securing greater freedom from constitutional checks—an issue which came to a head in the later fourteenth and early fifteenth centuries with the disputes between the *conciliaristae* and the *papalistae*—the terms seem to date from Laurence of Arezzo in 1440.[2] Nevertheless the weight of the Canonists, not least those of the Papalist wing, was generally thrown on the side of those who would limit the civil executive by law and popular consent. Their convictions went deeper than their motives about political expedience. Their temper was strongly constitutionalist. They were accustomed to the formal procedure of discussion and agreement. Their bias was toward deliberation and majority decision and away from the magic of majesty acquired by force or inherited by blood.

When St Thomas quoted the *Glossa Ordinaria* to the effect that the prince was above criticism, he capped it with the remark from Gregory IX's *Decretals*, that whatever law a man makes for another that he should keep himself.[3] This text marks his intermediate position between the old constitutionalism of feudal custom and the new absolutism of the legalist

---

[1] F. Kern. *Kingship and Law in the Middle Ages.* p. 73.
[2] *Liber de Ecclesiastica Potestate.* See A. H. Chroust and J. A. Corbett. *MS*, xi, pp. 62—76. Toronto, 1949.
   B. Tierney. *Foundations of the Conciliar Theory.*
[3] 1a–2ae. xcv, 5, *ad* 3.

lawyers. It cannot be alleged that the Canon Law was on the side of liberty as nineteenth-century Liberals conceived it. No Roman lawyer was for freedom in the sense that an English common lawyer used the term. Yet the canons favoured a show of reasonableness and the consent of subjects, and the civil law borrowed much from them, for instance in applying the maxim, *quod omnes tangit ab omnibus approbetur.*[1]

Monarchy was the normal type of government in the Middle Ages. Inside the universe conceived as a hierarchy of powers, the supreme temporal ruler gathered some of the awe due to divine majesty. The *Contra Gentes* made a passing reference to the *altitudo regiae dignitatis,* and the dedication to the King of Cyprus of the *de Regimine Principum* wonders, almost in the eighteenth-century fashion, what might be offered *regiae celsitudini dignum.*[2] Nevertheless there was no feeling that the prince personated Jupiter, no dread of the divinity that hedges in a king. The mystique of the Divine Right of Kings, of the Lord's anointed, of their Sacred Majesties, of Throne and Altar and the romantic ideals of legitimism were later sentiments not generally entertained by the medievals.

The Holy Roman Emperor had once been a *vicarius Dei* and almost a priest, but papal policy, mistrustful of a rival pontiff and a civic sacramentalism, had drily restrained the veneration paid to him: no indelible character was conferred at the coronation anointing. Legend might murmur of Barbarossa, not dead but sleeping in the mountain, and his cult was encouraged by Frederick II's party. But the climate in which St Thomas lived was not favourable to the imperial spell. Cologne was a trading city ruled by its Bishop and merchants, Paris and the Umbrian cities had their own pride, and Naples, though it rallied to Manfred and Conradin, was never part of the Reich. Men west of the Rhine and south of the Alps were not cowed by *Kaiserpolitik;* their princes were no mere *reguli,* and they met an arrogant imperialism much in the spirit of John of Salisbury's sharp rejoinder to Rainald of Dassel, 'Who then appointed the Germans to be judges over the nations?'

---

[1] M. Gaines Post. 'A Romano-Canonical Maxim ... in Bracton.' *Traditio,* iv, pp. 197–251. New York, 1946.

M. V. Clarke. *Medieval Representation and Consent,* p. 266. London, 1936.

[2] *III Contra Gentes,* 49. de Regimine Principum, Prologue. see 1a. cviii, 6.

It was acknowledged that a prince might be compared to a father; he was sire, and an almost involuntary respect for his grandeur conferred on the throne and kingdom the strength of patriarchal loyalty and confidence of race. All the same if St Thomas warmed to non-rational factors of social cohesion, he was cool about purely paternalist rule—political prudence differed from domestic prudence because the State was not a large household.[1] Indeed a Slave-State, apart from its abuses, was rather like a family in that subjects were not their own masters, whereas a true polity was composed of free men and the executive power was constitutionally limited, *coarctata secundum aliquas leges civitatis*.[2] The superiority of the ruler derived more from the excellence of his political virtue than from the glamour of his name, and the ranks of power were computed according to divine causality working through office and not according to ties of blood, emotions of abasement or any submissive sympathy. People should not crave to have their decisions taken for them. There was no *mein Führer* business, the sovereign's duties were rather those of a first magistrate—the thought was closer to Jefferson than to Bolingbroke and the idea of a Patriot-King.[3]

Three strands entered into the idea of monarchy, the central principle of unity, the mode of transmitting kingly power, and the restrictions, if any, on its exercise. As for the first, the arguments for having one person at the head of the community, to look beyond conflicting sectional interests and to direct the whole to the common welfare, were generally admitted; from this point of view, monarchy seemed as natural as the V formation of migrating geese.[4]

Secondly, the succession might be established by heredity, or election, or *coup de main* subsequently ratified. Theologians showed a preference for election, and this too was canonical form—even the absolutist lawyers harked back to a concession of power in the distant past. The imperial dignity itself was not dynastic. Elective representation was in accord with the

---

[1] *Politics*, i, 2. 1252 a 20. 1259 b 8–16.
[2] *I Politics, lect.* 1. *III, lect.* 7. *V Ethics, lect.* 8.
[3] *I Politics, lect.* 10. *de Regimine Principum*, i, 4. (Ptolemy of Lucca. iv, 8)
[4] *de Regimine Principum*, i, 2, 6.

political mood of the Church. It was supported by the moral
teaching that obedience was not submission to force, genial or
otherwise, but the free acceptance of authority as being one's
own and no alien imposition.

Thirdly, was the effective sovereign bound to abide by the
rules agreed on by the people or, the limits set by moral laws
being taken for granted, could his power be exercised abso-
lutely? That was to become a live question. A written constitu-
tition which can be amended only by a referendum and which
constrains both legislature and executive is a modern instrument
only sketchily anticipated in the Middle Ages. A law was a
measure agreed on by a community of freemen, and the ruler
had to observe its bounds. Respect for the liberties of Christian
men was expressed alike by the feudal lawyers and thirteenth-
century publicists, and confirmed by the teachings of Aristotle;
the ruler was subject to the interests of the polity of which he
was part.[1] The now powerful merchant classes shared the same
view: the men of Lincoln maintained that ill luck befell a king
who wore his crown within its walls.

Sparta was praised because the supreme council of State
arrived at its decisions on the basis of written rules set down in
legal form.[2] St Albert described sovereign authority in a
civilized State as being that of one man who accepted the task
of governing other men free like himself, and who did not
command them except according to the constitutional charter.[3]
There was no room for the hero or superman who declared that
the law was what he had in fact enacted. An edict, observed St
Thomas, which is not formed according to reason has the
character of violence, not of law; that is, it exacts a non-
voluntary response, whereas a truly lawful action is performed
reasonably and freely.[4] There was no mention of the
philosopher-king whose wisdom found no need to consult the

---

[1] *Politics*, iii, 6. 1278 b 32. St Thomas, *lect*. 15. Such also was the thought of the
Roman de la Rose.

[2] *II Politics*, *lect*. 14. (ii, 9. 1270 b 30).

[3] *I Politics*, *cap*. 9.

[4] 1a–2ae. xciii, 3, *ad* 2.
P. Halmos, 'Political Leadership and the "Abnorm".' *Towards a Measure of
Man*, pp. 128–143. London, 1957.

will of his subjects or who brought law out of his own bosom. Medieval sentiment was that of Plato's *Laws*, not of the *Republic*.

Left to itself the tendency of this political Aristoteleanism might well have been to transform the king into the first magistrate. It encountered contrary movements, however, set up partly by a mystique of kingship, but more, in the realm of ideas, by the development of the Roman Law. Justinian's *Princeps* became the new model of the ruler. The twelfth century had been robustly critical of kings who acted beyond their powers. The thirteenth century was tamer by comparison. Concerning tyrannicide St Thomas was more hesitant than John of Salisbury and almost, one might say, more prim. He spoke of the right of active resistance more decisively in earlier than in later texts.[1] Though he had nothing but condemnation for the lawless exercise of government and probably remained of the opinion that the people had not entirely alienated their power to the prince, he seemed to grow more sensitive, perhaps more deferential, about the prerogatives of the sovereign, even when they were exercised improperly.[2] No writ could run against the Prince, though he was rightfully subject to the direction of law; no effective power—apart from the Church— existed to dismiss him or coerce him into constitutional paths.[3] This situation has proved a perpetual embarrassment to those Scholastic moralists whose tenet has been that all rebellions are wrong—until they succeed.

Evidence of what St Thomas reckoned was the soundest form of government is furnished by the Constitutions of his own group, the Order of Preachers. He was prominent in its academic administration and was a member of legislative Chapters and Commisions. His whole thought has proved such a pervasive influence on their temper, clerical in discipline yet lay in sympathy, that the Dominicans seem to stem as much from him as from St Dominic. Their Constitutions, which were thoroughly systematized by St Raymund of Pennafort, the disciplinarian Master-General who succeeded the more dashing Blessed Jordan of Saxony (d. 1237), had already been shaped

---

[1] For instance, compare *II Sentences*, XLIV, ii, 2 and 2a–2ae. xliii, 2, *ad*. 3.
[2] 2a–2ae. lxiii, 3.
[3] 1a–2ae. xcvi, 5, *ad* 3.

in most essentials before the death of St Dominic in 1221. In
some ways the most impersonal of religious founders, St
Dominic with good grace had allowed his self-governing
institution to outvote him at a General Chapter on an important
question of property-administration. His Castilian background
was not that of the Inquisition and a centralizing court, but of
local *fueros* and free communes that were the nurseries of
European constitutional liberties. His Order was to grow with
the guilds, corporations, parliaments and universities of the
West, and to flourish most happily in the Free Cities and
Nation-States where free citizenship was least impeded and
the shadow of the Emperor did not fall. Ptolemy of Lucca was
not untypical in his admiration for the Republic of Venice.

There may have been some connection through Simon de
Montfort between the Dominican Constitutions and English
parliamentary institutions; certainly both are the fruits of the
same growth.[1] They are also said to have influenced the
American Constitution, through Benjamin Franklin who
studied them during his residence in Paris. The system combined a strong executive—the canonical *plena potestas*—with
the practice of electing to administrative office and holding
periodical inquests on the conduct of business. The spirit of
feudalism and paternalism was absent; after one experiment
with an abbot, *primus atque novissimus*, said Jordan of Saxony
cryptically, priors of houses and priors provincials of national
groups were elected who held office for a limited period, after
which they returned to the ranks. The rule was later extended
to the Master-General, the head of the whole order. Some
appointments were made by the executive: tensions later
developed between a free democracy and an efficient aristocracy, the former tending to lapse into easy-going ways, the
latter to stiffen into a concern for privilege and vested interest.
Nevertheless the ideal was that of authority welling up from
within the community and checked by constitutional laws
decided at periodical general assemblies, or Chapters.

The elective principle was of old standing and the functions
of a Chapter to advise an ecclesiastical ruler were well under-

---

[1] E. Barker. *The Dominican Order and Convocation.*
  W. A. Hinnebusch. *The Early English Friars Preachers.*

stood. Yet the bishop or abbot was a father, whereas the
Dominican prior was an official; an abbey was a family, the
Dominican priory a polity. The Dominican electorate not only
chose their higher rulers, but also periodically called them to
account, for a special place was assigned in Provincial and
General Chapters to special commissaries or definitors, *diffini-
tores*, elected for this purpose. They sat alongside the priors or
provincials in order to represent the non-governing class sentiment of the Order; they could be expected to be immune from
the official defensiveness of superiors and, if necessary, to be
properly critical of bureaucratic encroachments.[1]

Such was the mixed constitution of the group to which St
Thomas belonged. The brethren, or *populus*, elected the Master-
General, or constitutional monarch, through their representatives at the General Chapter, or Parliament. The same method,
scaled down, was adopted in the election of the Prior Provincial
at the Provincial Chapter or a Prior Conventual at the Chapter
of the priory. A definitor may be compared to the *defensor
civitatis* under the later Roman Empire, the justiciar in the
Spanish kingdoms, the *sindicatus* in late medieval Italian cities
who might call a retiring magistrate to account for any mis-
carriage of justice, and, in a sense, to the judges in Great
Britain who protect the public against the official machine.
The Masters in Theology, who were given a special advisory
and honorific status, were like an aristocracy.

The balance has not always been preserved, for most company
and service executives are inclined to strengthen their own
hand, usually in the name of efficiency, and, given easier means
of transmitting orders, an authoritarian temper grows at the
expense of local responsibility. It has happened in the
Admiralty, the Foreign Office, the highest religious institutions.
A governing class emerges, sometimes on the strength more of
achievement in the past than of capacity for the future. The
Dominican aristocracy in particular has at times been regarded
by the rest rather as the old Radicals regarded the House of

---

[1] M. D. Knowles. *The Religious Orders in England*, p. 154 sqq. Cambridge, 1948.

H. Denifle. 'Die Constitutionen des Predigerordens vom Jahr 1228.' *Archiv für
Litteratur und Kirchenegeschichte*, i, pp. 165–227. Berlin-Freiburg, 1885.

'Quellen zur Gelehtengeschichte des Predigerordens im 13 und 14 Jahrhundert.'
Ibid. ii, pp. 265–248.

Lords. The intellectual limits of obedience, however, have been consistently appreciated; the requirement has been satisfied that before ordinances can be issued evidence should be shown for them. The rigidity of standardization has been countered less by the indulgence of superiors than by the officially recognized instrument of dispensation, recommended without apology as the more reasonable and therefore the better course, not as a concession to human weakness. The tide of freedom has always run strong among the Dominicans, despite, or perhaps because of, the classical severity of their theology. St Albert refrained from condemning *democratia* in those parts of the *Ethics* and *Politics* where Aristotle was hostile; Lacordaire sat on the left in the Constituent Assembly of 1848, and declared before his reception into the French Academy that he hoped to die penitently religious but impenitently liberal.

The feeling for a true polity charged St Thomas's examination of prudence, the governing virtue of human practice.[1] It was divided into personal, domestic, and political prudence according to three different fields, namely, of the life of the individual, of the family, and of the commonwealth. The division was roughed out in the *Commentary on the Sentences* which quoted Aristotle and Cicero and echoed a phrase from Andronicus of Rhodes about *prudentia regnativa*, the governmental prudence the ruler should possess in his double office of laying down the law, *legis positiva*, and administering the political community. As yet there was only a vague reference to another kind of prudence which should be expected of his subjects, namely the statesmanship of the citizens themselves.[2] Some questions later, when the political virtues were discussed, they were taken to mean the ordinary moral virtues knit together to make a good man and neighbour; nothing, however, was said either about his public service or the common good.[3]

The examination moved closer in the *Summa Theologica*: there Aristotle's meaning was modified. Statesmanlike prudence, *prudentia politica*, was not reserved to the ruler, though his was

---

[1] T. Deman. *La Prudence. Somme Théologique*. Edition de la Revue des Jeunes, pp. 282, 319–24. Paris, 1949.

[2] *III Sentences*, XXXIII, iii, 1, iv.

[3] *III Sentences*, XXXVI, i.

that excellent type of it called *prudentia regnativa* matching his *justitia executiva*; it was that virtue of practical intelligence whereby citizens freely made their own the ordinances of political authority.[1] A text in the *Ethics* was alleged for a political prudence in subjects which corresponded to the ruling prudence of princes: in fact Aristotle was there merely drawing a distinction between the two functions of the governor, namely to command and to issue particular decrees.[2] Moreover the *Politics*, also quoted in this connection, seemed to restrict political prudence to the governor.[3] St Thomas was a careful exegete on the *Ethics* and avoided the misreading; on the *Politics* he was uneasy about the limitation of political responsibility.[4] In the *Summa Theologica*, however, he felt freer to expound his own sentiments even if that meant stretching what Aristotle had said. The *legis positiva* and the government was in some sense everybody's responsibility. Influenced by the recovered ideal of *urbanitas* and by his own doctrine that law should be reasonably shared in by those it directs, he thought of men acting like craftsmen—*chirotechnae*, said Moerbeke. They were citizens with a law rather than subjects under a law, for a subject, as such, was one who cannot command or freely dispose of his own doings, and to that extent cannot be responsible or prudent.[5]

Citizens were those who took an active part in politics. Thus political prudence, corresponding to general justice which served the Common Good, should be well dispersed and not concentrated in the official rulers of the State. Government should be broadly based, and its responsibilities, including the deliberative, judicial and executive functions, should be assumed not solely but jointly.[6] Why should the official technique of running the State be immune from comment by

---

[1] 2a–2ae. l, 1, *ad* 1.

[2] 2a–2ae. xlvii, 12 *sed contra. Ethics*, vi, 8. 1141 b 24.

[3] 2a–2ae. xlvii, 12, obj. 1. *Politics*, iii, 4. 1277 b 26.

[4] *VI Ethics, lect.* 6, 7. *III Politics, lect.* 3.

[5] *VI Ethics*, lect. 7. 2a–2ae. xlvii, 12, *ad* 1.

[6] *III Politics, lect.* 4.

    A. J. Carlyle, *Political Liberty: A History of the Conception in the Middle Ages and Modern Times.* Oxford, 1941.

interested amateurs? Hence the preference for a political régime which welcomed the participation of the ordinary man, an ideal like that of the high political thought of the Jews, that every man had in himself the nobility of a prince. It is true that only a minority is able or prepared to think hard and act effectively, and St Thomas showed himself well aware of the fact; nevertheless the ideal, like that of Christian holiness, is to be preached. Historically it has proved one of the successful myths of government.

Texts which seem to favour the idea of simple monarchy should be read as recommendations of its advantages in the abstract, not as flat historical judgments on contemporary institutions. Monarchy served the principle of unity as aristocracy served virtue and democracy served freedom. St Thomas can no more be described as an ardent royalist than as a sober democrat. He never alluded to the ins and outs of party government. One man one vote, that he never advocated—he had too strong a sense of graded responsibilities.

It was essential that the régime should be *for* the common good; for the rest he applied no doctrinaire political test. He had an eye for country. Aware that circumstances alter cases, he appreciated that the right style of government varied with climate, geography and history. The best political system was a compromise; the worst was when one section in the country predominated. Despotism was bad, the rule of mediocrities not much better.[1] Free play should be allowed the wisdom of a leader, *prudentia principis*; let him observe the laws without being hidebound. Men were faced with a balance of evils: if fearful of tyranny, they will lack the unity and dignity of monarchy; if they adopt a king then they must suffer the risk of suffering a tyrant.[2] He spoke sardonically of the doubtful blessing of monarchy to the Jews.[3]

From our standpoint we may say that his practical ideal resembled the constitutional monarchy of the nineteenth century, a *regimen bene commixtum* of the three streams of

---

[1] *VIII Ethics, lect*, 10.

[2] *de Regimine Principum*, i, 4.

[3] 1a–2ae. cv, 1, *ad* 2. (I Kings, 8).

monarchy, aristocracy, and what is now called democracy.[1] Roman and Christian writers—Cicero, Polybius, Dio Chrysostom—had drawn the same conclusion before him; political liberty implied some share in the government, State affairs in some sense were the business of all citizens.[2] Perhaps he might have agreed with Sir Winston Churchill that his preference has proved the worst form of government—except for the others that have been tried.

No fool-proof system can be devised: one must accept the risk of a monarch becoming a *roi soleil*, the aristocracy an East India lobby, the populace a class wanting something for nothing. That constitution is most tolerable which offers the most practical advantages. Unanimity, the strength of the State, was best served when as many as possible have a stake in the country and play their part in running its political life. Then stability was ensured, and fewer occasions for sedition were offered.[3] As with private property, where he adopted Aristotle's pragmatic criticisms of communism and added his own reason, namely man's dignity as a self-reliant and responsible producer created to the image of God, so with political government, he required a happy versatility, and a balance of majesty, nobility and popularity. *Melius* and *expeditius* went together—the best was also the most practicable.[4] For he was a utilitarian, in the sense that he related moral means to ends beyond morals, not an ethical formalist, for whom duty was to be done for duty's sake without reference to the stream of physical processes, and preferably in defiance of them.

The give-and-take of free citizens within the political community was brought back to the concept of justice, the self-controlling habit of dealing fairly. Admittedly some kind of *justum* existed within a slave-group or a family, for the members possessed some rights and could not be treated as though they were chattels, not human beings. (In passing we may notice that during the Middle Ages slaves were not uncommon in rich Italian households; there was a traffic in them from the Black

---

[1] 1a. xcv, 4.
[2] 1a–2ae. xc, 3.
  E. Demougeot. *Le meilleur régime politique selon saint Thomas*. Paris, 1928.
[3] 2a–2ea. lxvi, 1.
[4] 2a–2ae. xl, 2.

Sea.) What was lacking, however, was the rights of persons standing on their own for they were part and parcel of one another; hence only an imitation of full justice, a metaphorical justice, was engaged.

Were the country one great family or slave-system, as it would be according to the extremes of some conservative and communist theory, then, if the system were benign, everybody would be cared for and some sort of justice would be ensured. On the other hand its monolithic structure would permit no interplay of mutual rights and obligations, no function of free associations, no contracts between independent groups, no pluralism of fully constituted units, in short no truly political community.[1] For the act of justice, in the proper sense of the word, was free, and the *justum simpliciter* lay between equals who were their own masters. The political community was composed of citizens who stood on their own feet and were, with respect to essential political rights, equal: *habebunt partem in magno principatu*.[2] The ideal of a completely classless society was not urged, since equal shares in community-benefits or equal payment for community-services was not demanded by social justice. Instead fair shares and obligations should be distributed in varying proportions, not identical amounts, to match the value of the recipient. There was no question of 'to every man a penny'.

Only a community of responsible citizens could receive law strictly so called, for law was not merely a command to be carried out but also a reason to be consented to and possessed. It was not given to slaves or even to sons, but to freemen; it supposed 'civil conversation'.[3] They might be called subjects, though that perhaps was too passive a term; a better, because more active, was citizens. When Aristotle said they were the people who take part in politics, or that they were rulers and ruled in turn, he was not describing actual conditions.[4] Nor did the description apply in the Middle Ages, except for brief and turbulent episodes in the history of the Italian City-States.

---

[1] *II Politics*, lect. 5. 2a–2ae. lvii, 4.
[2] *II Politics*, lect. 14.
[3] 1a–2ae. xcviii, 6, *ad* 2. *VI Ethics*, lect. 7. *See V lect.* 11. *III Politics*, lect. 3, 4, 7.
[4] *Ethics*, vi, 8. 1141 b 2 8. St Thomas, *lect.* 7. 1a–2ae. cv, 3, *ad* 2.

Most men had their own work to do and enjoyed little time for narrowly political occupations.[1] More important than a rota of public jobs was a temper of freedom, confirmed by the law and defended by the leisure class or contemplatives. It cannot be said that the *clercs* of the thirteenth century betrayed their trust.

The terminology was not always consistent. St Thomas accepted the three classical types of a just regime, *regimen rectum*, namely *monarchia* or *regnum*, *aristocratia*, and *timocratia*, opposed to which respectively were the three deviation types, *regimina perversa*, or *tyrannis*, *oligarchia*, and *democratia*. Democracy sometimes had an unpleasant ring, as with Plato, and was treated as the decay of *timocratia*, but the two were not always distinguished.[2] The rule by men of property, called oligarchy by Plato, plutocracy by Xenophon and timocracy by Aristotle, entered into this preferred constitution. He agreed with Aristotle and favoured the limitation of responsibility to men with a stake in the country, as in Sparta, where the Council of State was chosen from certain families.[3] Carthage, too, was admired; there the aristocracy was popular with common folk and—another point of resemblance to the rule of the Whigs— men could go to the colonies to make their fortune.[4] His thought bears some points of resemblance to that of Catholic Liberalism during the first three decades of the *Risorgimento*: freedom-loving, yet with no more liking for mob-rule than for despotism. His man of property, of course, was not a man who lived on his rents and investments, nor was he quite a nineteenth-century freeholder, but anybody who was self-determining and responsible about his work and could support a family. A timocracy may easily go stodgy, and he saw no sin of sedition in upsetting it; he disliked bourgeois mediocrity.[5] One feels, however, that he would have preferred Louis Phillippe to Louis Napoleon.

He spoke well of *status popularis*—*populus* signified the *demos*,

---

[1] *II Politics, lect.* 9.
[2] *VIII Ethics, lect.* 10. *II Politics, lect.* 6.
[3] *Politics*, ii, 10. St Thomas, *lect.* 15.
[4] *Politics*, ii, 11. St Thomas, *lect.* 16.
[5] *VIII Ethics*, lect. 10.

or public as we say, that is the whole multitude rightfully united, not just the largest section of it. He did not differentiate within the upper classes between the numerically few, *oligoi*, the economically wealthy, *plousoi*, by culture and character the best, *aristoi*, who possessed prestige, *gnorimoi*, and were able to enjoy leisure, *epieikeis*; nor within the lower classes, who may make up the crowd, *plethos*, or rabble, *ochlos*, between the poor, *penetes*, the workers for hire, *thetes*, the manual labourers, *chernetes*, the artisans, *technitai*, the toilers and unleisured, *ascholoi*, and the men of the vulgar sort, *banausoi*. If we take the Dominican Breviary lessons for the feasts of medieval saints we find three titles employed to designate their family background. There were the *nobiles*—from which nearly three-quarters were recruited—or property-owners employing workers; the *pauperes* who had no capital beyond what they earned; and in between, the *honesti*, self-employed tradesmen and artisans.[1] Most Dominicans were townsmen, and this was an urban division.

Commending in turn now kingship, now aristocracy, now popular rule, but always as abstractions, he was committed to none of these three straight types of constitution. His final texts approved the *politia* in which they are blended: monarchy provided unity and personal disinterestedness, aristocracy enlightened policies and good administration, and democracy a general feeling of responsibility for the country's government.[2] When the common good was not the affair of one man alone then most will not think of it as another's care, but each as though it were his own. Hence he praised the rise of the Roman Republic and noted that the Jews were not altogether happy under their kings.[3] An exclusive insistence on any one of the three types of regime may make forceful doctrine, yet prove unworkable. He knew, as Aristotle did, that the type of constitution is not settled by weight of numbers. The formal sovereignty of an individual, or a minority or a majority does

---

[1] S. Bullough. 'Class Distinction among our Saints.' *The Life of the Spirit*. xi, 122, pp. 82–8. London, 1956.

[2] 1a–2ae. cv, 1. 2a–2ae. xl, 2. lxi, 2. *II Politics, lect.* 14.
   C. H. McIlwain. *The Growth of Political Thought in the West*. pp. 330–6. carefully discusses St Thomas's monarchism and does not understate it.

[3] *de Regimine Principum*, i, 4.

not give the State its deepest character. The one, the few, or the most considered merely as quantities are lesser matters than the psychological and moral qualities of unity, of dignity and of common consent which fosters agreement despite differences. Otherwise two nations may result, of consumers and producers, of overseers and workers, of commissars and the rest.[1]

He compared a healthy political community, centred on one authority which encouraged the gifted to assume office and the citizens to collaborate, to a happy family blended of the monarchy of the father, the aristocracy of husband and wife, and the democracy of the children.[2] Or again, to a balanced personality in which the psychological powers work harmoniously without one tyrannizing over another.[3] Aristocrats might possibly form a majority, the king might be a cabinet, but in fact the wise are few, and for ultimate authority one man is better than a board. In practice it is difficult to find an alternative to the counting of votes and the settlement of policy by majority-decision. Hence, just as positive laws have to be expressed in fixed terms and therefore miss the analogical values of equity, so this levelling down by the weight of numbers produced a dullness which is one of the prices to be paid for democracy. Such consequences were not examined by St Thomas—far less than Aristotle can he be compared with Tocqueville—nor did he relate the condition of the fine arts to the decline of patronage.

The will of the *populus*, which was not identified with any one class in the community, was not that of a proletariat or working class, not that of the bourgeois or the 'best people', and certainly not that of the dictator as such. It was expressed in law, which takes its meaning and force from the Common Good. Precisely as such it envisaged a classless society, inasmuch as all were equal under the law. That apart, equality of birth or of opportunity was not entertained. The monarchy issued the *constitutiones principum*, the aristocracy the *responsa prudentum*, also the *senatus consulta*, the democracy the *plebiscita*, yet law without

---

[1] *II Politics, lect,* 5.

[2] *VIII Ethics, lect.* 11.

[3] *V Ethics, lect.* 17.

qualification, and especially customary law, was commensurate
only with the *populus*.[1]

The spilling over of Aristotle's *prudentia politica* from the
governing class to the whole people was perhaps not uninten-
tional on St Thomas's part. He was rarely limited to the
authentic meaning of a text, and he was writing when a social
movement promised a wider citizenship than any known to the
Greeks. Slavery had almost gone, the revived Roman Law still
bore the print of its popular origins and theology was bringing
into jurisprudence the figure of the Christian man, freer and
more lawful than the citizen of Athens. Politics was in the air
and now beginning to be studied with some of the detachment
of Machiavelli's *Discourses*, but as yet with no intention of
setting up the tyranny of *The Prince*. If a liberal spirit were
fermenting no intoxication on the word *Democracy* resulted. In
those days political causes were no substitutes for religious
convictions, and St Thomas was typical in being a political
pragmatist. The organized national interest, that was the
people. It was the source and purpose of civil authority, which
was, therefore, in some sense elected, since under Divine
Providence nobody but the people could designate the ruler.
There was nothing sacred about an opinion which happened to
be identified with the sentiments of the majority. Whatever
else it meant, government by consent and representation was
not tantamount to the constant control of policy by the populace.

5. *Political Equity*

Inferior power should not act against superior within a *universitas* conceived as a hierarchy of powers descending from God.
The obedience commanded, however, lay within the bounds of
due observance, and these were drawn according to a scaled
gradation of competence within the system—the proconsul
should not be obeyed against the emperor, nor the bailiff
against the king.[2] What were the limits of a supreme civil
power which was legitimate by origin? When the question was
put it was assumed that the substance of authority was com-

---

[1] 1a–2ae. xcv, 4.
[2] Commentary, *Romans.*, *xiii*, *lect.* 1. 1a. cv, 1. cvii, 1. cx, 1. 2a–2ae. x, 10. civ,
6, ad 6. cv, 1.

municated by God in virtue of a man's office, not his personality.[1]

This teaching found support alike in current theology,
feudal custom and the aristocratic temper reacting against a
personal conception of kingship. There was then no cult of
genius which would substitute inspiration or force for government by charter applied by the power of due order and jurisdiction. Not even holiness could do that. The limits to supreme
temporal power appeared from two recognized abuses, of
government *contra legem Dei* and government *ultra vires*. If the
ruler commanded vice then the subject was bound not to obey,
for the only justification of civil authority was that it defended
and fostered virtue. If he went beyond his warrant, for instance,
if he exacted tribute or demanded service to which he was not
entitled, then the subject was not bound either to obey or
disobey.[2]

The conviction that the people had the right to resist actively
or passively was older than the idea that a formal agreement
existed between ruler and subject; it was rooted in custom
only afterwards rationalized in terms of contract.[3] The legitimacy of political power was conditional on its observance. The
twelfth century was prepared to disobey openly tyrannical
edicts which flouted the laws of God and traditional rights.
Later, when the deposing power of subjects had lost ground
before the advance of public authority personified in the
prince, the need for some form and method to remove a tyrannical or incompetent ruler was recognized.[4] The mood still
persisted into the fourteenth century, when a group of cardinals
cast about for ways and means of deposing the Pope.

In the thirteenth century those who declared that the
Emperor possessed the *coeleste arbitrium* were countered by
those Papalists who held that he was no more than a dis-
missable functionary, some of whom for their part were not
indisposed to erect the Papacy beyond the reach of the laws.
The extremists on neither side represented the main tradition

---

[1] *Contra Impugnantes*, 4.
[2] *II Sentences*, XLIV, ii, 2.
[3] F. Kern. *Kingship and Law in the Middle Ages*, p. xviii.
[4] *de Regimine Principum*, i, 6.

of the theologians and jurists, which remained faithful to the idea that no ruler, whether of Church or of State, could dispose of constitutional law and dispense from it as he thought fit. He must begin by learning to obey. The principle was applied to ecclesiastical government. The *Summa Theologica* stood stiffly against the power of the Pope to dispense from religious vows— its position was not sustained in later official practice.[1]

No thirteenth-century lawyer had to face the prospect of statute conflicting with religious truth or moral justice, nor even of the State denying the legislative competence—or even competition—of the Church through the Canon Law, which might be added to by new decretals or conciliar decrees. The honoured phrase, *lex injusta non est lex*, seemed a glimpse of the obvious. Not until the Tudor Act of Supremacy achieved a change of legal and political theory in England, and the Prince in Parliament became a self-sufficient omnicompetent legislative body, did men such as Fisher and More find themselves in the predicament of affirming that law was null when it traversed a higher law. They stood less for the freedom of conscience or for the old ideal of a unanimous Christendom than for the principle that no earthly ruler could change the nature of Christ's Church.[2]

Already, however, sovereign authority was becoming edged with a certain severity as authority lost its geniality and adopted an official demeanour. The transition from tribal and feudal institutions to the *estates* and *offices* of a legal and political organization involved a stylization of the *persona publica*. Whereas the rule of a father or patriot-king could be pliant, since his temperament counted for much and his virtue, benevolence and caprice were not vitrified by law, and whereas the accommodations of the community were more likely to be congenial to its members when they were regulated by old custom and not by a book of words to which the sovereign could make additions, the situation changed when the constitution of the State became more formal. Private moods should not colour official action and public administration, in a sense,

---

[1] 2a–2ae. lxxxviii, 10, *ad* 2, 11. *III Politics, lect.* 4.
[2] D. M. Knowles. 'The Limits of Law'. *Blackfriars*, xxxvii, pp. 402–12. London, 1956.

should be 'soulless'. No harm is done, but only on condition that it be accepted that the State covers an area narrower than the whole of man's social interests, and that its main duty is to maintain a framework in which his freedom can be secure.

The conception of the State as a juridical body, constituted largely by Positive Law the limits of which were well recognized, should in fact have proved a corrective to official aggrandisement. St Thomas required the State's action to be confined to what is external, public, and measurable by standard patterns —Aristotle might have wondered at the need for this insistence, but then the Greeks had never left the administration of justice in the hands of lawyers, and they were not faced with a great engine of State. St Thomas accepted the Roman Law, but was not disposed to extend its scope, or even allow the juridical State it created to take a lofty line. Its business was not to train its subjects, heart and soul, to what on the official view was the highest virtue. The State was for men, not men for the State; they were not its creatures to be shaped entirely to its needs or overawed. Even the *Jus Civile* of the Romans had not interfered in the internal affairs of the family.

Having so drawn its boundaries, he was then able to accord the legal State a workmanlike dignity. Let it be treated with respect in the name of social stability and with the confidence that such a limited instrument will not prove a sprawling menace. Nevertheless it was not neutral to morality. Its laws were not merely tolerable as patterns of outward behaviour to which the subject showed outward deference and which he observed merely because otherwise he might be found out and punished. For public authority had moral rights and expected moral responses. True laws obliged in conscience. The ultimate purpose of the political community was nothing less than the life of friendship, of men with God and among themselves, promoted through education and disciplined manners. Its immediate business, however, was less ambitious, and only this was it able to enforce. It was concerned with the social work, not with the mode of virtue; it could command certain virtuous deeds, but not that they should be performed virtuously. For men could make laws only on matters they were able to judge, and they were able to judge only external appearances. Hence the adage, the purpose of a precept does not fall within the law.[1]

St Thomas then, was not one of those who would extend the competence of public administration. He was sensitive to two dangers, of too improving a spirit on the part of legislators, and of indifference on the part of subjects. Citizens must watch with a certain vigilant irreverence for any signs of school-marm fussiness in their rulers, lest the police become our moral mentors and measure the length of bathing costumes on the beach, or sacristans prowl round our churches like invigilators. Nor must they allow the specialism of political and juridical action so to ramify that the whole of social life is covered leaving them mere onlookers, responsible only for matters of their own private conscience. Otherwise public life will proceed merely according to the impetus of the existing legal machine without respect for *humanitas* and *animus*.

Both threats were met by his doctrine of Equity. It was a virtue all citizens should exercise; it was not merely the exercise of a jurisdiction complementary to law, nor a special department of the judiciary. Most social philosophers, especially if they are Christians, will feel more at ease with *aequitas* than with the stricter Roman *fides*. To St Thomas, however, Equity was no mere ethical temper, foreign to the theory and practice of lawyers who like things cut and dried. It was prompted by the very genius of law itself, for fundamentally law is a humane measure transcending mathematical adjustments. It exists for persons, not for standardized units in a scheme. As the Greek theologians practised the principle of economy, and were prepared to tolerate various modes of expression without pushing a difference to an anathema, so Justinian and his assistants expected Christian humanity to temper the quasi-mechanical action of the laws.

A comparison of the *Summa Theologica* with the *Commentary on the Sentences* shows the transition towards a less rigid notion of justice. It was as though it was felt that freer-minded citizens were needed when the sovereign grew stronger, and that personal self-confidence was the remedy for too detailed a State intervention.

---

[1] 1a–2ae. xci, 4. F. Suarez, *de Legibus*, iv, 12–13.

That law itself postulated a certain elasticity was learnt from the teaching of Martinus, one of the four great doctors of Bologna who followed Irnerius. The leader of the 'Equity-Wing', his influence may be traced through his pupil Rogerius who taught Placentinus, who founded the School of Montpellier. This, together with the Schools of Orleans and Paris, was the home of a French jurisprudence rivalling the Italians in Civil Law and perhaps surpassing them in Canon Law. The early professors of Bologna admitted that *jus* was modulated by circumstances and that a spirit of fair play should breathe through the codes, but it was the French schools, strongholds of humanism and attracting churchmen as well as professional lawyers, which exhibited an easier and more theological mastery of their apparatus, and a less slavish adherence to the Gloss.[1]

It was in their temper that St Thomas approached legality. The movement, sensibility and living purposes appreciated by natural science and philosophy, the uncrimped prudence which quickened practical morals, all these entered into his unadorned discourse.[2] Set going by Aristotle's distinction between the just and the equitable, he began to speak more definitely about the need for the letter of the law to be charged with the spirit of equity.[3] The change took place within the space of one year, after 1269 when he was writing the second part of the *Summa Theologica*.

Positive laws, he held, should not be credited with the immutability of Natural Law, hence they called for constant reassessment in the light of a changing situation, though they should not be lightly repealed lest customs were unsettled and social stability shaken.[4] Codification was valuable, and for the reason later given by Locke, that government should proceed according to standing laws and not according to extempore decrees. All the same, what was needed was less a flexible law than a flexible mind in the citizens.[5] The topic was discussed

---

[1] H. Kantorowicz. *Glossators*, pp. 3, 24.
  C. K. Allen. *Law in the Making*. v. 'Equity.' Oxford, 1927.
[2] *II Ethics, lect,* 2. *VI, lect.* 6.
[3] *Ethics*, V, 10. 1137 a 32. St Thomas, *lect.* 16.
[4] 1a–2ae. xcvii, 1, *c. & ad* 1, 2.
[5] 2a–2ae. lxi, 5. 1a–2ae. xcvi, 6.

under three headings, first under Law, secondly under Prudence, thirdly under Justice.[1] Let us take them in order, noting that between the first and the second, in 1270, the *Summa Theologica* had treated of the Gospel Law and sent a breeze blowing through the rabbinical regulations.[2]

Human Law, based on what happens in the majority of cases over a long stretch of time, ordained a fixed standard of behaviour.[3] It wielded moral power, yet inevitably bore more heavily on the *proni ad malum* than on the *prompti ad bonum*, for the virtuous were like princes—beyond coercion.[4] It stuck to certain defined forms of justice, hence on occasion failed to fit some exceptional case.[5] The lawyers themselves used legal fictions to attempt to bend this rigidity. The theologians and philosophers, who had never reckoned law among the liberal arts and were disinclined to grant that law was sufficient unto itself, were perhaps more sensitive to the need for suppleness. The stock example was at least as old as Plato: a man who was engaged by law to return a deposit might refuse to do so because of the damage that would result, thus to restore a sword to somebody beside himself with rage. Legality was highly prized, yet most agreed that an exception should be made when the keeping of the letter would harm the commonwealth.[6] No code was a substitute for subjects keeping their wits. A judicial decision itself was an act of conscience, and no human law could override that.

So much was recognized practice. The theory was opened out in the treatise on Law in the *Prima Secundae*. Faced with an unusual crisis with which the ordinary forms of law could not deal, the preliminary observation was that, out of respect for public authority, recourse should be made to the proper dispensing authority; a dispensation was not a grudging concession to weakness but a favour which honoured the fair-mindedness of a superior and his sense of situation. This,

---

[1] 1a–2ae, xcvi, 6. 2a–2ae. li, 4. lx, 5, *ad* 2. cxx, 1, 2.

[2] 1a–2ae. cv.

[3] Hence it differed from privilege and 'case law'—*privilegia et sententialia*, 1a–2ae. xcvi, 1, 2, *ad* 2, 3. xcvii, 1, c, 2, 9.

[4] 1a–2ae. xcvi, 4, 5.

[5] 1a–2ae. xcvii, 1, *ad* 3.

[6] 1a–2ae. xcvi, 6. 2a–2ae. lx, 5, *ad* 2.

however, was not always possible, for time and place might not allow the procedure of appeal. Then the urgency of the case might carry its own dispensation—necessity knows no law, *necessitas non subditur legi*, and there were claims on us higher than keeping the positive law.[1]

The personal initiative here brought into action spelt no disrespect for the standing regulations or any suggestion that lynch law could be defended. Respect for legal processes was a medieval trait, and Socrates, that constant questioner, was venerated for his refusal to dishonour the laws or evade their consequences. The argument, therefore, acknowledged their dignity. Law was no mere form of words to be subscribed to when it paid us not to do otherwise. It expressed the conscience of the community. When, however, it encountered a situation it did not forecast, then Equity must be brought into play.

This was a judgment which took into account what the legislator supposedly intended, and decided in the light of higher principles than the law in question that it was better honoured in the breach than in the observance. It was neither an interpretation of the law nor an attempt at ameliorative legislation, both of which were matters for expert legists and competent officials; instead, less ambitious, it was merely a judgment here and now that the law in question was not engaged, a recognition, not that an exception proved the law, but that a law did not prove the exception.

The free spirit of the argument was put in legalist terms, as might be expected from its setting in the treatise on law: the public benefit was stressed, also an appraisement of the legislator's mind and the presumption of permission; it was noted that a petition for a dispensation should be made when practicable.[2]

The argument was less fettered by legality when it was repeated under the heading of Prudence. This was the virtue which supplied working rules of action in contingent matters where abstract certitudes, scientific and legal, were not available and which operated confidently and without straining

---

[1] 1a–2ae, xcvii, 4. c, 8.

[2] Consult the parallel passage, 'Whether the precepts of the Decalogue can be dispensed from?' *III Sentences*, XXXVII, i, 4.

after artificial reassurance.[1] Prudence played for truth, not
safety. After taking counsel, *eubulia*, the decision of ordinary
prudence, *synesis*, which sufficed in normal cases, might well
find itself at a loss in some odd conjunction of circumstances.
Then a special kind of prudence came into operation; it was
called *gnome*, a flair for judging the exceptional.[2]

Taking his stand on the teaching of the *Ethics* and confidently accepting the assurance that not a sparrow shall fall
without your heavenly Father knowing it, St Thomas was
sanguine that no puzzle of practice could be wholly unintel-
ligible when taken to the highest system of reference, however
baffling it appeared to proximate principles of interpretation.
Thus miracles and monsters, scandals to specialist science,
have their proper place in the wider drama of Providence;
thus, we may add, shaggy-dog stories which break the formal
rules of wit are relished by a larger humour. The ordinary
precepts of moral practice might fail to meet the case, but
prudence, lissom like an athlete and not square-drilled like a
Potsdam recruit, was well equipped to deal with exceptionl
ones. Its shrewd judgment was not formed only by standard
conventions. The just man, said Aristotle, is no stickler for his
legal rights, for laws are like the lead rules that can be bent to
Lesbian mouldings and adapted to the shape of the stones.[3]
When he acts, as it were, off the note let him not necessarily
apologise as though guilty of an aberration. The ability to
make such a decision was not regretted; on the contrary, for it
displayed a prudence out of the rut, a law which belonged to
the highest justice.

St Thomas might have been expected to hedge when he
returned to the topic in his treatise on Justice. Instead he was
more downright and generous. The exceptional case was
governed by that kind of justice called equity, or *epieikeia*.[4] It
would have been enough had he regarded equity as an example
of occasional and extraordinary justice, a rare flourish on the
surface of plain dealing, or a virtue, similar to liberality and

---

[1] 2a–2ae. li, 4. 1a–2ae. cv, 2, *ad* 8
[2] 2a–2ae. li, 1, 2, 3, 4.
[3] *Ethics*, V, 10. 1137 b 30.
[4] 2a–2ae. cxx. *V Ethics, lect.* 16.

subordinate to justice.[1] He did more. He affirmed that the
highest and most enduring type of justice was that which went
beyond the letter to reach the spirit of law.[2] St Albert spoke of
its possessors as *superjusti*.[3] Furthermore equity was not a
particular kind of justice dividing the field with legalistic
justice and acting as a kind of countercheck; rather it transcended, contained and inspired the workings of all law and
justice. The argument, though compressed, was carefully stated
according to the logic of analogy—the spirit of equity, not the
observance of a code, was the primary and supreme type of
justice: *de ea justitia dicitur per prius quam de legali*.[4]

How the lawyers reversed the relationship of equity and
legality in the fourteenth century is significant.[5] When the
State's supremacy was more massively legalized, justice according to the law was treated as the primary idea and equity was
reduced to a derivative and complementary function. Few were
found bold enough to question the official exposition and application of law when it ran counter to justice and expediency.
The ecclesiastical authors themselves submitted to this legalism,
and the effects were manifest in the manuals of moral theology.
But equity, as St Thomas conceived it, most nearly approached
God's own justice, which is his mercy.[6]

The severity of law was admirable only when it was true; the
good as such was not the difficult, and law was not meant to
be burdensome.[7] Equity existed in its own right, not merely to
mitigate the rigour of law; it was the prime social virtue. It was
the fortifying, not the softening, of justice. The *jus aequum* was
not a branch of law set apart from the *jus strictum*, but *jus* looked
at from the highest point of view and reflecting *humanitas* and
justitia. The just man was lawful and fair, *legalis et aequalis*. Were

---

[1] 2a–2ae. cxvii.
[2] 2a–2ae. cxx, 1, *ad* 1.
[3] *III Politics*, cap. 8.
[4] 2a–2ae. cxx, 2.
[5] W. Ullmann. *Lucas de Penna and the Medieval Idea of Law*, p. 12, note 4.
   C. N. S. Woolf. *Bartolus of Sassoferrato*, p. 390.
[6] 1a. xxi, 1. Commentary, *Psalms*, xxv, 1, xlii, 1.
[7] 2a–2ae. cxx, 1.
   1a–2ae, xcix, 1, *ad* 2, 2.
   X Ethics, lect. 14.

he politically just merely according to the laws and constitution he would be only partially just, *justus secundum quid.*[1] He must be *justus simpliciter,* just before God, if he is to be completely and freely just in his community. The confidence that law was the servant of freedom underlaid this doctrine. In Cicero's phrase, all were servants of law in order that we might be free. St Paul said much the same, at greater strength and depth.

---

[1] *V Ethics, lect.* 1, 2, 11.

CONCLUSION

CONCLUSION

THE POLITICAL DISCOURSE

ST THOMAS came after the humanism of the twelfth century with its delight in the whole sensible appearances of things and before the scholasticism of the fourteenth with its crabbed analyses of set books. When he wrote the logicians had not yet ousted the poets from the universities. His theology was both biblical and speculative. His political mood was later than that of John of Salisbury's delineation of the body politic composed of members tempered by human virtue and governed by a head with a personal conscience, earlier than that of Marsiglio of Padua and John of Jandun and their image of the State living in its own right. Augustinism was left behind him, secularism was still to come. From internal evidence alone he could probably be dated to the third quarter of the thirteenth century—after the grandeur of the *Dies Irae* and before the emotion of the *Stabat Mater*. Nevertheless few writers have been so consistently explained outside his period, perhaps because of a certain agelessness about his thought. It may be the mark of a great work to rise above history; it is well to set it back in its period to know what its author meant.

His arguments were not preoccupied with the political vogues of his time and provide no information about the turn of events. The Dominicans had been expelled from Naples by Frederick II in 1239, a few years before he joined them; he passed over the Holy Roman Empire without mention, and did not harp on the political prestige of the Papacy and the ambitions of the Canonists. He belonged to an Order traditionally not committed to party-lines. Such detachment, while a merit in pure theory, is an embarrassment when fitting him into his historical surroundings. It has been said that his thought was too transparent to cast a shadow.

1. *The Historical Effect*

So far as political theory was concerned the fourteenth century hurried men into preoccupations St Thomas had not entertained. He had never treated Church and State as though either could appeal to exclusive loyalties, and his political community belonged neither to the theologians nor to the lawyers, nor to the Canonists nor to the Civilians, nor to the landed lords nor to the merchants. Much lay outside the precepts of natural morality, much could not be reduced to Positive Law. He was Dante's guide in heaven, but not in the world of politics. To Lucas de Penna he was *sanctus doctor*—the Neapolitan pride was to be expected—and he was quoted occasionally by civil lawyers. Petrarch mentioned his name, coupled with that of St Bonaventure, only in passing and to remind the French what they owed to the Italians. No lasting institutions were the memorial of his social thought.

His reputation grew as a philosopher and theologian; the Council of Vienne vindicated his teaching on the psychophysical unity of man in 1312 and John XXII canonized him in 1323. He was the official theologian of the Dominicans, but they were but one of the professional corps of the Church in rivalry with others, and they suffered grievously from the Black Death. His wisdom became the tenets of one particular clerical school among others and lost its air of being as large as life.

> *Nostro datus, nostro natus*
> *Thomas est in ordine*
> *et in scholis conservatus*
> *sparso verbi semine,*
> *sui palmam doctoratus*
> *miro tulit omine*

Such was part of a parody in a Dominican breviary about 1500 of his eucharistic hymn, *Pange lingua*.

Before that, somewhat paradoxically, as Professor Knowles notes, while the English Franciscans excelled in speculative theology the English Dominicans were distinguished by their excursions into diplomacy.[1] They were royal confessors until the rise of the House of Lancaster, and rallied to the hopeless

---

[1] *The Religious Orders in England*, pp. 166–170.

causes of their patrons, Edward II and Richard II. St Thomas's contemporaries, John of Darlington, Hugh of Manchester and William of Hotham, were charged with the highest affairs of State. The French Dominicans sided with Philip the Fair in his quarrel with Boniface VIII. John of Paris spoke as a moderate in favour of the regal power, Ptolemy of Lucca was more of a Papalist but he was a communalist as well; both were first-generation Thomists who left their mark on political history. Perhaps the only Dominican team-work which impressed itself on actual policies was that of San Marco of Florence associated with St Antoninus (d. 1459) and Savonarola (d. 1498).[1]

St Thomas's credit grew with Vitoria and the great Spanish Thomists of the sixteenth century who helped to humanize the Spanish conquest of America; this classical example of the effective and beneficent influence of academics on politics earned for the University of Salamanca the grateful admiration of Dr Johnson. The pressing importance of the Church's social doctrine has been increasingly realized in the last hundred years and Leo XIII set the philosophy of St Thomas on the period of its greatest vitality. Consequently the phrase 'Political Thomism' sometimes appears, but it is doubtful if it bespeaks more than adherence to the social teaching of the Encyclicals.[2] Modern attempts to make of St Thomas a man either of the Left or the Right, in theology or in politics, have never looked even plausible.

His ineffectiveness in shaping the course of events has been shared by some of the greatest figures in the history of political thought, by Plato who trimmed the *Republic* with the *Laws*, and was strangely neglected for centuries; by Aristotle, whose main thesis on the naturalness of political institutions went underground for as long; by Cicero and Seneca, whose ideals, though acknowledged by Roman social philosophers and jurists, shone fitfully in the lurid gangsterism of Nero's reign.

Take his writings as they stand, or compare them with those of Giles of Rome or Marsiglio, then they seem unpromising material to the student of medieval constitutional or political

[1] B. Jarrett. *S. Antonino and Mediaeval Economics*. London, 1914.
[2] J. Haessle. *Das Arbeitsethos der Kirche nach Thomas von Aquin und Leo XIII*. Freiburg, 1923.

history. They never formed a ruling and representative system in the Middle Ages. Many secular thinkers followed the vein of Averroism; many religious thinkers, turning from the authentic Aristotelean philosophy to nominalism, prepared the way for a fideistic theology unable to produce a public check to the civil power. The State could do what it liked, leaving the individual to wrestle with his doubts in the privacy of his conscience. Even the interests of most Dominicans in the late Middle Ages seem to have narrowed to domestic Church affairs if we are to judge from their library catalogues which have come down to us. These include bibles, postils, commentaries on the Scriptures and *Sentences*, the Fathers, Canon Law, sermon books and lives of the saints, yet few works of immediate influence on the political community.

With social cohesion, as with sex, many factors, and these the most important, escape a closely topological treatment. Although St Thomas was the first Western writer to bring out the difference of politics from the other sciences and to distinguish the operation of Civil Law from Moral Law, his rudimentary political theory can be reduced to purely political techniques no more successfully than Shakespeare can be explained by the rules of prosody. Politics, it has been remarked, needs statesmen with philosophic gifts and philosophers with practical interests. Also, that bad doctrines are more damaging than bad actions to the common good. The end should determine the means and not be improvised as opportunity offers; consequently the good statesman is a man of principle, which is to say that he has some sort of philosophy or religion.

Social teaching should be seen as a whole, and the student should be prepared to delay on parts seemingly remote from the conduct of State-business. 'Is it not the fact,' asks Sir Ernest Barker, 'that Plotinus preferred to think of the flight of the Alone to the Alone, and had no attention to give to social and political life, itself a fact of first importance in the history of social and political ideas?'[1] The dogmas of religion which St Thomas discussed were what all men of his time felt to be true, powerfully if sometimes obscurely; their convictions did not always determine their actions but at least toned what they

---

[1] *From Alexander to Constantine.* p. ix.

thought about them. These doctrines are all profoundly social. They work in and through the fellowship. They are at once an introduction and an epilogue to politics. And they still stir in the modern world. He may be treated as a pure philosopher by a useful academic abstraction, but he was first of all a theologian, and to call him a political Aristotelean is about as true as calling St Augustine a Stoic or Mill a Lockian.

2. *The Three Social Phases*

St Augustine's social thought can be schematized by a diagram of concentric rings. In the middle is the *domus*, outside that the *civitas* and State, outside that the *orbis terrae* and wider still the *mundus*. Transcending the whole is the spiritual City of God. The fact of sin makes a break between the temporal and eternal; there the visible Church entered as a kind of mediatorial kingdom, 'partly seated in the course of these declining times and partly in the solid estate of eternity.'[1] It was the plan of an imperial intellect setting the powers and principalities in their places.

St Thomas's thought was basically physical, that is to say he started, as Aristotle did, with a science about the outside world of Nature. The principles, not the details, of the *Physics* determined his whole treatment, even, one may say, of systematic theology. And so in comparison with St Augustine his gaze was less sweeping. He took the social organism in front of him and sought to read its developing inner purposes. He was less given to forced contrasts, less haunted by the sway of evil. He saw a greater continuity in the social evolution. Three periods can be marked in the movement of his social dialectic, corresponding to three main types of human intercourse. They apply to the development of social life alike through nature and grace, in other words they can be adopted by ecclesiology as well as by political philosophy.

The first was the community-group; the parts were like members of a body, subservient to the whole. The second was *civilis conversatio* or partnership in the political-group which, while respecting the conditions of the community-group from

---

[1] *de Civitate Dei*, i, 1.

which it evolved, established laws which guaranteed the citizens' independence. It reached out to a third type of association, the society of fellowship where nothing personal was surrendered. Similarly there were three types of authority, of might to be feared, of political right to be obeyed, of the sight of truth to be loved; these in some respects corresponded to the distinction of kingly, priestly and scientific power.[1] So also there were three types of social virtue described in the *Secunda Secundae*; they began with the almost instinctive and childlike respect for family and country, and moved through the observance of political and juridical obligations into the free play of equity and friendship. Patriotism, social justice, divine charity, that was the order and plan. By filling in the details the whole of St Thomas's social and political philosophy may be described.

Our special interest is the political community, the *civitas* or *regnum* which gave form to the human mass, also a special character to the sins of schism and sedition.[2] It occupied an intermediate position between the extremes of pure community and pure society, from both of which it drew its being; both, as we have said, should be regarded as abstractions or logical models, not as complete historical situations. 'In the life of a nation,' writes Dr G. M. Young, 'we are aware of two elements which need to be kept in adjustment—the irrational elements of customs, tradition, habit making for stability, and the rational, critical elements making for improvement.'[3]

The healthy State respects both its origins and its ends; the civilized achievement is not cut off from its own agriculture nor closed to spiritual forces. It discourages elegances and artifices which estrange men from physical nature and refuses any doctrinaire break with the past. It may well be cautious about ameliorative legislation that looks well enough on paper but is likely to comfort to the detriment of national morale, sapped more easily by sophistication from within than by aggression from without. This, of course, is no argument against social

---

[1] Commentary, *Job* xii, lect. 2. *I Politics*, lect. 5.
    G. Fessard. *Autorité et Bien Commun*. Paris, 1944.
    B. de Jouvenel. *Du Pouvoir. Histoire naturelle de sa croissance*. Geneva, 1947.

[2] 2a–2ae. xlii, 1, *ad* 2.

[3] 'Essay on Government.' *The Character of England*, p. 85, Oxford, 1947.

reforms as such, merely a reminder that soft conditions do not make for strength.

There are some crises where above all it is necessary to keep your nerve though the appearances and even all reasonable expectations are against you, and when any surrender to or collaboration with alien forces, speak they ever so fairly, must be doggedly rejected. The old nations which survive, like the Poles under repeated misfortune, or the British against continental hegemonies, are those with profound memories, indefinite perhaps on detail but firm on fundamentals. They act by a sort of tribal intuition and achieve a collective exaltation, which, in their manner, they may treat as a sort of joke. A government is well-advised to look below the pattern of its laws and policies and observe these deeper rhythms. They vary, and solid self-interest will usually prevail. It was on the side of the Whigs when they beat the Tories to the tune of *Lillibulero*. It was still on their side when the Jacobites produced a better romance than the Hanoverians could manage, for Charles Edward was powerful enough only to leave a legend and move Queen Victoria.

Here the infra-rational forces of race and tradition and the supra-rational persuasions of religion meet together. As the government must cherish the first so must they protect the second. The State will not survive if it be insulated from higher influences, for, as Professor Jung remarks, without the idea of God the masses begin to breed mental epidemics. There is no true and lasting power in the earthly city which does not derive from the heavenly—hence the social mission of contemplatives to bear witness to the Communion of Saints.[1] That however is indestructible, and grace can look after itself much better than nature can. More vulnerable is wholesome social materialism, and its worst enemy calls itself rationalist materialism.

The *Ethics* noticed that natural friendship, a *philia* that went deeper than legal arrangements, held States together, and accordingly the wise legislator cherished unanimity no less than justice.[2] The Roman Law itself supposed fidelity and loyalty—

---

[1] *Quodlibets*, vii, 18. *Contra Impugnantes*, 2.
2a–2 ae. clxxxiii, 2. Inaugural address, *Rigans Montes*.
[2] *Ethics*, viii, 1. 1·155 a 23. St Thomas, *lect.* 1.

quid leges sine moribus? Behind the civilization of Plato and
Aristotle lay the Homeric phase of heroic barbarism. The
divisions of party politics are largely matters of emotive images
which command the allegiance of the steady voters on either
side. Even new countries find it necessary to create their myths
—Abraham Lincoln, Kemal, Gandhi, Stalin. Some wear better
than others. And so a sound constitution, even the legal artefact
of the State, is supported by an accumulation of blind and
unconscious racial pressures, of pre-rational affections deriving
from immemorial sources of terror and wonder, of a sense of
kinship and of honour, of usage and custom, of panache and
prejudice—*ut orare contra orientem apud omnes catholicos*,[1] which
may seem childish or superstitious or merely quaint to a rationalism which ignores the force of mythology.

Had he dwelt on descriptions of the natural origin of the
State St Thomas would have included the fabulous with the
primitive, for nothing seemed to him exotic. He differed from
his predecessors, alike by his psychology of the soul as the
substantial form of body, by his biological reading of law and
by his lack of morbidness about the instinctive motions of the
human organism. There was no radical corruption; the *massa
humana* was not a *massa damnationis*, and the God-given faculty
for legislation remained intact within it. The germ of Natural
Law appeared when men recognized that some events occurred
according to a settled order and not by the capricious intervention of unseen personal agencies. He had no dislike for or
illusions about the aboriginal, no hankering to have it artificially
tamed and clipped by State planning. He was alive to the
danger of the body politic ossifying under too much law.

Homo naturaliter pars multitudinis—a natural *impetus* caused
social cohesion before the entrance of the formal factors of law
and the inspiration of spiritual friendship.[2] Human beings
huddle together and exemplify the biological benefits of
crowding, observable in the lowest organisms.[3] The human

---

[1] Vincent of Beauvais. *Speculum Doctrinale*, vii, 58.
  VIII Ethics, *lect*. 11. 2a–2ae. cxliv–cxlv.
[2] *I Politics*, lect. 1.
[3] M. F. Ashley. 'The Origin and Nature of Social Life and the Biological Basis
  of Co-operation.' *Horizon*, xix, p. 384. London, 1949.
  M. Mead. *Co-operation and Competition among Primitive Peoples*. London, 1937.

mass-group is formed by drives from within, from impulses to cohabit and share, different from the forces from without which produce the mere conglobations, as they have been called, of moths round a lamp, flies on meat or cattle at a water-hole. There are in fact no truly solitary organisms, and this holds true even of such supposedly unsocial creatures as sharks and tiger-beetles.[1] Sharing the same reek—*in eodem fumo et eodem igne communicantes*—human beings produce and consume together, and are produced and consumed; they mingle with one another by *actio-passio* rather than by distinct awareness and affection.[2] St Thomas never seemed to have wrinkled his nose at the smell of humanity, which Palmerston, truer than he knew, called *esprit de corps*.

At this stage the operation of the group is determined accordingly. Its parts as such are not persons, separately conscious and self-determining. A baby, Freud said, is more aware of his mother's breast than of his own toes. The individual in such a mass is so subordinate to the purpose of the whole as to be borne onwards by its needs instinctively or willy-nilly. He incarnates the herd-instincts, lust, avarice, hate—all healthy in their place. And the leader in this type of community is the strong man, who is deposed, or expelled, or killed when his strength fails—as in an elephant herd.

Such a collectivity exists in a Slave-State organized solely for production and consumption under the rule of the strongest. There the Church, a *societas peregrina* uncommitted to the social processes around it, may work without agitating for political liberty, considering the slave sufficiently emancipated by the liberty of the Gospel.[3] Its happiest form is the family or *domestica multitudo*, which, precisely as such, is not a society of persons, but a biologically social unit, the shared life of male and female for the procreation of young.[4] It is, of course, designed to grow out of that condition into a partnership where there is a 'civil' relationship between husband and wife—St

---

[1] W. M. Wheeler. *Essays in Philosophical Biology*, p. 158. London, 1939.
W. C. Allee. *Co-operation among Animals*, p. 12. London, 1951.

[2] St Albert, *I Politics*, cap. 1. 2a–2ae. lxi, 4. 3a. xx, 1, *ad* 2.

[3] 3a. xx, 1, *ad* 2. 2a–2ae. lxi, 4. *V Ethics*, lect. 6. *I Politics*, lect. 11.

[4] 2a–2ae. clii, 4. cliv, 2. *V Ethcis*, lect. 6. *I Politics*, lect. 11.

Thomas wrote in a wife-beating age—and the children are being educated into adultness and friendship.

The fusion of individuals in mass-purposes, however, was not altogether destroyed in what comes after: thus the Dionysus Myth of the king who is killed was taken into Christianity. The sexual coupling, the being rooted in the same soil and being involved with the same material possessions, the ties of blood and sense of kinship, all these persisted when the ecological group was transformed into the neighbourhood group, and that into the political group. They were safeguarded even in the communications of divine charity. Evolving forms do not kick away the ladders up which they climb. Even a Pope remembers his country, and remains a Venetian like Pius X or a Milanese like Pius XI. In the ascending scale, *jugum legis, regula rationis, vinculum amicitiae*, there are no suppressions.[1]

The gradual separating of the parts of the community may be represented as a movement from barbarism to civilization as men assumed a diversity of functions and fulfilled them as responsible agents. The political community was not an ant-hill; there was no justice without a polarity of free persons.[2] It was barbarous, said Aristotle, to make no distinction between women and slaves; it was barbarous, added St Thomas, not to be ruled by civilized laws and not to hold liberal converse according to lawful idiom, which was why the Venerable Bede translated fine literature lest the English be reputed barbarians.[3] In general barbarism can be defined as a condition where the members of a community act from the compulsions either of brute force or of appeals to weakness. Men may be jingoes or pacifists, and their group may seek aggression or appeasement; in neither case is might possessed by right, and consequently civilization is not present.[4] Barbarism is a term of disparagement only when applied to a community which should be civilized but is arrested at the compulsive level or reverts to it. The same holds true of individuals.

---

[1] 2a–2ae. xxvi, 7. lxxvii, 4. *de Regimine Principum*, i, 15.
[2] 2a–2ae. lvii, 4.
[3] *I Politics, lect.* 1.
[4] R. G. Collingwood. *The New Leviathan. Man, Society, Civilization and Barbarism.* Oxford, 1942.

Among the factors of social cohesion which preceded political relations properly so called were the virtues of *pietas* and *observantia*—family loyalty, patriotism, and reverence for power.[1] Our attachment to kindred and country, *quoddam essendi principium*, of which we are begotten and nourished, was more binding than any bond tied by rational enactment—and more difficult to shake off. We were engaged before we chose, and our 'sympathy', *connaturalitas*, was no more to be explicated in the concepts of law than the works of mercy were to be couched in the forms of justice.[2] Treason is not just the abuse of legal protection, a mere matter of a passport, but an offence against one's own kin.[3] It is more damaging and strikes deeper than breach of contract. Traitor is an uglier term than rebel, or revolutionary, or recalcitrant, or recusant.

Patriotism may be contrasted with social justice, indeed may seem sometimes to conflict with it, as when a loyal soldier receives wrong orders, or like a stubborn German paratrooper fights on for his country though he knows the régime is unjust and the consequences will be more widespread disaster: conventions have changed, for in the days of classical war it was no dishonour to haul down your flag when further fighting would be plain massacre.[4] Patriotism and social justice have different objects and purposes; patriotism looks back to one's origins, rejoices in being a true-born Englishmen and hinges on the pride of nationality; social justice looks forward to the common good, serves the State and hinges on the principle of law. The Queen is the symbol of the first, the Constitution the symbol of the second.[5]

There were other connected social habits, primitive and not fully reasoned out, all healthy in their degree. While awe before mere fact of size and might should be controlled—the power of disposing of slaves, noted St Thomas, had not such grandeur about it that it should be venerated—the response to real greatness was expressed in sentiments of honour, glory, and

---

[1] 2a–2ae. ci, cii.
[2] 2a–2ae. ci, 1. *c. & ad* 2, s.
[3] Rebecca West. *The Meaning of Treason.* London, 1949.
[4] C. S. Forester. *The Naval War of* 1812. London, 1957.
[5] 2a–2ae. ci, 3, *ad* 3.

reverence.[1] Even fear could be bracing, though any servility in it, as when God was feared merely as the inflicter of punishment, was morbid.[2] Respect for power could be enhanced by the charismatical character it received from religious consecration: the king was anointed and crowned by the pontiff and his power was sealed by an oath of allegiance.[3]

These sentiments were not so fully deliberate as to possess the full quality of Aristotelean virtue. They were the pre-conditions of virtue, like the delicacy to which moralists appealed in defence of chastity. Thus, when St Thomas condemned incest he spoke of a *quaedam turpitudo honorificentiae contraria*.[4] When people condemn something as disgraceful we are apt to suspect prejudice; in truth, however, the argument from an affronted sense of decency, as in the case of incest, lies deeper than the reasons of social morality which are also advanced against it, namely, that it makes family relationships ambiguous and causes a psychological inbreeding which narrows the circle of friends.[5]

From these semi-instinctive responses to social authority a more deliberate attitude could develop, formed by a supervening set of virtues which corresponded to community-power less informally and more juridically presented. They clustered round the idea of obedience. This, in the strict sense of the term, was owed to civilized or political authority, not to patriarchal authority or *potestas dominativa*.[6] It was offered to an animate law and meaning, not to a brute fact, to a power that could explain itself, not to mere power in possession of superior force. It was not content with 'because father says no' or 'big brother knows better'.

Obedience responded to a precept, that is, a reasonable command, either tacit or expressed.[7] God's majesty was to be obeyed in all matters, but human authority only partially

---

[1] *I Politics, lect.* 5. 1a–2ae, ii, 2, 3.
[2] 2a–2ae. xix, 5.
[3] 2a–2ae. cii, 1. ciii, 1.
   M. Bloch. *Les rois thaumaturges*. Strassburg, 1942.
[4] 2a–2ae. cliv, 9.
[5] *Ibid.* See 2a–2ae. cxliv, clxv.
[6] *I Politics, lect.* 5.
[7] 2a–2ae. civ, 2.

reflected divine power.[1] We were not bound to obey another man in the private motions of our inner life, for, as Seneca said, to suppose that slavery falls on the whole man is wrong.[2] Obedience was not abject, it was the virtue of the good citizen and subordinate, not of the yes-man.[3] Conscience was not abdicated, we were not blindly committed, but pledged our reasonable service on appropriate occasions as the law commanded, that is, to legal superiors in their office of government.[4]

If we seek the exemplar of human happiness we must look where *beatitudo* is found. Not in *potestas*, for that is not ultimate enough: we can ask, Power for what? For good, we reply. But what is our good? It is not in this world, but only with God.[5] And so lifted above the mass and the political community, yet not despising them, are the communications of spiritual being within a fellowship without slavery, property or institutions. St Thomas went to Plotinus for an account of sublime virtue when he was introducing his treatment of the theological virtues, extravagances to the reasonable life described in the *Ethics*.[6] These are qualities of the spirit freed from the world, ranging unhampered by the complications of an organized scheme; these are the three theological virtues of faith which assents first to God himself and only afterwards to a dogmatic articulation; of hope which trusts him beyond all the sensible appearances; of charity which enters into friendship with the Divine Persons.[7] Though they inspire heroic detachment they are rooted in ordinary life, for faith preserves the reason, hope the desires and charity the natural friendliness of the human organism.

The Church as set forth by the medieval Canonists might look like a system of clerical offices—indeed critics sourly remarked that they were careerists who reduced it to a system of benefices—yet in truth the conception of a fellowship of believers, a *societas* quickened by the Holy Spirit, was not alien

---

[1] 2a–2ae. civ, 4.

[2] 2a–2ae. civ, 5, *c*, & *ad* 2.

[3] 1a–2ae. c, 5.

[4] 1a–2ae. vi, 4. xix, 5, 6. 2a–2ae. cii, 2, *ad* 2, 3. civ, 5.

[5] 1a–2ae. ii, 4, 8. iii, 8.

[6] 1a–2ae. lxi, 5. 1a–2ae. lxii.

[7] 2a–2ae. i, 1. ii, 3. xvii, 2, 5. xxiii, 1, 6. xxiv, 8, 9. xxv, 1. xxvi, 3.

to their thought. They worked alongside Christian philosophers and theologians. The political horizon was enlarged beyond the State and beyond the visible Church. Man was a true cosmopolite, a citizen of the whole universe, not because that was a society but because everything in it belonged to God, and by accepting him we entered into companionship with him in all his works. That companionship, which grew with divine charity and contemplation, formed a true society. It was not a State, not even an ideal State, such as More's Utopia or Campanella's City of the Sun. It was more like St Augustine's City of God built outside the boundaries of the present world. It was the intercourse of persons with God, who as Saint Bernard said, *amat ut caritas, novit ut veritas, sedit ut aequitas.*[1]

Any science of politics which thinks it can neglect this supra-political association will fall into the danger of talking merely about the trivial. It will certainly fail to analyse its principles. Happiness does not consist in being practical, but in what we are practical for.[2] What exactly do human beings want from their work and their social life? When the inquiry is pressed it will meet answers which imply judgments belonging to high philosophy and religion. They may be right or wrong, aspiring or merely comfort-seeking, confident or half-hearted. The society which alone could be man's true home may be drawn with the firm outlines of Christian dogma or brought out as a wish-fulfilment dream or left as a hazy ideal. No matter. Omit it, and the study of politics is left inadequate.

Aristotle noted that a city is most properly identified with its preponderant element.[3] Consequently an organized community of Christians, or of persons who know a dignity superior to State-service will be expected to differ from a closed system according to materialist or positivist theory: we must remember, of course, that in practice men are often both worse and better than their theories. They are wayfaring to a *communicatio amicorum*, a heavenly *urbanitas* surpassing civic friendliness or team work or the *amicitia utilis* of people banded together for a

---

[1] *de Consideratione*, v, 5. PL, clxxxii, 795.
   See *de Regimine Principum*, i, 4.
[2] 1a–2ae. iii, 5.
[3] *Ethics*. ix, 8. 1168 b 32. 1a–2ae. cvi, 2.

common job. At the best they will be the leaven in the mass. At the worst, one may reflect that it is better to be ruled by clerical than by lay commissars: priests at least daily confess their sins and are usually neither so grim nor ruthless. Matters so work out that religious countries appear strong in faith but weak in public spirit, and non-believing countries appear less tolerant of social abuses and jerrymandering. That may be an accident of history and racial temperament. There is another paradox: family feeling remains strongest, also folk-customs, art and the tang of nature, where the otherworldly virtues are most admired.

The spiritual and free society differs from a material and coercive community on three counts. First, it forms no collectivity, no mass greater than its components, no body of which the associates are members: it is compared to the leaven, the ferment, the living catalyst which appears at the end of a physiological reaction unaltered. As a consequence, secondly, the persons in a society are equals and not hierarchically arranged in due subordination. Thirdly, they are ruled by no coercive law, for they are freemen not bondmen, and the law they willingly receive is the Eternal Law, the Logos conceived in the mind of God, the name appropriated to the Son, and known directly in the companionship of the blessed.[1] Such is not the condition of the present civil community, as Plato the protagonist for the Inquisition, recognized; nor of the present religious community, for though the use of force to extend religion has usually proved disastrous, the Church must still accommodate itself to a world where most of us are children or mental or moral defectives.

The pure society is like the pure community; each is a real type which can engage philosophical inquiry without representing a complete concrete situation for the whole man, who is neither a pure soul nor a pure body, nor merely a friend nor a kinsman, but a centre of multiple relationships. Heaven is the end and examplar of the State, the forms and official practices of which have to be constantly tested in its light. Political courses anyhow are determined by convictions about

---

[1] 1a–2ae. xci, 5. xciii, 1, *ad* 2. 2, 4, *ad* 2. cvi, 1, *c & ad* 6.
  2a–2ae. xxiii, 1. lviii, 3, *ad* 2.

matters lying outside political organization. Magna Charta
can be traced from the teaching in the schools of Paris, the
French Revolution to the Encyclopedists, and the influence of
academic ideas on historical practice still continues. Are not
the physicists the masters of politics today?

Men are not only common and productive but also aristocratic and contemplative. How they should live together is
largely decided by what they think they are, and this turns out
to be a theological question whatever the answer given. Some
sort of utopia lurks in every political doctrine. Faulty ideals and
and false goals vitiate the details of practice, for social exemplars are not idle dreams but present realities, entering as ends
into the constitution of the community which is in movement
towards them. Restlessness moves to quiet, all rational association to friendship.[1] Human life is not more exhausted by the
pursuit of virtue than by practical activity. Beyond beckons
the friendship of God. Beyond, and yet already present in what
we do. St John of the Cross knew that courtesy was part of the
Christian life; were it lost among the Carmelites, he warned,
and superiors to rule harshly and by force, then the Order
could be mourned for as ruined. He quoted St Thomas that men
brought up under fear presently degenerate; they become
slave-minded, little-souled, incapable of strenuous and manly
deeds.[2] So it is with the political community, when active
debate and collaboration are superseded whether by the dictate
of tyrannical power or the drag of comfort.

The glow from the heavenly city, far from blurring the
earthly city in a haze, makes it clear and real; the authority of
God, far from reducing the exercise of political power to a series
of interim accommodations to a shadow-world, lends it authentic strength. For reality and causality entirely derive from
eternal sources. We can afford to exalt the power of the State
when we know that its extent is limited, we can stress obedience
when we know that it is not an end in itself, just as we can
admit no deviation from mathematical truths without being

---

[1] *II Politics, lect.* 1. *de Regimine Principum*, im 14.

[2] *Spiritual Sayings*, xi. Complete Works. ed. E. Allison Peers. iii, p. 314. London,
    1943.
    de Regimine Principum, i, 3.

overwhelmed by them. Justice, said Masaryk, is the arithmetic of love.

The higher form is at work in the lower as the lower in the lowest. One of St Thomas's favourite principles was that the superior does not dispense with the inferior; sensitive does not destroy vegetative, nor intellective sensitive. He would have approved the answer to the question in Lorca's poem: What makes the gloss on the horse's coat?—Sweat. He was not mistrustful of the self-love in which charity moves and which it surpasses, nor of economic factors in political processes, nor of the profit-motive in the service of the common good. Oppositions in his dialectic were not contradictions and exclusions, but complements. Friendship holds passion, and society the warmth of kinship. The resonances of the infra-rational and the supra-rational remain in the real truth of the reason; physical sympathy or *compassio* should be kept and spiritual freedom welcomed by the reasonable political community. If the claims of grace in the City of God do not destroy the primitive instinct for comfort, if the spirit blesses the flesh, still less should the arts and institutions of the civilized State be impositions on the natural group, like the rococo and palladian palaces peremptorily plastered by Peter the Great on the morasses of the Neva, and now called Leningrad.

3. *Summary*

It now remains to gather the fragments together and offer a compendium of what has been discovered from St Thomas's pioneering work in political philosophy. We began with the social ideas and moods of his political background. (Part One).

I. In their expression by the theologians, especially his immediate predecessors among the Paris schoolmen, a new awareness of the value of secular values was noticed, together with a feeling for the dignity of civil authority, though the Augustinian conviction persisted that dominion existed to mitigate the effects of sin (1)[1]. Their researches into the patterns of social life which followed the reception of God's Eternal Law by the human mind opened up questions of individual and social psychology, and gave precision to a Natural Law theory

---

[1] Roman numerals indicate chapters. Arabic numerals in brackets their sections.

governing political association which owed little to legal positivism (2).

II. At the same time the Jurists were exploiting and adding to the resources of the recovered Roman Law which was displacing folk and customary law. Some of the Canonists were running a political cause, a Papal Caesarism in matters temporal as well as spiritual. Here St Thomas stood apart, since he did not hold that all rights were communicated through the visible Church. It was rather from the spirit of the legal teaching common to all of them that he drew. The canonical insistence on the reasonableness of law was shown by the need for proper promulgation and display of evidence in its processes; on the responsibility of its subjects by their preference for due election to supreme authority as against hereditary or forcible acquisition; and on dispassionate administration by the distinction between person and office (1). The Civilians had not yet come to plenary political power. St Thomas owed more to the French than to the Italian Schools, notably in his respect for custom, desire for constitutional checks on government, and admission of equity which played above the letter of the law (2).

III. A sketch of his surroundings indicated how the feudal order was changing into a town-culture. Social life was becoming at once less rooted and more formal. St Thomas was not a cloistered monk, but at home in universities and courts (1). Yet the Dominicans were vagrants with a difference, for they were also canons, dedicated to liturgical observances and accredited preachers of orthodox theology (2).

IV. The twelfth century had given birth to a natural philosophy which addressed itself to a world of real not symbolic values (1). This was stimulated by the discovery of Aristotle known by Latin translation first from the Arabic and afterwards from the Greek. At a time when Western Christendom, united under Emperor and Pope, was separating into the Nation-States, the *Ethics* and the *Politics* inspired the ideal of a City of Reason which owed nothing to the Christian revelation (2).

That in résumé was the first part of this study. The theme then turned to the assimilation and transmutation of these

ideas and forces by St Thomas. It was divided into four
movements, theological, juridical, cultural and philosophical
(Part Two).

V. The investigations of the theologians had left the field
untidy, and it was his merit in jurisprudence to put it in order.
He achieved a comprehensive definition of law (2). Also a
classification of its various types which allowed for supra-legal
and infra-legal specimens—the Gospel Law and 'the law in my
members'—and included the historical category known as the
Jus Gentium (3, 4). But his chief contribution to the political
philosophy of law lay elsewhere, in his biological reading of the
social reason which united men in the political community.
This was not imposed on natural processes from outside; it was
neither the postulate of a mind which stood apart from them
yet had to domesticate their savagery nor was it a dictate of
will which checked sinful greed through the institutions of
private property and civil dominion. Rather it sprang from the
original drives of the human organism. When man was described as a social and political animal a real not an artificial
unity was signified (1). Moreover his subordination to the group
belonged to the essential things and was not due to the Fall.
This teaching departed from the common Christian persuasion,
deriving from St Augustine, that the right of the State to govern
resulted from a compromise with sin (5).

VI. Inspecting more closely the functions of law-making and
statesmanship, St Thomas, like all his contemporaries, did not
place them outside the framework of moral doctrine. Nevertheless they were unlike conclusions drawn by theoretic argument. Occupied with concrete situations which could not be
wholly elucidated by abstractions, they represented in the main
those pragmatic adaptations to environment which, according
to Aristotle, were elicited by art and prudence not by moral or
scientific doctrine. Hence they were not extensions of religion,
and could claim some immunity from clerical censorship (1).
They might claim obedience in conscience but were not to be
moralized. At the same time, not all morality was to be legalized
or made a matter of public politics. Not all sins were crimes,
since the power of the State to prescribe or punish was limited
to its own protection (2). Christianity revealed a City of God

beyond all earthly organization, hence the merely political *bonum commune*, if wider than the *bonum publicum* according to juridical Roman conceptions, was conceived in less inclusive terms by St Thomas than by the Greeks (3). His theological inquiry into the origins of authority scarcely went beyond the general statement that all lordship was from God and might be presumed to be present so long as nothing vicious was commanded. The possession of civil power did not in essence depend on ecclesiastical ratification. In so far as he followed the legal inquiry into the source of authority and law he was content to repeat that it lay with the people; the tenor of his thought suggests that he was opposed to the suggestion that they could abdicate this radical responsibility (4).

VII. Growing State centralization and officialdom gave new point to the perennial problem of individual responsibility for group-action. By his Christian conscience, his semi-feudal conception of honour and his philosophy of the dignity of the person, St Thomas could not allow the State to act out of human control; on the other hand it had a life of its own and followed ends which were not the total of those of its parts. The problem was broken up into pieces. The notion of official justice was related to the notion of contract involving personal responsibility (1). The divorce between private and public life was considered (2). There were distinctions between justice done by person to person, by person to group, by group to person (3). It was recognized that politics may have to be content with the second-best and to tolerate what it cannot abolish (4). With regard to the profound tension between part and whole, it was accepted that persons were somehow anarchic in any association lower than the City of God (5). The State was not a single organism, and only in a metaphorical sense was it a body in which human beings are subservient members (6). The ascription to it of a personality was no more than a useful fiction, though, as in the case of the human race considered as one group, the bonds could be so close that all may share in general guilt and penalties (7).

VIII. The philosophical stage was set by Aristotle. The full effect of the *Ethics* and *Politics* were beginning to be felt and the first commentaries were written (1). Yet the flourishing of the

Hellenic spirit was brief, and it was soon stifled in the schools by an excess of logic and law. The qualified acceptance of a strictly rational realism in theist and moral philosophy by the Dominicans was not that of the majority outside their ranks. Others who had gone the whole hog and were prepared to countenance contradictions to the dogmas of Christian faith were condemned. Some survived to join forces with the Regalist lawyers in attacking the civil supremacy of the Pope (2). The short-lived model of a Christian polity for which St Thomas assembled the parts was neither an improvisation nor a piece of scholasticism, if that means a speculative grid imposed rigidly on the world of fact. It was built on experience (3). It also matched noble social ideals of the thirteenth century, among them the rule of law freely accepted by subjects and government based on consent (4). The right to criticize and resist the abuse of power was also recognized, together with the overriding need for Equity lest the administration of law become hidebound (5).

The conclusion treated St Thomas's political philosophy almost as a period piece which exercised little influence on the history of the later Middle Ages (1). Its general dialectic was outlined according to three phases: the primitive condition of human solidarity formed by pre-rational factors which still persist; the condition of association freely entered into or accepted proper to the civilized State; and the ultimate condition of friendship beyond the dream of respectability and the threat of coercion. This was already prefigured in political processes (2). 'Charity', says St Thomas,[1] 'embraces in itself all human loves, those alone excepted which spring from sin. Hence love for relations and for fellow-citizens and for companions wayfaring together, or indeed for anybody however associated, can be from charity and worthy of heaven.'

---

[1] Disputations, *de Caritate*, 7.

INDEX

A

333

T